China's Civilian Army

China's Civilian Army

The Making of Wolf Warrior Diplomacy

PETER MARTIN

OXFORD
UNIVERSITY PRESS

Oxford University Press is a department of the University of Oxford. It furthers
the University's objective of excellence in research, scholarship, and education
by publishing worldwide. Oxford is a registered trade mark of Oxford University
Press in the UK and certain other countries.

Published in the United States of America by Oxford University Press
198 Madison Avenue, New York, NY 10016, United States of America.

Library of Congress Cataloging-in-Publication Data
Names: Martin, Peter (Reporter), author.
Title: China's civilian army : the making of wolf warrior diplomacy / Peter Martin.
Description: New York, NY : Oxford University Press, [2021] |
Includes bibliographical references.
Identifiers: LCCN 2021004587 (print) | LCCN 2021004588 (ebook) |
ISBN 9780197513705 (hardback) | ISBN 9780197513729 (epub) | ISBN 9780197513736
Subjects: LCSH: Diplomatic and consular service, Chinese—History. |
China—Foreign relations administration—History. | China—Foreign relations—1949–
Classification: LCC JZ1734 .M38 2021 (print) |
LCC JZ1734 (ebook) | DDC 327.51—dc23
LC record available at https://lccn.loc.gov/2021004587
LC ebook record available at https://lccn.loc.gov/2021004588

DOI: 10.1093/oso/9780197513705.001.0001

3 5 7 9 8 6 4

Printed by LSC Communications, United States of America

Contents

Acknowledgments

Of the many ways that attempting to write a book has humbled me, two stand out. One is learning just how much help I needed. The other is how lucky I am to be surrounded by people willing to provide it.

Jim McGregor took a chance on me a decade ago and has been a friend and mentor ever since. "Just slop it out" proved to be the sagest of all the advice I received during the drafting process (any remaining slop is my responsibility alone). My dear friend David Cohen deserves a running footnote throughout this book and everything else I write.

I likely would not have begun this project without the early encouragement of Charles Edel over dinner at Founding Farmers in DC. I would certainly never have seen it through without the unstoppable insight and enthusiasm of Jude Blanchette. Ken Wills, Lucy Hornby, Ting Shi, James Green, Steven Lee Myers, Nerys Avery, and Tom Pomeroy all struggled through early drafts, which must at times have been painful to read. They all offered invaluable advice and encouragement.

The book also benefited tremendously from the input of the following people whose expertise and experience improved the manuscript's style and substance: Chris Anstey, Alec Ash, Antony Best, Matt Campbell, Andrew Chubb, Alan Crawford, Rush Doshi, Alex Farrow, Carla Freeman, Chas Freeman Jr., Karl Gerth, Clara Gillispie, Andy Heath, Tim Heath, Ken Jarrett, Jeremiah Jenne, Betsy Joles, Dan Ten Kate, Jeff Kearns, Wes Kosova, James Mayger, Trey McArver, Richard McGregor, Jessica Meyers, Will Millard, Colum Murphy, Lance Noble, Junni Ogborne, Lena Schipper, Brendan Scott, Charlie Seath, Gerry Shih, Katie Stallard-Blanchette, David Wainer, Bob Wang, Dennis Wilder, and Keith Zhai.

I owe an immense vote of thanks to the many dozens of people who spoke to me during the course of this project who are either named in the footnotes or chose to remain anonymous. I would also like to thank Wang Wei, my wonderful Chinese teacher of many years who tolerates my strange desire to master Party-speak.

I am grateful to the Bloomberg Politics team for being supportive of this project, especially Brendan Scott, Dan Ten Kate, Ros Mathieson, and Wes

Kosova. Kristin Powers and Samantha Boyd have also been generous with their time and provided useful advice. All of the opinions in the book, though, are mine alone. Thank you also to David McBride and Holly Mitchell at Oxford University Press for commissioning this project and patiently helping me see it through to the end.

I would like to thank my partner, Alexandra, for being my best friend and constant inspiration, and my brother, Graham, for being a rock. Finally, I would like to thank my parents to whom I owe more than they will ever know. This book is dedicated to them.

Introduction

It was late afternoon when Rimbink Pato, Papua New Guinea's foreign minister, heard a loud commotion outside his door. Seconds later, four Chinese diplomats burst uninvited into his office, demanding last-minute changes to the communiqué of the 2018 Asia-Pacific Economic Cooperation summit, the Pacific's most important economic and political forum.

For Papua New Guinea to have even hosted a meeting of APEC, whose members represent around 60 percent of the world's GDP, was a feat in itself. The sprawling archipelagic nation in the middle of the South Pacific has a population of just 8.6 million people and is among the poorest on earth. With 850 languages and more than 600 islands, it was difficult to govern at the best of times. The capital Port Moresby had a reputation for violence, prompting the country's southern neighbor and former colonial overlord Australia to provide security for the event by stationing a warship in the harbor.

China had been meticulously building its influence in the resource-rich nation for years, ramping up investment and building infrastructure. Chinese loans had funded hospitals, schools, and hydropower stations across the country. By the time the summit took place in November 2018, the nation owed a quarter of its external debt to Beijing.[1] Further afield, China was promising more than $100 billion to finance infrastructure projects across the Pacific and Eurasia under its Belt and Road Initiative.[2]

It looked like the event would be an easy win for Xi Jinping, the president of China and head of the ruling Communist Party. President Donald Trump skipped the meeting, sending Mike Pence, the vice president, instead. Pence spent little time on the ground, instead stationing himself in nearby Cairns inland from Australia's Great Barrier Reef because of concerns about violence.

Xi was the first foreign leader to land in Port Moresby. Ahead of his arrival, local newspapers carried an op-ed in his name, which hailed the "rapid growth" in ties as the "epitome of China's overall relations with Pacific island countries."[3]

Xi made a grand entrance. His motorcade, which included two Hongqi ("red flag") limousines air-lifted from China, sped from the airport to the hotel along a Chinese-funded highway past the fluttering flags of both countries. Xi drove past crowds of cheering high school students and billboards of himself shaking hands with the country's prime minister. His hotel was decorated with red lanterns and an elaborate Chinese gate.[4]

At the summit, Xi delivered his standard speech on the importance of open markets and globalization. He'd used public appearances since Trump's surprise election victory in November 2016 to contrast China's approach to the "America first" protectionism espoused by his American counterpart, and APEC was no exception. The audience of global executives and political elites applauded when he told them, without naming names, that implementing tariffs and breaking up supply chains was "short-sighted" and "doomed to failure."[5]

This public display was largely under China's control. The ongoing behind-the-scenes wrangling over the summit's communiqué, however, was not. In a last-minute push to influence wording about "unfair trade practices" that they believed targeted Beijing, Chinese diplomats took matters into their own hands by requesting a sit-down with Papua New Guinea's foreign minister. He refused, arguing that bilateral negotiations with an individual delegation might jeopardize the country's neutrality as host. The Chinese tried again but were once more rebuffed.

Undeterred, four Chinese diplomats decided to push their way into the foreign minister's office, calling out that they just needed two minutes of his time. Security guards then asked the Chinese officials to leave and police were later posted outside the door. Publicly, Papua New Guinea's foreign minister sought to downplay the incident, telling reporters it was "not an issue." Privately, the country's officials described China's behavior throughout the negotiations as "bullying."[6] China's foreign ministry denied that the incident ever occurred, calling it "a rumor spread by some people with a hidden agenda."[7]

As reporters waited for the outcome of the summit, Canadian prime minister Justin Trudeau eventually confirmed that negotiations over the communiqué had collapsed. "There are differing visions on particular elements," he said with understatement. For the first time since leaders began attending the annual summit in 1993, no joint statement was issued.[8]

The APEC summit should have been an opportunity for China to boost its reputation. Trump had spent the two years leading up to the Port Moresby meeting undoing much of the goodwill the United States had developed in the region. Within days of his January 2017 inauguration, he had withdrawn from the Trans-Pacific Partnership, a twelve-nation trade deal that aimed to help America compete with China's engagement in Asia. He'd gone on to launch a trade war with China, forcing Pacific nations to choose between two powers they could not afford to offend. The president had also personally insulted America's partners across the region, hanging up halfway through a January 2017 phone call with Australian prime minister Malcolm Turnbull and branding Canada's Trudeau "very dishonest" and "weak." But instead of taking advantage of the opportunity, China emerged from APEC looking ever-more like a bully. Its diplomats—the very people who should have been most concerned about their country's reputation—only seemed to be making matters worse.

The APEC debacle was just one of a series of setbacks for Chinese diplomacy in the months before and after the summit. Two months earlier, at the Pacific Islands Forum in the Micronesian microstate of Nauru, China's envoy had walked out of a meeting when the host refused to let him speak ahead of another nation's prime minister. The president of Nauru described the Chinese diplomat as "very insolent" and a "bully."[9]

In the months after the Papua New Guinea incident, China's ambassador to Canada publicly accused his hosts of "white supremacy." China's chief emissary in South Africa declared that Donald Trump's policies were making the United States the "enemy of the whole world." Its representative in Sweden, Gui Congyou, labeled the country's police "inhumane" and blasted its "so-called freedom of expression." In the space of just two years, Gui was summoned by Sweden's foreign ministry more than forty times while three of the country's political parties called for him to be expelled. Unabashed, he told Swedish public radio, "we treat our friends with fine wine, but for our enemies we have shotguns."[10]

While these aggressive displays won plaudits at home, they compromised China's efforts to cast itself as a peaceful power. The foreign media began to brand this new confrontational approach "wolf warrior diplomacy" after a series of Chinese action movies that depicted Rambo-like heroes battling China's enemies at home and abroad. The second in the series, *Wolf Warrior 2*, told the story of a group of People's Liberation Army soldiers sent to rescue stranded Chinese civilians in a war-torn African nation. The 2017 movie was a huge success for China's film industry, making more than $854 million at the domestic box office.[11] Its tagline read, "Even though a thousand miles away, anyone who affronts China will pay."[12] The moniker captured the intimidating and sometimes bewildering nature of Chinese diplomacy as seen by the outside world, and it stuck.

The behavior of Chinese diplomats grew even more combative as Covid-19 spread around the world in early 2020. Beijing's envoys hit back hard at suggestions China was to blame for the spread of the virus. Some did so on Twitter: "You speak in such a way that you look like part of the virus and you will be eradicated just like virus. Shame on you," Zha Liyou, China's consul-general in Kolkata, India, tweeted at one user who criticized China.[13] Others vented their frustration through embassy websites: an anonymously authored text posted on the website of the Chinese embassy in France falsely accused French retirement home staff of leaving old people to die, sparking public anger in France and a rebuke from the country's foreign ministry.[14] Most provocatively of all, Zhao Lijian, a recently appointed foreign ministry spokesman, suggested that the virus might have been spread deliberately by the US Army, prompting fury in Donald Trump's Oval Office and worldwide alarm about Beijing's role in spreading disinformation.[15]

The behavior of Chinese diplomats helped fuel a global backlash against Beijing. Reinhard Buetikofer, a German lawmaker who chairs the European Parliament's delegation for relations with China, said the foreign ministry's "extremely aggressive" behavior combined with the Communist Party's "hard line propaganda" had helped turn European opinion against the Asian nation. Its conduct, he said, spoke to the "pervasiveness of an attitude that does not purvey the will to create partnerships, but the will to tell people what to do."[16] A global poll released in October 2020 showed that negative perceptions of China hit record highs in the United States and eight other developed economies including Germany, Britain, South Korea, Australia, and Canada.[17]

These setbacks matter. As global politics is increasingly defined by Sino-American rivalry, the ability to compete diplomatically will help shape the history of the twenty-first century. Taken together with economic, military, technological, and ideological prowess, diplomacy is a key part of what makes any power great. American strategists have long defined it as a core element of any nation's power: diplomatic, informational, military, and economic capabilities are often reduced to the acronym "DIME."[18]

Chinese diplomats play an outsized role in representing the country abroad. The Communist Party's top leaders speak to the world through a blend of empty-sounding platitudes about "win-win" cooperation or Marxist slogans that fall flat with foreign audiences, while China's civil society is too tightly constrained to present its own alternative. NGOs are closely regulated, while the country's media and cultural industries are heavily censored, and its business leaders studiously avoid politics. While the foreign ministry is widely seen as a weak bureaucratic player at home, on many crucial global issues, its diplomats are the face of the Chinese state to the world.

China knows diplomacy is important and it's spending big to compete. Between 2012 and 2017, Beijing nearly doubled its spending on diplomacy to $7.8 billion, even as the United States slashed funding for the State Department.[19] In 2019, its diplomatic network overtook that of the United States, with 276 embassies and consulates around the world. Just three years earlier it had ranked third behind America and France.[20] Still, instead of winning friends, its "wolf warrior" diplomats have become symbols of the threat posed by a rising China.

***

To understand what's going wrong, we need to step into the shoes of the country's diplomats. Chinese envoys are behaving so undiplomatically because they are unable to extricate themselves from the constraints of a secretive, paranoid political system which rewards unquestioning loyalty and ideological conviction. While their actions can sometimes seem aggressive— even bizarre—from the outside, they make perfect sense when seen from a domestic perspective. Understanding why involves looking at how China's political system has shaped the behavior of its diplomats since the earliest days of the People's Republic.

In 1949, Mao Zedong established Communist China after decades of bitter political struggle with Nationalist Party (Kuomintang) rivals. The Communists had spent much of this time living secretive, underground lives in fear of capture and persecution. After being nearly obliterated in 1934, they were forced into a humiliating retreat across China's remote heartlands before rebuilding their revolutionary movement and eventually seizing on Japan's 1937 invasion to stage a comeback. Despite the Communist Party's eventual victory in 1949, the new regime feared that its rule could be undermined by class enemies at home. What's more, it faced the threat of invasion by the Kuomintang, which had established a new capital on the island of Taiwan, and an increasingly hostile, anti-communist United States.

Still, Mao's new regime badly needed to build bridges with the outside world. Establishing ties with capitalist nations would strengthen its claim to be the sole legitimate government of China, a status contested by the Kuomintang on Taiwan. Strong diplomatic ties with the communist world could bring military protection for the new regime, as well as access to the crucial foreign technologies and expertise needed to modernize the country. Communist China's approach to diplomacy was forged by this imperative to establish relationships around the world while jealously guarding the Party's hard-won victory.

The man charged with squaring this circle was Zhou Enlai, one of the Communist Party's most experienced revolutionaries and the founding father of modern Chinese diplomacy. The task was especially daunting given that the new government had no diplomats to speak of. Acting on Mao's instructions, Zhou cast aside any Kuomintang diplomats who had opted to remain in mainland China, and instead set about creating a diplomatic corps from scratch. Other than a small group of Party officials who had experience dealing with foreigners, the bulk of Zhou's diplomatic corps would be made up of fresh college graduates, ex-soldiers, and hardened peasant revolutionaries. Most spoke no foreign languages and some had never even met a foreigner.

Zhou's task was doubly daunting because, domestically, diplomacy had often been associated with weakness and capitulation to foreign powers. Beginning in the mid-nineteenth century, Chinese envoys had represented the crumbling Qing Dynasty by signing agreements that gave foreign powers preferential access to the Chinese market, extra-legal privileges on Chinese soil, and even control over portions of the country's territory such as Hong Kong. The imperial capital of Beijing itself had been sacked on more than one occasion. The Communists came to power promising to end bullying at the hands of foreign imperialists and declaring that China had "stood up." In order to distance the new regime from this humiliating legacy, the diplomacy of the People's Republic would need to win the respect of other nations while never allowing its own diplomats to show weakness.

Zhou's solution was to model Chinese diplomacy on the military force that had propelled the Communists to power: the People's Liberation Army. He told the new recruits to think and act like "the People's Liberation Army in civilian clothing." They would be combative when needed and disciplined to a fault. They would instinctively observe hierarchy and report to their superiors on everything they did. When necessary, they would report on each other. Most important, the idea of working as a "civilian army" underscored the fact that the first loyalty of Chinese diplomats would always be to the

Communist Party. As every good Communist knew, when Chairman Mao declared that "political power grows out of the barrel of a gun," he had added that "the Party commands the gun, and the gun must never be allowed to command the Party."[21]

The idea of a "civilian army" proved a potent and lasting metaphor for Chinese diplomacy. It provided Zhou's ragtag group with a way to feel proud of what they were doing and some sense of how to do it. A little like the "mission statement" pinned to the wall of a tech startup, it gave them a way to scale their organization quickly while conveniently ignoring the fact that they didn't really know what they were doing.

"They applied the same discipline to the foreign ministry that they applied to the military," explained Gao Zhikai, a former foreign ministry interpreter. "The discipline applied to the organization and also to every individual. The pressure is huge: everyone is watching everyone else to make sure no one is fooling around."[22]

Using this rubric, the Communists found a way to communicate with the outside world while minimizing the risks of doing so. Zhou encouraged a style among his diplomats that one cadre aptly described as "controlled openness."[23] Chinese diplomats were expected to adhere to a rule that forbade them from meeting alone with foreign counterparts. Instead, they worked in pairs to ensure that if anyone deviated too far from the Party line, or shared sensitive information, the person next to them was there to report it. Diplomats were instructed to ask permission before they acted, even on the most trivial matters, and to always report what they said, did, and heard to their superiors. They were banned from dating or marrying foreigners. They were told to stick rigidly to pre-approved talking points, even when they knew these often failed to resonate with foreign audiences.

Born of necessity more than seventy years ago, these rules and practices are still in place today. Zhou's approach has survived and evolved through revolution, famine, capitalist reforms, and the rise of China as a global power. "We're very different from other ministries," one diplomat said. "We're unusual in that we've had a strong culture that's lasted since 1949."[24] Even within the secretive world of the Chinese bureaucracy, foreign ministry officials have a reputation for being unusually uptight and somehow more difficult to relate to than their peers in other ministries. Officials in the Ministry of Commerce sometimes jokingly refer to the Ministry of Foreign Affairs as the "Ministry of Magic" (*mofa bu*), a play on words in Chinese from the acronym MOFA.

The core of China's distinctive approach to diplomacy is the enduring martial ethos established by Zhou. "Our diplomatic corps is a civilian army," wrote one former ambassador in 1997. "It was trained and developed through education from the Party and under the care of Zhou Enlai."[25] In 2019, while touring the new military museum in Beijing, foreign ministry spokesperson Hua Chunying reminded her People's Liberation Army host of the ministry's roots as a "civilian army."[26] Today, as Chinese diplomats square up to the United States in an increasingly intense global rivalry, they still work off assumptions forged in the bloody revolutionary struggles of the twentieth century.

There are real strengths to China's approach. Its diplomats bring unrivaled discipline to the pursuit of their goals. "They can be very charming and professional," one European diplomat said. "Dealing with them can be exhausting because they won't deviate from the official line for even a second."[27] As a result, foreign interlocutors are never left in any doubt about China's stance on the country's core interests such as Taiwan, Hong Kong, and Tibet. What's more, China's disciplined approach to these kinds of issues extends all across its central government agencies, hiding most inter-agency conflicts from the world and enhancing China's ability to present a united front in negotiations. It's a powerful combination in a world beset by disruption and uncertainty.

At times, Chinese diplomacy has performed impressively. In the 1950s, China undertook a charm offensive that won it friends in the developing world and helped build support for the Communist Party as the internationally recognized government of China. In the period after the 1989 Tiananmen Square massacre, Chinese diplomats helped rehabilitate their country in the eyes of the world, kickstarting a nearly two-decade run of successes that culminated in China's hosting of the Summer Olympic Games in 2008.

Yet the system also has major weaknesses. China's approach to diplomacy makes its envoys effective at formulating demands, but poorly equipped to win hearts and minds. Their fear of looking weak in front of Party leaders and the Chinese public makes them focus excessively on small tactical wins at the expense of strategic victories; their constant repetition of official talking points is unpersuasive at best and, at worst, looks like bullying; and their limited space to improvise, show flexibility, or take the initiative leaves them unable to tailor their approach to different audiences.

These constraints matter because they cut to the heart of what it means to conduct diplomacy. Daniele Varè, an early twentieth-century Italian diplomat, described it as "the art of letting someone else have your way." Chas Freeman, a veteran American diplomat, elaborated on the point: "Diplomacy is a political performing art that informs and determines the decisions of other states and peoples. It shapes their perceptions and calculations so that they do what we want them to do because they come to see doing so as in their own best interest."[28]

Judged by these standards, China's political system sets severe limits on the performance of its diplomats. Ultimately, it's a system that's better at silencing critics than persuading others to share its point of view, a system that leaves the Party with tremendous international influence but few true friends. This is true for China on a state-to-state level—the closest thing it has to an alliance is with North Korea; its closest relationship is with Pakistan. It's also true on a personal level: "You know, I don't think I ever really got to know anyone well," another senior European official said at the end of a four-decade career dealing with Chinese diplomats. "I played tennis with a couple of people in the 1990s, but I wasn't able to sustain those relationships. There's no one I could really call a friend."

The system performs particularly badly at times of political tension in Beijing, when Chinese diplomats find themselves more concerned with avoiding charges of disloyalty than improving their country's reputation. These periods of political uncertainty at home have often been accompanied by the forceful assertion of domestic ideologies on the global stage—regardless of the reputational consequences for China. This impulse played out most dramatically during the 1966–1976 Cultural Revolution. As diplomats watched Mao push Chinese politics in an ever more radical direction, they followed his lead in their interactions with foreigners by barking slogans and handing out copies of the Chairman's "Little Red Book." Eventually, the tight discipline of the foreign ministry broke down so completely that junior diplomats locked ambassadors in cellars, forced them to clean toilets, and beat them until they coughed up blood.

Today, as Xi Jinping pushes China in a more authoritarian direction at home and promotes a new, more assertive, role for the country abroad, many of the forces that previously held back China's diplomatic progress are once again resurfacing. Unlike Mao, Xi favors domestic order over radical rebellion. Above all, he seeks political security for himself and a state apparatus that is responsive to his needs. In October 2016, the Communist Party declared Xi its "core leader," a title that had eluded his predecessor, Hu Jintao, and signaled the demise of collective leadership in the Party. In March 2018, it abolished term limits for the presidency, clearing the way for Xi to remain in power for life. These changes mean that any ambitious diplomat must appear to be on the right side of Xi's political agenda, as there is little prospect of waiting him out.

The costs of getting on the wrong side of Xi have also become ever more apparent. Under Xi, Chinese politics has become an increasingly repressive and frightening place. Since 2012, as part of an anti-graft campaign that treats political disloyalty as a form of corruption, more than 1.5 million officials have been punished. That's around four times the population of Iceland. Diplomats have had to sit through "self-criticism" sessions in the foreign ministry and "inspection tours" that test their loyalty to the Party and willingness to follow orders.[29] As such, the impulse for Chinese diplomats to follow Xi's lead is rooted in fear as well as ambition.

The easiest way for diplomats to work toward Xi's wishes is to assert Chinese interests forcefully on the world stage. Even before Xi became president, he used a February 2009 trip to Mexico to complain about "foreigners with full bellies who have nothing better to do than point the finger" at China's human rights record.[30] One of his first acts after becoming leader of the Communist Party in November 2012 was to lay out an agenda for "the great rejuvenation of the Chinese nation," signaling his ambitions for the country to retake its rightful place in the world. Since then, he has repeatedly instructed diplomats to stand up for China more aggressively than they did in the past, even crafting handwritten notes instructing them to show more "fighting spirit."[31]

As a result, the country's envoys have taken a more assertive and even belligerent tone to prove their loyalty to the leadership. They have handed out copies of books about "Xi Jinping Thought" at diplomatic events, echoing the way their predecessors behaved with Mao's "Little Red Book" more than four decades earlier; they have waxed lyrical about Xi's leadership in meetings with foreign counterparts; and they have shouted at and insulted foreign politicians rather than risk looking weak. "Beijing rewards diplomats that are aggressive advocates of China's views and scorns those that it perceives as overly timid," explains Ryan Hass, who served as a China expert on President Barack Obama's National Security Council. "We seem to be watching China's diplomats matching the mood of the moment in Beijing."

The trend has become even more pronounced as the world increasingly questions American leadership. In the space of less than two decades, the United States' authority has been dented by foreign policy mistakes in the

Middle East, an indecisive response to the Global Financial Crisis, paralyzing political gridlock at home, the "America first" populism of Donald Trump, and its fumbling response to the Covid-19 pandemic. At the same time, China's economy boomed and the country faced down the global pandemic more successfully than most Western nations. Many Chinese diplomats began to feel that their political system and development model were superior to those of the West, a belief reinforced by domestic propaganda. In May 2020, foreign ministry spokesperson Hua Chunying responded to State Department criticisms of China's crackdown in Hong Kong by simply invoking the final words of George Floyd as he lay pinned down by Minneapolis police: "I can't breathe."[32]

***

Given all this, you might expect Chinese diplomats to relish the "wolf warrior" label. They don't. To many, it's just the latest example of foreigners refusing to treat China fairly in the court of international opinion. "We think it's really unfair," said one foreign ministry official. "We work so hard to improve China's image and explain our policies, but it doesn't matter what we say. Whatever we do, America and its allies will criticize us."[33] Le Yucheng, the foreign ministry's top vice minister, called the term a "discourse trap that aims to prevent us from fighting back" in a December 2020 speech. "I suspect these people have not awoken from their dreams 100 years ago," he said.[34]

This frustration is understandable. In terms of credentials, today's Chinese diplomats are up there with the best of their international counterparts. Many hold advanced degrees from Georgetown University or the London School of Economics, and have spent years mastering foreign languages ranging from Czech to Bahasa. They have invested much of their lives studying the countries to which they are posted and often care deeply about China's reputation. On a personal level, they can be suave, sophisticated, and even funny.

Quietly, many understand that their behavior is contributing to a global backlash against China. Yuan Nansheng, China's former consul general in San Francisco, voiced the concerns of many inside China's foreign ministry in September 2020 when he warned that "if we let populism and extreme nationalism flourish freely in China, the international community could misinterpret this as Beijing pursuing 'China First,'" referring to Trump's "America First" policy. Yuan called for a return to the low-key approach to diplomacy the country had followed in the 1990s and early 2000s. "Chinese diplomacy needs to be stronger, not just tougher," he said.[35]

It was this contrast between the impressive abilities of many Chinese diplomats and the stilted way they behave in press appearances and official meetings that first drew me to this topic in early 2017. My curiosity only grew as the behavior of some Chinese envoys became ever more brash and aggressive. How could such a sophisticated and well-informed group of people so consistently act in ways that clearly undermined their country's reputation? Why was this emerging superpower struggling to take advantage of the diplomatic opportunities presented to it at an unprecedented moment of global change?

In many ways, Chinese diplomats seemed like a microcosm of their country's broader inability to communicate. The more I explored the topic, the more convinced I became that it was the Chinese system, not the shortcomings of any particular individual or group of individuals, that was holding the country back. I decided that I'd try to understand what it feels like to work as a Chinese diplomat, and to think about what—on an individual level—was making Chinese envoys behave so strangely. In a word, I hoped to put a face on Chinese diplomacy.[36]

This book is a result of that effort. It is based on my experiences as a reporter in China, as well as dozens of interviews with current and former diplomats in Beijing, Washington, and London. Just as important, it draws on research that uncovered a wealth of sources in Chinese government bookstores and on the websites of secondhand booksellers: the memoirs of retired Chinese diplomats. I started out with the books of major figures in Chinese diplomacy such as former foreign ministers Li Zhaoxing and Tang Jiaxuan, but quickly discovered more than one hundred such titles by both senior and junior diplomats. The most useful books were published between the mid-1990s and the mid-2000s, a period of relative political openness, and many have—to my knowledge—never been used before in studies of China's foreign relations. Even when these books have been used, they've usually served to tell a story about the grand sweep of China's foreign policy without pausing to look at the inner worlds of those who implement it.[37]

The books aren't much fun, I concede. Published under the watchful gaze of Chinese censors, some of them written under pseudonyms, the books are cautious and often dull. But hidden among accounts of long meetings, travel logistics, and even family vacations, they contain small moments that paint a rich portrait of China's struggle. Many contain personal stories that mirror China's own trajectory from abject poverty to power and status. Some bear the inscriptions of authors to friends or colleagues who have since sold them to secondhand bookstores or whose children may have done so after their deaths. Others have stamps from the libraries of Chinese embassies around the world. Some even have chunks of text crossed out by readers or faces scratched out from pictures.

Taken together, the books and interviews reveal deep-seated feelings of inferiority and frustration at the difficulties of making China's case to the world. They provide glimpses of diplomats' fears as China's revolution turned on its external representatives and their awkward embarrassment at being forced to lie to foreign counterparts or defend policies they themselves believed indefensible. Above all, they help put a human face on the interactions between a closed society and a more open outside world. Arrogant but brittle, entitled but insecure, Chinese diplomats are in many ways a microcosm of the kind of power China is set to become.

1

The Founder

When he took the stage in China's new foreign ministry on the evening of November 8, 1949, Zhou Enlai knew he had a problem.[1]

He had just become foreign minister and premier of a new revolutionary state whose future looked uncertain. The Chinese Communist Party had established a new government in Beijing, but a rival regime on the island of Taiwan made up of members of the defeated Nationalist Party (Kuomintang) was still seen as the legitimate government of China by all but a handful of nations. Worse, the Nationalists were cultivating American support to invade the mainland and dislodge the Communists. America itself, which had long seen itself as a kind of benevolent tutor to China, was immersed in angry recriminations about who had "lost" the country to Soviet influence.

A handsome man with bushy eyebrows and a good command of English and French, Zhou had spent time in Japan, Britain, France, and Germany by his mid-twenties. Cultured, sophisticated, and quietly confident, Zhou was a natural diplomat. The same was not true of the ragtag group of recruits seated in front of him that night.

At small tables arranged in a semi-circle in the auditorium were some 170 fresh college graduates, local administrators, and hardened peasant revolutionaries. Most of the group had never been overseas and many spoke no foreign languages. They would soon be joined by a cohort of generals and officers from the People's Liberation Army who knew even less about the outside world.

The recruits cut a stark contrast with the elegant white building the Communists had commandeered for their foreign ministry. Erected in the late nineteenth century by Qing Dynasty officials to host visiting German dignitaries, the building's entrance was decorated with two traditional Chinese stone lions in front of European-style neoclassical pillars. It had later served as the foreign ministry of a subsequent republican government in Beijing.

Still, the group was all Zhou had as he prepared to win the new government a place in the world. Addressing the recruits from a makeshift speaker's table with a portrait of Chairman Mao looking down over his shoulder, Zhou was honest about the scale of the challenge ahead. "Most of you are fresh graduates," he said. "We had some contact with foreigners in the past, but before we were engaged in guerrilla warfare. This is diplomacy. It's different."

The recruits were new to diplomacy, but in a sense that didn't matter: Just as the revolutionary state sought to remake Chinese society at home, its diplomacy would represent a radical break with China's past.

Raising his voice, Zhou told the group that "China's last hundred years of diplomatic history is the history of humiliation, of reactionary governments kneeling on the floor to conduct diplomacy." The Communists wanted nothing to do with this legacy. To them, their predecessors had all been some combination of capitalists, traitors, or cowards. The "new China," as they called it, would do things differently. It would cast aside the work of its predecessors and build a diplomatic corps from scratch.

Zhou's desire to start anew served the interests of the regime at home. By portraying his predecessors as traitorous cowards, he could present the Communists as the nation's savior. Instead of looking to the past, the Communists would conduct diplomacy by drawing on strengths that secured them victory in China's long Civil War. "Armed struggle and diplomatic struggle are similar," Zhou told the group. "Diplomatic personnel are the People's Liberation Army in civilian clothing" (*wenzhuang jiefangjun*).[2]

For Zhou, this was much more than mere propaganda. It reflected a genuine and widespread sense of despair about the state of China and its place in the world. During Zhou's lifetime, the once powerful Qing Dynasty had collapsed, the country had plunged into decades of civil war, and China had been forced to cede territory to foreign powers. After reeling from an invasion in which Japanese soldiers were instructed to "kill all, burn all, and loot all," China found itself engulfed in the Civil War from which the Communists had emerged victorious. China's GNP per capita was just $50, compared with $60 in India, and its average life expectancy was just thirty-six years.[3]

Zhou was motivated by a powerful desire to transform the condition of China through the revolutionary potential of the communist state. This would mean a push to industrialize China's economy through a program of socialist modernization and the imposition of a one-Party dictatorship, which would in theory rule on behalf of the Chinese people. It would also mean a complete rethink of Chinese foreign policy and Chinese diplomacy. As part of that effort, Zhou established a diplomatic corps based on the idea of a "civilian army"—a culture that still endures today, more than seventy years after the founding of the People's Republic.

Just as J. Edgar Hoover molded the modern FBI, Zhou's personality and policy choices continue to shape how China's foreign ministry interacts with the outside world today. One diplomat's memoirs described Zhou as "the great helmsman" of Chinese diplomacy, an honorific usually reserved for Mao himself.[4] Zhou is still revered today. "In the foreign ministry, you can criticize Mao Zedong, but you cannot criticize Zhou Enlai," said one diplomat.[5]

***

Zhou Enlai was born in 1898 to a struggling but genteel family in a once-great empire. The ruling Qing Dynasty had been reduced to signing a string of humiliating "unequal treaties" that granted the British and other imperial powers extensive trading rights in China and legal extraterritoriality on Chinese soil, beginning with the Opium War of 1839–1842. Just three years before his birth, China had signed what many regard as the most humiliating of all these agreements: the 1895 Treaty of Shimonoseki, which ceded control of Taiwan to Japan. A string of internal rebellions left tens of millions dead and many more destitute.

The Zhou family home was in the city of Huai'an on the fertile central plains of coastal Jiangsu province. Zhou was raised by a loving and doting aunt whose husband had died before the couple could conceive. They lived in the family's ancestral home, together with Zhou's biological parents.[6]

The aunt had great aspirations for her nephew. She enforced a strict routine, teaching him to read at three and waking him every morning at dawn to practice. She read him fairy tales, stories about Chinese history, and Tang dynasty poetry. Zhou quickly developed a relentless curiosity that would stay with him his whole life.

It wasn't an easy childhood. By the time Zhou was ten, his aunt had died of tuberculosis and his biological mother of cancer. His father left to seek work in faraway Hubei only to lose his job, leaving the family deeply in debt.

Zhou quickly took on family burdens far beyond his age. He cared for two younger brothers; put food on the table; and met with creditors, pawning his late mother's belongings to keep them at bay. He was left to remember family birthdays and the anniversaries of deaths, coordinating gifts for these occasions.

In 1910, Zhou's uncle—an official in the industrial city of Shenyang (then Fengtian) in Northeast China—invited the boy to live with him. Zhou, now aged twelve, found himself in the land then known as Manchuria, a nearly 900-mile journey north of the temperate plains of Jiangsu. To the north was Siberia; to the south, the snow-capped Changbai mountains bordering Korea. Zhou's uncle enrolled him at the best school in the area, the newly opened Yingang Academy.

Zhou's strong southern accent immediately marked him out as different and he found himself targeted by bullies. "I had to come up with my own strategies," he later remembered. "These essentially consisted of efforts to be-friend whomever I could and employ my new allies in my counterattacks."

Zhou's childhood experiences left him with an impressive ability to forge connections with almost anyone he met. A 1974 CIA profile described him as an "urbane pragmatist" who could communicate "reasonableness to his hearers" and "exude an air of charm while working under great stress."[7] Even the famously cantankerous Soviet leader Nikita Khrushchev had a soft spot for Zhou. "We all considered him a bright, flexible, and up-to-date man with whom we could talk sensibly," he later wrote.[8] Others, though, felt there was something a little too slick about Zhou: some in the Kuomintang referred to him as "*Budaoweng*," a weighted toy that always lands upright.[9] Peng Dehuai, a talented and outspoken Red Army general, would later tell Zhou to his face that he was "too sophisticated, too smooth."[10]

As a young man, Zhou also developed the personality traits that would help define his later style of leadership: an engaging and polished but always carefully controlled manner, combined with unrelenting fastidiousness and an uncanny ability to absorb information.[11] As foreign minister and premier, Zhou worked extraordinarily long hours, often finishing for the day as late as three or even four the next morning.[12] When he grew tired, he would place a wet cloth on his face, paste tiger balm on his temples, and even tug at his own hair to keep himself alert.[13] Zhou would go on to mold China's diplomatic corps in this image. Those around him were forced to keep similar hours as they tried to keep up.[14] (This hasn't changed. A 2015 survey by the Chinese ride-hailing app, Didi Chuxing Technology Co., showed that foreign ministry employees worked among the longest hours of any central government ministry.)[15]

On a personal level, Zhou was a study in self-control. Even at the height of the Beijing summer, he always fastened all his shirt buttons and made sure to wear socks with his sandals to avoid the impression of scruffiness, one of his secretaries remembered.[16] Unusually for a man of his generation, Zhou didn't smoke and even kept a sign on his office desk asking that others refrain from doing so.[17] He could handle his liquor, but almost never drank to excess.[18] Sometimes during dessert, he would sprinkle a few drops of China's fiery *baijiu* liquor on his ice cream.[19]

Zhou prepared extensively for every meeting and practiced attention to detail, which bordered on obsessive. As foreign minister, he routinely corrected small mistakes by translators, taking individuals aside for pep talks on how they might improve. On occasion, he even rearranged flowers in meeting rooms before guests arrived after complaining they weren't "natural enough." He sought to institutionalize his meticulous style with a phrase diplomatic trainees still learn today: "there are no trivial matters in diplomacy" (*waijiao wu xiaoshi*).[20]

But there was also a deeply caring side to Zhou's fussiness. He made a point of remembering his diplomats' names, asking after their families, and even placing food on the plates of his translators at banquets to ensure they were able to eat as they worked. At times, he was almost paternal. "Premier Zhou asked me if I practiced family planning," remembered one translator. "He suggested I have two children at most and said that male comrades should control themselves."[21]

***

By the time Zhou reached adolescence, China was several decades into an experiment with European diplomacy that hadn't always come naturally. From the outset, the country's modern diplomatic corps developed as a direct response to foreign incursions and domestic turmoil. Its very existence was a testament to China's weakness.

After the Qing defeat to the British in the second Opium War (1856–1860), the embattled dynasty established a body called the Zongli Yamen, a proto-foreign ministry, in response to British demands for a government department with which Western diplomats could interact. Imperial China had traditionally dealt with foreigners through an array of government departments depending on the nature and function of the relationship. It had no tradition of posting permanent emissaries to foreign countries.

The learning curve was steep, but Qing diplomats adapted quickly. In 1864, they used extracts from American jurist Henry Wheaton's classic book, *The Elements of International Law*, to extract compensation from Prussia after a Prussian warship seized Danish merchant vessels moored at a Chinese port.[22] From the 1870s onward, Chinese diplomats were posted permanently abroad for the first time, where they achieved successes such as helping to curb the exploitation of "coolie" Chinese laborers in Cuba and Peru.[23]

Still, China's new diplomats were powerless to stop the erosion of sovereignty and territory that stemmed from Western imperialism, Qing government mismanagement, and technological backwardness. In 1879, Beijing's envoy to Russia even ceded some 1,200 square miles of the far-western region of Xinjiang to Russia despite explicit instructions to the contrary.[24] There was every reason to think that further incursions would follow: in Africa, European powers were engaged in a "scramble" for territory, while the United States would soon annex Hawaii and take the Philippines from Spain.

The greatest humiliation of all came with the 1895 Treaty of Shimonoseki. The treaty was signed by Li Hongzhang, China's leading political and diplomatic leader between 1870 and the end of the century. A classically trained scholar, Li had passed China's imperial exams in 1847 before becoming a distinguished military commander. He helped to put down the Taiping rebellion, a thirteen-year domestic revolt that claimed more than 20 million lives, and went on to become the governor of several important Chinese provinces. Li was a patriot and a pioneer of the "self-strengthening" movement, which sought to save China by improving China's knowledge of Western military technologies as well as governing techniques such as international law.

These reforms were not sufficient, however, to prevent China's crushing defeat when it went to war with Japan over its influence in Korea in 1894–1895. China had traditionally exercised strong influence in Korea, whose leaders had traditionally sent three tribute missions a year to Beijing.[25] On paper, the situation looked good for Beijing. China had invested heavily in its navy, which was about twice the size of Japan's and included some of the most powerful battleships in the world, but China's forces were poorly organized and inadequately supplied. In the end, these weaknesses proved decisive. Beijing suffered at least 35,000 casualties and deaths during the course of the conflict, seven times more than Japan; the Chinese fleet was virtually destroyed; and the commanding Chinese admiral, who had been seriously injured by a shell from his own ship, committed suicide.[26]

The two sides met to negotiate a peace in March 1895 at the port city of Shimonoseki on the southwestern tip of Japan's main island of Honshu. The talks themselves were a visual representation of how far each power had embraced change. Itō Hirobumi, the prime minister of Japan, wore Western-style dress uniform, complete with a sword and medallions; Li, in contrast, looked every bit the Confucian scholar, clad in traditional Chinese robes with his trademark white beard and mustache.[27] The Japanese pushed Li hard. The resulting treaty, signed in April, forced Beijing to recognize Korean independence, as well as to cede the Liaodong peninsula in Northeast China, the Penghu Islands, and—most important—the island of Taiwan to Japan (Liaodong was returned after a Russian intervention). It also had to open up more treaty ports to Japan and allow Japanese-run factories in China.

Japan's victory turned East Asia's long-established order upside down, ending any pretense of Chinese primacy and transforming Taiwan into a symbol of China's weakness. For more than a century, reunifying Taiwan with mainland China has been an almost sacred mission for Chinese nationalists everywhere. Li Zhaoxing, foreign minister from 2003 to 2007, tells a story in his memoirs about a senior colleague who would get drunk and continuously repeat, "the world only has one China," in reference to Beijing's rival regime on Taiwan. "These words show the weight Chinese diplomats attach to the Taiwan issue," Li wrote. "People tell the truth when they're drunk." For Li and other Chinese diplomats, China will never be able to consider itself a true great power until Taiwan returns to the motherland. "Unlike other major global powers, China is not fully united," he wrote. "This is something that Chinese diplomats must never forget."[28]

Li Hongzhang's legacy would prove equally enduring. Despite devoting his life to strengthening China, Li would be remembered as the personification of Chinese weakness. During his negotiations with Margaret Thatcher over the return of Hong Kong nearly a century later, China's paramount leader, Deng Xiaoping, told the British prime minister that he would not become another Li Hongzhang.[29] In 2019, when China's top trade negotiator, Liu He, sought to strike a deal with the Trump administration, online commentaries emerged comparing his willingness to compromise with that of Li Hongzhang.[30]

In 1901, foreign pressure once again resulted in changes to China's diplomatic apparatus. After an eight-nation army sacked and looted Beijing in the wake of the anti-foreign Boxer Rebellion, Western nations instructed China to convert the Zongli Yamen into the country's first official foreign ministry.[31] A subsequent republican government established its own foreign ministry in the very building where Zhou delivered his November 1949 speech that established Communist China's foreign ministry and vowed to break with the diplomacy of "humiliation."

Zhou experienced these foreign encroachments firsthand. Russian troops had stayed on in northeast China after joining the eight-nation army that put down the Boxer Rebellion. When his teacher told the young Zhou about Russian designs, Zhou responded with anger: "Every citizen must bear the burden of determining the life and death of the nation."[32]

China's international prestige continued to decline. It had now signed "unequal treaties" with countries as diverse as the United States, France, Russia, Prussia, Portugal, Denmark, the Netherlands, Spain, Belgium, Italy, Brazil, and Mexico.[33] Japan operated with impunity in China's backyard as it rushed to fill a power vacuum left by the Qing Dynasty's waning power. It inflicted a stunning defeat on Russia in 1904–1905 and annexed Korea in 1910, further encroaching on an area of traditional Chinese influence, which shared a lengthy border with Manchuria, the ancestral homeland of the ruling Qing Dynasty.

The Qing Dynasty was now so weak that it was unable to persuade Chinese provinces to fund the reforms needed to redeem itself. In October 1911, a rebellion that began with a bomb plot in central China's Hubei province quickly spread. In a desperate bid to save itself, the imperial court called on its top military commander, Yuan Shikai, to put down the rebellion. Instead, Yuan turned on the regime and helped to establish the Republic of China in January 1912 with the famed revolutionary organizer and Nationalist Party leader Sun Yat-sen as provisional president. In February, the last Qing emperor—a six-year-old boy named Pu Yi—abdicated his throne at the insistence of Yuan Shikai. Sun, recognizing that he lacked Yuan's military strength, handed the soldier the presidency of the new republic.

Hopes for the new government were soon dashed as the new republic proved even weaker than its Qing predecessor. Yuan inherited a splintered country with weak public finances. He tried to extend his power by appointing close allies to key government posts, eliminating opposition to his rule, and eventually by proclaiming himself emperor in 1915. Ultimately, his efforts failed. China continued to fragment and rapidly descended into rule by powerful regional warlords. The government in Beijing was able to exert authority over only a section of northern China. All the while, the once great empire's global influence and reputation continued to slide.

Zhou Enlai's political education took place against this turbulent backdrop. He followed events closely in the *Shengjing Daily* newspaper. Now fourteen years old and a student at Dongguan Model School in Shenyang, Zhou read works by reformers such as Kang Youwei, a famed advocate of constitutional monarchy, and Liang Qichao, a leading disciple of Kang whose despair over the physical and spiritual weakness of China led him to dub it the "sick man of Asia"—a term later used by Westerners to scorn the country.[34] Zhou was drawn in particular to a book called *The Revolutionary Army* by Zou Rong, a revolutionary hero who had died in prison in 1905, which called for the Chinese people to rise up and overcome their humiliation. When asked why he attended school, Zhou replied with a simple but powerful quotation from Zou: "so that China can rise up."[35]

In 1913, Zhou moved to the northern port city of Tianjin when his uncle took up a new job. After a few months of intense study for the school's entrance examinations, Zhou was accepted by Nankai Middle School. Modeled on British and American private schools, Nankai sought to develop a strong sense of personal discipline in its students: they rose at 6:30 A.M. before undertaking physical exercise, time in the classroom, and self-study, with lights out at 10 P.M. Classes were conducted in English. Zhou was a straight-A student and continued to read widely including thinkers such as Montesquieu, Rousseau, Adam Smith, and Charles Darwin. At the same time, he was increasingly gripped by political events and his strengthening conviction that China needed to be saved.[36]

It is impossible to understand the way Chinese diplomats think and act without appreciating the power of this conviction. "National humiliation" has become a mainstay of the Communist Party's domestic propaganda, which amplifies and sometimes distorts events. But for Zhou and many of his contemporaries, humiliation was a lived experience.

Wu Jianmin, who would later serve as a senior Chinese diplomat, was one of many who experienced life as a second-class citizen in his own country. Guards at the French Embassy in Nanjing once even set a dog on Wu and his childhood friends as they played outside the embassy's grounds in the 1940s. This scarring episode stayed with Wu into his adulthood, when he was appointed China's ambassador to France.[37]

Experiences like this have helped shape the mindset of China's diplomatic corps. "Historically, the Chinese people were bullied into being afraid, into a somewhat unhealthy mindset where they're overly sensitive to the evaluation of the outside world," Wu wrote in 2015. "If someone says we're good, we're delighted and get all puffed up. If someone says a couple of bad things about us, we're incredibly sad or angry. It expresses a lack of confidence."[38]

The desire to separate themselves from what they saw as the shameful way China had been bullied by foreign powers has instilled Chinese diplomats with an extreme sensitivity to slights and a strong desire for symbolic equality on even the most trivial matters. When Zhou himself toasted Richard Nixon during the US president's historic visit to China in 1972, he was careful to toast the president's glass at exactly an equal level to his own to signify equality between the two powers.[39]

This sensitivity to small gestures and symbolism continues today. Sometimes, it borders on the absurd. Tang Jiaxuan, foreign minister from 1998 to 2003, wrote up a revealing incident in his memoirs. After finishing a meeting with his Indonesian counterpart in 1998, both men visited the men's room. The Indonesian foreign minister turned on the faucet for him and passed him a towel. "This kind of action is extremely rare in diplomatic circles," Tang wrote more than a decade after the fact. "It not only reflected his respect and friendship for China, but also his wish to establish a personal friendship from deep within his heart."[40]

***

China's experience of the First World War would only strengthen the country's sense of humiliation. It would also prove Zhou's making as a revolutionary.

Now divided up between powerful warlords and rival regional governments, China joined the conflict relatively late, in the summer of 1917. It sent some 140,000 laborers to aid the Allied war effort in the hope of regaining control of German territorial concessions on its own territory.[41] As one British officer explained, the Allies were happy to accept the laborers because "they are excellent material, as can be seen by a visit to one of the coolies' battalions." When the Chinese cabinet offered military assistance to the allies, however, British officials argued that transporting the men would amount to "wasting allied tonnage for which they will receive no military return whatever."[42]

Still, the Beijing government hoped that its contribution might be rewarded by the victorious Allies at the end of the war, and dispatched a delegation to the Paris Peace Conference of 1919, which was held at Versailles. Many in Beijing—especially students—shared this sense of optimism, not least because they read about President Woodrow Wilson's "Fourteen Points," which called for self-determination and equality among nations. Chen Duxiu, an intellectual who became one of the founding figures of the Chinese Communist Party, described Wilson as "the number one good man in the world."[43] These high hopes would soon be cruelly dashed.

China's position at Versailles was weak from the outset. The country was now so divided that its delegation to the peace conference was made up of representatives from competing governments in China's north and south. What's more, whereas China had contributed laborers, Japan had spilled blood for the Allies: when Tokyo joined the conflict in August 1914, it declared war on Germany and attacked its Jiaozhou lease on China's Shandong peninsula, which juts out onto the Yellow Sea near Korea. Most important, China's case was undermined by secret agreements Japan had reached with Allied nations to secure recognition of its territorial claims in return for military support.

The country's diplomats performed impressively under the circumstances. One of them was Wellington Koo. Aged thirty-two, he had grown up in the international settlement in Shanghai where he attended St. John's College school, an independent liberal arts college set up by American missionaries, before studying in the United States where he earned a PhD in law and diplomacy from Columbia University. France's prime minister Georges Clemenceau described Koo as "a young Chinese cat, Parisian of speech and dress."

Still, China's representatives at Versailles were unable to sway the great powers. Germany's Jiaozhou lease was turned over to Japan while Koo and the rest of the delegation refused to even sign the treaty. China's diplomats took away a powerful lesson from their experiences in Paris as articulated by the head of the delegation, Lu Zhengxiang: "weak countries have no diplomacy."[44]

Back in China, the response to events at Versailles was explosive. Student protesters massed in Beijing and across the country on May 4, 1919, to demand that China fight for fairer treatment in international affairs, with protesters even torching the house of Cao Rulin, the Beijing government's communications minister, who they believed was too close to Japan.[45] The student protests soon developed into nationwide industrial strikes and a boycott of Japanese goods. The campaign was later dubbed the May Fourth Movement.

Zhou had been watching events unfold from Japan. After he finished high school, he had left for Tokyo in the fall of 1917 to enroll in a Japanese-language school. Like many other young Chinese, Zhou's relationship with Japan was deeply ambivalent. Although the country was already an object of Chinese nationalist anger, it nevertheless provided a model for how Asian nations could strengthen themselves in a world dominated by Western imperialists.

Japan also provided a haven for radical young Chinese who aspired to remake their nation. It was in Japan that Zhou discovered Marxism. Just one month after his arrival, the October Revolution unfolded in Russia. Zhou was mesmerized. He followed the revolution closely, taking notes in his diary as events unfolded. He also read American journalist John Reed's account of the turmoil, *Ten Days That Shook the World*, which was published in 1919.

Zhou returned to China in April 1919 on the eve of the May Fourth Movement. He was swept up by the nationalist fervor gripping the nation as well as the free flow of radical ideas on how to save it. He quickly became a leader of the Tianjin student movement, organizing boycotts of Japanese goods and protest marches against the city authorities. In 1920, he was jailed for six months after leading more than 5,000 students in a march to the local governor's office. In prison, Zhou delivered lectures on Marxism to fellow inmates. He had become a revolutionary.[46]

After his release from jail, Zhou headed to France on a work-study program along with many hundreds of other young Chinese. Like many of his generation, Zhou idealized France's revolutionary heritage. He wrote of the country as the "birthplace of freedom" in a poem to one student who'd set sail ahead of him. "One day you will return, and unfurl the banner of freedom," he predicted.

The France he found shocked and disappointed him. In letters home, Zhou remarked on France's social unrest, widespread unemployment, and the exploitation of its working population. Worse still, many young Chinese in the city faced discrimination, even at the hands of the workers whose radicalism they hoped to emulate.[47]

Nevertheless, Europe's intellectual climate was inspiring. Zhou read widely on political ideas ranging from the gentle gradualism of British Fabian socialism to violent anarchism. In spring 1921, Zhou joined the Paris cell of an underground organization that would soon become the Chinese Communist Party. The cell was under the tutelage of the Comintern or Communist International, then under the control of the new Soviet government in Moscow.

Zhou helped to establish the European branch of the Chinese Communist Youth League the following year. He was put in charge of propaganda and took to wearing a Western business suit paid for by the Comintern.

While in Europe, Zhou also spent time in Britain and Germany. He developed relationships with other future Communist leaders such as the legendary guerrilla commander, Zhu De. He also met future paramount leader Deng Xiaoping, who was struggling with French while laboring in a Renault auto manufacturing plant. Zhou also found his own idealistic way of proposing to his future wife, Deng Yingchao, a student activist he'd met before leaving China. On a postcard depicting the French revolutionary Robespierre, he wrote, "someday we too will meet together to confront the guillotine arm-in-arm."[48]

Much of Marxism's appeal for Zhou lay in its promises of social equality. He was perhaps even more moved by its prospects for promoting China's national renewal. During his time in London he wrote admiringly about the ongoing Bolshevik Revolution in Russia, predicting that just as the Renaissance, the Reformation, and the French Revolution had presaged the rise of the West, Lenin's revolution might help propel China to global prominence.[49]

There was something especially captivating in Lenin's revolution for those who sought to strengthen their own countries. It was a powerful example of how a disciplined "vanguard" party could remake a backward society and mobilize its people toward rebirth. The power of Lenin's approach was evident to the Communists' most bitter enemies. "Communist parties all over the world have long been working underground," the leader of China's nationalist Kuomintang Party Chiang Kai-shek wrote in his diary in 1938. "They have a tightly organized structure and an iron discipline that defies other parties."[50]

For Lenin and many of his early twentieth-century contemporaries, the modern military epitomized the mobilizational power of strict discipline. Communists often dressed in military uniforms for official occasions and even refashioned their capital cities by building giant military parade grounds at the center.[51] Accordingly, when Zhou came to think about how Chinese diplomacy should work, he chose the People's Liberation Army as his inspiration. By the time he delivered his November 1949 speech to the first class of Chinese Communist diplomats, the army had the added advantage of having defeated the Kuomintang government in the country's protracted Civil War.

***

In fact, Zhou had been putting similar ideas into practice for decades before the Communists won. In the late summer of 1924, Zhou returned to China, taking up a role at the Whampoa Military Academy in Guangzhou. The academy was organized by the Kuomintang and supported by the Comintern, which at that time saw the party as a route to influence in the country.

Encouraged by the Soviet agent, Mikhail Borodin—who supplied Bolshevik skills, weapons, and advisers—the Communists and the Nationalists, then led by Sun Yat-sen, had agreed to join forces in the city. The plan was to create a national revolutionary army that would end warlord rule and unite China under one government.

Zhou was appointed as the academy's political commissar, an experience that gave him real military credentials and a taste of enforcing political discipline on a revolutionary army. Whampoa and its teaching methods were modeled on those of the Soviet Red Army and Soviet advisers were on hand to ensure that their models were followed.[52] It was at Whampoa that Zhou saw firsthand the potential for military training to focus the mind and build character.

Whampoa was led by Sun Yat-sen's protégé, Chiang Kai-shek, a military commander who would become head of the Kuomintang after Sun died in 1925. Chiang was born to a family of salt merchants in 1887 in the port city of Ningbo, just south of Shanghai. Chiang internalized his traditional Confucian education far more than many of his contemporaries, developing a lifelong respect for discipline, hierarchy, and authority. He received military training in Japan before returning to China in 1911 and going on to serve under Sun Yat-sen. A fervent patriot and natural autocrat, Chiang had an almost unshakable faith in his own destiny and a fervent desire to free China from imperial influence and warlord rule. Over time, Chiang came to see communism as a severe threat to the country's future: he grew resentful of the cautious attitude of Soviet advisers in Guangzhou as he planned a military campaign to reunite China. Communists inside the Kuomintang, he said, "are not open and do not deal honestly with us."[53]

In August 1925, Zhou and Deng Yingchao married. Deng, herself an experienced revolutionary and now a leader in women's circles in Guangzhou, soon became pregnant. Unwilling to sacrifice her political work to stay at home, she aborted the fetus with drugs she bought from a street vendor. Zhou was away on a military campaign against a local warlord at the time and was furious when he learned of her decision. Deng later suffered miscarriages and the couple was never able to have children.[54]

By 1926, the period of training was over. In July, the Nationalists—now led by Chiang after Sun's death the previous year—launched a "Northern Expedition" to eliminate warlord power and end the unequal treaties. Their forces conquered China's populous and wealthy eastern provinces before ending their campaign near Nanjing, where they set up their capital.

Chiang now felt able to rid himself of the Communists. Relations between the two parties had been strained for more than a year, and, in April 1927, Chiang ordered a massacre of his erstwhile allies. The purge, known as the "white terror," killed some 500 Communist cadres in Shanghai, the cosmopolitan coastal city where the Chinese Communist Party had been founded just six years earlier. Chiang ordered a nationwide manhunt for Communist leaders and Zhou was on the list.[55]

The campaign was a massive setback for the Communists whose urban apparatus was now destroyed. In its aftermath, a new leadership came to the fore. Zhou emerged as a central figure, charged with handling the Party's military affairs. After the massacre, Zhou began living as an underground revolutionary. Like other activists, he lived under constant threat of arrest, torture, and execution by the Kuomintang's secret police. He attended Party meetings only after 7 P.M. or between 5 A.M. and 7 A.M. Zhou never showed himself in public places and often traveled disguised as a businessman, sometimes sporting a beard.

In Shanghai, Zhou and other leaders also began clandestine efforts to rebuild the Party apparatus. He helped organize safe houses for the 200 underground revolutionaries scattered throughout the city as well as to build out the Party's intelligence capabilities.[56]

Zhou's life in Shanghai was punctuated by his leading role in a disastrous military uprising in the city of Nanchang in 1927 during which the Communist troops briefly took control of the city. But their plan to ignite a broader uprising across neighboring regions faltered, and they were forced into a humiliating retreat. It was the first major engagement in a multidecade civil war between Chiang Kai-shek's Nationalists and the Communist Party. In the aftermath of the failed uprising, Zhou was reprimanded by the Comintern but reemerged as one of the most influential figures in the Party following a 1928 meeting in Moscow.

After a period of disagreements with the Comintern over strategy, as well as factional jostling inside the Communist Party, Zhou and other underground leaders were eventually forced to flee Shanghai. Their cover had been blown after the Nationalists captured a member of the Party's intelligence apparatus.

In December 1931, Zhou undertook a dangerous journey to the isolated mountains of Jiangxi province in southeast China. His destination was a Communist base area where Mao Zedong was advocating a peasant-led revolution—a shift from the Communists' earlier strategy of urban insurrection. After stopping at safe houses along the way and even traveling through Hong Kong, Zhou reached the area, known as the Jiangxi Soviet, a few weeks later.

Zhou went to work standardizing and professionalizing the Red Army, which would only later take the name the People's Liberation Army. Zhou's efforts focused heavily on "political education," strict organizational discipline, and professional intelligence gathering. It was an approach he would later employ when organizing Chinese diplomacy.[57]

When Zhou arrived in Jiangxi, he was unquestionably Mao's superior in the Party hierarchy, sometimes imposing orders on Mao with which the future chairman disagreed. Mao would later remind Zhou of these incidents when he wanted to put him in his place.[58]

The Communists remained under intense pressure in Jiangxi. Between 1930 and 1934, the Nationalists launched a series of encirclement campaigns. The Communists were able to repel these at first, using guerrilla tactics, but by 1934 the pressure had become too much.

In October, the Communists set out on a prolonged retreat, known later as the "Long March." It was a journey of some 4,000 miles, crossing rivers and mountain ranges during which troops faced starvation, skirmishes with Nationalist forces, and aerial bombardment. The March would later assume a place in Chinese political mythology akin to George Washington's wintering at Valley Forge.

During the Long March, Zhou made a fateful political transition. In the course of the journey, Mao consolidated his hold over the Party, especially after the January 1935 Zunyi Conference of the Party leadership. Always closely attuned to shifts in the political climate, Zhou retreated into the role of loyal lieutenant—a role he would continue to play until his death in 1976.[59] Zhou's transition spoke to a deep instinct for self-preservation that would enable him to outlast almost everyone else in Mao's inner circle.

Zhou made himself useful and indeed often indispensable to Mao by mediating conflicts and organizing the Party's bureaucracy. He implemented Mao's policies and liaised with outsiders. Zhou's talents also bred resentment. His response was extreme deference to Mao which sometimes bordered on sycophancy.[60]

"I have always thought, and will always think, that I cannot be at the helm and can only be an assistant," Zhou told Mao when the chairman politically persecuted him in later life.[61] Sidney Rittenberg, an American communist who stayed behind in China after the revolution, remembered Zhou once crawling around on the floor in front of Mao to show him points on a map.[62] Mao's personal physician, Li Zhisui, even described Zhou as a "slave" to the chairman.[63]

This instinct extended to foreign affairs. When meeting foreign guests, Zhou took pains to attribute China's successes to Mao's leadership, playing down his own role.[64] He would also consult Mao on the most trivial of matters, sometimes surprising even his own staff. Years later, Zhou suffered a rare loss of self-control, throwing up after drinking too much with Soviet leader Nikita Khrushchev in Moscow. When Zhou returned to Beijing, he immediately reported the incident to Mao, a move a longtime translator thought odd. Mao didn't seem to care.[65]

On another occasion, Poland's communist government said it wanted to give Zhou an award during his 1954 visit to the country. Zhou wrote a special cable to Mao asking whether he should accept. When a diplomat asked Zhou why he didn't just accept and tell Mao later, Zhou replied, "This is a matter of discipline. How could I not report this to the chairman?"[66] Zhou permitted no portraits of himself to be displayed inside the foreign ministry; when he once discovered a painting of himself alongside that of Mao in an overseas Chinese embassy, he immediately ordered that his image be taken down.[67] He knew it would be unwise to display too much self-regard.

Zhou's actions were carefully calculated. For one thing, deference to Mao would allow him space to pursue policies he considered important and, where possible, to protect those he cared for. The approach was likely also necessary for Zhou's political survival. "On some level, Mao hated his servant, who, he knew, was not only far too smart, but also inscrutable in his devotion," wrote Gao Wenqian, Zhou's former official Communist Party biographer who later moved to the United States to work as a human rights activist. "He always kept his eyes half-open for a chance to humiliate him."[68]

Zhou's deference to Mao should not be confused with weakness. Like most of those who succeeded in the underground Communist movement, Zhou was also capable of chilling ruthlessness. In 1931, he had ordered the execution of the family members of a defector to the Nationalists.[69] In 1955, he left the crew and passengers of an airplane—including Chinese and foreign journalists—to be blown to pieces over the Pacific Ocean after deciding not to board himself because of a bomb plot.[70]

The exact truth about Zhou Enlai's relationship with Mao remains a closely guarded state secret, even in today's China. With the reputations of so many revolutionary leaders stained by famines, crackdowns, and political oppression, Zhou remains a pristine model communist for the regime to promote. As Gao, his biographer, puts it, Zhou is the Chinese Communist Party's "last perfect revolutionary."[71]

***

After just over a year in retreat across China, the battered Communist forces arrived in the northwest province of Shaanxi in October 1935. During the journey, they had passed comrades buried in shallow roadside graves, picked the meat off dead horses to survive, and chewed at the leather of their belts to suppress hunger.[72] Just 8,000 of the original 80,000 who had set out on the journey had made it to the country's remote and barren northwest, where they would set up camp and begin the task of rebuilding a revolution that seemed on the brink of failure.

The Communists' efforts to rebuild took place as much of the world seemed intent on tearing itself apart. In March 1935, Adolf Hitler had announced that he was re-forming the Luftwaffe, the German air force banned under the Treaty of Versailles. In October, Italian dictator Benito Mussolini launched an invasion of Ethiopia, one of Africa's few remaining independent states. The Soviet Union, already weakened by years of mass starvation and political repression, was on the brink of Stalin's Great Terror, a breathtaking purge that claimed the lives of about a million people.[73]

Against this bewildering backdrop, the Communists found themselves weakened and more isolated than ever. To have any hope of saving the revolution, they would need international support and recognition. The task of securing this would fall to Zhou Enlai. His first significant step would involve a young student organizer named Huang Hua, who found himself in the right place at the right time.

2

Shadow Diplomacy

One summer day in 1936, Huang Hua slipped out of his dormitory with a single leather suitcase in hand, telling no one of his departure. The twenty-three-year-old student's destination was the Communist Party's remote revolutionary base in the badlands of Shaanxi province.[1]

Born Wang Rumei in 1913, the bright-eyed student with a broad toothy smile had grown up in Hebei province on the vast North China Plain. Civil war had disrupted his studies in his hometown, forcing him head to the country's Northeast to continue his education, only to see that too cut short by Japan's invasion of the region in 1931. Huang and his classmates watched trainloads of Chinese students retreating south in the face of the advance by their stronger Asian neighbor.

In 1932, Huang had enrolled in Yenching University in Beijing (then "Beiping"), a school run by American missionaries. At Yenching, Huang mixed with left-wing professors and got hooked on books about Marxism. In short succession, he'd marched against Japanese aggression, joined the Communist Party, experimented with homemade explosives, and found himself imprisoned for subversive activities. Huang's support for the Communists spoke to a passionate, almost visceral desire to remake his country through revolution and restore it to a place of dignity. Like many of his contemporaries in the underground Communist movement, he adopted a new name on joining the Party. Wang Rumei became Huang Hua.

Now a senior at Yenching, Huang had agreed to act as translator for the American journalist Edgar Snow, who was on his way to meet the already legendary guerrilla leader, Mao Zedong. For Huang, the journey would mark the start of a lifetime representing Chinese Communism to the world. He'd go on to serve as China's first ambassador to the United Nations and eventually foreign minister. For now, though, Huang would need to make it across the country without being caught.

His first stop was Xi'an, an ancient walled city at the eastern end of the Silk Road that had been the capital of multiple ancient dynasties. Xi'an was now a battleground for local warlords and a den of Nationalist government spies. Its ancient streets teemed with beggars, colorfully dressed prostitutes, villagers selling hand-spun clothes, and merchants delivering goods to Western department stores.[2]

After traveling to the city separately, Huang and Snow agreed to rendezvous at Xi'an's West Capital Hotel. The pair decided that Snow and his friend, the American doctor George Hatem, would carry on ahead in a military truck while Huang would wait for instructions from underground contacts.

At one point, Huang narrowly evaded capture by Kuomintang agents patrolling the city. Two men knocked at his door, demanding that he explain his business in Xi'an and show them his papers. Thinking on his feet, Huang dropped the names of local dignitaries to signal that he was politically well-connected. "You're welcome to enter and search my things," Huang said, projecting confidence he did not possess. "No, it seems you're one of us," one of the agents replied. When Huang recounted the story to his local contacts, they told him it was time for him to get out of the city. "Xi'an is not safe. You shouldn't stay here any longer," one told him.

Three tense days later, it was time to leave. Huang's contact picked him up in a military truck, together with a friendly colonel who would help them get through the city's checkpoints. Once they reached the outskirts, they donned the uniforms of the local warlord's army and set out on a 200-mile journey through some of the most lawless parts of rural China.

Huang and his companions drove for three days until the road literally ended. The colonel headed back while Huang and his contact continued on foot along a mud road, climbing ridges and crossing rivers barefoot.

Although both were tired and hungry, Huang's companion told him it was too dangerous to stop: the risk of encountering armed bandits was just too high. At one point, an unknown voice cried out from behind: "Give me the password or I'll shoot." Huang's contact ignored the voice and kept walking. Huang Hua followed.

When Huang eventually arrived at the Communist Party's base area centered on the town of Bao'an (they later moved to nearby Yan'an), he was greeted by Party spymaster Li Kenong, who quizzed him about his background and Party connections.[3] Once Li was satisfied that he was not a spy, Huang was cleared to begin exploring his new environment. And some environment it was.

The area surrounding Bao'an, was one of the poorest and most technologically backward parts of China. Farmers eked out their livings from arid hillsides during the five frost-free months of the year, but often found their efforts washed away by flooding in July and August. Ineptly governed for centuries, the area had been further decimated by warlord and bandit attacks after 1911. Many peasants lived in the rubble of deserted towns and villages linked by crumbling roads.[4]

It was in this most hostile of environments that the Communist Party set the tone it would impose on China's future and the country's diplomacy. Knowing that it needed international legitimacy to survive, the Party put together a coterie of foreign affairs specialists, including Huang Hua, who would go on to emerge as the core of the foreign ministry's leadership in 1949.

Many of the practices and cultures laid down by this group continue to shape Chinese foreign policy today—for better and for worse. Communist leaders charmed overseas guests using hospitality techniques that endure today. They enticed foreigners, especially Americans, with promises of political liberalization that they had no intention of keeping.

Most important, this period saw Mao Zedong's overweening political influence begin to shape the Party's diplomatic culture, just as he shaped almost all other aspects of political life. In the years that followed, China's fledgling diplomats experienced methods of political control that would recur periodically inside the foreign ministry, most dramatically during the Cultural Revolution and more recently under Xi Jinping. First, though, Edgar Snow had arrived at the Party's base area and he was in need of entertainment.

***

Snow's arrival at the revolutionary base presented the Party with an opportunity to try its hand at what we now call public diplomacy.

When Zhou Enlai had put out feelers for a foreign journalist willing to travel to Shaanxi, Snow seemed like the perfect fit.[5] Born to a middle class family in the leafy suburbs of Kansas City, Missouri, Snow dropped out of college to join an advertising firm in New York at the height of the Roaring Twenties. He'd soon saved enough for a trip to Asia and set sail in 1928. "I knew nothing of foreign peoples," he later remembered. "I didn't know a communist from a Catholic when I went to China."[6]

Snow traveled across Asia, earning money as a writer before moving to Beijing with his new bride in 1933. Once there, he used his media connections to help left-wing Chinese writers get published in the West and raise money for local labor unions. Genuinely distressed by the poverty and inequality he witnessed in Nationalist China, Snow had become strongly critical of Chiang Kai-shek and was doggedly pursuing an interview with Mao Zedong.[7]

In Snow, the Party saw an opportunity to raise its profile in elite circles in the United States. Its treatment of Snow helped establish an enduring model where flattery and careful stage management secured the support of foreign "friends."[8]

Step one was flattery. When Snow and his companion Hatem arrived at the base, they were treated like international statesmen. A marching band played as Red Army troops lined the streets and crowds shouted, "Welcome, American comrades!" An array of top Communist leaders greeted the pair after their long journey before treating them to a banquet.[9]

"The effect pronounced on me was highly emotional," Snow wrote in his diary. "It was the first time I had been greeted by the entire cabinet of a government, the first time a whole city had been turned out to welcome me."[10]

The Chinese government continues to deploy flattery as a diplomatic tool today. When President Donald Trump announced his first official visit to Beijing in November 2017, Cui Tiankai, China's ambassador in Washington, played to the president's ego by promising a "state visit-plus," suggesting a level of access and decorum not usually afforded to foreign dignitaries. During the visit, Xi Jinping hosted Trump for dinner in the Forbidden City, making him the first foreign leader the People's Republic had invited to dine in the palace that housed Chinese emperors for nearly 500 years. Trump and his wife Melania were treated to afternoon tea in the Hall of Embodied Treasures and a private performance of Peking Opera in the Belvedere of Pleasant Sounds, a theater once used to entertain the imperial family.[11] Trump would later describe the visit as "one of the most incredible of my life."[12] He was just one in a long line of foreign guests wined, dined, and flattered by Communist Party leaders using the model tested on Edgar Snow.

Snow's arrival in Shaanxi was a validation for the Communists too. When Snow and Hatem delivered a speech to members of the Red Army, attendees unfurled banners in both English and Chinese that read, "We are not isolated. We have the support of international friends."[13] For a political Party that had spent so much of its history isolated and on the run, Snow's visit was an uncommon moment of international recognition.

Once Snow was settled, the Communists arranged for him to tour the base area, assigning Huang Hua as his handler. Huang accompanied Snow to meetings with Red Army commanders and soldiers on the front line where the American heard stories about the Long March as well as the Party's redistributive programs. Mao also met with Snow every day for ten days to impart his life story.[14] Throughout the trip, Snow's experiences were carefully choreographed. His writing was personally reviewed and censored by Mao using translations provided by Huang.[15]

By the time Snow first met him, Mao was forty-three years old. Born in the rustic village of Shaoshan in rural Hunan province, Mao was the son of a rich peasant farmer whose domineering personality he grew to despise. A voracious reader from a young age, Mao became interested in the works of nationalist reformers as an elementary school student. He later became acquainted with the founding members of the Chinese Communist Party while serving as a librarian at Peking University, and went on to become one of its earliest members.

With messy hair parted in the middle and a thick Hunan accent, Mao stood above most of his contemporaries at nearly six feet tall. He was in many ways the opposite of Zhou Enlai, especially in his distrust of intellectuals and contempt for discipline. Throughout his career, Mao's commitment to social justice was matched by a restless desire to dismantle the social and political institutions of traditional China, which he believed had kept the country weak. Mao also had a remarkable capacity for personal and political grudges and an overpowering drive for revenge.

Initially overlooked by Soviet advisers and even shunned by other revolutionaries, Mao's belief in peasant revolution had been vindicated after the Party's previous Soviet-backed policy of urban insurrection took it to the brink of extinction in 1934. By the end of the Long March, Mao was unquestionably the dominant force in the Party. The power of his personality and his vision for China's revolution would shape Chinese politics for decades to come.

Snow turned the interviews into a book, *Red Star over China*, which became a bestseller after its publication in 1937. The book marked the beginning of Mao's transformation into an international revolutionary icon. It praised Mao as a "Lincolnesque" leader who could "awaken" China's population to "a belief in human rights."[16] The Party's first major attempt at public diplomacy had gone better than it could have hoped.

***

The "Yan'an years," named after the small city where the Communist Party moved its headquarters in 1937, would later take on a mythical quality in Party history. They came to represent a pure kind of communist idealism that flourished before the leadership was led astray in the Great Leap Forward and Cultural Revolution—an image that people like Edgar Snow helped cultivate.

In reality, though, it was during these years that the Party developed techniques for political and ideological control that have endured through today. It was in Yan'an that Mao began to lay the foundations for his future cult of personality, working with Party propagandists to develop "Mao Zedong Thought." It was also in Yan'an that Mao first read the *History of the Communist Party of the Soviet Union (Bolsheviks): Short Course*, a book compiled and published in 1938 at Stalin's direction. The book would play a formative role in Mao's approach to politics and economic policy in the decades that followed.[17]

Snow was just one of many overseas visitors entertained in Yan'an— other groups included students, members of progressive political parties, and overseas Chinese leaders. As each group was welcomed to the base, cadres assessed their political attitudes and figured out how they could be useful. Many dined with Mao and Zhou and were treated to the best meals the Party could offer. One group of students was even treated to a cocktail party in a peach orchard.[18]

Snow's glowing reviews of his visit helped win him a special status: as an "old friend" of China. He'd be deployed again and again by the Party to send messages to the outside world. These ranged from attempting to persuade the world that there was no famine during the disastrous Great Leap Forward of the late 1950s to Mao's furtive signals that he was open to closer ties with the United States in 1970.

The "old friend" moniker would later be assigned to leaders like Richard Nixon; Henry Kissinger; Singapore's founding prime minister, Lee Kuan Yew; and King Juan Carlos I of Spain.[19] It's still used now. In December 2016, when Terry Branstad was proposed as a candidate for US ambassador to China, China's diplomats seized on his relationship with Xi Jinping even though this consisted only of a brief visit to America in the 1980s. Nevertheless, Branstad too became an "old friend of the Chinese people."[20]

It's a designation with a very precise meaning in the Chinese system. "Friendship for them means you're someone who will give them the benefit of the doubt," said Robert Suettinger, a former senior CIA China analyst. "It's about having a foreigner who will tell you things he might not otherwise tell you. It's very structured. It's very transparent. They use the term over and over again to soften you up because they know you understand it differently from them."[21]

"Friendship" proved so useful that it helped bridge the worlds of diplomacy and intelligence for Party leaders. During training classes on intelligence-gathering techniques given to Chinese military attachés in the 1950s, Li Kenong and other instructors showed Soviet intelligence textbooks that advocated the use of money and beautiful women to gather information. Li told the recruits, however, that China would instead rely on the technique of gathering intelligence by making "friends."[22]

The designation of friendship also confers on the recipient an obligation not to transgress the relationship. A classic 1985 study of Chinese negotiating behavior conducted for the RAND Corporation identified the careful application of pressure to "old friends" as a core tactic. When President Ronald Reagan entered office in 1981 after campaigning for a tougher China policy, China assiduously pressured his vice president, George H. W. Bush, knowing that Bush considered his role in establishing friendly Sino-American ties in the 1970s a major professional achievement. Just after Reagan's inauguration, Chinese premier Zhao Ziyang wrote to Bush expressing his hope that "in view of the part you played in promoting the normalization of China-U.S. Relations" he would "make significant contributions to the further development of our relations."[23]

**

After finishing up his time as Snow's minder, Huang briefly returned to Beijing, before permanently moving to Yan'an and devoting his life to the communist cause. After a period studying subjects from propaganda to guerrilla warfare, he eventually got a job as secretary to the Red Army general, Zhu De, one of the Party's greatest military leaders.[24]

Life in the rural backwater was spartan. Cadres were fed millet and boiled turnips, sometimes potato. Huang grew so thin that when a colleague bumped into him, he assumed Huang was carrying a pistol. In fact, he'd grazed up against Huang's hip bone.

Huang would later describe the mood in Yan'an as "relaxed." But life was highly regimented. Students and cadres were woken with a bugle call at 6 A.M. before running, eating breakfast, and working or taking classes. Lights went out at 10 P.M. after a brief period of free time. "All institutions led an army-style life," Huang remembered. (Even today, foreign ministry recruits undergo one month of military training before joining China's diplomatic service.)[25]

Huang had arrived in Yan'an just as the Communists were starting to think seriously about the outside world. In 1927, the Party had established regular (although intermittent) radio contact with the Soviet-led

Communist International through an organization labeled the "Village Work Department" to disguise its true function. In 1928, it began building links with overseas revolutionary movements.

In 1931, the Jiangxi Soviet—the Party's main base before the Long March—had established a proto-foreign ministry under the leadership of Wang Jiaxiang (who would later go on to serve as ambassador to the Soviet Union). But the new institution, which was set up in a village building, found itself with little to do except manage occasional dealings with local foreigners.[26]

Now, after reestablishing a permanent base area following its 1935 arrival in Shaanxi, the Party once again looked to the outside world as it welcomed guests such as Snow.[27]

The real turning point for the Party's foreign relations came two years later, in July 1937, when Japan invaded China. Over the next eight years, the war would divert the bulk of Chiang Kai-shek's forces from fighting the Communists and provide crucial breathing space for the revolution to strengthen. Having previously agreed to work together against Japan in 1936, the Communist Party and the Kuomintang were now on the same side—at least in theory.

The struggle against Japan helped to alleviate Yan'an's isolation and created conditions for the Communists to expand their international reach. Zhou, who was now the Party's official representative in its coalition government with the Nationalists, used his presence in China's wartime capital of Chongqing to develop relationships with American, British, and Soviet diplomats. He also met with foreign journalists and international organizations.[28]

During the war with Japan, Zhou began to set up a number of outward-facing organizations that would help train many of China's future top diplomats. In March 1938, the Communists set up a liaison office in the border region around Yan'an to handle visits from foreigners and non-communist Chinese.[29] In 1939 and 1940, Zhou instructed the Party's Southern Bureau and its Yangzi Bureau to set up departments specializing in international propaganda. They would later be renamed Foreign Affairs Bureaus.[30]

Zhou chose his recruits well. One of them was a brilliant English-speaking revolutionary named Gong Peng. Gong had previously helped translate Edgar Snow's *Red Star over China* into Chinese. Gong said the tasks of the new bodies were to gather intelligence on foreign countries, publicize the Party's foreign policies, and to "make friends and expand influence."[31] She would go on to play a leading role in early Communist China's relations with foreign journalists. Peggy Durdin, a pioneering foreign correspondent, would describe her as "the most impressive public relations figure I have ever met."[32]

By the time these organizations were up and running, China's fight against Japan was on the way to becoming part of a global conflict as Hitler pushed a reluctant Europe toward war and tensions mounted between Washington and Tokyo. Japan's surprise attack on Pearl Harbor in December 1941 brought the United States into the conflict, turning the tide against the Axis powers and winning Nationalist China a powerful new ally against Japan.

For now, Mao's Communists and Chiang Kai-shek's Nationalists were at least nominally on the same side, although both parties expected a final battle for China's future to ensue as soon as the war with Japan ended. In the meantime, Chairman Mao was focused on extending his grip over the Party apparatus, including its nascent foreign affairs organizations. By late 1941, Mao had established personal control over the long-range radio linking Yan'an to Moscow.[33] Now he sought more complete authority, and his weapon of choice was terror.

****

In the spring of 1942, the Communist Party's nascent foreign policy apparatus experienced its first purge as Mao launched a "Rectification Campaign."[34] Aimed at further unifying the Party behind Mao, the movement sought to weed out "subjectivism, dogmatism and factionalism." Paradoxically enough, it also targeted "indulgence in jargon."[35]

At first, many cadres were confused by the campaign, especially young recruits. Still, they followed their superiors' leads, using the Leninist techniques of "criticism" and "self-criticism" to attack those who fell short of Mao's standards and to confess their own shortcomings.[36] Prominent intellectuals and writers whose views diverged from the Party leadership's were viciously and publicly attacked. Some were sent off for "reform through labor."[37]

As the campaign spread, Huang Hua briefly found himself in political trouble. A fellow Communist reported him to his superiors for using his boss's official seal without permission (the equivalent of faking a signature). Huang managed to avoid serious repercussions as his boss, Zhu De, vouched for him. Many others were not as fortunate.[38]

The Rectification Campaign intensified after April 1943, as Mao's internal security chief—Kang Sheng—led a hunt for "hidden enemies" in the Party's ranks. Many were forced to falsely admit they were enemy agents.[39] An atmosphere of fear and uncertainty spread across Yan'an as the campaign engulfed the Party. Even officials from Stalin's Soviet Union found the new mood distasteful. Peter Vladimirov, a Russian journalist and Soviet agent based in Yan'an, said that the purge had led to an "oppressive, suffocating atmosphere."[40]

Zhou Enlai was expected to participate in the campaign just like everyone else, and returned to Yan'an to do so. In addition to joining in the self-criticism sessions, Zhou wrote a 50,000-character document outlining his "new" understanding of Party history.[41] In a speech, he told assembled officials that "all those who opposed Mao" had now been "proved utterly wrong."[42]

After working so hard to build ties with the outside world, the Party now shifted its focus inward. The flow of foreign guests to Yan'an slowed significantly, leaving the Communists' base area a more isolated place and cutting the Party off from access to the intelligence foreigners brought with them.[43]

The relationship between political repression at home and foreign policy setbacks would prove an enduring one for China. The Rectification Campaign provided an early lesson to the country's budding diplomats that their personal and professional actions would be closely watched. Ties with the outside world were important, but foreigners had to be handled with caution. A sharp sense of political realities would be necessary for Chinese diplomats to stay safe.

"The influence of the Communist Party, its guiding ideology and its internal power struggles have impacted the composition and behavior of its diplomatic corps from day one," said Suettinger, the former CIA specialist. "They've never put aside the idea that they have enemies who need to be dealt with—inside and outside of China."[44]

Still, it was clear to Mao and everyone around him that international relationships could be crucial to the Communists' future chances of success against the Nationalists. Fortunately, an opportunity was developing in Washington.

***

As the war against Japan progressed, American policymakers were growing increasingly skeptical about the dependability of Chiang Kai-shek's

Nationalists. Concerned about reports of corruption and even that Chiang might be hoarding American military supplies for a future fight against the Communists, some in Washington wondered if it might make sense to send aid to Yan'an.

To this end, Washington dispatched a US Army Observer Group in July 1944 to assess the Communists' politics and military capabilities.[45] The group was led by Colonel David D. Barrett and made up of military officers, service personnel, and diplomats. The mission arrived just one month after Allied troops landed on the beaches of Normandy and as the United States was starting to think seriously about what the world might look like after the end of the war.

The fact the visit was even taking place was a breakthrough, marking the first official contact between the American government and the Chinese Communist Party. As Huang Hua later recalled, "The dispatch of the United States Army Observer Group to Yan'an signified that the United States government had in fact given somewhat official recognition to the Communist Party of China."[46]

It was also a significant challenge: officials in Washington were closely aligned with Chiang Kai-shek and suspicious of all stripes of communists.

The Party's previous contact with the United States had been limited. A Chinese bureau was established inside America's Communist Party in 1935 to help publicize the Chinese Communists and track the political mood in America. The Party had also sent delegations to the United States to promote the impression of military professionalism in the face of Nationalist incompetence.[47]

The US Army Observer Group's visit to Yan'an was something altogether different. Zhou believed that the visit necessitated a new organization and a more rigorous and professional approach to foreign affairs. A Foreign Affairs Group was set up under the Red Army to receive the guests. Huang Hua was put in charge of translation.

The first group of Americans arrived in July, landing on a specially expanded airstrip outside of the city's east gate. They were greeted by a host of top leaders including Zhou Enlai, and later met with Mao, Zhu De, and others.

The Communists prepared a welcome banquet for their guests, providing the best selection of Western food they could muster, including jam, milk, steak, and eggs. For accommodation, they were given what the Communists considered the best caves in Yan'an, which they furnished with a radio antenna, a power generator, and the Stars and Stripes flag.[48]

The Party's new diplomats were instructed to be welcoming, answer questions positively, and exchange ideas with the American visitors. They were told to approach the relationship as one of equal allies where China was neither superior nor subordinate, and foreigners would have to be respectful of China's "national dignity."[49]

The visiting Americans were shown the resistance bases of Communist troops and briefed on the condition of the Red Army. They did not seem to pick up on the brutal Rectification Campaign that had just taken place. John Service, a foreign service officer who had pushed for the visit, described Mao as "modern" and "Western" and took his claim to support democracy seriously. "There is no feeling of restraint or suppression," he wrote. Most striking of all, Service wrote admiringly that there was "no criticism of party leaders."[50]

Zhou quickly moved to formalize the Party's forays into international diplomacy. In August 1944, he drafted a directive entitled "On Diplomatic Work," which hailed the success of the mission and proclaimed "the beginning of our work in foreign relations." The directive emphasized the importance of winning international recognition for the Party and stressed the need to cooperate with the US Army. At the same time, it noted that Chinese diplomacy should not lose sight of "self-respect and self-confidence."[51]

***

In August 1945, the atomic bombs that dropped on Hiroshima and Nagasaki ended the Pacific War. The defeat of Japan left a vacuum in those areas of China that had been controlled by Tokyo. The Nationalists and Communists rushed to seize the opportunity by picking up the conflict they'd waged off and on since the 1920s. During the war, the Communist Party had gained popularity and governing experience, and had seized important weapons from the Japanese while the Nationalist government had become increasingly beset by corruption.

The two sides began fighting again just as tensions between the United States and the Soviet Union were increasingly dividing up the world along ideological lines. Although Stalin had initially been hesitant to throw his full support behind the Chinese Communists, he became increasingly willing to offer support as he watched the United States occupy Japan. The Communists' cause was also aided by Stalin's decision to withdraw from Manchuria, which gave the Communists an advantage in a strategically crucial area.

Even before the resumption of hostilities, America had been attempting to create a durable peace between the Kuomintang and the Communists. It initiated two ultimately unsuccessful mediation missions: the Hurley Mission, which lasted from September 1944 until November 1945, and the Marshall Mission from December 1945 to January 1947, led by war hero George C. Marshall.

On Marshall's arrival in Chongqing, Zhou treated the American general to a dose of his trademark charisma, stressing the Communist Party's interest in peace and democracy, and even offering Marshall a toast to "lasting freedom." A few months later, when Marshall visited Yan'an, he met with Mao, Zhe De, and other leaders, with Huang Hua acting as translator. Marshall was also treated to a banquet and a two-hour performance of revolutionary songs. As the American prepared to leave the city, Mao told him that "the entire people of our country should feel grateful and loudly shout, 'long live cooperation between China and the United States.'"[52]

It was not to be. Peace talks collapsed in 1946 and the civil war resumed in earnest, becoming just one part of a much broader battle for influence as the world slid toward the Cold War. American and European policymakers were distressed at what seemed like relentless Soviet expansionism in Eastern Europe and worried parts of Western Europe as well as Asia would fall next. In March 1947, President Harry Truman announced a doctrine that promised to "support free peoples who are resisting attempted subjugation by armed minorities or by outside pressures."[53]

By 1948 it was clear to Truman's advisers that Chiang Kai-shek could not win against the Communists. Marshall, now back in Washington as secretary of state, laid out the stark choices facing the Nationalists to Wellington Koo, China's onetime delegate at Versailles and now the Republic of China's ambassador to the United States. Chiang "is losing about 40 percent of his supplies to the enemy," Marshall said. "If the percentage should reach 50, he will have to decide whether it is wise to supply his own troops."[54]

By 1949, the Nationalist government was a mess and the Communists were sweeping across China. The Republic of China's diplomats overseas had not been paid for six months. Diplomats in the embassy in Paris were in a state of rebellion and were attempting to persuade Nationalist diplomats elsewhere to switch allegiance. In October, the group sent a telegram to the Communists, saying that they had cut off contact with the Republic of

China's foreign ministry and would await instructions from Beijing.[55] That moment would come soon enough.

***

In anticipation of victory, Zhou had made sure he kept China's nascent diplomatic corps together. In 1947, he established a new iteration of the foreign affairs group that had welcomed the American visitors to Yan'an three years earlier. Although the Party's contact with the outside world was now limited, Zhou busied the group with tasks such as translating Mao's writings into English and monitoring events outside China. This time, the group would report directly to Party leaders instead of the military.[56]

"Zhou Enlai believed that this group of cadres had some foreign affairs experience and had some foreign language skills," one participant remembered. "They could become the backbone of the new China's diplomacy."[57]

As victory approached in January 1949, Zhou gathered his foreign affairs group in the revolutionary base of Xibaipo outside of Beijing. He delivered a speech outlining how foreign diplomats in Beijing should be treated and laid down his expectations for the new diplomats of the soon-to-be-born People's Republic.

"Foreign affairs cadres are the People's Liberation Army in civilian clothing," Zhou told the assembled recruits, stressing the need for absolute discipline and obedience to the central leadership. "Diplomatic authority resides with the center, no region is permitted to act on its own authority," he added.[58]

***

Mao's forces took control of the Nationalist capital of Nanjing in April 1949. Mao issued a proclamation that still stands today: that to have relations with the new China, countries would need to break relations with the Nationalist government, which was then reassembling on Taiwan.

Huang Hua was sent to head up the Communist Party's foreign affairs operations in the city. He began taking over the Republic of China's foreign ministry and shipping reams of its official documents to Beijing. He was also given another mission in Nanjing: Mao authorized him to meet with John Leighton Stuart, the US ambassador who Huang knew from his days at Yenching University.[59] Thirteen years after he'd arrived in Yan'an as a bright-eyed student, Huang was now on the front lines of the new communist power's diplomacy with the most powerful nation on earth.

Mao trusted Huang with this mission because he had now developed the extraordinary self-control the Party expected of its top diplomats. He had a practiced persona for every occasion. The American communist Sidney Rittenberg, who had known Huang since Yan'an, remembered him as "haughty, distant and somewhat aloof."[60] American negotiators who dealt with Huang in the early 1950s remembered him for the "rudeness" and "ferocity" of his negotiating style, which they described as "intolerable."[61] Henry Kissinger, conversely, remembered Huang for his "extraordinary human warmth and reliability."[62]

For Huang's meeting with Leighton Stuart, Mao instructed him to "listen more and speak less." If the US ambassador was friendly, Huang should reciprocate but make sure not to be too warm.[63] Perhaps predictably, the talks went nowhere. Given the Communists' close ties to Moscow and Washington's growing anxiety about Soviet expansionism, they probably never had much chance of success.

Events moved quickly after the Communists' capture of Nanjing. On September 21, Mao declared that the new China had "stood up," signifying an end to the country's humiliating experience of civil war and external encroachments. On September 30, the Foreign Affairs Group was disbanded in preparation for the establishment of a new foreign ministry. (In reality, day-to-day control remained in the hands of Wang Bingnan, a key member of Zhou's Yan'an Foreign Affairs Group whom Zhou had once described as his "ears and mouth.")[64]

On October 1, 1949, Mao declared the founding of the People's Republic of China. Zhou, who was fifty-one, became the country's first premier and foreign minister. In their first official act after the country's foundation, China's new diplomats were sent out across the city on bicycles to deliver the news to foreign embassies.[65] Huang Hua stayed on in Nanjing, before being transferred to head up foreign affairs in Shanghai, where a significant foreign population remained. Huang stayed in Shanghai until 1953, when he would once again face American interlocutors across the negotiating table at the end of the Korean War.

The new country entered a world beset by uncertainty and intensifying ideological competition. Stalin's Soviet Union was victorious in war and pushing for influence from Berlin to Tehran. Japan's collapse had left a power vacuum in Asia. The United States was settling into a dramatically expanded global role and embarking on an international struggle against communism. Europe was in ruins and receiving reconstruction aid under the Marshall

Plan. Old empires were crumbling as a raft of new nations struggled for independence.

The new government in Beijing, by choice, lacked a single diplomatic relationship. In a bid to rid the country of "feudal influences" and what he saw as the Nationalists' servile relationship with foreign powers, Mao had opted not to recognize any of the Republic of China's diplomatic relationships. It also began systematically reducing foreign influence in China—from missionaries and media outlets to foreign diplomats—through a policy he described as "cleaning the house before inviting guests."[66]

Mao also opted not to use a single one of the hundreds of talented Nationalist diplomats in the new China's diplomatic corps. With the exception of the small circle that had shadowed Zhou since Huang Hua's arrival in Yan'an, the group of some 170 individuals Zhou addressed at the ministry's founding ceremony on November 8 had only limited experience in dealing with foreigners. The complex tasks of establishing a network of overseas embassies or conducting international negotiations would have seemed even more alien. But, ready or not, it was time for China's new diplomats to meet the world.

3

War by Other Means

As Chairman Mao greeted Romania's new ambassador to China in March 1950, ten former People's Liberation Army generals peeked through small holes in an ornate door.[1]

Romania, along with a slew of other Communist nations, had just established diplomatic ties with the newly established People's Republic of China. It was now time to exchange ambassadors. Making that formal would involve an arcane ceremony developed in Europe and practiced around the world: the designated ambassador would hand over a letter to the other country's head of state and ask to be accepted as the official representative of his nation.

The generals watched carefully, craning their necks as the ambassador presented his credentials. It was a bewildering experience. "How can anyone remember all that gibberish?," Geng Biao asked his colleagues when it was over. "You can just say anything you want. The other side won't understand anyway," countered Ji Pengfei. "Just make sure the comrade translating says the right thing."

The generals were about to become some of the very first Chinese ambassadors posted overseas after the foundation of the People's Republic and they were there to learn. They had spent most of the last two decades living out of caves and engaged in near-constant fighting with better-equipped enemies. Mastering the niceties of diplomatic protocol hadn't exactly been a priority.

Now, they found themselves in Zhongnanhai, the palatial imperial compound next to the Forbidden City, which the Communists had commandeered as their headquarters after years of squalor and hardship.

China's newly minted diplomats would venture out into a world increasingly divided between hostile capitalist and communist camps. In the last year alone, Senator Joseph McCarthy had whipped up public hysteria about communism in the United States, warning that hundreds of Soviet spies had infiltrated the State Department; America had marshalled its European allies to establish the North Atlantic Treaty Organization, a mutual defense pact aimed at countering Soviet aggression; and the Soviets had conducted their first nuclear test, spurring President Truman to counter in January 1950 by announcing that the United States aimed to develop a hydrogen bomb.

After the ceremony concluded, Zhou Enlai introduced the generals to Mao, who recalled each of their contributions in battle. Zhou then explained the rationale for picking the generals. China's diplomatic corps was "purer than other ministries," he said. They were all "frontline proletarian soldiers."

Mao looked pleased. "Ambassador generals are good," he said. "Ambassador generals won't run away."

After the meeting, it was time to practice. The generals lined up to present their credentials to a colleague who was pretending to be the Indian president. No one had wanted to take the risk of pretending to be Mao.

***

The ambassador generals weren't the only ones confused about their new roles. Strange as it might seem, the new government had begun building a foreign ministry with a deliberate shortage of diplomats. Mao had said that as well as "cleaning out the house before inviting guests," they'd also need to "build a new kitchen."[2]

Unlike some other ministries, which took on Nationalist officials together with new recruits, there was no space for Kuomintang diplomats in the new China's foreign ministry.[3] Instead, Zhou Enlai and his Yan'an recruits set about creating a new diplomatic corps from scratch: a "civilian army." The project saw the melding of Zhou's embrace of disciplined routine and Leninist party-building techniques with the life experiences of real Chinese soldiers and practical tips from the Soviet Union. As always, Mao's vision of revolution loomed large over everything.

For Mao and the rest of the regime's leadership, starting anew was an obvious choice. As they sought legitimacy in a largely hostile world, political purity and loyalty to the Communist Party were paramount.[4] Over the past three decades, the Party had learned that secrecy was necessary for survival. They couldn't run the risk of diplomats defecting and threatening the revolutionary project at home.

"Diplomatic work requires strong professionalism, but it also requires strong politics," a military officer explained to one of the new recruits. "The KMT's diplomats understood professional business, but they did not have the moral qualities of the new China's diplomats. We would have failed if we relied on them to conduct diplomacy."[5]

Even those who had been with the Party for decades were subject to suspicion. Indeed, Mao once remarked that one future foreign minister, Qiao Guanhua, who had been involved in the Party's foreign affairs since the Yan'an days, "knew too much" to be an ambassador.[6]

If China's new leaders saw starting from scratch as a political necessity, that didn't make it any easier. China was losing virtually all of the institutional knowledge about Western diplomacy that it had accumulated over the last century. Undeterred, Zhou and his Yan'an confidants began pulling together the ministry. The Yan'an group would largely stay on in Beijing: as the only members of the group with experience doing anything that remotely resembled diplomacy, their expertise would be needed in the capital.

They were supplemented at the top of the ministry by individuals such as spymaster Li Kenong, who had greeted Huang Hua on his arrival in Shaanxi. Li went on to become one of Zhou's deputies as vice foreign minister while retaining his leading role in secret intelligence.[7] The Soviet-trained Wang Jiaxiang and Zhang Wentian, who had both previously held top leadership positions in the Communist Party, took up crucial roles. Wang became China's first ambassador to the Soviet Union, while Zhang was made China's representative to the United Nations (a position he would never take up as China was still represented by the Republic of China on Taiwan).

At the working level, Zhou brought across local administrators who'd served in Communist base areas and had at least some experience navigating bureaucracies. Others were fresh graduates—mostly language majors—from universities in Beijing.[8] A small minority, including Ji Chaozhu and "Nancy" Tang Wensheng, who both went on to translate for Mao, were Chinese-born students who had grown up overseas and had returned to serve the revolution.[9]

Then there were the ambassador generals who'd been recruited to lead China's new embassies overseas. Of the seventeen ambassadors appointed between October 1949 and 1952, twelve were senior military officials and nine were survivors of the Long March. Only three had ever been abroad.[10] More junior officers from the military would be appointed as political counselors and secretaries in embassies or serve as military attachés.[11]

Like the decision to build a foreign ministry from scratch, the rationale for appointing generals as ambassadors was also political. Mao was only partly joking when he observed that the group who had watched the Romanian ambassador present his credentials wouldn't run away. Only the military—which swore (and still swears) its loyalty to the Communist Party, not the country—could be relied on for its loyalty and ability to keep secrets.

The appointment of the generals would also help to make Zhou's call for a "civilian army" a reality. The aim, as one diplomat put it, was to "plant the Party and military's excellent traditions and style into the roots of China's diplomatic corps."[12]

That's not to say that the military recruits were happy about their new civilian assignments. When General Han Nianlong told military commander (and future foreign minister) Chen Yi that he did not want to go abroad to serve as an ambassador, Chen told him to "cut the crap, follow orders, and get moving." Others, including Ji Pengfei, a future acting foreign minister, held out hopes that they would return to military service.[13]

Ultimately, it wasn't up to them. As Vice Minister Li Kenong repeatedly told a group of military recruits, "a member of the Communist Party must keep up with the circumstances and submit to the Party's assignment. You go where the Party tells you and should not have any individual plans." Characteristically, Zhou Enlai was more conciliatory. "Changing from military to diplomatic struggle is simply a matter of changing the front on which one conducts conflict," he reassured them. "It is not a matter of giving up struggle."[14]

***

Many of the recruits brimmed with excitement as they arrived in Beijing. Whether they were fresh graduates or battle-hardened soldiers, most had never been to the capital before. Some had never even visited a city. Others saw multistory buildings, electric lights, telephones, and flushing toilets for the first times in their lives.[15] One recruit from southern China recalled hearing stories as a kid about how you needed to carry a stick in Beijing in case your pee froze in the city's winter and you needed to knock it free from your private parts.[16]

Some new arrivals were disappointed by Beijing's narrow streets, bad traffic, and dilapidated buildings.[17] The foreign ministry building itself only seemed to underline the problems: the shower rooms in the basement of the ministry and the cafeteria frequently suffered power cuts.[18] Conditions for the junior recruits were especially spartan. Ji Chaozhu, who had returned from America to serve in the revolution, recalled sleeping in a dormitory with some twenty other men, sprawled out on a long wooden platform made of planks laid on top of stools. The floor was slick with spit.[19]

Hygiene aside, there was a levity to post-"liberation" Beijing. After thirty years of struggle, the Communist Party had achieved victory against daunting odds. Its new diplomats would have the chance to play a part forging Chinese society anew.

At first, the atmosphere in Beijing was one of relative openness, even fun. Officials from the country's new ministries walked back and forth freely between buildings to drop in on wartime friends in other departments. The foreign ministry even held Saturday night dances in the hall where Zhou had delivered his speech founding the ministry. One Xinhua journalist remembered dancing there to the jazz classic "In the Mood."[20]

But free movement and jazz was not what Mao Zedong had in mind for his revolution, which he'd famously promised would not be a "dinner party." He wanted to see Chinese society remade and purified through his peasant revolution. Getting rid of foreign influences seemed like a good place to start. "If you compared our country to a home, you'd find its interior dirtied with firewood, garbage, dust, fleas, bedbugs, lice and more," Mao told a Soviet visitor in early 1949. "After liberation, we need to have a good clear-out."[21]

Before long, bright-eyed excitement gave way to solemnity. Employees across ministries were issued with multiple sets of identity cards, questioned about their business as they visited colleagues, and repeatedly told that there were spies everywhere. Within six months of its establishment, the ministry found itself in the midst of a criticism and self-criticism campaign reminiscent of the "rectification" movement in Yan'an, this time focused on insufficient discipline and laxness with official secrets.

In the foreign ministry and in government organizations across the city, the mood began to darken. "We became suspicious of strangers and of each other, so that it was no longer comfortable to see each other, because it would mean a long report back on what we talked about," remembered the Xinhua journalist who had danced in the foreign ministry. Officials became "insular" and retreated to their own places of work. "Even the Saturday night socials were held within the confines of one's own organization," she remembered. "Friendships made during army days gradually faded away."[22]

***

If the regime felt the need to chasten political and social life in Beijing, it saw the need to be doubly cautious when it came to sending people abroad. The first lesson in store for China's new diplomats was learning their place in China's political system and the meaning of discipline.

Discipline meant doing exactly what was asked of you: nothing more and nothing less. The German sociologist Max Weber described it as the "exact execution of the received order in which all personal criticism is unconditionally suspended."[23] The French philosopher Michel Foucault went even further, describing it as an automatic response that bypasses understanding: "the order does not need to be explained or formulated; it must trigger off the required behavior and that is enough."[24]

It was a message Zhou and other leaders stressed early and often. Zhou's 1949 founding speech was crystallized in a motto that summarized his expectations for Chinese diplomats: "Stand firmly in position; master our policies; know the details of your work; and strictly observe discipline."[25]

This imperative flowed from the top of China's political system down to its lowest levels. Zhou summarized the approach in another phrase he constantly repeated to his trainee emissaries: "diplomatic authority is limited" (*waijiao gongzuo shouquan youxian*).[26] Diplomats were to be the messengers who delivered the Party's line on foreign affairs; their room to improvise was almost nonexistent.

This approach came naturally to the ambassador generals. China's first ambassador to East Germany and later acting foreign minister, Ji Pengfei, later described his desire to make his embassy staff "truly become the People's Liberation Army in civilian clothing." When one counselor at the embassy decided to go skiing without permission, Ji immediately reported him to the foreign ministry's leadership, which had him sent home.[27]

The idea that the Party should maintain strict discipline in its conduct of foreign affairs at all levels proved enduring. When liberal reformer Hu Yaobang was removed as the Communist Party's general secretary in 1987, one of the charges levied against him was making unauthorized foreign policy decisions, specifically the invitation of a group of Japanese schoolchildren to China.[28]

These same messages are repeated to trainee diplomats today. Recruits are still taught Zhou's motto emphasizing discipline and instructed that "diplomatic authority is limited." Li Zhaoxing, foreign minister from 2003 to 2007, summarized this approach in his 2014 memoirs: "For many years, the foreign ministry has always emphasized discipline. Every employee must study the 'Five Major Disciplines Handbook' which touches on discipline in politics, organization, dealings with the outside world, secrecy, and financial affairs."[29]

The approach is both a strength and a weakness for Chinese diplomats. On the positive side, it allows them to press China's position with relentless consistency and stamina. "The Chinese process is very disciplined and very complete," said Susan Thornton, a former acting assistant secretary of state for East Asian and Pacific Affairs who dealt with high-level Chinese officials for two decades. "They are very good at delivering their messages across multiple levels, in multiple locations. They kind of blanket the airwaves with their message. There's no mistaking what the official position is on X issue."[30]

Sometimes, this approach also provides China with an edge in negotiations. "They gain a great advantage in being able to keep secrets, in keeping their inter-agency fights away from the outside world," said Thornton. "When they come to the table to face their foreign counterparts, they have a very clear set of guidelines and whether they agree or not they all pursue them and there's no leaking."

There are also serious disadvantages. First, Chinese officials, even at ministerial level and above, have very little room for initiative, leaving their counterparts in the driver's seat on most issues. "One of the things they complain about is that the US is always bugging them to do stuff, but they never bug us to do anything. But it's because they never have any ideas," said Thornton.

More important, the relentless repetition of talking points regardless does not necessarily guarantee their persuasiveness. It can even be counterproductive. The deference to authority "narrows their scope to come up with persuasive points," said Thornton. "US negotiators are always trying to find ways to explain things in a different way, but the Chinese just come back to repeating the same talking points."[31]

It also makes cultivating future leaders more difficult. Li Zhaoxing was nervous after being made chargé d'affaires, or acting ambassador, in Lesotho in the early 1980s because he had no idea how to lead. "Many years of education from the Party taught diplomats to obey the organization," Li wrote. "Whatever the organization said, we would do."[32]

The focus on obeying orders from above has one final important consequence: when Chinese diplomats find that their limited talking points fail, they resort to making demands.[33] More concerned with evaluation from their colleagues than their impact on foreigners, their drive and discipline can blind them to a core art of diplomacy: listening.

When then President Hu Jintao visited Ottawa in 2010, Chinese officials were under intense pressure to present him as an international statesman. When Canadian officials said the TV camera following Hu around could not enter the country's cabinet room, Chinese diplomats were incredulous. "It has to happen," they told their Canadian interlocutors. They repeated the demand some six times and were rebuffed each time. Eventually they just went ahead and sent the camera crew in behind Hu, only to be blocked by security guards. Hu continued the meeting as if the small brawl behind him wasn't happening.[34]

***

Once China's new diplomats had been taught the parameters of their professional persona and existence, they needed to think, look, and act the part.

First up, they needed to learn something about international politics. New ambassadors were lectured on topics such as international law and diplomatic protocol by internal speakers such as Zhou Enlai and Li Kenong.[35]

Aware that the diplomats would be heading out into the world with less specialist knowledge and experience than their foreign counterparts, one lecturer offered a few crude words of reassurance. "International law my ass," he said after lecturing the recruits on the topic. "We only believe in Mao Zedong law."[36]

The foreign ministry supplemented these lectures by inviting ambassadors from other Communist countries like the Soviet Union, Romania, Poland, and Hungary to talk with the trainees on subjects ranging from politics to economics and the day-to-day workings of embassies. Mao's Russian-speaking son acted as translator.[37]

It was natural for China to look to the Soviet sphere for guidance. Of the fourteen top officials who served on the Politburo between 1945 and 1969, nine had spent time either studying or working in Moscow. Two of Mao's sons, a daughter, a brother, and one of his wives (who was later estranged and committed to a Soviet psychiatric hospital) had spent time in the Soviet Union before the revolution.[38] Zhang Wentian, China's second ambassador to the Soviet Union, had a Russian wife and child from his time as a student in Moscow.[39]

Next, China's new diplomats had to learn how to dress. They would need to win international respect while staying true to the values of the Chinese revolution. In the end, the regime decided that men would wear Mao suits (known as "Zhongshan" suits in Mandarin after Sun Yat-sen) and women were to wear qipaos on formal occasions. Western suits and one-piece dresses would be acceptable on informal occasions.[40]

Then there was food. The recruits, most of whom hailed from poor rural backgrounds, were taught how to hold a knife and fork and eat Western food.[41] Lessons continued along these lines for many decades, often to the initial bemusement of the students. "At first, I was pretty confused. Who can't eat? We have to study this?," Li Zhaoxing remembered thinking after attending protocol training in the 1960s. "But after taking the class I realized there was a lot to learn about eating." In particular, he found the lesson on staying quiet while you eat helpful. As a Shandong native, he'd always slurped his noodles noisily.[42]

There were even compulsory dancing lessons, instruction on how to tie neckties, and guidance on how to behave at cocktail parties. The ministry then held mock diplomatic receptions where the budding diplomats could put their newly acquired skills into practice.[43] One ambassador was called out for putting his knife in his mouth, while others were told to refrain from getting spittle on counterparts as they spoke.[44]

As Chinese society increasingly integrated with the outside world, less and less of this kind of training was necessary. Eventually, the etiquette lessons were replaced with a simple written test before being scrapped altogether.[45]

Still, the ministry continues to offer constructive suggestions to recruits. One handbook written by a former envoy (and endorsed on the back cover by five current and former senior foreign ministry officials) suggests that diplomats refrain from asking foreigners personal questions such as what car they drive or how much money they earn—a commonly accepted practice in China. It also instructs them to avoid hoarding food at buffet dinners and cautions against "unharmonious noises" while eating.[46]

***

Learning on the job continued as diplomats began heading overseas in late 1949 and 1950. Upon arriving for their assignments after long train and boat journeys, many found sparse conditions.[47] China's first ambassador to Poland, Peng Mingzhi, even used a sheet of wood on an old bathtub as a desk.[48]

More disconcerting was the awkward sense that they didn't know what they were doing. China's ambassador to Hungary said that he and his staff had no idea what they were supposed to do in the embassy.[49] Diplomats in Moscow quickly became bored, struggled with the language, and joked that they needed only four members of staff—enough to play Mahjong.[50]

Some diplomats were shipped overseas before receiving any serious language training. In Burma, Chinese diplomats asked a member of the overseas Chinese community to teach them the language.[51] Lacking a translator, diplomats in Poland carried dictionaries with them.[52] Their colleagues in Romania were forced to translate everything into Russian before then rendering it in Chinese because they couldn't find a Romanian-to-Chinese dictionary.[53]

Perhaps inevitably, they learned by making mistakes. In Indonesia, one military attaché broke convention and suffered embarrassment when he arrived in Indonesia without informing the local ministry of defense that he was on his way.[54] In India, the wife of a senior diplomat was severely reprimanded after she accidentally shook hands with an American diplomat. "At that time, if you shook hands with the wrong person, it could become a political problem . . . it made us all nervous," remembered one of her colleagues.[55]

In Beijing too, they made a lot of mistakes at first. On several occasions, cleaners inadvertently pushed garbage carts out in front of foreign guests as they walked and held discussions with Zhou. Ministers from across the government would show up to meetings with foreign counterparts hours late—sometimes they failed to show up at all.[56]

Still, many of the department's leaders took a systematic approach to learning on the job. China's ambassador to Moscow, Wang Jiaxiang, arranged for Soviet diplomats to lecture his staff on diplomatic protocol and international law. Wang sent the transcripts of each lecture back to the foreign ministry, which used them to develop training materials. Diplomats heading to countries in Eastern Europe often stopped off in Moscow for additional instruction, while other groups of trainee diplomats were sent to study in the city.[57]

The new diplomats also turned to their Soviet counterparts for less theoretical advice. China's first ambassador to Sweden, Geng Biao, didn't know whether to reply to a letter he had received from the Danish foreign ministry and so asked contacts in the Soviet, Polish, and Romanian Embassies what to do. In India, where the average age of Chinese diplomats in 1950 was thirty, a junior diplomat was assigned the task of getting regular advice from Soviet diplomats based in the country.[58]

As China's diplomats turned to the Soviets for help, so too did Chairman Mao. He embarked on a nine-week visit to the Soviet Union in December 1949, the first trip he'd taken abroad in his life. After cooling his heels for weeks, Mao managed to extract a pledge of Soviet support if China found itself attacked, but he was forced to allow the continued Soviet occupation of ports in Manchuria. Stalin also refused to help the Communist Party conquer Taiwan, although he promised crucial economic aid and the dispatch to China of Soviet experts to help the country industrialize.

***

Establishing a diplomatic network wasn't just a matter of technical skills. It was also an exceptionally delicate political task. China needed diplomats as a bridge to the outside world: its leaders—like many authoritarians who preach revolution—craved diplomatic recognition as an endorsement of their rule. This desire for outside contact had to be balanced against ensuring that diplomats would remain loyal to the revolution. For this reason, political "purity" and "reliability" were made the top selection criteria for the first diplomats sent overseas.[59]

One aspect of commanding loyalty came down to instilling fear of the outside world. To be sure, the new recruits were apprehensive about the capitalist world in its own right: "diplomats working in capitalist countries were hypernervous as soon as we were out of the door," wrote one diplomat posted to the Netherlands. "It felt as if somebody would try to incite a defection or kidnap you at any time."[60] The ministry did its best to accentuate these fears. "Some journalists from capitalist countries are frightening. They will spread rumors with bad intentions," a group of diplomats heading to India was told in 1950. "You must be careful."[61]

Loyalty also flowed from diplomats' fears of their own political system. They knew, for example, that they would be strictly reprimanded for accepting even minor meetings with foreigners without permission or deviating from the official political line.[62] One ambassador was sent back from Indonesia within a year of arriving in 1950 for being photographed by a journalist drinking a beverage with his shirt off—the central leadership decided it didn't fit the image that China sought to project. "Even if people disagreed deep down, they couldn't express an opinion that was different to that of the leader," remembered one diplomat.[63]

Punishments could have life-changing consequences. When one young diplomat who had been given coupons to buy a dress for her first posting in Romania selected a design with flowers instead of the standard-issue outfit, the ministry accused her of "capitalist thought." It redeployed her to war-torn Vietnam to "experience challenge."[64]

Today, political loyalty remains the single most important criterion in the foreign ministry's selection of recruits. "The first quality that the Ministry of Foreign Affairs looks for is loyalty, political loyalty," one applicant who failed the later stages of the process told an interviewer in 2018. "One's political loyalty and discipline is one of the most important considerations," confirmed a Chinese diplomat.[65]

Inside embassies, Party organizations monitored diplomats' behavior. At regular meetings of the Party branches, diplomats were expected to take part in confessional-style self-criticisms in front of their colleagues, just as they had done in Yan'an.[66]

Still, the country's diplomats would not be effective if they were driven by fear alone. They needed to help China communicate with the world and that meant engaging in dialogue with their foreign counterparts. Zhou's way of squaring this circle was to encourage a style among his diplomats that one former cadre aptly described as "controlled openness."[67]

The most distinctive part of this approach was a rule requiring that Chinese diplomats move around in pairs, known as "two people move together" (*er ren tong xing*). Zhou and the ministry's leadership insisted on this rule from the outset, delivering pep talks to diplomats preparing to head overseas that they should only venture outside in pairs.[68] Wang Jiaxiang, China's first overseas ambassador, who was posted to Moscow, led by example: despite his extensive experience in the city as a student, he took others with him to every meeting. He even made sure that he was accompanied when he went out for casual walks.[69]

While almost all countries place some restrictions on diplomats' foreign contact, China's system was extreme by any measure. "This is supposed to be for our protection, though the notion is absurd," Offred says of a similar rule about traveling in pairs in Margaret Atwood's dystopian novel, *A Handmaid's Tale*. "The truth is that she is my spy, as I am hers."[70]

The buddy system quickly became part of daily life. Sometimes its implementation was even comical. When one trainee diplomat in Vietnam was asked on a date by a local woman in 1961, he immediately reported the invitation to his superiors. The embassy "earnestly researched" the woman's request and eventually ruled that he could go on the date as long as four other Chinese students accompanied him. He didn't get a second date.[71]

While enforcement of this rule has varied over the years, it is still in place today. The first chapter in a 2009 book on diplomatic protocol by former diplomat Zhang Guobin teaches readers that diplomats are not permitted "any kind" of private contact with their hosts on overseas visits.[72] In Xi Jinping's China, the buddy system has been enforced with renewed zeal. "Strictly implement the two people move together rule," one senior official instructed a group of early career diplomats in 2017 before they headed overseas to study for master's degrees.[73]

From the outside, it's easy to see the rule as an embarrassing inconvenience ("I feel kind of sorry for them," said one former senior American official).[74] It's more complicated than that for anyone inside the system: "It's a kind of protection," explained one former Chinese diplomat. "It makes it difficult for others to accuse you of leaking information."[75]

Chinese diplomats, like their counterparts across the country's political system, were also deliberately kept in informational silos. They were briefed in detail only on their own immediate area of work and discouraged from talking to each other about their assignments. ("Don't say what you shouldn't say. Don't hear what you shouldn't hear. Don't see what you shouldn't see," one trainee diplomat was told in the 1980s).[76] The practice limited the damage that any potential defectors or rogue actors could do, but also meant that lower-ranking diplomats were often in the dark about the broader purpose of their work.

The buddy rule and the general political restrictions that China places on its diplomats limit their effectiveness. "Broadly speaking, Chinese diplomats are reserved, overly cautious and insufficiently open," China's former ambassador to France, Wu Jianmin, wrote in 2015. "The best foreign diplomats tend to have a freer hand."[77] It's no small irony that a country whose diplomacy puts so much stress on "friendship" maintains such onerous barriers to the development of meaningful personal relationships with foreigners.

***

As its diplomats fanned out across the world, China was confronted with a significant foreign and military challenge: war on the Korean Peninsula. North Korean leader Kim Il-sung's June 1950 invasion of the South had been met with a far more determined American response than he, Stalin, or Mao had bargained for.

When American forces—operating under a United Nations mandate for the first time in the organization's young existence—crossed the 38th Parallel and pressed on toward the Yalu River in October, Beijing decided to fulfill earlier promises to assist the North if its troops floundered. Mao sent an order for Chinese troops to "repel the attacks of the American imperialists and their running dogs." China would dispatch more than 3 million troops as "volunteers" to Korea during the war, commanded by a veteran guerrilla general, Peng Dehuai.

Chinese leaders were concerned about national security, but they were also focused on China's place in the world. "If we consider North Korea's position in the East, we cannot but offer it assistance," Zhou explained to a Party meeting a few days later. "If we consider that our relationship is as close as lips and teeth we cannot but offer assistance."[78]

In November 1950, as fighting was escalating rapidly in Korea, Chinese diplomats got the chance to put their side of events to the United Nations. It was an opportunity that wouldn't come again for more than two decades. The general-turned-diplomat Wu Xiuquan was chosen to represent the People's Republic. A long-time associate of Zhou Enlai, the forty-two-year-old Wu had studied in the Soviet Union and had his face scarred by a bullet fighting the Nationalists in the Civil War. He arrived in New York leading a team of nine. They were the first official representatives of Communist China ever to set foot in the United States.[79]

At the time, the United Nations did not recognize the Beijing government, and Wu and his team had virtually no knowledge of the organization. Zhou instructed them to talk with "great confidence."[80] Wu relished the challenge. American anti-communists "had always portrayed the Chinese Communists as a group of terrible bandits," Wu later wrote. "Now we could let the people of the world take a look for themselves."[81]

"It was clear to us that both geographically and politically, this was a completely different world," Wu wrote of his arrival in New York. They stayed in nine adjoining rooms in Manhattan's Waldorf-Astoria at a price Wu described as "shocking." They ate room service most days and ventured outside only to hold conversations away from the listening devices that they assumed were laced throughout their hotel rooms. New York City provided the group with security guards. "We knew they had two tasks," Wu remembered. "To protect us and to surveil us."[82]

On the afternoon of November 28, Wu made his first address to the United Nations Security Council at Lake Success on Long Island (the organization's Manhattan headquarters was still under construction).[83] Wearing a black suit, Wu rose from the horseshoe-shaped table to deliver an address on American "aggression" on Taiwan. "I am here in the name of the central government of the People's Republic of China and the representative of the Chinese people to accuse the United States government of the unlawful and criminal act of armed aggression," Wu began.

Wu rocked his head up and down and wagged his finger energetically as he addressed the room for a full 105 minutes. "The American imperialists have always been the cunning aggressor in their relations with China," Wu said before demanding that the United States withdraw from Korea. He closed the speech, which *Time* magazine dubbed "two awful hours of rasping vitupera-tion," by demanding that America face sanctions for its behavior.[84] As would happen so often in Chinese diplomacy, Wu was playing more for the crowd back home than the crowd in the room.

By mid-1951, troops on the two sides had fought each other into a bloody stalemate around the 38th Parallel where the conflict had begun. The combatants began to talk about an armistice as the fighting dragged on. It was time for Chinese diplomats to head to the front.

Ji Chaozhu, a returnee from the United States who'd recently studied at Harvard, made his way to Kaesong as a translator for the negotiations. Along the way, he passed bomb craters and heard echoes of machine-gun fire. At one point, he and his colleagues hid in a ditch as American fighter planes passed overhead. Upon arrival at the Chinese embassy in Pyongyang, he found the building to be nothing more than a bunker with brick walls, a damp earthen floor, and heavy wooden pillars holding up the roof. Most of its rooms were lit with candles.[85]

On-again, off-again negotiations at the border dragged on for the next two years in these spartan conditions, as the talks became stuck over a va-riety of issues, in particular the return of prisoners of war from both sides. The diplomatic corps' physical hardship was a point of pride for the ministry. "Although they were frail scholars, these bookish people who couldn't fire guns or throw grenades, they had wills of steel," remembered one diplomat posted to the negotiations. "Zhou Enlai called the Foreign Ministry's cadres, 'the People's Liberation Army in civilian clothing.'"[86]

On March 5, 1953, China received news that would change the course of the talks: Stalin was dead. The initial reaction was one of shock and remorse. The Soviet dictator had been a kind of North Star for many of the country's revolutionaries on their journey to power. Diplomats at the Chinese embassy in Islamabad cried uncontrollably when they found out.[87] Chinese flags flew at half-staff across the country for three days.[88]

Stalin's passing also represented an opportunity for China. Moscow al-most immediately softened its stance on the negotiations, freeing up China and North Korea to do the same.[89] Finally, after three years of horrendous conflict, the armistice was signed in July 1953.

China was in a state of exhaustion. It had been at war almost continuously for some twenty years. Conflict in Korea had delayed the task of economic reconstruction at home after the end of the civil war.[90] The countryside was still recovering from Mao's brutal land reform campaign and a series of political purges aimed at subduing landlords and other groups the Party deemed disloyal. By the summer of 1953, China was also facing a severe grain shortage.[91]

As it looked to rebuild at home, Beijing began working closely with Moscow on a Five-Year Plan for economic development. Zhou visited the Soviet Union to gather insights for the undertaking, while the embassy in Moscow sent back a steady stream of information gleaned from the Soviet experience.[92] Thousands of Soviet advisers, teachers, and workers came to China to transfer new technologies, set up factories, and build infrastructure as the plan was implemented.[93]

Stalin's death also made a new kind of Chinese diplomacy possible as the Soviets launched a "peace offensive" in 1953. The initiative saw the Soviets settle some of their most pressing territorial disputes and adopt a less rigid ideological attitude toward the developing world.[94]

The only place for Chinese diplomacy to go was up. While the country had won a degree of grudging international respect by fighting the Americans to a standstill in Korea, China was viewed as more of a pariah than ever by the West. By 1954, Mao had concluded that "our house has been cleaned, and now we can invite guests."[95]

4

Chasing Respectability

In late spring 1954, Zhou Enlai and a group of Chinese diplomats dressed in black Mao suits arrived at Montfleury Villa just outside Geneva, Switzerland. An elegant white building with tall glass windows and two chimneys that peeked out on the Swiss countryside, it was an unlikely setting for the emissaries of a communist state.

Nevertheless, Montfleury would be their home for the next few months as they prepared for the most important international meeting so far in Communist China's short history: the Geneva Conference. A Soviet-initiated meeting of the "big five" victors of the Second World War (the United States, Britain, France, the Soviet Union, and China), the conference was held between April and July 1954. It aimed to settle the future of postwar Korea, as well as Indochina, where China had been helping the Vietnamese Communists fight the French and America was growing alarmed at the prospect of Communist victory.[1]

The stakes were high. Both Korea and Vietnam bordered China and impacted its immediate security environment. In addition to negotiating over Korea, Beijing hoped to prevent America from intervening in the escalating conflict in Indochina and ensure that Communist Vietnam continued to act as a buffer state. Longer term, it also hoped to persuade the United States to disengage from Taiwan.[2]

The importance of the Geneva Conference for China went far beyond these interests. It also represented the country's first major foray into diplomacy with the capitalist West. To succeed at boosting China's image and upholding its interests in Asia, Zhou and his diplomats hoped to engage the United States, Britain, and France as equals. China was now playing in a new league and its diplomats needed to look, think, and act the part.

It wouldn't be easy. China lacked full diplomatic ties with Britain, France, and America, whose leaders had initially been vehemently opposed to Chinese participation at Geneva. President Dwight D. Eisenhower had told British prime minister Winston Churchill that he opposed allowing "the bloody Chinese aggressor into the councils of peaceful nations."[3] Secretary of

State John Foster Dulles said he would not meet with Zhou at Geneva "unless our automobiles collide."[4]

Still, Zhou was clear about the opportunity Geneva represented for Chinese diplomacy. Declassified documents drafted by Zhou shed light on his plans. China would seek to capitalize on "contradictions" in the positions of the United States, Britain, and France over the Indochina issue. China would try to reach agreements at the conference, even temporary ones, and above all look for opportunities to provide the country with greater international exposure.[5]

Zhou also saw the conference as a major opportunity for China's fledgling diplomatic corps. One diplomat who attended the conference said that Zhou and the foreign ministry's leadership saw it as an opportunity to train Chinese diplomats and showcase China's "great diplomatic strength." As such, Zhou beefed up the delegation to almost 200 people to allow more to take part.[6]

Foreign ministry preparations were painstaking. Before they set out from Beijing, Zhou gave the delegation a pep talk. "Although we had experience in domestic negotiations in the past, and we had experience in quarreling with the Americans, that was a performance without restrictions," he told them. "This is a formal performance . . . we need rhythm, we need orderliness, and we should maintain harmony."[7]

Each member of the delegation was fitted for a simple Western suit—the first most of them had ever owned.[8] Members of the delegation were lectured on diplomatic protocol, Swiss politics and customs, and best practices for ensuring secrecy.[9] They were reminded to dress smartly when meeting other diplomats, to take their hats off indoors, and to cover their mouths when sneezing.[10]

Despite these detailed instructions, fitting in wasn't an easy task once the delegation arrived. Zhou and the rest of the delegation decided to arrive in Geneva wearing Mao suits to convey a sense of seriousness, but some locals mistook them for missionaries because of their austere and unfamiliar dress.[11]

The sense of difference was only exacerbated by the Chinese government's profound sense of mistrust for these strange new surroundings. The delegation was instructed to speak softly indoors. Zhou conducted many of his meetings outside in case of electronic listening devices, despite having access to a specially constructed room for secure communications built by Chinese intelligence officials.[12] The diplomats also set up a special room to test for poison they feared might have been laced in with the locally bought food, drinks, and cigarettes.[13]

The decision to rent Montfleury Villa itself spoke to China's desire to prove itself on the international stage while keeping the capitalist West at a safe distance. The foreign ministry had decided that it would need to rent a villa after hearing that the Americans and the Soviets had done so. Chinese diplomats fitted the building with calligraphy, pottery, and engravings borrowed from the Forbidden City in Beijing in a bid to showcase China's ancient culture.[14] Montfleury itself was chosen because its large garden would allow for outside meetings, which would avoid the bugs they assumed were planted throughout.[15]

Despite the West's hostility and China's initial trepidation, the Geneva Conference was a major success for China. On the substantive issues, Zhou's willingness to compromise with France on the line of control between North and South Vietnam helped make an agreement on Indochina possible, even as an agreement on Korea remained out of reach.[16] Throughout the process, Zhou consulted closely with Soviet foreign minister Vyacheslav Molotov. When they met at the Chinese villa, aides would play distorted noise in the background in case of listening devices.[17]

Even more important than the agreements reached was the image China projected. Zhou succeeded in initiating dialogues with Britain, France, and, most important, the United States. These talks enhanced the regime's international legitimacy and developed relationships that would later provide China with options beyond the Soviet sphere. The meetings in Geneva eventually led to more formal dialogues between the American and Chinese ambassadors in Poland.

Geneva was a huge success for China's public diplomacy. Both Huang Hua and Gong Peng gave press conferences in Geneva, while Zhou Enlai wined and dined the comic movie star Charlie Chaplin in his villa.[18] Chaplin had moved to Switzerland after being hounded by the FBI as part of the McCarthyite crackdown on communists. The pair watched a movie of the Chinese love story *Butterfly Lovers*, while dining on Peking duck and exchanging toasts of China's fiery *baijiu* liquor. Chaplin told Zhou that he didn't usually eat duck because he liked to mimic the way they walked.[19]

The international response to China's performance at the conference was testament to Zhou's success. Kingsley Martin, editor of Britain's center-left *New Statesman* magazine, wrote that China had emerged as a "world power."[20] Domestically, the *People's Daily* boasted that China's "international prestige has been greatly enhanced."[21]

There were lessons here for the future. Li Kenong, a veteran spy and vice foreign minister, believed the foreign journalists and dignitaries Chinese diplomats had met at the conference could prove a useful source of intelligence. On returning to Beijing, Li declared that the information gathered from these interactions had "a relatively high value for understanding the future foreign policies of our enemies."[22] Zhou ordered the foreign ministry to set up an "Information Department" to deal with foreign journalists, expanding on the responsibilities of the "Intelligence Department" he'd established in the ministry in 1949.[23]

The Geneva Conference was just the start of a much broader charm offensive, which lasted from the end of the Korean war through to the beginning of the Cultural Revolution in 1966. The core part of this push was a strategy aimed at winning over developing countries through traditional diplomacy and a range of distinctively communist tactics borrowed from the Soviet Union and honed during China's revolution. Chinese diplomats also made progress with rich industrialized nations and ended the period with a far more knowledgeable and experienced diplomatic corps than it had started out with.

The charm offensive heralded the beginning of an enduring theme in Communist China's foreign relations: the drive for international respectability.[24] Derailed multiple times by political strife at home, the push would eventually culminate in Beijing's labeling of itself as a "responsible major power" in the 1990s and its public advocacy for status quo institutions such as the United Nations and the World Trade Organization.

Many of the tools Chinese diplomats practiced during the 1950s are taking on renewed prominence in its foreign policy today. The country's push to win over the developing world in many ways foretold China's decision since 2013 to pivot toward Eurasia under the Belt and Road Initiative. Its use of distinctively communist methods for building influence overseas have recently stoked controversy in the United States, Europe, Australia, and beyond.

Progress wasn't smooth with China's 1950s charm offensive. Successes were limited by China's paranoid political system, which regarded the outside world as a source of ideological impurity, and by the increasingly radical direction of its domestic politics. Even as it tried to win over world opinion, Beijing engaged in periods of diplomatic and military aggression. Only two months after Geneva, China ramped up tensions with Taiwan to remind

Washington of its claim to the island. In late 1954 and early 1955, Chinese batteries lobbed shells at two Kuomintang-controlled islands, Kinmen and Matsu, each of which sits just miles from the coast of southern China's Fujian province. It was a self-defeating show of military strength that undermined much of the goodwill Zhou's cadre of diplomats had achieved.[25]

Still, for now at least, the charm offensive continued. When Zhou explained his foreign policy to the first meeting of China's National People's Congress in the fall of 1954, he stressed that a "peaceful international environment" was needed for China to develop its economy.[26] To realize the country's potential, China would need to dramatically improve relations with its neighbors and begin to develop partnerships outside the Soviet bloc. An opportunity to do so would come the following year with the Afro-Asian Conference held in Bandung, Indonesia.

***

Today, it is difficult to imagine the excitement surrounding the Bandung Conference given the stale and repetitive format of most diplomatic gatherings. For its founders and participants, the meeting represented a profound new juncture in global history.

The withdrawal of Britain, France, and other colonial powers from Asia and Africa created an explosion of newly independent states with no firm allegiance to either the West or the Soviet bloc. The conference, held in April 1955, was attended by twenty-nine newly independent states from Asia and Africa (including six future members of the Group of 20). Indonesia's president, Sukarno, declared it the "first intercontinental conference of colored peoples in the history of mankind."[27]

For China, in particular, the opportunity was huge. Mao had been theorizing since at least 1946 about the potential for China to work with the "vast intermediate zone" between the capitalist and communist camps whose political sympathies were still in play.[28] In Bandung, China would have the chance to represent itself to these nations free of American hostility and independent of Moscow.

The foreign ministry was clear-eyed about how to get the most out of the gathering. Zhou's plan was to "isolate the American forces, win over the 'peaceful and neutral' countries, and try to split the countries closely following the United States and hostile to China."[29]

The Americans were alarmed. As the British embassy in Tokyo reported, the United States feared that Bandung would "offer Communist China an excellent propaganda opportunity before the representatives of countries not formally committed to either the Free World or the Communist Bloc."[30]

Chiang Kai-shek was even more jittery, and he decided to do something about it. After five long years camped out on Taiwan waiting for an opportunity to exact revenge for his humiliating retreat from mainland China, his security services hatched a plot aimed at Chiang's former Whampoa Military Academy colleague: they were going to kill Zhou Enlai.

In late March 1955, agents from Taiwan's Number Five Liaison Group approached an employee at Hong Kong's Kai Tak airport. They offered him 600,000 Hong Kong dollars and refuge in Taiwan in exchange for planting a bomb on an April 11 Air India Constellation flight scheduled to take Zhou Enlai to Indonesia.

The employee agreed and the bomb went off as planned, killing all eleven passengers. Fortunately for China, Zhou was not among the passengers. After receiving a tipoff about the plan, he changed his travel plans at the last minute and opted for a different flight. The group of junior Chinese diplomats and journalists who boarded the plane died somewhere over the Pacific.[31]

Zhou arrived in Bandung in mid-April 1955. He had seen off the immediate threats to his safety, but still faced considerable suspicion from other participants. Thailand, in particular, was closely aligned with the United States, while Ceylon's prime minister was toying with closer ties to Taiwan and warning of communist "subversion."

Understanding the scale of the challenge, Zhou took an uncharacteristic risk on the second day of the conference: he set aside the notes for his carefully drafted speech and rose to deliver an entirely different address.

"The Chinese Delegation has come here to seek common ground, not to create divergence," Zhou told the audience. "Is there any basis for seeking common ground among us? Yes, there is. The overwhelming majority of the Asian and African countries and peoples have suffered and are still suffering from the calamities of colonialism."[32]

Zhou pointedly avoided one markedly divisive issue the participants expected him to highlight. He did not belabor the status of Taiwan or China's lack of representation at the United Nations.

Zhou's speech also laid out a set of ideas designed to steer China's relations with developing countries: the Five Principles of Peaceful Coexistence. The five principles were first enunciated during negotiations with India over the status of Tibet between 1953 and 1954. They called for mutual respect for territorial integrity and sovereignty, mutual nonaggression, noninterference in other countries' internal affairs, equality and mutual benefit, and peaceful coexistence.[33]

Bland as they might sound, the "five principles" resonated beyond China's borders, especially with Nehru's India. The five principles articulated a new-found empowerment for non-Europeans as post-colonial states struggled to find their way in a brave new postwar world. Zhou was drawing on the Communist Party's own experience of persecution and triumph to outline a future where all states would be treated with dignity.

Zhou's pitch worked. "I felt a definite change in the room's atmosphere," remembered one Chinese attendee. "The applause grew more frequent, and when Zhou finished and sat down the entire crowd gave him a standing ova-tion. It was a moment of great rhetorical and diplomatic triumph."[34]

Over time, the principles Zhou outlined in his Bandung speech would also gain traction with other communist governments. The reformist commu-nist leader of Hungary, Imre Nagy, would later write about the appeal of the principles, including the pledge of mutual non-interference, in his book *On Communism* after the Soviets ousted him in March 1955.[35] The principles re-main a standard part of China's diplomatic talking points today. The foreign ministry even held an anniversary ceremony to honor them in 2014, where President Xi Jinping described the principles as "the cornerstone of China's foreign policy."[36]

Meanwhile, Zhou also succeeded on the sidelines of the gathering. He quietly worked the room, addressing the concerns of attendees from other countries and putting a human face on communist China. Ceylon's out-spoken prime minister John Kotelawala – who had gone into the conference pledging to ask Zhou "tough questions" – publicly raised the possibility of self-rule for Taiwan and railed against communist "imperialism." Zhou met with him, listened to his grievances, and convinced him to soften his tone.[37]

Foreign diplomats were impressed. Filipino diplomat and anti-communist intellectual Carlos P. Romulo wrote grudgingly that Zhou had "comported himself as one who has taken a leaf from Dale Carnegie's tome on *How to Win Friends and Influence People*."[38] O. C. Morland, the British ambassador to Indonesia, told London that Zhou's "demonstration of sweet reasonableness" had persuaded all but the most resolutely anti-communist governments that "Communist China might really have no aggressive intentions."[39]

The impact of Zhou's diplomacy went far beyond the conference room. China dominated media attention: Zhou's name appeared four times more frequently in Western coverage than India's Nehru.[40] *Time* magazine dubbed

Zhou's performance a "triumph" and his speech a "masterpiece of diplomatic dexterity."[41] Indonesia's *Star Weekly* gushed that "people could not stop talking about Zhou's eyebrows which were thick and black."[42]

A series of breakthroughs soon followed. In its neighborhood, China established diplomatic relations with Nepal in 1955 and with Cambodia in 1958 following positive encounters between Zhou and Cambodian leader Norodom Sihanouk at Geneva and Bandung. It also improved ties with Indonesia and Pakistan, opening the way to an eventual close alignment with the latter against India.

Success in Bandung also opened the door to closer relations with the strategically crucial Middle East. China and Egypt, then the most powerful Arab state, signed a trade agreement after a meeting between Zhou and Egyptian president Gamal Abdel Nasser at Bandung; full diplomatic relations would follow the next year. This in turn helped China establish diplomatic ties with Syria and Yemen.[43]

Taiwan's diplomats could only look on with dismay. Ho Feng-Shan, a longtime ambassador who represented the Republic of China on Taiwan, was booted from his post in Egypt after Zhou's successful courting of Nasser. At his next posting in Mexico, Ho watched the People's Republic invite movie directors, actresses, and writers to Beijing as well as facilitate trade delegations. Eventually, the Nationalists were booted from Mexico too. "Although I had many small victories, the circumstances were too poor," Ho later reflected. "I finally lost to Zhou Enlai."[44]

"The Bandung Spirit" still animates Chinese diplomats today. The country's continued self-identification as a developing country reflects the way its leaders see themselves as aligned with the developing world. Sometimes it's even a source of controversy in China's relations with America and the European Union. At the World Trade Organization, for example, the United States contests China's designation as a developing country.[45] China's push to craft an image as a champion of developing world interests is also expressed through its efforts to shape global development through institutions like its Asian Infrastructure Investment Bank, launched in 2014.

***

Breakthroughs at Geneva, Bandung, and elsewhere made it necessary to expand and reorient the foreign ministry whose staff swelled from the initial 170 in 1949 to nearly 2,000 in 1960. The ministry's structure was also altered as new nations gained their independence from former colonial masters and became targets of Beijing's charm offensive. A new department for West Asian and African Affairs was established in 1956 (previously Western European and African affairs had been handled together).[46]

Gradually, under Zhou's close supervision, the ministry began to lay down the kinds of standard operating procedures by which bureaucracies live and die. These included subjects ranging from the department's official responsibilities to training guidelines.[47] The protocol department scoured every book it could find on the topic, including Nationalist Chinese, Soviet, and Western precedents to develop a guide on how to deal with foreigners.[48]

Zhou also sought to formalize the way China made its foreign policy as part of a broader push to regularize policymaking. In March 1958, he established a Central Foreign Affairs Leading Small Group to bring together foreign policy decisionmakers from across the government, the military, and the Communist Party. Headed by Chen Yi, the group reported directly to the Politburo.[49]

To train future generations of diplomats, the government had set up the Beijing Foreign Studies University in 1949 and the College of Foreign Affairs in 1955.[50] The triumphs at Bandung prompted Zhou to shift the focus of language training in these schools toward the needs of Asian and African nations. Zhou also sought to deepen China's diplomatic expertise by establishing a think tank overseen by the foreign ministry, the Institute of International Studies, as well as a publishing house specializing in foreign affairs, the World Knowledge Press, in 1956 and 1957 respectively. All these institutions remain active today.[51]

The post-Bandung hiring spree made it necessary to draw Chinese diplomats from a wider range of backgrounds. Over time, the diplomatic corps became less reliant on hires from the military. An increasing proportion of the seventy-seven new ambassadors appointed between 1954 and 1966 were now drawn from other government ministries, provincial governments, universities, or inside the foreign ministry itself.[52]

Even so, Zhou did not turn his back on the foreign ministry's militaristic discipline. He constantly reminded cadres that they needed permission to act, often returning to military metaphors to explain the importance of discipline and focus.[53] New recruits were taught the motto that had come to summarize the spirit of his 1949 speech, which articulated the ministry's bedrock principles: "Stand firmly in position; master our policies; know the details of your work; and strictly observe discipline."[54]

In early 1958, Zhou handed over day-to-day control of the ministry to Chen Yi, a celebrated military veteran and mayor of Shanghai. In many ways, the double-chinned former guerrilla could hardly have been more different from Zhou. Often pictured wearing sunglasses, Chen relished sharing strong opinions and thought himself too outspoken to be a diplomat.[55] He couldn't help himself. "He was one of only one or two people I knew of who would talk back to Mao," American communist Sidney Rittenberg remembered.[56]

And yet, as foreign minister, Chen adopted Zhou's style. When Zhou handed over the reins, he emphasized the core understanding that "diplomatic authority is limited." Chen would later repeat the line again and again to diplomats under his command.[57] Like Zhou, Chen also practiced extreme deference to Mao on matters of foreign policy. Briefing a new ambassador in 1965, he explained that ambassadors' powers are severely limited, adding, "forget about ambassadors, I have limited authority as foreign minister. . . . Chairman Mao personally concerns himself with our country's diplomatic policies and developments which Premier Zhou keeps in hand."[58]

***

As Chinese diplomats gradually became accustomed to the rarified world of international diplomacy, a gap opened up between the ministry's culture and the rest of Chinese society.

Many countries fret about the gap between their diplomats and the countries they represent, but the issue caused particular problems in Mao's China. Not long after his peasant soldiers had entered Beijing in 1949, Mao beseeched them to "always keep the style of plain living and hard struggle" that had characterized the Party's path to power.[59] The same would be expected of the country's diplomats, regardless of what their day jobs might entail.

"For regular people, the gate of our country's foreign ministry seemed sacred and mysterious," wrote one diplomat. "The diplomats inside seemed arrogant: coming and going from the country, holding their diplomatic passports, socializing and attending banquets."[60]

Chinese diplomats were also separated from their families. Many of those sent abroad in the early years found it difficult to find romantic partners. Trips home often involved rapid courtships, followed by short weddings and quick pregnancies. When the kids were born, regulations required that they stay in China: many attended the foreign ministry's kindergarten in Beijing.[61]

They learned of births, deaths, graduations, and weddings from the infrequent visits of diplomatic couriers.[62] "I didn't carry out my responsibilities as a father," one diplomat reflected at the end of his career. "I didn't carry out my responsibilities as a husband."[63]

Diplomats' distance from daily life in communist China could be dangerous. Many were unknowingly accumulating political "crimes" simply for doing their jobs. Gong Peng, one of Zhou's Yan'an associates who brilliantly courted the foreign media, would later be targeted for her willingness to draw on intellectuals and overseas returnees to staff her department.[64] Similarly, Wu Xiuquan, China's ambassador to Yugoslavia from 1955 to 1958, developed an impressive personal relationship with Marshal Tito, the country's fiercely independent dictator. The pair went hunting together and even visited Tito's private island, where Wu sampled wines from Tito's private collection. All of this would later become evidence of Wu's "treasonous relations with foreign countries."[65]

***

For all of the charm offensive's early wins, China was still a pariah to much of the world. It lacked diplomatic relations with most Western European countries, Japan, the United States, and any nation in Latin America. Still, Zhou was confident that if the governments of these countries refused to establish formal relationships with China, parts of their societies could be persuaded to establish less formal ties.[66] To pursue these groups, Zhou turned to a set of distinctively communist practices that traced their roots back to Lenin: the use of "united front" diplomacy.

United front activities have deep roots in the global communist movement. The Soviets had long used overseas front organizations and Party-controlled "friendship societies" to covertly influence events overseas.[67] The Party had previously communicated with the West through foreigners such as Edgar Snow. In 1942 it had created a United Front Work Department, which Zhou briefly headed before the Communist victory in 1949.[68] The organization worked with friendly domestic groups to broaden the basis of the Communist Party's support in China, as well as to build networks of support overseas among the Chinese diaspora and through foreign civil society groups.

After the revolution, the Party's united front apparatus expanded considerably and was often staffed by current or retired diplomats. This included the Chinese People's Institute of Foreign Affairs, which was set up in 1949, and the Chinese People's Association for Friendship with Foreign Countries, founded in 1954. Both of these organizations, together with the United Front Work Department, are still active today. Together, they form part of a web of Communist Party and Chinese government departments that make up the country's "foreign affairs system" (*waishi xitong*).

United front activities targeted groups ranging from overseas Chinese to left-wing political organizations, as well as foreign artists, movie stars, and scholars. Targets were invited to Beijing or received visiting delegations from China. The aim was to marginalize anti-China voices and smooth the way for formal diplomatic ties.

Although the Chinese government liked to characterize these exchanges as "people-to-people," there could be no doubt that the Communist Party was in charge. One official history of the international ties of the All-China Federation of Trade Unions is explicit on this point: because China is a socialist country, "the interests of its trade unions are the same as those of the government." The language used to describe the body's overseas activities closely mirrored the language Zhou had used to keep the foreign ministry in its place, stressing strict "discipline" and the "limitations of diplomatic authority."[69]

The star performer of united front diplomacy was without question Pu Yi, who was the last emperor of China and whose life was depicted in Bernardo Bertolucci's 1987 movie *The Last Emperor*.

Born in 1906, Pu Yi was just six years old when the dynasty that he was born to lead collapsed. He initially continued to live in the imperial palace, where he was tutored by the former British imperial official and scholar Reginald Johnston, who tutored the now teenage boy on topics ranging from the use of tanks in battle to etiquette for aristocratic tea parties. Under Johnston's guidance, the former emperor also adopted Henry as his English name.[70]

In 1924, Pu Yi was forced to leave the imperial city as violence between competing warlords intensified. He took up residence in the Japanese-controlled concession in Tianjin. In 1932, he accepted a role as the nominal leader of the puppet state of Manchukuo that Japan set up in his ancestral home of Manchuria. At the end of the Second World War, he was imprisoned by the Soviets after they pushed Japanese troops out of Manchuria. The Soviets handed him over to the Chinese in 1950, months after the Communist Party's victory in the Civil War.

The big question on Pu Yi's mind as he returned to the land he once ruled was how long he had to live. After he crossed the China-Russia border, he was met by local foreign affairs officials who placed Pu Yi in a third-class railway carriage with papered-over windows. They sat with the emperor throughout the journey, making small talk but refusing to answer the former emperor's questions about how and when he would be killed.

In fact, China's leaders believed Pu Yi was far more useful alive than dead. He underwent a period of political "re-education" for five years in China's northeast, where he studied Marxism and visited farms and factories to learn about the socialist economy.[71]

By the late 1950s, he was ready for prime time. Pu Yi became the star attraction for foreign groups brought to tour China as part of united front work. One former foreign ministry Spanish-language interpreter remembered escorting dignitaries from such countries as Bolivia, Argentina, Peru, and other Latin American nations to meet the former emperor. Dressed in a Mao suit, Pu Yi would tell the guests about the weight of China's past humiliations and the transformation it was undergoing under the Communists. Under the Party's tutelage, he could now look after himself and was no longer a "parasite," he would tell his guests.[72]

Within ten years of Communist China's foundation, united front activities spanned the globe. The Latin American Friendship Association organized visits to China for Latin American economists, cultural figures, and journalists,[73] while the Chinese People's Committee for World Peace hosted African-American activists such as W. E. B. Du Bois, Robert F. Williams, and Elaine Brown.[74] The Britain-China Friendship Association invited trade unionists, journalists, and activists[75] to China while others courted retired French politicians and Japanese legislators.[76]

The Communist Party described these visits as cultural activities, but they were tightly controlled by the government and their aims were always above all political. As Zhou told China's national table tennis team in 1963, their aim was "not victory in sports skills, but political influence."[77] Less than a decade later, the team would be helping to develop ties with Nixon's America.

Drawing from the same playbook they'd used with Edgar Snow in Yan'an, the Communist Party treated guests like movie stars. Retired, even disgraced, politicians were received as noble emissaries for their home societies. They were treated as honored guests at banquets in Beijing and rewarded with access to parts of China where most foreigners could not go. They also received a level of political access in China that they could only imagine in most countries: Mao himself met with the delegations of Latin American trade unions at least seven times between 1959 and 1966.[78]

For retired politicians, this access to top leaders provided a way to stay relevant at home. Of all the individuals courted in this fashion by Beijing, perhaps the greatest success story has been Henry Kissinger. Kissinger, who has held no significant political office since President Gerald Ford lost the 1976 election, has met with every top Chinese leader since Mao. After Donald Trump's election in 2016, Kissinger visited Beijing to share his insights into the American political scene before returning to share his thoughts on China with Trump.

Chinese students and journalists from the Xinhua News Agency were also vehicles for Beijing's influence. They were especially useful in countries where China didn't yet have formal diplomatic ties. Before the independence of Ghana, Guinea, and Mali, for example, Zhou sent Xinhua journalists to gauge attitudes toward China and prepare to establish formal ties.[79] They were also useful for tracking local politics. In communist Hungary, Xinhua journalists and Chinese exchange students worked together to track the movements of political dissidents around the country.[80]

Journalists in state media have been assigned quasi-diplomatic tasks ever since. Xinhua reporters went on to act as a kind of de facto embassy for communist China in the then British colony of Hong Kong, reporting on developments to the mainland and acting as a mouthpiece for Beijing in the city. Today, Xinhua journalists still file secret reports to the Communist Party leadership from the secure rooms in some Chinese embassies.[81]

There was also a more sinister side to China's 1950s influence operations. The threat of the People's Republic endorsing insurgent movements worked hand in hand alongside the power of China's conventional military force as a complement to Beijing's diplomacy.

China provided extensive military aid and training to the Vietnamese communists in the lead-up to the Geneva conference, including rocket launchers the Viet Minh used to defeat the French at Dien Bien Phu in 1954.[82] China supplied more than 150,000 weapons to the Front de Libération Nationale in the French colony of Algeria[83] and held training courses for Thai Communists in Beijing.[84]

Still, there were limits to Beijing's support for global revolutions at this stage. Before the Cultural Revolution, Beijing tended to support insurgencies in countries where it saw the incumbent government as unfriendly, while sparing those it saw as sympathetic. By 1965, Beijing endorsed armed struggle at least implicitly against the governments of twenty-three countries—twelve explicitly. The policy had the advantage that countries that were not targeted were constantly kept on their toes.[85]

Since coming to power in 2012, Xi Jinping has reinvigorated united front organizations. In 2014, Xi echoed Mao in describing united front work as a "magic weapon."[86] Unlike in the past in which armed groups in developing countries gained Beijing's favor, today political parties and organizations in wealthy nations receive much of Party's largesse. "Friendship" associations set up by the Chinese government overseas are increasingly attempting to court political influence in countries such as Australia and New Zealand.[87] A 2018 report by a committee of experts in the United States reported that Chinese diplomats had pressured universities to cancel events deemed offensive to China and exerted influence on the intellectual output of American think tanks.[88]

***

As Zhou charmed the world, Mao grew increasingly troubled by changes taking place in other communist nations.

After Stalin's death in 1953, Chinese diplomats had begun reporting a troubling shift in attitudes toward the late dictator inside the Soviet Union. China's ambassador to Moscow, Zhang Wentian, sent back a series of reports noting a shift away from the cult of personality in the Soviet Union. Mao showed great interest and concern.[89]

At the same time, other diplomats noticed that some socialist countries were more equal than others. In Yugoslavia, Ambassador Wu Xiuquan reported to Beijing that Tito's image seemed far less ubiquitous than Mao's in China or Stalin's in Russia. What's more, the country's leader was referred to simply as "comrade Tito" or "President Tito" rather than honorifics such as "great leader" or "great helmsman," which were routinely bestowed on Mao.[90] Like a good diplomat, Wu reported the discrepancy to Beijing.

As Mao ruminated on what these changes might mean for China, Soviet leader Nikita Khrushchev delivered his explosive February 1956 "secret speech" on Stalin. Delivered at the 20th Congress of the Communist Party of the Soviet Union, the speech denounced Stalin's cult of personality and criticized his use of the Gulag.

The message was shocking for a country that had long venerated Stalin. More important, its delivery smacked of disrespect. The Chinese side first heard about the denunciation when a Soviet leader verbally briefed Deng

Xiaoping and other leaders in Moscow after the fact. They didn't get to read the full transcript until they saw it in the *New York Times*.[91]

Mao didn't disagree with everything in the speech, but he worried that it might damage the unity of the communist bloc. Worse, it could undermine his own efforts to build up a cult of personality at home. Stalin had been 70 percent right and 30 percent wrong, Mao told his colleagues.

Mao also doubted the wisdom of Khrushchev's policy of "peaceful coexistence" with the West. Beijing was—at the time—willing to reduce tensions with the West when it suited its interests, but believed that any more fundamental accommodation would constitute an ideological betrayal.[92]

Then there was the awkward feeling that Khrushchev was somehow just more annoying than Stalin. While the new Soviet leader seemed sincere about improving relations with China, even increasing military aid to the country, Mao like many others found his personality grating. ("Khrushchev is a person with little capacity for detecting nuances and subtleties," read a 1961 CIA "personality sketch.")[93]

As Mao and his colleagues debated Soviet actions, long-standing grievances began to surface. Wang Jiaxiang, Communist China's first ambassador to the Soviet Union, said the country had a history of "great power chauvinism," while many Chinese ambassadors felt that the Soviets cared too much about Europe and looked down on Asia.[94] Mao and other leaders were also concerned about what unrest in Poland and Hungary might mean for the global communist movement. Industrial unrest across China only exacerbated their fears.[95]

Layered on top of all of this was Mao's deepening frustration with the direction of his revolution at home. Mao believed that the diplomatic successes of Geneva and Bandung had opened up space for a rapid push to industrialize, but China's post–Korean War economic recovery seemed plodding and cautious to him. He now accused some colleagues of "walking like a woman with bound feet."[96] Mao also faced signs of pushback against his authority at home. At a meeting in September 1956, the Party emphasized collective leadership and even removed a reference to "Mao Zedong Thought" from the Party constitution. State media began to criticize "the cult of the individual" and "the practice of idolization."[97] It was almost as if Khrushchev was shaping China's domestic policies.

Mao responded with the "Hundred Flowers" campaign," which encouraged Chinese citizens and officials to share their opinions on the state of the Party and the country. The aim was to improve the government's work. Large handwritten posters, known as "big character posters," began to appear on the walls of the foreign ministry as diplomats joined in.[98]

The campaign didn't develop as Mao hoped. Stung and apparently genuinely surprised by the fact that some participants voiced strong dissatisfaction with his regime, he shifted gears in the summer of 1957.[99] The "Hundred Flowers" campaign now became an "anti-rightist" campaign aimed at restoring ideological orthodoxy and punishing those who had spoken out.

This campaign hit the foreign ministry hard. Like other workplaces across the country, the ministry set quotas for finding and punishing "rightists." The foreign ministry's quota was 5 percent. In other words, one in twenty of the diplomats Zhou had assembled in a short eight years would be designated targets.[100]

An atmosphere of fear and paranoia set in. "From then on, life inside the Party became less and less normal," remembered one diplomat.[101] The new "abnormal political mood," as top economic planner Bo Yibo described it, stretched across the whole government apparatus and would come to profoundly shape how officials interacted with Mao as he pushed an increasingly radical line. "No Party members or regular people were permitted to voice different opinions," Bo remembered.[102]

Inside the foreign ministry, a number of important officials were targeted. Vice Minister Zhang Hanfu was criticized, as were the Yan'an veterans Gong Peng and her husband Qiao Guanhua. "No one dared to speak to them," wrote one official.[103] Despite the temporary ostracism, all three ultimately survived. Pu Shan, a Harvard-educated official at the ministry who had translated for Wu Xiuquan at the United Nations in 1950, and his wife were less fortunate. They were branded "bourgeois rightists" and removed from the ministry. Pu was reassigned to a job in a research institute.[104]

Just like during the Yan'an "rectification campaign," some went along with the criticisms even if they hated doing so.[105] Others seemed to embrace it with zeal: "We are trying to blunt the edges of intellectuals like you," one diplomat was told by a colleague.[106] In the end, the best anyone could do was keep their head down. "In this poisonous atmosphere, millions of us kept our doubts to ourselves, even among family and friends," recalled the returnee translator Ji Chaozhu. "There was no benefit from complaining, and no one to complain to."[107]

***

In November 1957, as Mao radicalized China's domestic politics, he paid a second visit to the Soviet Union. Whereas previously Mao had been forced to wait for weeks for an audience with Stalin, during this visit Khrushchev personally escorted Mao to the Kremlin Palace, where he was to stay, the former residence of an empress. The Chinese leader sensed that the power dynamic between the two countries had shifted. "Look how differently they're treating us now," he told his entourage. "Even in this communist land, they know who is powerful and who is weak. What snobs!"[108]

Mao used the visit to showcase his evolving views of global politics and his burgeoning ambitions for the Chinese revolution. Buoyed by the Soviet launch of the Sputnik satellite a month earlier, he declared that "the east wind is prevailing over the west wind." In response to the Soviet pledge to overtake America in in absolute and per capita production by 1970, he declared that China would overtake Britain in fifteen years.

The Soviets, however, were alarmed by what they heard from Mao, especially his callous attitude toward conflict. "If the worst came to the worst and half of mankind died, the other half would remain while imperialism would be razed to the ground," Mao said of nuclear war.[109] His words rattled his hosts, not least because Khrushchev had just signed a secret agreement to deliver a Soviet atomic bomb to China by 1959. The bomb would never be delivered. Within a year, the Soviets would be questioning Mao's mental stability.

5

Between Truth and Lies

In the autumn of 1961, Li Jiazhong set out to have his first suit fitted. The twenty-four-year-old had been given coupons to buy it at a tailor's shop in Beijing's Wangfujing shopping district and clear instructions on what kind to purchase.[1]

Until recently, Li had been a French major, but he'd been reassigned to study Vietnamese after the foreign ministry decided it needed more Asia specialists. After learning the language, Li would be posted to China's new embassy in Vietnam. He wasn't thrilled by the sudden shift at first, but reassured himself by thinking of a line he read in a Soviet novel about a tractor station: "you stand where the Party places you."

Li was excited to head overseas but had no idea what to expect. His visit to the tailor suggested one thing, though: his first posting was likely to involve more food than he was getting at home.

The old man who fitted Li's suit told him he'd make it a little loose-fitting, as a lot of young men seemed to gain weight overseas. It seemed a strange comment to make about someone heading to China's poor, southern neighbor of Vietnam. Yet the tailor's words spoke to a fact that both men understood but neither could voice: China was in the midst of a colossal famine.

It wasn't just Li and his tailor who didn't feel able to acknowledge the truth: before departing for Vietnam, Li and other students were given a pep talk by officials in Beijing. China's situation was "completely good," the officials told them. The Great Leap Forward, Mao's push to industrialize China at breakneck speed, was progressing well. Li and the tailor had managed to forge a quiet human connection among the slogans and lies flying around China.

As the Great Leap caused enormous suffering, hardship, and famine, the Chinese government was still trying to push ahead with the charm offensive it had launched after the end of the Korean War. To accomplish this feat, China's diplomats had to lie to their foreign counterparts, to each other, and even to themselves. By 1962, an incomprehensible 45 million people had starved to death or died of beatings and executions.[2]

families. Others broke with the foreign ministry's strict discipline and stole food from the cafeteria to get by (those who were caught were immediately fired).[17] When the ministry's kitchen ran out of cooking oil, it tried to borrow from other government departments, only to find that they too had run out.[18]

Mao pushed ahead, even as he received reports of famine. At a March 1959 meeting in Shanghai, he pushed for higher agricultural targets.[19]

Chinese diplomats posted overseas continued to receive updates telling them that "the situation with the 'Great Leap Forward' is excellent." The foreign ministry brought groups of ambassadors home on carefully choreographed tours of the countryside to showcase the bumper crops and impressive new steel smelting capacity.

Once again, the country's envoys found themselves caught between two worlds. Wang Guoquan, China's ambassador to East Germany, participated in one of the ministry's tours before returning to East Berlin, where he told a local official about the extraordinary advances China was making.

The German official went quiet, but his wife spoke up. The results sounded scientifically impossible, she said. Wang realized she was probably right and resolved not to talk about the achievements of the Great Leap outside of the embassy.

Wang later reflected on his initial credulity. "The country had just been through the anti-rightist struggle," he wrote of Mao's recent political campaign. "If someone expressed a different opinion, they'd be immediately attacked."[20]

***

By July 1959, some of China's leaders had decided to confront Mao over his policies. The leadership met at Lushan in the cool wooded mountains of northern Jiangxi province. Developed as a retreat for European missionaries in the late nineteenth century, Lushan had been a favorite destination for both Chiang Kai-shek and Mao, who made a point of occupying his former rival's villa. It was in this serene setting that Peng Dehuai, China's famed Korean War hero, took the lead in challenging the chairman's policies. What followed would provide a brutal warning about the dangers of speaking truth to power in Mao's China.

In small group discussions that Mao monitored from a distance, Peng was characteristically outspoken. "We all have a share of responsibility, including Mao Zedong," Peng said. "The steel target of 10.7 million tonnes was set by Chairman Mao, so how could he escape responsibility?"[21]

Mao defended his policies in a speech on July 10. "Doesn't everybody have ten fingers? We can count nine of those fingers as achievements, and only one as a failure." Zhou placated Mao, telling attendees that the Party was quicker to discover and solve problems than the Soviet leadership.[22]

But Peng disagreed. He had seen the starvation and misery firsthand during a trip home to Hunan province. Peng had also discussed the situation with others, including Vice Foreign Minister Zhang Wentian, who agreed that the situation was dire.[23] And while difficult to interpret, remarks he'd made during a trip to Poland later struck one junior diplomat as prophetic: "Will we see you again, Marshal Peng?" the diplomat had asked him. "No, you won't see me again," Peng replied.[24]

Peng decided to write to Mao. As Mao slept on the night of July 14, Peng dropped off a letter at his residence. The pair had known each other since before the Long March and Peng admitted that he'd never been as agreeable as Mao would have liked. "I am a simple man and I am crude and lack tact. For this reason, you should decide whether this letter is of value for you," he wrote. Peng then heaped praise on Mao before pointing to the wastefulness, inflated production claims, and "leftist errors" of the Great Leap.[25]

Mao was furious. He had thought Peng arrogant ever since Yan'an and long harbored suspicions about his loyalty.[26] He had the letter distributed among participants and called for other cadres, including Chen Yi, to join from Beijing. One by one, with just a few minor exceptions, the assembled leaders spoke out against Peng and praised Mao's policies.

Then came Zhang Wentian's multi-hour intervention on July 21. The vice foreign minister spoke through heckling as he told the truth: targets had been too high, production numbers were fake, the backyard furnaces had been a costly failure, and the quality of production was poor. Peasants were dying. "The shortcomings outweigh the achievements nine to one."[27]

Zhang, like Peng, was not your average yes-man. One of the Party's strongest intellectual voices, Zhang had studied abroad in Moscow in the 1920s and had once been general secretary of the Communist Party.[28] He was a member of the Politburo when he was appointed as ambassador to the Soviet Union in 1951. From Moscow, he sent back the cables detailing the 1953–1955 rollback of Stalin's personality cult that had caught Mao's interest. He also harbored doubts about the Great Leap Forward for months before the Lushan meeting.[29]

Mao's sense of grievance against Zhang ran deep, as it did with Peng. Zhang had been one of the Party leaders who Mao felt had snubbed him in the early

1930s. Mao had even excluded Zhang from his 1938 wedding to Jiang Qing after he suggested in a discreet note that she might not be a suitable choice.[30] When Mao targeted Zhang in his Yan'an "rectification campaign," Zhang dared to tell Mao his treatment had been unfair.[31]

Just as Mao faced up to this opposition at home, he began to smell conspiracy abroad. On July 19, Mao received a report from the foreign ministry that detailed widespread misgivings about the Great Leap among Soviet officials. He had it distributed to the leadership without comment.[32] A few days later, Mao learned of a speech by Khrushchev criticizing the establishment of communes in Poland. Given the importance of communes to the Great Leap, Mao interpreted the speech as an attack on his policies. Once again, he had the materials circulated.[33]

Mao came out swinging. In a rambling three-hour speech on July 23, Mao rebutted Peng and issued an extraordinary threat: "If we deserve to perish," he said of the Party leadership, "I will go to the countryside to lead the peasants and overthrow the government. If the People's Liberation Army won't follow me, I will find a Red Army. But I think they will follow me." The assembled leaders would have to choose between him and Peng, he said.[34]

Over the ensuing weeks, small groups of senior leaders were convened to denounce Peng and Zhang.[35] Some suggested they had been working in concert to challenge Mao.[36] Although many in the leadership—including top diplomats such as Wu Xiuquan, who had recently returned after serving as ambassador to Yugoslavia—were sympathetic to their colleagues, they did not dare to speak out against the denunciations.[37] Zhou, of course, fell in line behind Mao.

As the days rolled on, even Peng was broken by the sheer force of the "criticism" sessions. He issued a letter in which he confessed to "anti-party, anti-people, anti-socialist mistakes of a rightist opportunist nature."[38]

The Lushan Conference closed by passing a resolution that found Mao's opponents guilty of conspiring against the Party, the state, and the people. Peng was replaced by the far more pliant Lin Biao, who had been scathing about the Great Leap in his private diary but fawned over Mao in public.[39] Mao then unleashed a hunt for "rightist" elements in the Party that led to the removal of Zhang from his position in the ministry. Many thousands of others were accused of "right opportunism." Zhang's long-term associates in the foreign ministry were either demoted, disciplined, or dismissed.[40]

The whole affair was a brutal warning about the dangers diplomats could face if they spoke their minds. "It was clear that the Great Leap Forward was wrong, but we didn't dare to say much," remembered one Chinese ambas-sador. "If you met someone, you'd just say 30 percent of what was on your mind."[41] In September, China's ambassador to North Korea told his Soviet counterpart that China's "difficulties" were the result of "natural disasters."[42]

***

As Mao lashed out at rightists at home, China's relations with the communist world took a sharp turn for the worse. In June 1959, Khrushchev had failed to deliver on his promise of an atomic weapon for China while continuing to make nice with the United States. Mao even began to see parallels between Khrushchev's brand of socialist thought and American ideas of chipping away at the ideological foundations of Communist Party rule through its policy of "peaceful evolution."[43]

Khrushchev traveled to Beijing in 1959 for the tenth anniversary of the People's Republic, for which Beijing had constructed a new complex to host international visitors—the Diaoyutai State Guest House—despite the famine.[44] The visit was tense, as the two sides clashed over Soviet attempts to mediate in China's increasingly tense border dispute with India.

By the summer of 1960, the two sides were slugging it out in public. In June, Deng Xiaoping acted as Mao's attack dog before a trade union meeting in Beijing, launching an hour-and-a-half-long attack on "Soviet revisionism" in front of a Soviet representative. A few weeks later, Khrushchev personally replied at a Romanian Communist Party Congress in Bucharest. "If you want Stalin, you can have him in a coffin!" he shouted at Beijing's representative, Peng Zhen. "We'll send him to you in a railway car!"[45]

"When I look at Mao Zedong, I simply see Stalin," the Soviet leader mused to his companions back in Moscow. "He is an exact copy."[46]

In July, Khrushchev withdrew the Soviet advisers who had been so central to China's modernization push. At the same time, Mao's determination to pay the Soviets back for their assistance projects only served to worsen the famine.

That month, Zhou and other Party leaders began working on a new trade policy that aimed to reduce China's dependence on the Soviet Union. They managed to persuade Mao to import more grain from capitalist countries, including Canada and Australia, exhausting the country's reserves of foreign currency.

Party leaders also began to quietly adjust China's economic policies. In October 1960, economic planner Li Fuchun presented Mao with a report on mass starvation in the county of Xinyang in Henan province where later investigations would show that up to one in eight residents had died.[47] In November, the communes were weakened, allowing villagers to keep private plots of land and engage in side occupations. China also began to curtail its exports of grain to ease hunger at home, although Zhou and other Party leaders insisted on fulfilling China's obligations to the communist governments of Albania, North Korea, North Vietnam, Cuba, and Mongolia to "facilitate the development of our diplomacy."[48]

The quiet retreat from the Great Leap didn't mean it was time for an honest conversation. Out of concern that the famine might dent its international reputation, the Chinese government turned to its old friend, Edgar Snow. Snow was now living in Switzerland along with other American socialists who had been hounded by McCarthyism in the United States. He was taken to communes, factories, and schools across the country in an attempt to dispel the reports of mass starvation that were now widespread outside China. Snow lived up to Party's expectations when he wrote about the visit. "I diligently searched, without success, for starving people or beggars to photograph," he wrote. "One of the few things I can say with certainty is that that mass starvation such as China knew almost annually under former regimes no longer occurs."[49]

Privately, Snow had his doubts. "I realized what it is that is strange about these meetings," he wrote in his diary. "I am cordially received and given every co-operation technically correct. But no intimacy is established, no spark of human warmth established," he wrote. "It is as if you knew that you were never going to see the person again and it cannot be the beginning of a friendship."[50]

Snow was right to be suspicious. Foreign ministry planning documents analyzed by the historian Julia Lovell detail the Party's clinical assessment of Snow's professional predicament. "In recent years, he has suffered repeated professional frustrations and setbacks" and he would likely seek "fame and fortune by writing a book" about China, the documents said. The ministry was also clear about the right approach for dealing with Snow once he arrived: "On the surface we should seem relaxed; inside, we must be tense," read one of the documents. "We will let him see some of the things that we allow him to see, to bring him to understand a few things that we have prepared for him to understand."[51]

Xia Kunbao, a student at Beijing Foreign Studies University and a future environmental diplomat for China, was present when Snow visited his college cafeteria. Xia and his classmates had been surviving on meager daily rations of grain. Their bellies and limbs had swollen from hunger and the school had ordered them to stop running or playing basketball during physical education classes to preserve energy. On the day Snow passed through, the grain rations were replaced with meatballs and a big bowl of rice. "It seemed Snow was completely satisfied with the happy lives of Chinese college students," Xia later remembered.[52]

Contrary to the government's assurances, the reality in 1961 was that many millions were still starving across China. Jiang Benliang, a young diplomat whose mother had starved to death two years earlier, was sent home to the Hebei countryside to take part in physical labor that year. He found peasants searching desperately for their next calorie. Soon, Jiang too would be foraging for food. His body swelled up as fluid leaked from his blood vessels into his limbs. He ate wild grass and tree bark just to fill his stomach.[53]

Old tactics die hard. In 2010, after a string of self-immolations in Tibet, the government invited journalists on guided tours of the region to showcase how harmonious the region had become (foreign journalists are forbidden from traveling to Tibet on their own).[54] In 2019, after international critics, including the United Nations, reported that China had imprisoned up to one million members of its Uighur minority in "re-education" camps in Xinjiang, the government invited foreign journalists on carefully choreographed tours of the region. Security checkpoints were removed and guard towers taken down from the camps.[55] Chinese foreign ministry officials were themselves taken on similar tours by the Xinjiang government.[56]

***

Wang Jiaxiang had been watching the disaster unfold from his new role heading up the Communist Party's International Liaison Department.

After returning from his post as ambassador to Moscow in 1951, he had become the department's founding head. Created to develop ties with communist parties across the world, its initial cadres were drawn from the United Front Work Department. By 1956, the group had developed relationships with some sixty other communist parties, all the while staying almost completely out of the Chinese press.[57] Even today, the International Department plays an important role in liaising with ruling parties in countries such as North Korea and Vietnam, as well as an increasingly diverse range of other political parties, from social democrats to right-wing populists.[58]

From Wang's perspective, Chinese politics was headed in the wrong direction. In addition to escalating tensions with the Soviet Union, there were border tensions with India and China's involvement in an increasingly dangerous proxy war against America in Vietnam. He had also become increasingly frustrated with his day job as Mao's feared security chief, Kang Sheng, encroached on the Liaison Department's work and spread rumors about Wang and his wife among the ministry's staff, seeking to undercut him. With increasing tensions against the Soviet Union occupying Mao's attention, influence over party-to-party ties was a valuable political prize.[59]

Wang decided it was time to speak up. It wasn't an easy decision. As Mao himself would later reminisce, Wang had played an important part in the dictator's rise to power. He'd also been central to the development of "Mao Zedong Thought" in Yan'an, helping to lay the foundations for Mao's future cult of personality.[60]

Still, Wang felt the situation had become urgent. In spring 1962, after having the department conduct research on the direction of China's foreign policy, he took the unprecedented step of proposing an alternative foreign policy in letters to Zhou Enlai, Deng Xiaoping, and Chen Yi. He argued that the government should issue a statement saying that its policy had always been one of peace. He also argued that China should seek to prevent Khrushchev from reaching a compromise with the United States that might leave China isolated.[61]

Wang's act of conscience met predictable consequences. To Mao, Wang's arguments all sounded a lot like the Khrushchev-style revisionism that Mao was increasingly fixated on defeating at home and abroad. At a Communist Party meeting in September 1962, Mao accused Wang of revisionism, together with the head of the Party's United Front Department, Li Weihan. Wang and his family were later told to move out of the Zhongnanhai leadership compound.[62]

Contrary to Wang's hopes, Mao continued to push Chinese foreign policy in a confrontational direction, especially with the Soviet Union. Khrushchev blunted Mao's ability to celebrate over China's swift victory over Indian troops in the October 1962 border war, for example, by urging restraint on both sides in the run-up to the conflict. To Mao, it sounded as though Moscow was siding with Delhi.[63]

The conflict had taken place just as Khrushchev decided to compromise with President John F. Kennedy by removing Soviet missiles from Cuba after the two sides had come close to nuclear war. Beijing used the opportunity to needle the Soviets.[64] Communist Party newspapers compared the Soviet leader's dealings with "American imperialists" to Britain's appeasement of Hitler at the 1938 Munich Conference.[65] At a Soviet reception in Beijing, Chen Yi counseled his hosts against "wishy-washiness" in foreign policy.[66]

Needling wasn't enough to satisfy Mao's frustrations with Moscow. He decided to respond with the communist equivalent of a face slap: an ideological polemic. Starting in 1962, the *People's Daily* published a series of essays edited by Mao and other top leaders that detailed their theoretical objections to Soviet "revisionism."[67]

Beijing also attacked Moscow face-to-face in an increasingly bizarre series of party-to-party meetings. The last of these occasions, held in Moscow in July 1963, followed the Soviet expulsion of three Chinese diplomats for distributing anti-Soviet material. Deng Xiaoping led the Chinese side. The two sides held eleven meetings over fifteen days, during which they delivered lengthy diatribes packed with ideological invective. On July 19, Mao's longtime security chief, Kang Sheng, read a speech approved by Beijing that praised Stalin as a "good" comrade and criticized Khrushchev for calling the late dictator a bandit, a gambler, a despot like Ivan the Terrible, a fool, a piece of shit, and an idiot. One eyewitness said the "strange" talks were "difficult even to call negotiations."[68]

Beijing's split from the world's most powerful communist state also worsened its relationships with other socialist countries. Only Albania, which had itself split from Moscow in 1960, offered unalloyed encouragement to Beijing.[69] Even those who hoped to stay neutral, such as the Cuban Communists, were compelled to take sides and eventually criticize Chinese "splittism." Chinese embassies throughout much of the Eastern Bloc came to resemble "lonely islands," one diplomat remembered.[70]

Ideological war meant a constant state of high alert. China's diplomats in Cuba, who had until recently enjoyed hosting Fidel Castro on his impromptu visits to pick up Chinese food at their embassy, were now under strict orders to walk out of any event where China was criticized.[71] On one occasion, an over-eager Chinese delegation stormed out of an event after hearing the word "China," wrongly assuming that their country was about to be criticized.[72]

***

China's split from the Soviets left it more in need of foreign friends than ever. After 1962, the famine had receded as Mao stepped back from the front line of Chinese politics and technocracy kicked back in. Like before, Beijing needed effective diplomacy to pursue its development goals.

Zhou undertook a thirteen-nation tour of African and Asian countries from late 1963 to the spring of 1964. The trip helped pave the way for a later agreement that would see China help build the Tanzania-Zambia railway after the World Bank refused to provide the country with financial aid to link the country with seaports. Despite early suspicions toward China, Zambian president Kenneth Kaunda would go on to describe China as a "reliable all-weather friend." Each new relationship on the continent provided China with one more vote toward replacing Taiwan in the United Nations.[73]

By far the biggest breakthrough was China's establishment of diplomatic relations with France in January 1964. After beginning with economic and cultural exchanges, China had successfully seized on the opportunities created by de Gaulle's desire to showcase France's independent foreign policy. China and France also shared frustrations over the Limited Test Ban Treaty between America, Britain, and the Soviet Union in 1963, which both China and France saw as an effort to diminish their global roles.[74]

It was a big win and China knew it. It represented China's first full diplomatic relationship with a major capitalist power and opened up the possibility of further breakthroughs in Western Europe as well as French-speaking African nations. "Far from being isolated, [we are] now in a progressive situation," read a 1964 foreign ministry memo.[75]

The good news kept coming. In October 1964, two positive developments occurred on the same day: Khrushchev was ousted and China successfully tested a nuclear weapon. The mood in the foreign ministry was one of elation. "We felt like there was an invisible force encouraging and helping us," one ambassador remembered.[76]

Khrushchev's removal wasn't only satisfying because it removed Mao's bête noire. It also opened up the possibility that China could resume its charm offensive with other communist states and perhaps even Moscow itself. After all, several socialist states—including North Vietnam and North Korea—were already drawn to China's emphasis on sovereignty and national development over models dictated by Moscow.[77]

Before long, Chinese diplomats in other communist states began to notice the difference. The embassy in Prague found that "people were willing to talk with us and listen to our opinions."[78] Others were beginning to look to Beijing as a potential bulwark against Soviet aggression. Romania, for instance, urged Zhou to visit the country as soon as possible in early 1966 as its own relationship with the Soviet Union worsened and its leaders began to see the Sino-Soviet split as an opportunity.[79]

The foreign ministry moved into a set of buildings in Beijing's Dongjiaomin Lane, just East of the Forbidden City, after an earthquake damaged the old building in 1966.[80] It would remain there for the next four years. The ministry now oversaw relations with forty-nine countries and the future looked bright.

***

As the famine eased, a semblance of normality returned to political life in China. New recruits continued to join the ministry. Their passion, even after the revolution had inflicted such suffering on its own people, is a testament to the mix of deeply personal, even banal, motivations that power any political movement.

For Dai Bingguo, the Russian-language student whose skin had turned a sickly yellow during the famine, joining the ministry was a life-changing opportunity. Born into brutal poverty in a small mountainous village in Guizhou province, he saw four of his five siblings die before adulthood and had raised money for his college fees by walking village to village to borrow from relatives and officials.

Becoming a diplomat gave Dai access to otherwise unimaginable opportunities. When he finally arrived in Beijing to work at the foreign ministry, Dai found that his hair turned black for the first time in his life: until then it had always been yellow from malnutrition. "There were no children of high-ranking cadres. Most came from regular families," Dai later wrote of his incoming class at the ministry.[81] For students like Dai who made it to Beijing, the Party had delivered on its promises of social equality and opportunity.

For others, becoming a diplomat was a route to international adventure. The secrecy and restrictiveness of Party life even seems to have been part of the allure. One fresh graduate who joined the ministry in 1962 was dispatched on a secret mission to Tibet as a translator during the Sino-Indian border war. Told not to ask where she was going, she was instructed to keep "the Party and nation's secrets" and given just over two hours' notice before setting off. As she proudly wrote in a note to her husband, "This is the first time the leaders have treated me as a member of the People's Liberation Army in civilian clothing."[82]

Many more saw becoming a diplomat as a chance to serve international communism. One official at China's water and electricity department remembered feeling a "rush of excitement" when learning that he "would become a member of the 'PLA in civilian clothing," after being offered an ambassadorship in 1965. "I would become the eyes and ears of the center," he thought.[83]

The ministry's strong culture was matched by camaraderie in many embassies overseas. Zeng Tao, China's ambassador in Algeria, remembered his embassy as "one big family" when he looked back at this period. "Everyone from the ambassador on down all ate the same food in the same cafeteria. We were with each other from dawn to dusk," he wrote. "Embassy staff respected their leaders, and the leadership looked after the staff." They even went on beach outings together.[84]

The good times didn't last. Back in Beijing, Mao was starting to feel that bureaucrats like them had it too cozy. If the Great Leap Forward had stretched the ministry's tight discipline, the Cultural Revolution would snap it.

6

Diplomacy in Retreat

In June 1966, Foreign Minister Chen Yi ushered a group of young diplomats into a room inside the Zhongnanhai leadership compound. Not long out of training, they included Secretary of State Hillary Clinton's future counterpart, Dai Bingguo, then a twenty-five-year-old Soviet specialist who'd pulled himself out of brutal poverty in the southern Chinese countryside and made it all the way to the foreign ministry.

Chen knew they were disturbed by the increasingly tense mood in the capital and wanted to reassure them. Mao had just declared the start of the Cultural Revolution and its effects were already being felt inside the ministry. Still, Chen said he'd seen trouble before and was sure this too would pass. "I've seen the biggest storms thousands of times, so why be afraid that a little storm will capsize the boat?"[1]

Despite Chen's reassuring words, things were about to get much worse. China was on the brink of a decade of political chaos motivated by Mao's desire to save his revolution from what he saw as a descent into technocracy and to reinforce his centrality to the country's political life.

This was the start of the most destructive period in the diplomatic history of the People's Republic. The Cultural Revolution would bring down much of what had so far been achieved and leave indelible scars on multiple generations of diplomats—just as it left scars across the country. China's progress in establishing diplomatic ties with the outside world ground to a complete halt from the middle of 1966 until the end of 1969.[2] By the end of 1969, even Mao complained that "now we are isolated. No one will listen to us."[3]

Before it was all over, Chen would be dead and countless others would be imprisoned, beaten, and publicly humiliated. Dai and most of his colleagues would be shipped off to labor camps. One of Mao's translators described the period as "our *Lord of the Flies*."[4] "At the time, many foreigners said China had gone mad," another diplomat remembered. "It was true. China had gone mad."[5]

***

The Cultural Revolution began in mid-May 1966. Mao issued a directive warning of "revisionists" in the Party who aimed to create a "dictatorship of the bourgeoisie." Within weeks, a new "Central Cultural Revolution Group" had taken over the country's cultural policies and was pushing for the violent overthrow of the status quo. The group—later dubbed the "Gang of Four"— was led by Mao's wife Jiang Qing, together labor activist Wang Hongwen, cultural critic Yao Wenyuan, and Shanghai Party Secretary Zhang Chunqiao.

Most Chinese diplomats didn't understand how important these developments would turn out to be for them. Foreign ministry staff paid little attention at first, holding a few cursory "study sessions" to feign compliance. Diplomats charged with "political work" in the ministry, however, sensed something bigger was afoot and urged the ministry's leadership to pay more attention.[6]

Gradually, others sensed a change too. The head of the Information Department, Gong Peng, and her husband, Vice Minister Qiao Guanhua, began throwing out old books, magazines, and records, as well as all of Gong's pointed shoes—anything that might be deemed feudal, capitalist, or "revisionist."[7] Chen Yi began encouraging cadres to take a more active role in the emerging political movement despite his private doubts. By late June, more than 18,000 big character posters—hand-painted signs that were the mainstay of any public protest—had appeared in the foreign ministry alone.[8]

The signals were harder to interpret for those posted overseas. Chinese diplomats in Yugoslavia tried to piece together information from official documents and foreign media reports.[9] The foreign ministry, for its part, tried to stop its diplomats overseas from getting too distracted: it sent instructions forbidding them from putting up big character posters and suggesting that they focus on studying "positive things."[10]

By August, however, the Cultural Revolution had halted normal life. Across the country, student "Red Guards" were attacking schools, universities, and anything else they considered "feudal." In mid-August the Party's Central Committee officially called for the overthrow of "those within the Party who are in authority and taking the capitalist road."

Then Mao received a letter from Austria that sealed the ministry's fate. A member of that country's Communist Party had written to Mao telling him that Chinese diplomats in Vienna were driving around in Mercedes cars and that the men were wearing Western suits while the women donned high heels. Another letter from Tanzania leveled similar criticisms.[11]

On September 9, Mao issued a simple written instruction to Chen Yi: "revolutionize or there will be danger." Chen immediately instructed embassies to reform their behavior in meetings and their protocol. As soon as China's embassy in Poland received the instruction, it ordered its diplomats to change clothes. "No one dared not implement the September 9 instruction," recalled the ambassador.[12]

Embassies were told to promote "Mao Zedong Thought" and the Cultural Revolution.[13] All diplomats were now required to wear Mao suits as well as Mao badges.[14] Political "study sessions" were stepped up.[15] The embassy in North Vietnam specified that the Mao suits be made of plain cloth to symbolize their suffering together with Vietnam in its fight against America.[16] China's embassy in Mongolia hired a local construction company to cover its exterior walls with giant red boards featuring quotations from Chairman Mao in large gold font. They began distributing copies of Mao's "Little Red Book" at diplomatic events.[17]

Almost immediately, the ideological ardor pushed Chinese diplomats further away from their foreign counterparts. The new rules meant that attending many formal and even social events with other embassies from black tie galas to dances and hunting trips became unthinkable. For diplomats who had spent so long trying to fit into the rarefied world of international diplomacy, the shift was downright embarrassing. "In their eyes, not caring about clothes or appearance was a sign of being uncivilized," one diplomat said of her foreign counterparts. "It hurt our personal dignity and our national prestige."[18]

In Chinese embassies, just as in schools, homes, and government buildings across the country, items deemed ideologically improper were destroyed. In Pakistan, the military attaché led the embassy's support staff in breaking "feudal" items inside the embassy and criticizing the ambassador.[19] In Nepal, rebel diplomats destroyed anything they could find that was old, including calligraphy and antiques.[20] A statue in the Chinese embassy in Cuba was smashed, as it represented the pre-Communist society the rebels hoped to destroy.[21]

An almost religious fervor for "Mao Zedong Thought" swept through the foreign ministry as it did across the rest of the country. Media reports circulated of instances where Mao thought helped restore sight to the blind, reattach severed hands, and restart hearts that had stopped beating—all without any professional training.[22] One young diplomat from the Russian section of the foreign ministry's Translation Department boasted to a colleague that he had just operated on a patient despite his lack of medical credentials. It was "so simple and easy," he said.[23]

As the disaster unfolded, the outside world responded with a mixture of alarm and confusion. China's top diplomats sought to play down the movement's impact. Chen Yi tried to reassure the French ambassador in November 1966 by placing the events in the context of the sweep of history, citing the French, Russian, and Chinese revolutions as precedents and even comparing events to the Paris Commune of 1871. Facts and experience would help to reassure skeptics of the Red Guards, he said.[24]

In truth, even China's fellow communist countries could make little sense of what was happening. "We also know very little of what is going on over there," one Soviet leader told his Polish counterpart. "Our embassy is working in exceptionally difficult conditions."[25] Even the North Koreans were fazed. "The Great Proletarian Cultural Revolution has seriously alarmed us," the country's supreme leader and founder Kim Il-sung told the Soviet ambassador in November 1966. He warned that members of his Korean Workers Party were "not so experienced as to correctly understand everything."[26]

Although it was dangerous to admit it, foreign ministry officials in Beijing were worried too. "My friends at work and I were horrified at what was going on, and even more disturbed that there were radical elements in the foreign ministry who sympathized with the Red Guards," remembered one official. "Everyone knew someone who had been or might be a target."[27]

By the winter of 1966, rebels in the foreign ministry proclaimed themselves the "Foreign Ministry Revolutionary Rebel Station." They soon declared their intention to overthrow the ministry's Party Committee. They also started to monitor everyone's work.[28] As events unfolded, Chen Yi became a particular focus after he was targeted by Mao's wife Jiang Qing and as he worked to limit the influence of foreign ministry rebels. Always more willing to speak his mind than Zhou, his directness made him a ripe target for punishment.[29] He also served as a convenient proxy for attacks on Zhou himself. In January 1967, Zhou advised Chen not to venture outside unless it was essential.[30]

***

In early 1967, the foreign ministry began recalling ambassadors to Beijing to take part in the Cultural Revolution. As they approached the capital, the discipline of China's diplomatic corps was stretched to breaking point.

China's ambassador to Yugoslavia, military veteran Kang Maozhao, was among their number. He and about half of his embassy staff headed home by train in early 1967. They all got along well enough on the road and junior officers continued to treat him with respect.

When Kang's train arrived in Beijing, he found a city covered in political posters. There was—unusually—no one from the ministry to greet him at the station. His home too was empty, with his children out to participate in the Cultural Revolution. Not long after arriving back, his colleagues turned on him. Denouncing him, they said that he had been too close to Chen Yi and was a "capitalist roader."[31]

Kang's experience was typical. Ambassadors and other senior diplomats were locked up, had their houses ransacked, and their savings stolen. They were forced to scrub toilets, kicked and beaten in front of their peers, and publicly criticized and bullied into confessing their "crimes" both by students and by staff from their own embassies.[32] When Gong Peng, the brilliant diplomat who had courted foreign journalists in Geneva, collapsed during one of the multi-hour criticism sessions aimed at her, younger diplomats spat at her and shouted "she's playing dead."[33]

By summer 1967, Huang Hua, now posted in Egypt, was China's only remaining ambassador overseas, staying on in his post on Zhou's insistence as Egypt and Israel went to war. Chinese students in Cairo had smashed statues inside the embassy, while rebel diplomats called for the downfall of Chen Yi and told Huang they would be supervising his work. Ever the studious communist, he traded quotations from Mao's "Little Red Book" with rebels in a bid to assert his authority.[34]

China's now leaderless embassies were left guessing what to do. Unsure how to respond, the skeletal staff left at the embassy in Laos put up big character posters to demonstrate their revolutionary credentials and held meetings to discuss whether they were indulging in "revisionist" diplomacy. At one point, they began growing their own vegetables in order to show that they were "practicing production."

The diplomats in Laos received contradictory and confusing messages. At one point, cables from Beijing told them that their allowances would be cut off, while others said things were back to normal. On another occasion, they received a call from Beijing condemning their decision to attend a diplomatic event before they had even reported it to the ministry. The diplomats began to search the embassy and discovered listening devices inside the roof beams of their accommodation, hidden in the walls of the embassy, and concealed inside desk lamps in their offices.[35]

Back in the Chinese capital, the situation was spiraling out of control. In August, rebel diplomats attended a series of meetings in the foreign ministry criticizing Chen Yi. At another meeting on August 11, thousands of students gathered to denounce Chen in the massive Great Hall of the People towering over Tiananmen Square. The once pudgy general now looked gaunt and pale.[36]

In mid-August, the rebel group attempted to seize power in the ministry, paralyzing its political department for more than two weeks. They managed to apprehend Chen's top deputies, forcing Ji Pengfei and Qiao Guanhua to write confessions and even sell newspapers on the street.[37] On one occasion, Qiao was beaten until he coughed up blood.[38]

At another struggle session on August 26, the rebels let the air out of Chen's car tires to prevent him from leaving the ministry. He hid in a shower room and eventually escaped through the back door. The next day, the rebels planned to grab Chen and drag him into the streets, but Zhou Enlai personally intervened: "If you try to seize Chen Yi, I will block you at the door of the Great Hall," Zhou told them. "You can do it by stepping over my chest."[39] A CIA memo from that time asked simply: "China's Foreign Policy—Who Is in Charge?"[40]

In the spring of 1968, it was the turn of Vice Minister Zhang Hanfu. Zhang had served in the ministry since 1949 and acted as a kind of chief operating officer. Now recovering from an illness, he was dragged from his home by Red Guards and rebel diplomats with no opportunity to say goodbye to his family. He died in prison dressed in tattered rags four years later.[41]

Zhou tried his best to hold the ministry together as mentees turned on mentors and friends betrayed each other to stay safe. Always, there was the fear of what the following day might bring. Like many of his colleagues, Fu Hao, the deputy head of the personnel department, was unable to sleep at night without the aid of sleeping pills. After one of Fu's friends in the ministry committed suicide, Zhou urged him to stay positive, worrying that he might also take his own life.[42] Zhou himself was now consistently working eighteen-hour days.[43] In a bid to protect his personal staff, he advised that they mimic the wording of official Party documents when they spoke to others, lest they land themselves in trouble.[44]

As their world collapsed around them, Chinese diplomats found their most profound beliefs challenged. "Many comrades found it hard to believe that Chairman Mao could have been wrong" in launching such a disastrous campaign, remembered one of Zhou Enlai's Yan'an foreign policy recruits.[45] "I felt pretty low back then," one ambassador remembered, "but I couldn't say anything. I didn't dare to say anything."[46]

**

Even more painful than the violence and humiliation aimed at the ministry's leadership was the brutality directed at their families.

Wang Jiaxiang, the former ambassador who had dared to question Mao's foreign policies, saw his son targeted. Criticized in public "struggle sessions," his glasses smashed, his face painted black, and forced to stand for hours in the painful "airplane" position—doubled over with his arms stretched out behind his back—Wang's son eventually took his own life. Wang himself was imprisoned for nineteen months, pushed and shoved in front of crowds of more than 1,000, and forced to adorn his home with posters listing his crimes. Three of his grandchildren became Red Guards and chose to distance themselves from him.[47]

Wu Xiuquan, the former general who had successfully wooed Tito in Yugoslavia, saw his children punished for his "crimes." His pregnant daughter was forced to undergo "re-education through labor." His ninety-year-old mother's house was covered in political posters and bombarded with loudspeakers barking political slogans. Wu himself was beaten, forced to clean public toilets, and to chop wood in Beijing's freezing winter. After initially being imprisoned in his office in the Party's International Department, he was taken to an undisclosed location, where he was shut in a room for seven years and allowed no contact with his family. The room's windows were boarded over and bright lights shone down on him twenty-four hours a day. He became so lonely that he tried to communicate with other prisoners by coughing until the guards banned it. His captors refused to use his name, instead simply calling him "number 42."[48]

Then there was Wang Bingnan, who had led the ambassadorial talks with the United States in Poland. Already accused of conspiring with a foreign spy before the outbreak of the Cultural Revolution, Wang was locked in a cellar as ministry rebels focused on his wife, Zhang Yuyun. Day after day, they criticized, beat, and humiliated her. She was tough, escaping twice from her captors. But eventually she too reached breaking point and hanged herself in the bathroom with her belt.

Wang was released briefly to see his wife's body. He found it covered in cuts and bruises with half her hair shaved off. Resisting the politically dangerous urge to embrace her body, he held back tears until he was returned to the cellar. The rebels allowed him ten minutes to tell his children about their mother's fate, all under close rebel supervision.[49] (One of Wang's sons, Wang Boming, went on to become one of the founding fathers of China's stock markets and to bankroll Caijing, a groundbreaking investigative business news organization.)[50]

It wasn't just senior diplomats who were at risk. Anyone suspected of having too much foreign contact was in danger. One teacher at Beijing Foreign Studies University—the Foreign Ministry's main feeder university—found herself accused of having suspicious foreign contacts. After three months of imprisonment and forced confessions, she snapped and threw herself in a canal still holding a copy of Mao's "Little Red Book". The next day, the rebels took her husband to the site where her body was found, forcing him to participate in one last round of criticism against her corpse.[51]

***

The Red Guards trampled on China's hard-won diplomatic gains both in Beijing and in global capitals, where student activists and radicalized officials clashed with local authorities.

Most dramatically, the British mission in the Chinese capital was stormed and torched by Red Guards. When protests broke out outside the Chinese embassy in London, young Chinese diplomats ignored the instructions of senior diplomats and engaged in hand-to-hand combat with the protesters outside. British television news captured an image of a Chinese diplomat waving an axe.[52] "Red Diplomats Armed with Mao Tse-tung's Thought Are Dauntless," boasted a headline in the official Peking Review the following month.[53]

The provocations extended to other communist countries and China's newer friends in developing countries. The Soviet embassy in Beijing was put under siege by Red Guards and German diplomats were beaten up in the streets.[54] Rebels damaged the Polish ambassador's car,[55] while the Czechoslovakian ambassador was detained at the airport, his car forced open and the national flag ripped off.[56] In Ghana and Indonesia, Chinese representatives were expelled for their provocations.[57]

As these events unfolded, China's senior diplomats had to pretend that all was well when they met foreign counterparts. In the summer of 1967, China's ambassador to Hungary was hauled into a meeting with the country's foreign minister who recounted an attack on the car of the Hungarian ambassador in Beijing. The envoy had then been dragged out of the vehicle and marched to a police station—a flagrant violation of international legal protections reserved for ambassadors. The Chinese ambassador didn't know the facts of the matter, but the report seemed credible enough given what he'd heard about events in Beijing. Still, he couldn't say this to a foreigner. Stuck between the need to maintain a good relationship with a fellow socialist country and the more pressing imperative of staying safe, he simply replied, "the Red Guards of my country have been trained and educated. They know what should and shouldn't be done."[58]

As the violence escalated, Zhou Enlai tried to keep Chinese diplomacy on track. Instead of traveling abroad, he visited foreign embassies inside Beijing. Spotting a potential win for China after the Soviet Union's 1968 invasion of Czechoslovakia left other European Communists nervous, Zhou attended Romania's national day celebrations in Beijing that year. His speech criticized the aggression of the "Soviet revisionist clique."[59]

***

By late 1968, Mao had decided that things had gotten out of hand. Millions of urban youth were sent down to the countryside for "re-education" and the military was brought in to restore order to the cities.

China's foreign policy, which had been radicalized by the Cultural Revolution, also needed a reboot. It was undermining the country's most basic and long-standing policy objectives and had become a major threat to national security. China faced a hostile United States, embittered by Beijing's military support for North Vietnam, and a hostile India on its Southwest border after the pair's 1962 border war. By March 1969, Chinese and Soviet troops were exchanging shots on the border. Soviet leaders were even considering a pre-emptive nuclear strike against Beijing.[60]

Zhou began planning for a return to normal. Anticipating the rebuilding of China's diplomatic relationships, starting with infrastructure at home, he commissioned the "Beijing Diplomatic Projects" in 1969, including an International Club, a "Friendship Store" that would sell foreign products unavailable to regular Chinese, and a Diplomatic Residence Compound on Jianguomen Outer Street, about three kilometers east of Tiananmen Square. In keeping with the mood of Chinese politics, the designs of the buildings veered toward international modernist themes instead of Soviet influences.[61]

Even more profound changes were taking place behind the scenes. While reading his regular summary of foreign media in late 1967, Mao had spotted an article by the former American vice president and lifelong anti-communist, Richard Nixon. Published in *Foreign Affairs*, the article argued that "there is no place on this small planet for a billion of its potentially most able people to live in angry isolation." Intrigued, he recommended the article to Zhou.[62]

Nixon dropped another hint in his January 1969 inaugural address. "Let all nations know that during this administration our lines of communications will be open," he said.[63] China's leaders got the message. Chinese state media panned the speech, denouncing Nixon as the "jittery chieftain of American imperialism," but—acting on Mao's orders—it also took the unprecedented step of publishing the speech in full.[64] Quietly, the chairman was beginning to see stronger relations with the United States as a way to protect China against the Soviet threat.

On Mao's instructions, Zhou pulled together a committee of "four marshals"—Chen Yi, Ye Jianying, Xu Xiangqian, and Nie Rongzhen—to evaluate the international situation.[65] Zhou brought Chen back from the factory where he'd been living outside of Beijing in a bid to stay safe.[66] He told Chen and the other marshals to meet weekly and think big. After several months of meetings and with some coaxing, they reported that, contrary to Chinese propaganda, neither the United States nor the Soviet Union was likely to attack China and recommended an expansion of China's diplomatic activities overseas.

In late 1969, Zhou began to send some diplomats abroad again. Addressing one group headed to Cuba, he criticized "leftists" and admitted that Chinese diplomacy had experienced setbacks.[67] These were hopeful signs, of course, but most diplomats knew nothing of Mao's broader rethink on foreign policy. What they did know was that most of the diplomats still left overseas were extreme left-wingers and many were nervous about heading back to face them.[68] Indeed, when China's ambassador to Congo had arrived at his post that summer, his diplomats had refused to even meet with local elites.[69]

Still, going abroad was a good option when the alternative was being sent to the camps.

***

In 1968, the Party began establishing re-education camps all across China to rewire the thinking of the country's bureaucrats. Named "5.7 cadre schools" after the May 7 date on which Mao gave the order, between 70 and 90 percent of central government employees—including China's diplomats—were sent to study at these "schools," which were in effect labor camps.[70] When they arrived, with no knowledge of what might come next, many diplomats assumed they would spend the rest of their lives in the countryside.[71]

The thirty-year-old diplomat Zhang Bing was sent to one such camp in the spring of 1969.[72] Born in a rented cottage in a northern Chinese village, she dreamed of one day seeing the ocean, perhaps even the world. She taught in a middle school after graduating from college, but when her husband joined the foreign ministry in 1965, she began studying in her spare time, even taking her three-month-old baby to lectures. After just a year of preparation, she was accepted by the ministry.

When she left on the train for Beijing with her child in her arms, Zhang imagined a future in Beijing and capitals around the world. Instead, after just a few years in the ministry, she'd been shipped off to the "Foreign Ministry 321 Cadre School," in Taiping Village in Heilongjiang Province, which borders Siberia. Some 500 foreign affairs cadres were sent to Taiping and the neighboring villages, including teams from the foreign ministry, the Diaoyutai State Guesthouse, the foreign ministry's in-house think tank, and its publishing house.

Twenty people were crammed into Zhang's dormitory. They shared two large "kang" beds, hard heated platforms used to stave off the biting winters of northern China. Zhang and her colleagues covered the platforms in straw to soften the surface and put up a curtain to separate men and women. Nighttime was difficult as colleagues snored, farted, slapped mosquitoes, and talked in their sleep. They worried about wolves.

The days were harder. They toiled in the fields and built bridges, roads, and homes for locals. The work was grueling and none of them knew what they were doing. When they weren't laboring, Zhang and her colleagues engaged in re-education and self-criticism sessions where they would study Mao's works and dissect the shortcomings of "revisionist" thought.

The work was especially tough for older diplomats, who were often injured in the process. One prominent veteran revolutionary and social scientist, Chen Hansheng, was forced to deliver newspapers and clean the school's toilets. He was so short-sighted that he had to press his face up against the excrement-covered surfaces in order to clean them.

The food was terrible. Lacking fresh produce, the diplomats ate whatever salted vegetables were available. On special occasions they ate bean sprouts.

Some suffered diarrhea and others serious constipation. Most avoided taking laxatives in order to avoid spending too much time around—and perhaps falling inside—the open pit toilet filled with maggots.

But amid the adversity, there were little moments of joy. A future ambassador, Shi Wushan, managed once to smuggle a can of meat into the camp. Once he and his friends had devoured its contents, Shi filled the can with stones and threw it into the river to hide the evidence. Displays of loyalty to Mao could win rewards: one of Zhang's colleagues obtained an accordion that Red Guards had stolen from the home of Vice Minister Ji Pengfei to play music venerating the chairman. Her colleague was permitted to leave the camp to perform in nearby towns and villages.

By November 1969, China's tense relationship with the Soviet Union and the cadres' inability to grow anything in the fields of northern China saw Zhang's whole camp uprooted and sent to Mao's home province of Hunan.

Her story was not unusual. Another diplomat at a camp in Hubei remembered colleagues suffering from malnutrition after eating carrots for every meal. They drank water from a hole next to the public toilet, which would overflow when it rained; they once killed a dog for its meat.[73] At some camps, diplomats were used in place of oxen to pull plows.[74] One vice minister, Chen Jiakang, even died at a 5.7 school.[75]

Occasionally, Zhang and other colleagues were called back to the ministry when extra staff were needed. But even these brief moments of reprieve could be humiliating. When Zhang was called back to staff a banquet for Pakistani dignitaries in Beijing, she served pork to the guests. No one had ever told her that Muslims didn't eat the meat. "I didn't even have the most basic diplomatic knowledge," she wrote later. "I embarrassed the foreign ministry and embarrassed the Chinese people!"

In 1971, the camps began to be dismantled.[76] Zhang stayed on until 1972 when she fell ill and was sent to Beijing. A few months later, when she was assigned to train for a new job in the ministry, she felt like she had nothing to contribute. "If they sent me back to the foreign ministry, what could I do?" she asked herself. "How can someone who can only shout slogans, write big character posters and do manual work in the fields be a diplomat?"

Zhang was by then thirty-four years old and six months pregnant. "In a flash, six years had gone by and the golden years of my life had pointlessly drifted away," she wrote. For her and many millions of other young Chinese, the Cultural Revolution raised painful questions about the new society they'd been told they were building.

Zhang went on to serve in diplomatic posts in Sweden, Canada, and New Zealand, traveling widely and fulfilling her dream of seeing the world. Still, her experience in the camps left her with an uneasy feeling. "I've thought about it hundreds of times," Zhang wrote after her retirement. "Is history true or is it just a story? As a regular Party member how should I treat the Party's history?" She looked back at the slogans she had been told as she'd headed out to the 5.7 school: " 'The 5.7 soldiers are glorious.' 'The 5.7 road is heroic.' These were all lies to trick people," she wrote.

Mao, of course, felt differently. "The foreign ministry was a mess. Control was lost for a month and a half and power was in the hands of the counter-revolutionaries," he later recalled. "Most of it was good, but there were some bad people."[77] In any case, Mao's mind was focused on other things at the time: while Zhang and others had languished in the countryside, Chinese diplomacy had moved on without them.

***

On July 16, 1971, Mao's grandniece, the thirty-two-year-old Wang Hairong, and American-born interpreter Tang Wensheng ("Nancy Tang") walked into the foreign ministry cafeteria looking pleased with themselves. News had shot through the ministry that Secretary of State Henry Kissinger had just completed a secret visit to China and these two young female diplomats had been in the small group that accompanied him from Pakistan. The pair had emerged as the aging dictator's eyes and ears in the ministry and it seemed likely they'd be in the know. They quickly found themselves surrounded by a crowd.[78]

It's no wonder that their colleagues wanted details. Kissinger's visit was a massive shock for those on the front line of Chinese foreign policy. America was China's sworn enemy. The two sides had concluded a major war less than twenty years earlier and had been sparring through proxies in Vietnam. When Chinese diplomats ran into their American counterparts around the world they would turn their backs and leave.[79] Beijing was covered in posters calling for the fall of "American imperialism."

After the initial public flirting that had followed Nixon's election, the hunt began for an effective channel between the two powers. It was a sensitive political matter for both sides after decades of hostility. And with no effective working channels, it was also logistically tricky.

The unlikely moment for a breakthrough was a December 1969 Yugoslavian fashion show in Warsaw. A group of Chinese diplomats from the embassy in Poland attended the event, led by attaché Jing Zhicheng. They saw two Americans pointing at them across the room. Unaware of the strategic rethink taking place in Beijing and hoping to avoid the appearance of being too close to Nixon's America, they stood up to leave. To their surprise, the Americans pursued them, shouting in Polish that Nixon wanted to resume talks with China. Jing and his associates began to run, but the ambassador to Poland, Walter Stoessel, caught up with Jing's interpreter, telling him that he had an important message for the embassy.[80]

Two weeks later, Lei Yang, China's acting ambassador in Warsaw, met with Stoessel to suggest reopening the ambassadorial talks first established after the Geneva Conference. The two sides resumed discussions in February 1970 but failed to yield the breakthrough either side was looking for. When America launched military incursions into Cambodia as part of its efforts in Vietnam, Mao canceled the talks altogether.[81]

Nearly as suspicious of bureaucracies as Mao, Nixon turned to backchannel diplomacy. In July 1970, he used an extended overseas visit to tell Pakistan's president, Yahya Khan, and the Romanian leader, Nicolae Ceauşescu, that he sought high-level exchanges with China. Kissinger, meanwhile, asked a former French official to pass on the same message to China's ambassador in Paris, Huang Zhen. Beijing also tried to pass messages to the American embassy in Oslo and Kabul. Still, neither side bit.[82]

Then, in August, Mao tried a more familiar tack: he invited Edgar Snow back to Beijing. Snow, now aged sixty-five and recovering from surgery, was met by Huang Hua just as he had been more than three decades earlier in the badlands of Shaanxi province. Huang and other colleagues who had just returned from "re-education" in a 5.7 school told Snow that Chinese society had been remade: "We disdain money and possessions. We desire to create a socialist society and a new and nobler man," they said.[83]

During China's National Day celebrations on October 1, Snow stood next to Mao during a parade in Tiananmen Square. Mao also granted Snow an interview with an embargo of three months in which Mao said he would be delighted to meet with any other senior official willing to travel to China. Mao presumably expected Snow to pass the message to the American government. Snow never passed on the message and Washington missed the significance of his public appearance with Mao, dismissing him as a "Beijing propagandist."[84]

In December, Mao decided the time for signals and backchannels was over. Zhou wrote directly to Kissinger in a handwritten message delivered via Pakistan. The note invited an emissary to Beijing to discuss Taiwan. One month later, a similar note appeared through the Romanian channel. Kissinger responded by welcoming the idea of an emissary.[85]

All channels then went quiet for a few months until, in April 1971, Beijing invited the American ping-pong team to tour China. Zhou received them in the Great Hall of the People, saying that their visit had "opened a new chapter in the history of relations between the Chinese and American peoples." Zhou followed up with another note via Pakistan inviting Kissinger to Beijing. In May, the United States accepted.

Before Kissinger's arrival, Zhou immersed himself in the details of Nixon's and Kissinger's lives. He read Nixon's book, *Six Crises*, which detailed Nixon's role in public life from his position on the House Un-American Activities Committee through to his "kitchen debate" with Khrushchev. Zhou even watched the president's favorite movie, *Patton*, which had just been released.[86]

In July 1971, Kissinger pleaded illness during a trip to Pakistan. He then slipped away to fly to Beijing. He was met unannounced at the airport by a team of five Chinese diplomats, including Wang Hairong and Tang Wensheng.[87] Beijing itself was still covered in posters calling for the fall of "American imperialism." Workers' militias were even using images of Americans for target practice.[88]

During Kissinger's two-day visit on July 9 and 10, Zhou played him beautifully, talking extensively about history and the principles of diplomacy. Foreign diplomats often find themselves irritated by these theoretical digressions by Chinese diplomats, which they see as distractions, but they appealed to Kissinger's ego and intellect. Zhou was "one of the two or three most impressive men I have ever met," Kissinger later remembered. "He moved gracefully," Kissinger swooned, "and with dignity, filling a room not by his physical dominance (as did Mao or de Gaulle) but by his air of controlled tension, steely discipline, and self-control, as if he were a coiled spring."[89]

The combination of meticulous research and targeted flattery remains a powerful tool in Chinese diplomacy. Before Trump's inauguration in January 2017, Chinese officials used VPN networks to jump over China's Great Firewall that censors the Internet and scour Twitter for clues about his strategy.[90] China's powerful vice president Wang Qishan later told American officials and businessmen in Beijing that he had watched the movie *Three*

Billboards outside Ebbing Missouri to familiarize himself with Trump's voter base.[91]

The Kissinger visit felt like a slap in the face to some of China's few remaining friends, despite Zhou's efforts to reassure them. North Vietnam described it as "throwing a life buoy to Nixon, who almost had been drowned," while Albania described it as a "betrayal" of the world proletarian revolution.[92]

The move to strengthen ties with America coincided with a broader recalibration of Chinese foreign policy. In the fall of 1969, Zhou met with Soviet representatives at Beijing airport in a meeting arranged by North Vietnam. The two sides addressed each other as "comrade"—a sign of at least grudging respect. In January 1970, China sent a special envoy to a royal wedding in Nepal while Zhou visited North Korea that April and sent a telegram to Indonesia to express condolences over the death of former president Sukarno in June.[93] Small as these moves might seem, they were significant gestures in the context of the Cultural Revolution.

But returning to normal wouldn't be simple. The political atmosphere inside China was fraught. One diplomat headed back overseas in fall 1971 settled on a strategy for self-preservation: "no matter what our counterparts said, no matter whether or not what they said was accurate, so long as they suggested China had done anything wrong or should change its behavior, I would rebut it all without exception. Then I would decide on what to do after seeking instructions from the center."[94] It's a common tactic for Chinese diplomats even today.

The starkest reminder of the confused state of Chinese politics came in September 1971 when Mao's designated successor, Lin Biao, attempted to flee China. Lin had been rewarded for his long-standing sycophancy toward Mao when he'd replaced Peng Dehuai as defense minister in 1959. He had briefly emerged as Mao's heir apparent after Liu Shaoqi, Mao's previously anointed successor, had been violently shoved aside in the Cultural Revolution.

Even today, the details of Lin's actions remain shrouded in secrecy. Official sources say he and his son had been planning a coup against Mao. At a minimum, Lin decided that Mao was out to get him. On September 13, 1971, Lin boarded military plane with his wife and son and ordered it to fly north. Unclear where Lin was headed, Zhou told diplomats in Beijing to monitor all foreign radio broadcasts closely without elaborating on what they were listening for. Mao and Zhou stayed up through the night, waiting for news.

On September 14, Chinese diplomats in Ulaanbaatar had just finished breakfast when they received an unusual report from their Mongolian counterparts. A plane had crashed near a small mining town some 350 kilometers from the Chinese border. After waiting for permission from Beijing and the Mongolian authorities, a team of Chinese diplomats was dispatched to the crash site. They found the wreckage of the plane strewn across a large blackened section of the green Mongolian steppe, together with nine charred and disfigured bodies. After a later investigation, Beijing determined that body number five was Lin Biao.[95]

Lin's attempt to flee created a major political problem for Mao. He needed something to divert attention from the ugly fact that his once designated successor had betrayed him. Luckily for the aging dictator, good news was on the way.

***

Just after Kissinger boarded his plane at the end of his second visit to China on October 26 1971, the foreign ministry received a cable from New York: the People's Republic of China had been admitted to the United Nations.[96]

The ministry's leadership had some idea the breakthrough was coming. A team of diplomats had long been charged with calculating the outcome of the annual vote on Chinese membership based on reports from embassies and newspaper clippings. In 1971, they cautiously reported to their superiors that a win was possible.[97]

Chinese diplomats knew that this was a huge breakthrough. It bestowed a new level of international legitimacy on the regime and formalized its status as a major power. It was also a huge vindication of the country's post-Bandung bid to woo the Third World. But there was a major obstacle. Mao had consistently insisted that China was in no rush to join the United Nations. In fact, the Chinese had made a point of not proactively raising the matter with Kissinger during his secret visit.[98] As China's senior diplomats agonized over what to do, the complex politics of the Cultural Revolution muddied every available option.[99]

Mao alone could break the impasse. The task of coaxing him to have China join the United Nations would require all of Zhou's diplomatic prowess, as well as his formidable powers of ingratiation. Knowing that Mao needed a win after the Lin Biao affair, but also acutely aware that all the glory for securing this victory would need to belong to Mao, Zhou set off for the chairman's residence.[100]

The safest bet, of course, was simply to quote Mao's words back to him. "Participating now does not fit the chairman's teaching to 'not fight battles for which you have not prepared,'" Zhou said after arriving with a group of aides. Perhaps a safer option would be to send an advance team to study the situation in New York before dispatching a full delegation.

"Didn't the UN Secretary General send us a fax?" Mao replied. "We will send a delegation." Zhou's pitch had worked.

Mao seemed amused as he surveyed the list of countries which had voted for China's admission. "Britain, France, Holland, Belgium, Canada, and Italy have all become Red Guards, rebelling against America and voting for us," he said.

In high spirits, Mao talked with the aides for nearly three hours, citing Chinese classics like *Romance of the Three Kingdoms* and repeatedly quoting himself. "I have said that you should not fight battles for which you are not prepared," he told them. "I have also said 'learn to fight during war.' Please will the Premier now urgently prepare?"[101]

In the two-week window before the delegation was due to depart, Zhou did just that. He set up a small group to lead preparations for the trip, which would be the first time mainland Chinese officials had set foot in America since 1950. The fifty-two-strong delegation would be led by Qiao Guanhua, while Huang Hua would stay on as China's permanent representative in New York. The group would wear Mao suits inside the United Nations building and Western suits while walking around New York.

With little time to prepare, the group brought along such a heavy load of reference materials that diplomats had to cut down on personal possessions so they didn't overload the plane. They packed dictionaries, records of government announcements, and more than ten years of *Peking Review* back issues in case they needed to check anything. Zhou personally edited the first draft of Qiao's speech, incorporating instructions from Mao.[102]

The delegation was scheduled to leave the morning of November 9, but Mao wanted to meet with its leading members before they set off. It was a big moment for everyone involved. One second secretary who was too junior to attend the Mao meeting slept fully clothed just in case the leadership changed its mind.[103]

Those who were able to attend entered Mao's study in Zhongnanhai at around 8 P.M. on the evening of November 8. They found him wearing a white flannel dressing-gown—a common sight for anyone used to working with the chairman. After greeting the group, Mao sat himself down in an armchair. Picking up the tea he'd placed next to a lit cigar, he began talking history.

When the meeting wrapped up at around 10 p.m., Mao fired off a set of instructions for the group's departure the next morning: they should be seen off by the entire Politburo, department heads from across the Party, government, and military, and a crowd of "a few thousand."

Zhou then took the group to the Great Hall of the People where they were each given a bowl of noodles and a pep talk that lasted until the sun rose over Tiananmen Square. As the diplomats set off from the airport on their two-day journey to New York, the assembled crowd chanted: "Long live the victory of Chairman Mao's revolutionary diplomatic line!" "Long live chairman Mao!"[104]

Before the delegation left Chinese territory, the group's leader, Qiao Guanhua, issued a final set of instructions: they should maintain "strict discipline" and "secrecy."[105] He knew they were in for a shock.

7

Selective Integration

When China's diplomats arrived in New York in 1971, they may as well have landed on another planet.

What first struck many of them were the colors. On clothing, in shop fronts, and on neon signs, they saw a world that seemed physically and even morally jarring compared with the monochrome uniformity of communist Beijing. For the first time in their lives, the group of mostly middle-aged men saw pornographic theaters, prostitutes, strip clubs, and sex stores with lurid "items that made you sick," one of them remembered.[1]

It was all a long way from Mao's China. This was the New York City of *Shaft*, the crime action thriller that came out that year, and of *Jesus Christ Superstar*, the rock opera that had just opened on Broadway. The world's first electronic stock exchange, the NASDAQ, had opened in February, and the newly topped out twin towers of the World Trade Center dominated the city's skyline. Crime raged in the streets below as the murder rate once again set a record; mob boss Joseph Colombo had been shot in the head at Columbus Circle just a few months before the delegation's arrival.

Chinese diplomats knew they were out of place. "To Americans, the arrival of the Chinese delegation seemed like the sudden appearance of aliens," one of them later wrote.[2]

The experience wasn't just eye-opening for these new arrivals in America. It was also a pivotal moment for Chinese foreign policy. China's entrance into the United Nations helped spark a process that would eventually see it establish ties with virtually every other country in the world. It would also see Beijing sign up to treaties and multilateral organizations that helped define the status quo of international politics.

China integrated with extraordinary speed. The People's Republic was a member of just one intergovernmental organization in 1971. By 1989, it was a member of 37 and had signed more than 125 international treaties—compared with just six in the country's first two decades of existence.[3] By 2001, the process had helped precipitate such transformative changes in the country's political economy that the communist nation could join the World

Trade Organization. In 2008, China's national defense white paper boasted that its role in multilateral affairs was "notably elevating its international position and influence."[4]

China's participation at the United Nations likewise grew precipitously. In 2019, it surpassed Japan as the second-largest contributor to the organization's budget.[5] It provides more personnel to peacekeeping operations than any of the four other permanent members of the Security Council even as it lobbies with Russia to cut human rights posts in peacekeeping missions.[6] Chinese diplomats are also pushing to have Xi Jinping catchphrases included in UN resolutions.[7]

China's integration into the global economy and international institutions was a hopeful sign for many Western elites that the country might one day become more like the West by embracing market economics and eventually liberal democracy. But most Party elites in Beijing never saw things that way. Chinese leaders from Mao and Zhou through Xi Jinping have always seen participation in international organizations and groups as validation of their rule—never as a slippery slope to wrest the Communist Party from power. These mismatched expectations have led to confusion, hurt feelings, and bitter disappointments on both sides from the Tiananmen massacre to China's crackdown on human rights activists in the years after the 2008 Olympic Games.

In 1971, all of this was decades away. The first diplomats to touch down in New York were watched closely for their political loyalty and even held at arm's length by their own government. Their immediate task was to make sense of the strange city in which they found themselves.

With no consulate building in New York, the delegation booked nearly the whole fourteenth floor of the Roosevelt Hotel near UN headquarters from which to live and work. This small area became a little enclave of Communist China, hermetically sealed—as best they could manage—from the world outside. Everyone except the very top leaders was paired off in twin rooms. No member of staff was permitted to leave the hotel except for official meetings. Even recreational walks were forbidden after a while.

The basics of life in New York City were tough for the delegation at first. Diplomats found it hard to sleep with the roar of city life outside the window and none of the three drivers they'd brought with them had valid driver's licenses. They had to rely on yellow New York taxicabs to move around the city.[8]

The diplomats watched television news and read the *New York Times*, but the cultural gap was difficult to overcome.[9] Western diplomats would talk about "new movies, music, entertainment, and fashion, as well as women," remembered a translator in the group. "But the Chinese delegation observed strict discipline and, even though we were overseas, we couldn't watch movies or entertainment shows. There was a gap with contemporary Western culture. We found ourselves with nothing to say when these topics came up."[10]

Working at the United Nations presented Chinese diplomats with the steepest learning curve they had faced since their very first missions overseas in 1949. One of them compared it to a school for Chinese diplomats where they could learn for the first time how the national interests of countries around the world fitted together.[11]

Back in Beijing, officials in the foreign ministry and across the government raced to read reports sent back by the delegation. Each one contained new information about the outside world.[12]

As much as its envoys had to learn, it was clear that China's admission to the global body was a breakthrough for the country's international standing. When Qiao Guanhua delivered China's first speech to the organization, one participant remembered, "We could feel China's international status increasing."[13]

And, indeed, it did. A wave of diplomatic recognition followed, each new relationship representing a victory over Taiwan. In the Middle East, Beijing established relations with Iran, Kuwait, and Lebanon in 1971. Jordan switched recognition to Beijing in 1977, followed by Libya and Oman in 1978.[14] In Europe, it expanded ties to include Italy, Austria, Belgium, Greece, West Germany, Spain, Portugal, and Ireland. Before the end of the decade, the People's Republic had normalized relations with Canada, Australia, New Zealand, and Japan as well as dozens more countries across Asia, Africa, and Latin America, bringing the total to 120 countries.[15] Most important, it gained the official recognition of the United States in 1979.

***

It wasn't only in New York City that Chinese diplomats found they still had a lot to learn. Envoys returning to posts around the world were tasked with rebuilding ties damaged by the turmoil of the Cultural Revolution and prizing away Taiwan's diplomatic partners. Making progress was difficult. At every turn, they faced reminders of how far China had fallen behind and just how mistrusted their revolutionary rhetoric had left them.

In Canada, where diplomatic relations were established in 1970, it was difficult for diplomats to separate truth from their own propaganda. One immediate if unlikely challenge presented itself right next to the embassy in Ottawa in the form of what appeared to be an old folks' home.

After curiously observing the building from the outside for some weeks, a group of embassy staff ventured inside to investigate. On the surface, conditions inside seemed good. The rooms were warm and clean. Each room was equipped with a sofa, a carpeted floor, and a button for calling staff. The building's elevator ran day and night, connecting residential floors with a small bar, a recreational room and a library.

Their conclusion was clear: the home was a ruse designed to deceive China about conditions in the capitalist West. Only later did the truth dawn on them, as the diplomats discovered similar facilities all over the country: this was just what life was like for Canadians.

"At first, we thought the old people's home was a Canadian propaganda display for foreigners," remembered one military attaché. "But later we came to understand that there were old people's homes just like this in every city across Canada and that supply was sufficient to meet local needs."[16]

The diplomats' behavior resembles how other governments often deal with Beijing: they project assumptions about how their own political system works onto China. In foreign policy jargon, it's called "mirror imaging." It's a pitfall CIA analysts are cautioned against in their training and is a near-permanent feature of Western relations with China.[17]

In the 1980s, Chinese diplomats would head into meetings with the State Department's China Desk and instruct the officials to "please do something about your Congress" when lawmakers asked difficult questions about the country.[18] In the run-up to the 2008 Summer Olympics, China's then top diplomat, Dai Bingguo, asked his French counterparts why they hadn't done more to stop the country's media from smearing China over its record in Tibet.[19] If only American and French diplomats had such powers.

Things were no different across the developing world. Chinese diplomats arriving in Venezuela were struck by the number of tall buildings around the country. Those dispatched to Kenya saw air conditioners, taxis, and commercial parking lots for the first time in their lives.[20]

Even more humbling, many began to realize that they didn't understand even the basics of diplomacy. Most of the senior staff were old revolutionaries who couldn't speak foreign languages while younger staff had seen their language skills slip during the Cultural Revolution. They were sent to represent

China in societies that felt threatened by the aggressiveness they'd seen from China during the Cultural Revolution.

The experiences of China's future foreign minister Li Zhaoxing give some sense of the problem. By the time Li, thirty, arrived in Kenya in 1970, the country had limited China's Nairobi embassy to eight staff members and routinely subjected them to searches despite their diplomatic status.

It was little wonder. Just a few years after establishing diplomatic relations with China in 1963, Kenyan diplomats had been threatened in the streets of Beijing. In 1967, the country withdrew its diplomatic staff from China and expelled a Chinese diplomat after the embassy distributed copies of Mao's "Little Red Book" in Nairobi.

During a routine visit to a local tax office, Li discovered that embassy staff had been erroneously paying land taxes to the Kenyan government for years, despite the exemption granted for diplomatic property under the Vienna Convention on Diplomatic Relations, which he'd learned about in college. No one in the embassy had thought to apply this basic tenet of diplomatic practice. "We didn't tell you to pay tax, but you came to pay and so we took the payment," a local tax officer told Li.[21]

The situation was disquieting inside embassies too. China's diplomats—just like the rest of the country—had spent half a decade embroiled in brutal factional fighting and personal attacks. Now they had to return to work as if all was normal.

With the Gang of Four still in power in Beijing, there couldn't yet be any official reckoning with the events of the Cultural Revolution—the diplomats would have to work it out on their own. When China's ambassador to Ghana arrived back at his post in 1972, one of the cadres who had attacked him in Beijing was sent to work as his subordinate. The young official apologized for his actions and went back to work.[22]

In Beijing too there were signs that the worst might be over. On January 6, 1972, Chen Yi died after a long battle with cancer. He was a political *persona non grata* right up until the end. His doctors spent months insisting there was nothing wrong with him to avoid the political risks associated with taking him on as a patient. His memorial on January 10 was to be a low-key affair given what were seen as his questionable political loyalties. Mao would not attend and neither therefore would most senior diplomats who had worked with him for so long.

But on the day, the seventy-eight-year-old Mao suddenly announced that he planned to attend the funeral instead of taking his regular afternoon nap.

Still wearing his pajamas, he donned an overcoat and set out. Lacking a comb, Mao's bodyguard straightened the chairman's greasy hair with his fingers and they set off for the cemetery.

Zhou also sprang into action. He had his staff notify everyone who'd been told they couldn't go that they could now attend and he arranged for journalists and photographers to rush to the cemetery to greet Mao on his arrival. Zhou's Hongqi limousine raced ahead of Mao's on the road so that Zhou could personally ensure every detail of the arrangements was perfect. State media announced Mao's visit in a cryptic sign that change was afoot.[23] What happened next was less ambiguous.

***

On February 21, 1972, Richard Nixon touched down in Beijing. There were no crowds to greet him. But Zhou was there dressed in a gray Mao suit with a group of some twenty-five officials and a marching band. After asking Nixon about his flight, he spotted Kissinger: "Ah, old friend," he said.[24]

During the car ride into the city, Zhou turned to Nixon and said, "your handshake came over the vastest oceans in the world—twenty-five years of no communication."[25] Nixon was taken to the Diaoyutai State Guest House, the complex where Khrushchev had stayed when the People's Republic of China celebrated its tenth anniversary—and a compound still used today for large or sensitive diplomatic meetings.

Not long after they ate lunch, Zhou approached Kissinger to tell him that Mao wanted to see Nixon "soon." They set off with Zhou to meet the chairman in Zhongnanhai. Originally scheduled to last fifteen minutes, their encounter lasted for more than an hour.

"Your book, *Six Crises*, is not a bad book," Mao told him. "I voted for you during your election. I like rightists." But when Nixon tried to discuss bilateral relations with Mao, he referred him to Zhou. "Those questions are not questions to be discussed in my place. They should be discussed with the Premier. I discuss philosophical questions."[26]

Nixon was taken to tourist sites around Beijing as well as to the cities of Shanghai and Hangzhou. Like the foreigners who inspected China during the Great Leap Forward, Nixon and his group found a heavily manicured China. US journalists on the visit discovered that the "tourists" at the Ming tombs and the Great Wall had been arranged by the government and taken around on a bus.[27] In Shanghai, residents had been ordered to stop drying their laundry outside during Nixon's visit to ensure that the city looked more cultured than cluttered.[28]

This instinct for putting on a show has a long tradition in China. Visitors to Beijing for Xi Jinping's Belt and Road Summit in May 2017 were met with unusually perfect blue skies as factories were ordered to shut down ahead of the event. Tourist sites, major intersections, and subway stations were monitored by security services that ranged from the feared People's Armed Police down to retired Beijingers sporting red armbands. Nightclubs were shuttered while establishments in the popular Sanlitun bar area were ordered to halt strip shows until the event had finished.[29] "Every visit to China was like a carefully rehearsed play in which nothing was accidental and yet everything appeared spontaneous," Henry Kissinger later remembered.[30]

Staged or not, Nixon's visit was the crowning achievement of Zhou's diplomatic career—the culmination of his work over decades from Yan'an to Geneva. Delivered in the middle of domestic turmoil in China, the visit helped change the course of the Cold War and transformed China's position in its struggle with the Soviet Union.

Success also brought problems in Mao's China. When the state-run Xinhua news agency celebrated the trip by reprinting international praise of Zhou's role in the visit, Zhou immediately smelled danger and reprimanded the agency.[31] China's political system was built around the official veneration of just one individual and that was Mao. No one was allowed to shine brighter than the chairman.

Zhou was right to sense danger. In the aftermath of the visit, Mao had his grandniece, Wang Hairong, and his interpreter, Tang Wensheng (Nancy Tang)—the pair who had appeared in the foreign ministry cafeteria looking smug after Kissinger's secret visit—monitor reviews of Zhou in the foreign media. Mao also began grumbling that the foreign ministry was insufficiently attentive to his views on world revolution.[32] Not long after, rumors began to spread in the ministry that Mao had ominously referred to the department as an "independent kingdom."[33]

***

As Mao seethed over Zhou's prominence, China's ties with Nixon's America continued to improve. The relationship began to broaden out beyond the secret channels initially used to negotiate the historic détente. In February 1973, the two countries announced that they would set up representative offices in each other's capital cities, a prelude to the establishment of full diplomatic ties. China's first representative in Washington was the ambassador general Huang Zhen, while Nixon's man in Beijing was David Bruce.[34]

Intelligence agencies in both countries also sensed an opportunity. China agreed to allow the United States to post one intelligence officer in its representative office in Beijing in exchange for the right to do the same in Washington. The United States selected longtime CIA China hand and future ambassador to China James Lilley for the job, while—according to Lilley—Beijing selected the English-speaking foreign ministry official, Xie Qimei. Xie was posted in the representative office's cultural section—the usual home for Ministry of State Security agents even today.[35]

Beyond relations at the top, the countries began to develop sub-governmental ties. This included the establishment of organizations such as the US-China Business Council and the National Committee on US-China Relations.

No one was more enthused by the turnaround in relations than the American business community. Long seduced by the prospect of hundreds of millions of Chinese customers, they began to plot their China strategies. Among them, the most doggedly persistent was perhaps the legendary CEO of Coca-Cola, John Paul Austin.

No sooner had Huang Zhen arrived in Washington than Austin dropped by to pay him a visit, insisting that the former general try his product. Huang demurred, saying that he preferred tea, but Austin had the company's Washington office deliver the drink to the representative office every week. He even supplied the diplomats with a refrigerator to keep the bottles cold.[36]

***

Although China's diplomacy had begun to normalize, the atmosphere inside its diplomatic apparatus remained fraught. Political struggles inside the ministry had now boiled down to what contemporaries called the "Lord Qiao" and "young girl" factions.

"Lord Qiao" referred to Qiao Guanhua, the journalist-turned-diplomat who'd played a key role in Chinese foreign policy since the 1940s and the husband of Gong Peng. Qiao was made foreign minister in 1974, taking over from Ji Penfei who had stewarded the ministry after Chen Yi's death. The "young girl" group was a reference to Wang Hairong and Tang Wensheng, the Mao favorites who had been keeping tabs on Zhou's international media appearances. Their direct access to Mao made them politically untouchable and left Qiao struggling to exert control over the ministry. At one point, he even wrote to Mao pleading for help.[37]

"Working at that time was like walking a tightrope. Any small act could prompt censure,"[38] recalled one diplomat.

Life was most complicated for Chinese diplomats in the Soviet Union. China's ties with the country were caught up in the domestic politics of Mao's moves to crush "revisionism." Staff at the embassy in Moscow were instructed to leave any event immediately if China or its leadership were criticized and failure to do so would constitute a "serious political mistake." On one occasion, foreign media reported that ambassador Liu Xinquan, a former general, had bowed as he left the room after China was criticized. When the foreign ministry telegrammed Liu to ask if the report was true he exploded with rage. "I, Liu Xinquan, was not afraid to lose my head in battle, how could I bow to Soviet revisionism?"[39]

It wasn't just factions inside the foreign ministry that were creating problems. Foreign policy—especially toward the United States—became a central symbolic battleground that pitted those like Mao's wife Jiang Qing and the rest of the "Gang of Four" who opposed closer ties with America against those who hoped for a more pragmatic relationship. No issue was too petty.

Jiang Qing inserted herself into the smallest details of foreign affairs. In 1973, a group of visitors from China inspected a television screen factory in the United States, where they were given glass snails as a gift. In an effort to derail China's relationship with the United States, Jiang Qing framed the gifts as a deliberate affront to China, implying that the country crawls. The foreign ministry conducted two investigations into the meaning of snails in American culture and concluded that the gift was not offensive. Mao agreed.[40]

Zhou increasingly became a focus of Mao's spite. When Zhou was diagnosed with bladder cancer in May 1972, Mao would not allow him to be treated, telling his personal physician that cancer could not be cured. "Leave the patient alone and let him live out his life happily," Mao said.[41]

Still, Zhou kept working and continued to meet foreign delegations even as his cancer progressed and he routinely found blood in his stool.[42]

The previous year, he had begun planning for the future of Sino-American relations. In an act of genuine strategic foresight, Zhou selected a small group of students to study in the UK at the University of Bath and the London

School of Economics to improve their English and their understanding of the West.

The first cohort arrived in the fall of 1972 and began taking classes in subjects including international relations, history, and development studies. The students, who wore Mao suits to class, at first found history lectures particularly frustrating: "The Chinese students took a while to accept the absence of an authoritative explanation," Michael Yahuda, professor emeritus of international relations at the LSE, told the *South China Morning Post*. Privately, some admitted to being disturbed by developments taking place at home.[43]

The group would go on to serve as the backbone of the foreign ministry's Americas department, producing, among others, the future ambassador to Washington and foreign minister Yang Jiechi; Zhang Yesui and Zhou Wenzhong would also go on to become ambassadors to the United States, while Wang Guangya ended up as ambassador to the United Nations. Yang Jiechi, in particular, would go on to be a force to be reckoned with in the foreign ministry, eventually making it all the way to the Politburo. In a strange way, Zhou would continue to influence top appointments in Chinese diplomacy from beyond the grave.

Zhou's political troubles continued to mount. In June 1973, he took a Vietnamese delegation to Yan'an, revisiting the city for the first time since the Communists had left near the end of the Civil War. Zhou found his old living quarters locked up and closed off to the public.[44] He was being penalized for getting on the wrong side of Mao.

In November, the Politburo held a meeting criticizing Zhou. Mao believed he had committed "rightist errors" during his meetings with Kissinger.[45] The chairman grew increasingly withdrawn. By this point, he was communicating with the leadership by having Tang Wensheng and Wang Hairong pass messages to Zhou for him to relay to the Politburo.[46]

In 1974, Mao decided to send Deng Xiaoping, who had been politically resurrected less than a year previously, to the United Nations instead of Zhou. Zhou's former official biographer, Gao Wenqian, describes the decision as a deliberate act of cruelty on Mao's part, although Zhou's cancer diagnosis was also likely a factor.[47]

Diplomats stationed overseas could only guess at what was really going on in China's domestic affairs based on scraps of information from back home. One diplomat recently posted at the United Nations felt a burst of excitement about Deng's 1974 visit after reading about it in a cable. He guessed that it meant more positive changes for Chinese foreign policy.[48]

During the visit, Deng delivered the Maoist line with characteristic precision, railing against Soviet hegemony and elaborating Mao's theory of the "three worlds." He also made brief trips to New York's suburbs and even to Wall Street. He provocatively suggested to his aides that China could learn from the United States.[49]

Other signals pointed in the opposite direction. In late 1974, the Gang of Four transferred a Chinese ambassador from Cambodia to Mauritania to "feed the mosquitoes" as punishment for being too deferential to Zhou during the "criticize Confucius" campaign.[50] In late 1974, diplomatic missions received instructions that they must take part in the "criticize Deng" campaign pushed by the Gang of Four, which opposed his rehabilitation. In Washington, the representative office held meetings, but no one wanted to stand up and speak.[51]

Mao openly talked about the fighting inside the foreign ministry during a 1975 meeting with President Gerald Ford in Beijing. Ford politely told Mao that he appreciated the work of China's liaison office in Washington and hoped that its head, Huang Zhen, would stay on. Mao responded by telling him, "There are some young people who have some criticism about him [Huang] and these two [Wang Hairong and Tang Wensheng] have some criticisms of Lord Qiao. And these people are not to be trifled with."[52]

It was an exhausting and bewildering cycle. Each twist of political drama was made more draining by the venal pettiness of the political targeting combined with the high stakes involved for all participants. By mid-1975, Zhou was too ill to take part in diplomatic activities.[53] Something had to give.

***

In the months from January 1976 to December 1978, China was hit by what seemed like an unending series of political shocks. The eventual outcome of these events would stabilize Chinese diplomacy and unleash the market reforms that would set the country on a course to superpower status.

That outcome seems natural enough in hindsight, but would have felt unlikely—perhaps even unthinkable—to Chinese diplomats at the time. The fate of their country hung in the balance and the harrowing experience of the last decade left them in no doubt about the stakes involved. All they could do was wait and respond to political signals from Beijing, balancing their convictions against the risks of picking the wrong side.

The first shock came on January 8, 1976, when Zhou Enlai finally died. When news reached the foreign ministry that morning, officials throughout the building broke down in tears. As the news spread to Chinese diplomats overseas, they too began to weep.[54]

The sadness was natural. Zhou was the founding father of Communist China's diplomacy and had overseen every aspect of its operations since before the People's Republic of China even existed. He had been a kind and even gentle presence for a group that often felt threatened both by the outside world and by their own political system.

But there were no innocent acts in Mao's China. Mourning Zhou meant taking a political stance. Even crying meant expressing a political doctrine. As if to underline the point, the Gang of Four immediately banned diplomats from joining those paying tribute to Zhou in Tiananmen Square. Many went anyway. The foreign minister, Qiao Guanhua; China's representative in Washington, Huang Zhen; and scores of junior diplomats made their way to the square to pay their respects.[55]

The foreign ministry's Party Committee also sent instructions forbidding the copying or propagating of poems or tributes to Zhou, while embassies were barred from flying their flags at half-staff.[56] The Gang of Four even tried, unsuccessfully, to have news of his death relegated to page four of the *People's Daily* and any reference to the need to "learn from" Zhou removed from his official obituary.[57]

Chinese diplomats around the world ignored these orders: in Italy, diplomats mourned Zhou for more than the permitted time; in Japan and Malta, they demonstrated their objection by deciding not to fly the flag at all.[58]

Inconsequential as they might seem, each of these decisions required a small act of courage. Embassy staff had discovered over the course of the last decade how serious the costs of sending the wrong political signals could be, but they did so anyway. And with Zhou gone, there was no one to protect them from what might come next.

In April 1976, Deng Xiaoping once again lost all of his positions and was placed under house arrest. In July, Zhu De, the revolutionary general who helped style Mao's tactics for guerrilla warfare, died. And then, later that month, the industrial city of Tangshan in northern China was hit by a devastating earthquake, which set off a seismic wave equal to 400 times that of the atom bomb dropped on Hiroshima.[59] Some 100 miles away in Beijing, the foreign ministry was so badly damaged that meetings with visiting dignitaries had to be held in tents set up outside the main building.[60] Every time they went inside, diplomats would watch the lights hanging precariously overhead and listen for unusual noises as they braced for aftershocks.[61]

All of this would pale in comparison to the political volcano that was about to erupt.

***

On September 8, 1976, Zhang Bing was staffing a banquet for Samoa's head of state, Malietoa Tanumafili II, when she noticed that the wait staff were running as they delivered the food.

The self-made diplomat, who'd been languishing in a labor camp just a few years earlier, was on duty in the Great Hall of the People, the gigantic Stalinist epicenter of Chinese state decorum off Tiananmen Square. Also on duty at the Great Hall was the twenty-six-year-old Yang Jiechi, who had returned from studying in England and was now working as a translator in the foreign ministry.

The fact that the staff were running was highly unusual: food and drink at Chinese state functions are delivered with practiced precision over the course of painfully drawn-out proceedings that often last around three hours. But for some reason the staff had been told to hurry today. Within an hour, the entire banquet was over.

Something else seemed off to the junior diplomats in the room that night: the leaders present looked worried. Especially Vice Premier Hua Guofeng. And little wonder, as they knew what Zhang and other junior officials would not find out until the next day: Mao Zedong was dying.[62]

Mao, then eighty-two, had been diagnosed with a form of motor neuron disease in 1975. He was already half-blind from cataracts, suffered from numerous sexually transmitted diseases, and had heart disease after decades of gorging on fatty pork. He suffered a heart attack on September 2 and began palpitating on September 7. Members of the Politburo began a deathwatch by his bedside. He died at ten minutes past midnight on September 9.[63]

The next morning, Chinese diplomats staffing the Samoan leader's visit were told what happened while preparing to see the Samoan leader off. They paused in shock before breaking down in tears.[64]

Mao left instructions that he be cremated, but he was too central to the legitimacy of the communist state for officials to let that happen. Instead, the Politburo decided that his body should be preserved like Lenin's.[65] The problem was that no one knew how to do it.

ǀ

China's acrimonious relationship with the Soviet Union meant that simply asking Soviet doctors how they had done it was out of the question. Instead, diplomats in the Soviet Union were twice dispatched to the Lenin library to search for the formula that had preserved the dead Bolshevik hero. But they returned empty-handed.[66] The Vietnamese communists were somewhat more helpful. Chinese diplomats in Hanoi persuaded local officials to explain the approach they'd used to embalm their national founder, Ho Chi Minh.[67]

Presciently, the government also sent out researchers to prepare for the possibility that the process would fail. Researchers in London were dispatched to Madame Tussauds to study British waxwork technology, but returned with the frustrating conclusion that China's wax working capabilities had already surpassed those of the United Kingdom.[68] In the end, doctors in Beijing figured it out for themselves through a messy process of trial and error in which Mao's body was pumped so full of formaldehyde that it oozed from his pores and the Chairman's neck swelled to the width of his head.[69]

Interpreting signals from Beijing became even more difficult as a power struggle played out between Mao's designated successor, Hua Guofeng, and the Gang of Four. Hua, a relatively obscure vice premier and minister of public security from Mao's home province of Hunan, was an uninspiring choice, to say the least. But he had the virtue at least of not being one of the Gang of Four. ("He looked and acted like the tough chief of security of a communist country," Singapore's founder, Lee Kuan Yew, had said of Hua after meeting him before Mao's death: "His turgid, clichéd rhetoric jarred.")[70]

The Chinese embassy in Rome first heard rumors from Beijing that the Gang of Four had fallen on October 6, but no official announcement came. Every night, diplomats would gather to listen to domestic and foreign radio programs. They would transcribe anything they heard about events in Beijing on notes that they posted in various patterns on the embassy walls to try to glean some sense of what was unfolding back home.

Eleven days later, the news finally came: the Gang of Four had fallen.[71] Hua had managed to gather the support of crucial Party elders and military leaders. The gang had been arrested one-by-one by Chinese troops loyal to the elders.

The response across China and inside the foreign ministry was euphoric. Diplomats from Washington to Paris, like many other Chinese who could afford it, ate crabs—three male and one female—to mark the Gang's demise.[72] The animal, known of course for its sideways walk, was often depicted in Chinese stories as a bully that blocks the path of others.[73] China's ambassador to Venezuela, Ling Qing, who had followed Zhou from Yan'an to his final days, summed up the mood: "The Cultural Revolution had been like a nightmare and, finally, it was over."[74]

Qiao Guanhua, the foreign minister, was among the casualties of the Gang's demise. In a desperate attempt to put the ministry under his own control and to survive the second purge of Deng Xiaoping, he had attempted to form an alliance with Jiang Qing ("a wise man responds to his circumstances," he'd said in response to a friend's disappointment). In Qiao's place, Huang Hua—the radical student who'd taken Edgar Snow to Yan'an—became foreign minister in December.[75]

Even if the Gang of Four was gone, China's future direction seemed far from certain. Although Deng was politically rehabilitated in July 1977, many embassies, in the absence of new orders, continued to propagandize criticisms of him.[76] In a meeting with the United Nations secretary-general in August 1977, Huang Hua insisted that nothing had changed: the Chinese people would stick to Chairman Mao's revolutionary line under the leadership of Hua Guofeng.[77]

Hua's time at the top proved short-lived. He inherited a country yearning for change, but failed to offer any alternative vision for its future: his key slogan, known as the "two whatevers," consisted of fulfilling "whatever policy Chairman Mao decided upon" and implementing "whatever directives Chairman Mao issued." This unimaginative approach to politics quickly lost Hua the support of the moderate Party figures who had helped him eliminate the Gang of Four, while his lack of personal charisma prevented him from winning over others. Deng Xiaoping quickly outmaneuvered Hua by seeking out Zhou's old allies across the bureaucracy and promoting a message that cleverly used a Maoist slogan to promise pragmatism and change: China, Deng said, should "seek truth from facts."

The task ahead of Deng was huge. China had been torn apart by a decade of scarring political conflict that had alienated many of the friends its diplomacy had won in previous decades. China was one of the poorest countries in the world in 1978: its GDP per capita was just one-fortieth of the equivalent figure in the United States and one-tenth of that in Brazil.[78] China accounted for just 4.9 percent of the global economy, barely up from the meager 4.2 percent it had represented in 1949.[79]

In December 1978, a crucial Communist Party meeting set the stage for two decades of extraordinary economic reform. The "Third Plenum" of the Eleventh Communist Party Central Committee declared that "practice was the sole criterion of truth"—a cryptic way of signaling a decisive shift toward pragmatism in Chinese policymaking.[80] Although Hua retained his official titles, Deng was now effectively in charge. Key Deng allies were promoted to the ruling Politburo, including reformer Hu Yaobang. Zhou Enlai's widow, Deng Yingchao, was also appointed to the body.[81]

Deng Xiaoping had been born in 1904 to a genteel family in Sichuan province. He'd studied in France as a young man, where he met Zhou Enlai, and later in Moscow before returning to China and enduring the Long March. Mao had long appreciated Deng's technocratic competence and political ruthlessness. In 1951, Mao had even reined in Deng's enthusiastic killings of "counterrevolutionaries" in Southwest China. Just five feet tall, Deng had been purged multiple times during the Cultural Revolution. His youngest brother had committed suicide and his son, Deng Pufang, had become a paraplegic after throwing himself out, or being pushed out, of a fourth-story window.[82]

Gradually, the political changes in Beijing started to filter through the foreign ministry bureaucracy. Embassies were told to begin emphasizing the "Four Modernizations," a program for economic development publicly proposed by Zhou in the mid-1970s and later endorsed by Deng. The "modernizations" laid out a blueprint for China's agriculture, industry, science, and technology sectors to catch up with the rest of the world. To help meet these goals, embassies were told to begin researching economic and technological development in their host countries.[83]

Stapleton Roy, a mid-level foreign service officer who went on to become America's ambassador to China, witnessed the changing political landscape firsthand as he accompanied congressional delegations to China in 1976, 1977, and 1978. "Each year the political line was totally different," said Roy. "The first year, Deng was a capitalist roader. The next year the Gang of Four were purged and Deng was no longer criticized. By the spring of 1978, Deng was the good guy."[84]

Deng took Mao's place as the ultimate arbiter of foreign policy and his command brought some certainty about the future of Chinese foreign policy and the role of its diplomats after a decade of enervating turbulence.

As the Chinese government tried to move on, diplomats were offered some limited opportunities to discuss what had happened. The closest they ever came to a reckoning took place in June 1979 at a meeting of ambassadors in Beijing. The foreign ministry organized the gathering to criticize the excesses of the Cultural Revolution, and some of the perpetrators and their victims ended up facing each other in small group discussions.[85]

Deng's approach to foreign policy, as with domestic policy, was pragmatic. Just as Zhou's 1950s charm offensive had made space for China to develop economically after decades of war and revolution, Deng's foreign policy would make space for economic development at home. This time, though, instead of learning by importing knowledge about five-year plans from the Soviets, Communist China would begin a series of experiments with markets and other capitalist practices.

Just after the Third Plenum concluded in December 1978, the United States and China finally established full diplomatic ties. Less than a week after the agreement was made public, Coca-Cola announced that it had reached its own agreement with the Chinese government to start selling its sweet, carbonated beverage.[86] A major symbolic step in its own right, the Coke deal was just the beginning of a wave of capitalist mores and Western political ideas that flooded into the country. The changes would enrich China's people, but also gave lie to the country's most sacred founding myths.

8

Rethinking Capitalism

In January 1979, Huang Hua found himself on a chartered airplane headed to Washington, DC. He was accompanying Deng Xiaoping, China's de facto leader, on an official visit to the United States—the first since the two countries had officially established diplomatic ties just a few weeks earlier.[1]

As the Chinese delegation flew across the Pacific, Deng was uncharacteristically chatty. At one point, he turned to an aide and reflected on this moment of opportunity. "As we look back, we find that all of those countries that were with the United States have been rich, whereas all of those against the United States have remained poor," he said. "We shall be with the United States."[2]

The visit represented an extraordinary turnaround, both for Huang and for China. As a young man, Huang's advocacy for the Communist Party had involved him living in caves and reaching out to the United States through unofficial channels like Edgar Snow. At Geneva and again during the Cultural Revolution, Huang found himself acting as the representative of a pariah state. Now, he was foreign minister for a government that had been in power for some three decades and increasingly found itself in what Kissinger dubbed a "tacit alliance" with America.

The grandeur of Deng's reception in Washington was a testament to the scale of the shift. President Jimmy Carter greeted Deng and his aides on the South Lawn of the White House. They walked along a red carpet and beamed with pride as their national flag was raised in America's capital. Deng met members of Congress and signed copies of the recent *Time* magazine cover with his face on the front. Carter received him in the Oval Office.

The visit was a rare breakthrough in a world which in many ways seemed stuck. The United States and Britain were plagued by low growth and runaway inflation. The Soviet Union had abandoned the reformist impulses of Khrushchev, settling instead into a long stagnation under the leadership of Leonid Brezhnev. The breakthrough of the Camp David Accords, which brought peace between Egypt and Israel, would soon be eclipsed by the upheavals of the Iranian Revolution and the Soviet invasion of Afghanistan.

Deng was determined to get his country unstuck. His decision to make "practice the sole criterion of truth" at the Third Plenum meeting a few weeks earlier in Beijing had laid the domestic groundwork for a dramatic turn in Chinese history, while his geopolitical shift toward the United States would provide him with breathing space to pursue reform at home.

Deng was already looking to draw lessons on how to reform China's economy during his trip to the United States. He visited a Boeing factory in Seattle, where he told his hosts that China had "many things to learn from the innovative industrial culture of the American people." Deng also asked if he could see a state-owned enterprise and was taken to the National Mint, although it was closed for the weekend when he arrived. He also demonstrated a knack for engaging the American public when he donned a ten-gallon hat in Houston.

Deng's domestic economic reforms and his outreach to the West marked the start of an extraordinary period of learning and experimentation in China.

***

Diplomats were at the vanguard of this process. Far more exposed than even the most powerful Beijing officials to just how far China had fallen behind, they found themselves confronted with unsettling truths: the capitalist model they had long reviled had delivered greater prosperity and higher living standards than communism. Some even began to question the Communist Party's monopoly on power.

One of the most open in his thinking was Ke Hua, Xi Jinping's soon-to-be father-in-law. Posted to London in 1978, at the tail-end of Prime Minister James Callaghan's embattled Labour government, Ke found himself on the front lines of the neo-liberal moment. In Britain and across the world, the prosperity and stability of the postwar economy had given way to new risks and surprises as policymakers began to lose faith in Keynesian economics. As workers went on strike and sometimes rioted in the streets, prominent think tanks such as the Center for Policy Studies and the Adam Smith Institute were pushing for Britain to free markets from state control.[3] By May 1979, Margaret Thatcher would be prime minister. Before long, Augusto Pinochet was pushing markets in Chile and Ronald Reagan was campaigning for the White House against Carter's policies that had led to high inflation and low growth—"stagflation."

Ke's revolutionary credentials were impeccable. As a student, he'd become involved in political activism, traveled to Yan'an, and served in the Red Army. After taking up roles in local government after 1949, he was transferred to the foreign ministry, where he weathered the Great Leap Forward and the Cultural Revolution before being appointed to London just as China's reforms were getting started. His daughter, Ke Xiaoming (also known as Ke Lingling), would soon marry Xi Jinping, the son of another high-ranking official, Xi Zhongxun. (The couple went on to fight "almost every day" and eventually divorced when Ke Xiaoming moved back to England, but Xi refused to move with her).[4]

From the outside, there were few signs that Ke was doing much serious thinking about his situation. When he met and dined with British officials in London, he was personable and courteous, but stuck closely to his talking points.[5] Inside the embassy, he was experimenting with heresy.

At first, Ke's observations about Britain were highly personal. When his son fell ill, he found that all of the healthcare costs associated with the treatments—even including fruit and milk—were taken care of by the UK government, despite the fact that the family were not even citizens. It got him thinking about whether the system he was looking at was really as evil as he had believed for most of his life. "It seemed that we needed to rethink capitalism," he later recalled.[6]

These were brave thoughts for an official from a country where challenging the Party's stance could be dangerous. Although Deng had begun pushing market reforms at home, no one knew how this experiment would work out or even how long he would be able to stay in power.

Chinese diplomats across the world were having similar experiences. Some dwelled on how different social and economic habits were in the capitalist West. In Chicago, diplomats saw twenty-four-hour stores, shopping carts, bar codes, and car trunks filled up with perishable goods all for the first time in their lives.[7] In New York, they saw their first Western-style "white weddings" (in traditional Chinese weddings, the bride usually wore red).[8]

Others focused on the lessons China could take from these experiences. In Norway, diplomats were struck by the country's apparently constant flow of students traveling overseas and returning with new ideas.[9] In the Netherlands, China's first female ambassador, Ding Xuesong, sent Beijing reports on the kinds of technology China would need as it modernized based on her visits to Royal Philips NV factories and Royal Dutch Shell Plc's natural gas fields.[10] China's first ambassador to Ireland, Gong Pusheng, helped alert

Beijing to her host country's experiment with the kind of free trade zones that would later inspire China's Special Economic Zones in Shenzhen and elsewhere.[11]

Ke felt that simple factual reporting on what he saw wasn't enough. Instead, his cables back to Beijing challenged Marxist doctrine head-on: "Contrary to what we were taught in books, capitalist profits have not been derived from expropriating the surplus value of labor for quite some time," Ke wrote. He added that there was no chance of revolution in the UK or any other European nation.

Telling the truth wasn't always easy. In fact, it was often painful for staff in the London embassy. As Ke's own beliefs began to shift, he encouraged those under him to challenge theirs. "You must all speak the truth," he told his diplomats. "After the 'Cultural Revolution,' speaking the truth is not easy. Everyone likes to speak falsehoods without even thinking about it. If any of you think telling the truth is too difficult, then at least speak fewer falsehoods or don't speak at all."

It was a sign of the times that Ke's conclusions on economics didn't land him in trouble at home. But there were still limits. Ke had wanted to cable Beijing with his observations on the advantages of "capitalist democracy," but none of his colleagues wanted their names attached to something so sensitive. Ke ended up keeping these observations to himself.

His colleagues were right to be concerned. Deng Xiaoping's government had rounded up activists in Beijing and across China after they called for free elections in 1979. In an important statement in 1981, Deng and the rest of the Party's leadership would rule that any opposition to the Party's continued monopoly on power would not be tolerated.

Undeterred, Ke spent his spare time compiling information on the workings of inter-party competition and a free press. "I'm personally very clear that the question of democracy is unavoidable for this generation and subsequent generations," Ke later wrote. Quietly, many in 1980s China were reaching similar conclusions. For now, though, Chinese diplomats had to deal with a new occupant in the White House who was causing problems for Sino-American relations.

**

Ronald Reagan, America's new president and the former governor of California, entered office in 1981 promising a more confrontational approach with the communist world, and that included China. Reagan had visited Taiwan two years earlier and met with the island's then president Chiang Ching-kuo, the son of Mao's longtime rival Chiang Kai-shek. On the campaign trail, Reagan even suggested that he would support the reestablishment of "official relations" with Taiwan.[12] Throughout Reagan's Republican Party—particularly on the right—fondness remained for "free China" on Taiwan as a bulwark against the Communist mainland.

When Reagan took office in January 1981, his government began considering selling fighter jets to Taiwan. China responded angrily, threatening to downgrade relations with Washington as it had just done with the Netherlands after its sale of submarines to the island. Old China hands in the administration—such as Vice President George H. W. Bush and Secretary of State Alexander Haig (a Kissinger mentee)—began to worry that the progress made over the last decade might now be at risk. These doubts represented an opportunity for China to gain leverage. Its diplomats pounced.

Huang Hua issued Haig an ultimatum at the North-South Summit on poverty reduction held in Cancun that October: the United States should set a date for ending all arms sales to Taiwan or China would downgrade relations. America would need to limit both the quantity and quality of arms supplied to Taiwan to the level of the Carter administration and then reduce these sales year by year, Huang said. Chinese state media complemented Huang's pressure tactics with a series of hostile articles.[13]

When Haig accepted one key demand—that arms sales be limited to Carter administration levels—China pushed for more. In a series of terse negotiations over the following months, Huang told Haig that "nothing" had been accomplished in recent months. When Bush visited Beijing in May 1982, Huang "battered" him, accusing the vice president of pursuing a "two-China policy." Huang insisted that the administration name a date by which arms sales would end.[14]

Chinese diplomats convinced Haig and many others at the State Department that America should meet China's demands, but Haig's dismissal in June, following frictions with the White House, scuppered the deal. Reagan instead offered China a vague written agreement that referenced the need for a "final resolution" of the arms sales issue but stopped short of offering a date. It was established in a Sino-American communiqué in August 1982 and remains an active point of contention to this day between the two countries.

Throughout the negotiations, Huang employed a classic Chinese negotiating tactic: displays of performative anger designed to exert pressure on the other side. Jeff Bader, a China hand who served in the Obama administration, describes such "verbal assaults" as "theatrical expressions of outrage."[15] Huang himself had used the tactic for decades before he tried it out against Haig. In December 1953, he deployed what an American interlocutor described as a "calculated harangue" in the negotiations that would lead up to the Geneva Conference. The diplomat, whom previous CIA reports had described as "well-liked" among Americans, spent six straight hours accusing the United States of "conniving," "perfidious actions," and "treacherous designs." At one point, he dared his American counterpart to walk out.[16]

Huang combined the outrage with another common Chinese negotiating ploy: the insistence that responsibility for the health of diplomatic relations belongs solely to the other side. "It is up to the United States to take the initiative," Deng Xiaoping told Richard Nixon with more than a bit of chutzpah during a visit to Beijing by the former president after the 1989 Tiananmen massacre. "America is capable of taking some initial steps."[17]

Yang Jiechi, the young interpreter who was sent off to England to study in 1973 and later served as a tour guide and handler for George H. W. Bush's visit to Tibet, accompanied Huang on many of his overseas visits during these years.[18] In time, he would go on to become a leading practitioner of both tactics as foreign minister.

The Mongolian foreign ministry, which had been on the receiving end of many such diatribes during the Sino-Soviet split, looked on at Chinese foreign relations with a sense of knowing familiarity. "The Maoist nature of policies remains unchanged," one of its diplomats wrote in a report. "In terms of foreign policy, one can say it is the matter of "wiping the foam and leaving the beer."[19]

China's relations with the United States stabilized after the 1982 communiqué on arms sales, but the country's leaders would never again hold the degree of optimism Deng had displayed in his trans-Pacific flight in 1979. In any case, quiet developments in the Eastern bloc now presented China with other options.

***

On March 24, 1982, Leonid Brezhnev delivered a speech in Tashkent, Uzbekistan, which caught China's attention. The Soviet leader stood by his country's previous criticisms of China, but also expressed hope that relations might improve. "We remember well the time when the Soviet Union and the People's Republic of China were united by bonds of friendship and com-radely cooperation," he said. "We have never considered normal the state of hostility and estrangement between our two countries."[20]

In their own mechanically socialist way, Brezhnev's words were tanta-lizing. Deng Xiaoping immediately spotted the signal that the Soviets were ready to improve ties and gave instructions for the foreign ministry to re-spond.[21] The task fell to the head of the ministry's Information Department, Qian Qichen.

Shipped off to Moscow in 1954 as a twenty-six-year-old student, Qian had personally experienced the emotional and political whiplash that had char-acterized the past three decades of Sino-Soviet relations. He'd first arrived in the Russian capital excited to visit the "sacred" site of Lenin's revolution, but he found that for people who lived in a socialist paradise, Soviet citizens seemed to spend a lot of time complaining. He witnessed the fallout from Khrushchev's 1956 "secret speech" and the onset of the Sino-Soviet split. When he returned to the country in 1972 after a stint in a labor camp, it felt as though the place had made little progress.[22]

The ministry decided to respond to Brezhnev with a press conference. Held two days after the Soviet leader's speech, it was something of a make-shift affair. Although the ministry had tried its hand at media relations in the past, press conferences were still an unusual occurrence. With no official venue, Qian stood without a podium to deliver his message to some eighty assembled journalists who, in the absence of chairs, were also forced to stand. Qian said that China had noted Brezhnev's comments, before adding that "we resolutely refute the attacks on China in the speech." Then came China's own oblique signal that it would consider improving ties: "In Sino-Soviet relations and international affairs, we value real actions from the Soviet Union."[23] Li Zhaoxing, a future foreign minister, translated Qian's remarks into English.

The press conference turned out to be the start of a multi-decade process through which Chinese diplomats gradually became accustomed to working with foreign media. In 1983, the government decided that all ministries with an outward facing role should designate official spokespeople.[24] Foreign ministry press conferences went on to become weekly, twice-weekly, and eventually daily from Monday through Friday, as they are today.[25] Although these events are now equipped with chairs and usually last longer than seven minutes, officials still deliver messages in much the same way. When asked about the state of agricultural purchases under a 2019 US-China trade truce, spokesperson Hua Chunying's remarks were remarkably similar to those of Qian nearly three decades earlier: "We hope the United States will honor its commitments by taking real actions," she said.[26]

The continuity is deliberate. In 2005, an official in the Information Department wrote a book explaining the ministry's strategies for press conferences. Drawing on a mixture of standard public relations techniques and Chinese diplomatic clichés, the book included tips for providing vague answers and pivoting the conversation to other topics. Classics of the genre include "Our stance is clear and consistent" (*women yiguan renwei*) and "We will release the relevant information in due course" (*women jiang hui zai shishi fabu youguan xiaoxi*).[27] The formulaic language is an outcome of the foreign ministry's culture of always asking permission before acting. "This reading of stock phrases doesn't happen because the spokespeople are unfamiliar with the topic," explained Wu Jianmin, a former spokesman, "but because the stock phrases have been officially approved."[28]

Within a few weeks of the press conference, Qian was promoted to vice foreign minister charged with supervising ties with Eastern Europe. The foreign ministry instructed the head of its Soviet Department to plan a trip to Poland so he had an excuse to stop off in Moscow on the way. (The same tactic was used in 2017 to present Xi's visit to Trump's Mar-a-Lago estate as a natural extension of his hastily planned trip to Finland.) The trip marked the start of a multi-year process of improving Sino-Soviet ties. Deng instructed Qian that he was in no rush.[29]

In the fall of 1982, China took steps to formalize its new relationship with the Americans and the Soviets, announcing at the 12th Party Congress in September that it would pursue an "independent foreign policy" instead of aligning with either superpower. Hu Yaobang, a prominent reformer and the formal head of the Communist Party (Deng never took the title), declared that China "never attaches itself to any big power or group of powers, and never yields to pressure from any big power."[30]

Hu stressed continuity by referencing Zhou Enlai's Five Principles of Peaceful Coexistence in the speech. But he was also impatient for change, increasingly believing that some in the foreign ministry were incapable of keeping up.

***

Hu's frustrations with the foreign ministry had been building for a while, especially with the now nearly seventy-year-old foreign minister, Huang Hua.

When Huang had accompanied China's reformist premier, Zhao Ziyang, to Cancun for the North-South Summit in 1981, he'd received instructions from the premier to soften the country's go-to anti-Soviet talking points—Zhao didn't feel that they would resonate well in a region where the United States loomed so large.

The change of approach made Huang and his deputy, Pu Shouchang, uncomfortable and the pair decided to stick to the standard anti-Soviet playbook they had been using for decades. Zhao saw their behavior as an open challenge to his authority, according to foreign ministry official turned scholar Liu Xiaohong.[31]

Younger diplomats were also growing frustrated, in one case with terrible consequences. Tang Jiansheng, the son of an official and a young diplomat in China's embassy in Mozambique, had become enraged with his supervisor, an older diplomat who spoke no foreign languages. The pair often clashed. After being ordered to conduct multiple rounds of "self-criticisms" in the embassy over his lack of respect toward his superiors, Tang snapped. He borrowed a gun from the local military and went on a killing spree that left his boss and eight other diplomats dead.[32]

The continued use of Maoist talking points and the sense of inertia within the system were too much for the country's new reformist leaders to tolerate. Hu called a meeting with senior diplomats and demanded the "rectification" of the foreign ministry. In contrast to previous rounds of "rectification" in the ministry, the focus this time was on making the department less ideologically rigid and more open to new ideas.

Others who had grown frustrated with the system sensed an opportunity for change and seized it. Deng Xiaoping's daughter, who was working at the time in the Chinese embassy in Washington, wrote to "Uncle [Hu] Yaobang," criticizing what she saw as the sloppy and inept way the embassy was being run.[33]

It was time for Huang Hua to go. He had served as foreign minister for nearly five years, capping a diplomatic career that stretched back to his accompaniment of Edgar Snow to meet Mao in 1936. Huang's last act as foreign minister was to attend Brezhnev's funeral in Moscow in November 1982. It was the most senior Chinese delegation sent to the Soviet Union since Zhou Enlai had visited in 1964. Huang was met with a motorcade, provided with a deputy foreign minister as a personal guide, and given a special standing arrangement at the funeral.[34] On his return to Beijing, Huang was replaced as foreign minister by Wu Xueqian, who was eight years Huang's junior and closely associated with Hu Yaobang and other reformers.[35]

Even after his official retirement from the foreign ministry, Huang remained active in "friendship diplomacy" until his final days. At ninety-six, he met with his "old friend" Henry Kissinger during the 2008 Olympic Games in Beijing, embracing him with a hug. Huang died two years later from lung and kidney failure. His funeral was attended by President Hu Jintao and other dignitaries, including the future president, Xi Jinping.[36]

China's leaders also reformed the way foreign policy was made. As part of a broader shake-up of the Party and the government, the Central Foreign Affairs Leading Small Group was resurrected in 1981—Zhou had established the group in 1958, but it had ceased to operate during the Cultural Revolution.[37]

The foreign ministry too was reformed to reflect the new focus on professionalism and efficiency. In 1982, the number of vice ministers was reduced from ten to six, bringing down the average age of its top officials from sixty-five to fifty-eight.[38] In addition, the ministry began pushing standard practices for retirement. From 1983, diplomats who were older than sixty were automatically retired unless they had reached the rank of vice minister. Top jobs also increasingly went to professional diplomats over military veterans, as the original ambassador generals retired.[39] Crucially, wages were adjusted, providing a boost in income for diplomats living overseas and rewarding those who assumed greater authority.[40]

Slowly, diplomats began to undo the damage of the Cultural Revolution. When Zhang Wenjin arrived in Washington as ambassador in 1983, he found the ambassador's residence empty. No one had dared to live in it for fear of being labeled politically incorrect. Its gardens were filled with weeds, its carpets filthy, and its front wall was decorated with a crude ink wash portrait of Mao that bore no resemblance to the deceased chairman. Neighbors had complained that "no household on the same street is as dirty and disordered as the residence."[41]

Zhang and his wife began the slow process of cleaning up the embassy and professionalizing the way it worked. As they did so, American spy agencies looked on and began to notice the change. "Since 1983, Beijing has transformed its Embassy in Washington from a fledgling establishment designed merely to monitor bilateral relations into an organization that pursues China's national interest with increasing effectiveness," the CIA reported in 1986. The agency noted the increasing independence of the Commercial and Science and Technology sections from the Political Section, signifying the increased importance it attached to specialized technical expertise. The CIA also noted there was an increasing willingness to depart from official talking points. Some diplomats were even allowed to skip Communist Party meetings.[42]

The ministry also began the slow process of specialization. One important area was arms control where a small group in the International Affairs Department began to work full-time in the early 1980s. The ministry also began rotating diplomats and government scholars to the Geneva Conference on Disarmament, providing them with an opportunity to learn from global experts. But despite some progress, by the mid-1980s, the foreign ministry still lacked equivalents to the State Department's Bureau of Economic and Business Affairs or its Bureau of Political-Military Affairs.[43]

Streamlining and specializing didn't mean the ministry's long-standing culture of discipline and secrecy would change. The instructors who taught Gao Zhikai, who joined the ministry in 1983, told the recruits, "Don't say what you shouldn't say. Don't hear what you shouldn't hear. Don't see what you shouldn't see." If other colleagues asked what you were working on, the recruits were told to respond with, "I have an activity" (wo you huodong).

Discipline extended to physical appearance. Gao had let his hair grow long in college, but he quickly realized that "there were to be no politically incorrect hairstyles like yuppies or hippies." He headed to the barber shop in the courtyard at the back of the ministry to get the same crewcut haircut as everyone else. The ministry even sent its own barbers to larger overseas postings to ensure that its standards were met. "It was quasi-military," Gao later said.[44]

Yet despite some positive changes, the ministry was still hobbled by long-standing weaknesses and limitations. A 1984 CIA report noted that the Chinese delegation to the United Nations was "hampered" there and at other international gatherings because its diplomats "are given little discretionary authority" and "relied on instructions from Beijing."[45]

***

With a modernizing diplomatic corps and neither the American nor Soviet superpower standing in its way, China continued to make headway with its diplomacy. Every relationship, old or new, represented an opportunity to learn. Just as diplomats in Moscow had sent notes back home about Soviet economic planning methods in the 1950s, Chinese diplomats studied American systems as they experimented with capitalism in the 1980s.

"They wanted to understand all these basic civics questions," said Hank Levine, a former official who worked on the State Department's China Desk in the mid-1980s. "They wanted to learn from the US, to understand how urban planning is done, how our social security system was structured. They had questions about the legal system, the healthcare system, the role of state governments versus the federal government. It was an effort to understand how America worked with an eye to understanding which practices could be applied to China."[46]

Every trip, sometimes every spare moment, was a chance to learn. Conscious of their need to build specialist expertise in their foreign service, the country's budding environmental envoys learned about waste disposal during a trip to Denmark in 1985.[47] Diplomats in Zimbabwe took driving lessons.[48] Diplomats posted to the United Nations took copies of Paul Samuelson's seminal economics textbook home and would study it at night when they realized they were behind the curve on Econ 101.[49]

Learning about capitalism didn't mean that Marxism no longer mattered. Many of the country's working diplomats maintained their faith in the creed. In London, even as he watched the Thatcher revolution unfold around him, one first secretary at the Chinese embassy quietly made his way to Highgate Cemetery on May 5, 1984, to celebrate Karl Marx's 166th birthday.[50]

China's leaders also felt the need to defend their doctrine in public. In her speech welcoming Hu Yaobang, the Communist Party's general secretary, to London in 1986, Margaret Thatcher joked that even Marx had not been a Marxist and warned about the dangers of ideology stifling "practical ideas."[51] To Thatcher, the remarks likely seemed innocent enough, but her Chinese audience took them as a serious ideological challenge. After earlier reviewing a draft of the speech supplied by Thatcher's aides, Hu had his diplomats stay up until the early hours of the morning to alter the contents of his speech for the next day. The new draft emphasized China's firm commitment to "socialism with Chinese characteristics."[52]

As China's leaders tried to navigate the new challenges of capitalism, the diplomatic momentum continued. By the late 1980s, China was even readying the groundwork for relations with South Korea, despite its treaty commitment to the communist North and the fact that until recently Chinese diplomats had made a point of ignoring South Korean diplomats at official functions.[53] In 1988, Deng Xiaoping declared that the time was right to establish relations, setting in motion a series of events that would culminate in the establishment of official bilateral ties in 1992.[54] After decades of struggles and numerous setbacks, China was moving quickly toward its long-standing goal of winning respect and recognition around the world.

Relations with both the Americans and the Soviets also continued to improve. Reagan had visited China in 1984 after previous tensions over Taiwan stabilized. More good news followed when China's "old friend" George H. W. Bush was elected president in 1988. The two countries continued to cooperate in Afghanistan, as well as in Cambodia, where they found common ground—perversely—in supporting Pol Pot's ousted government against the Vietnam-backed (and therefore Soviet-aligned) regime in Phnom Penh. Goodwill filtered all the way down to the working level: in the late 1980s, the head of the Political Section at the Chinese embassy in Washington even became bold enough to visit the homes of officials on the State Department's China Desk to play mahjong.[55]

The warm feelings and close contact helped the United States cultivate ties with the rising star of Chinese diplomacy who had until recently been overseeing China's improving ties with the Soviet Union: Qian Qichen.

A dignified and cultured man with bright eyes and a firm handshake, Qian spoke in a slow and measured style. He possessed a rare talent for phrasing Chinese talking points in a way that made sense to Americans. He was also a skilled listener. After meeting with foreign dignitaries, Qian would ask his aides, "What was his real point? What was he really up to?" He would wait to hear their assessments before offering his own.[56]

After hearing a rumor that Qian would likely become the next foreign minister, staff on the National Security Council took him to watch the John Adams comic opera *Nixon in China* at the Kennedy Center on the banks of the Potomac River in Washington. Most of the group from the Chinese embassy sat in stunned silence as actors sung their way through scenes depicting the Cultural Revolution through song and as Mao's estranged wife Jiang Qing even got sexy on stage in a bid for the chairman's attention. Qian laughed the whole way through.[57]

After his promotion to foreign minister in 1988, Qian became the first head of the ministry to pay a formal visit to the Soviet Union since 1957. His mission was to lay the groundwork for the historic meeting between Deng Xiaoping and Soviet leader Mikhail Gorbachev slated to be held in Beijing the following year.[58] He would need all of his formidable diplomatic skills for what was to come next.

***

The year 1989 wasn't an easy one to be a Marxist. A sense of unease had been building throughout the communist bloc for some time.

Starting in the early 1980s, Chinese embassies began sending cables to Beijing questioning the health of socialism in the Eastern bloc. In 1984, the embassy in East Germany noted "growing independent tendencies" in the country. Moscow's control of Eastern Europe seemed far weaker than in the past. The health of Eastern European communism was a matter of heated debate at China's conference of ambassadors in 1985, after which an increasing number of embassies began sending back reports that detailed growing "contradictions" in the Eastern bloc. As good Marxists, officials in Beijing knew that that political and social "contradictions" could drive profound historical change.

Chinese leaders watched with confusion as the Soviet leadership failed to treat the reemergence of the Solidarity movement in Poland with the same ruthlessness it had shown toward Czechoslovakia in 1968. Leaders in Beijing were dismayed by the Soviet bloc's "centrifugal tendencies," one former ambassador wrote.[59]

At the same time, the political atmosphere in Beijing became increasingly fraught. Rapid inflation, anger at official corruption, and uncertainty about the country's ideological direction all contributed to a growing sense of frustration with the government across the country. In the preceding years, the children of top officials had been arrested for crimes ranging from graft to murder and sexual assault. In 1984, Hong Kong media reported that Yao Xiaogang, the son of Deputy Foreign Minister Yao Guang, had been arrested for smuggling pornographic videotapes to Beijing from Yemen, where he worked for a Chinese state-owned airline.[60]

While some mourned the loss of stability that had accompanied China's shift away from a strictly planned economy, others—especially students— were increasingly attracted to liberal democracy. This emerging trend worried China's leaders. In January 1987, Deng Xiaoping and other Party elders forced the resignation of General Secretary Hu Yaobang over doubts about his commitment to one-party dictatorship. Although Hu's own attitudes on politics were never quite what pro-democracy activists imagined, his dismissal cemented his standing as a symbol for a gentler and more pluralist vision of politics for the People's Republic.

Developments overseas reinforced the worries of China's ruling elite. In May 1988, Hungary's aging dictator, János Kádár, was forced from office. In Poland, the country's leadership entered direct negotiations with the

Solidarity labor movement in early 1989 and scheduled elections for later that year, which the Communists would go on to lose.[61]

The Chinese leadership's reaction to the American invitation of astrophysicist and dissident Fang Lizhi to a banquet during George H. W. Bush's visit to Beijing in February 1989 exposed just how tense the political atmosphere had become. The foreign ministry initially threatened to boycott the dinner before agreeing that Fang could attend if he sat in an out-of-sight part of the dining hall. In the end, Fang never made it to the dinner. Two blocks from the venue, his car was stopped by armed plainclothes police officers. China's deputy chief of mission in Washington told senior State Department officials that they did not understand how "volatile" the situation had become.[62]

Things were about to get much worse. Hu Yaobang's death from a heart attack in April 1989 provided an opportunity for protesters to air their grievances at the country's direction—as many had done following Zhou Enlai's death in 1976. The initial mourners in Beijing's Tiananmen Square were soon joined by thousands of university students, workers, and even government officials. By early May, tens of thousands of students in major cities across the country were calling for democracy in China. The Politburo Standing Committee seemed paralyzed by indecision on how to deal with the unrest.

In Beijing, Chinese diplomats tried their best to continue with business as usual, but their attempts to present a calm front only underlined the regime's insecurities. "The situation is under control," diplomats told the American embassy in Beijing. "This is not a counterrevolutionary moment. China will not descend into chaos."[63] Their words rang hollow. By mid-May, students in the Square were on hunger strike.

Inside the ministry, a group of young diplomats organized more than 100 officials to send donations to the protesters in Tiananmen Square under the banner of the ministry.[64] Some diplomats in Washington were openly sympathetic toward the demonstrators and even discussed the evolving situation with their State Department counterparts.[65]

On May 15, Mikhail Gorbachev arrived in Beijing. The first Sino-Soviet summit in thirty years, the visit was a historic turning point for Chinese foreign policy. It was also a poignant personal moment for Deng Xiaoping, Mao's onetime attack dog against Moscow. As usual, the visit had been planned down to the tiniest details. Acting on Deng's behest, the foreign ministry had told the Soviets that Gorbachev should expect a handshake rather than a hug from Deng as the most fitting expression of the current state of relations.[66]

Foreign Minister Qian Qichen was forced to receive the Soviet leader at Beijing airport as protesters disrupted Tiananmen Square, the usual location for receiving such a dignitary. Still, with some 1,200 journalists from around the world gathered in Beijing to witness the historic meeting, the Chinese attempted to pull off the visit according to plan.[67]

As May rolled on and a crackdown seemed increasingly likely, the American ambassador and a former CIA officer, James Lilley, met with Qian in Beijing. "If things go wrong," Lilley warned him, "the Western media will go after you like a mad dog." Qian just smiled.

9

The Fightback

In the end, Qian Qichen learned that tanks had rolled into Tiananmen Square from CNN. Away on a visit to Ecuador, he was unable to get through to Beijing. All he could do was watch the wall-to-wall coverage on cable television showing vehicles on fire, dead bodies in the streets, the People's Liberation Army firing on civilians, and chants of "fascists" hurled at China's communist leadership. Eventually, he reached his deputy in the foreign ministry who helped him piece together events. It was only the next day that he received an official account from the leadership.[1]

Other Chinese diplomats posted around the world were also in the dark about what transpired in the square on June 4, 1989. Xinhua had stopped sending out reports on the country's domestic situation. Just as they had been in the most tumultuous days of the Cultural Revolution, diplomats were left to piece together events from Western media.[2] Officials at the Chinese embassy in Washington stayed up all night waiting for news from Beijing; even the ambassador didn't know what to tell them.[3]

Back in the Chinese capital, there was turmoil and confusion. Wu Xiaoyong, the son of former foreign minister Wu Xueqian, took it upon himself to set the record straight. Wu was so appalled by the scenes he witnessed on his way to work at Radio Beijing's English-language service on the morning of June 4 that he broadcast an unauthorized message. "A most tragic event happened in the Chinese capital, Beijing," he told listeners. "Thousands of people, most of them innocent civilians, were killed by fully armed soldiers." The crackdown, he said, was a "gross violation of human rights" and a "barbarous suppression of the people."[4] Wu was suspended from his job the next day and arrested in August.[5]

For some foreign ministry employees stationed overseas, the traumatic events were too much to take. Some twenty-five diplomats and embassy staff defected and asked for asylum in their host countries. Three couples from the Chinese embassy in Ottawa defected together in a van, while Xu Jiatun, the head of the Xinhua News Agency's Hong Kong branch (China's de facto embassy in the city), fled to the United States where he lived out the rest of his life.[6]

The defections represented the most serious breakdown in discipline among Chinese diplomats since the Cultural Revolution. The overall numbers were limited and most were from agencies other than the foreign ministry.[7] Still, the defectors were publicly voting with their feet against their own political system at a time when communist regimes were crumbling all over the world. One former diplomat later wrote that China's leaders saw the defections as a warning about the need for absolute political discipline in the country's diplomatic corps. "Foreign affairs cadres are on the front lines of interaction with the outside world," he wrote. "They often interact with foreigners and must accept education on strict discipline and secrecy."[8]

Despite China's violent political past, defections had always been extremely rare. When China's chargé d'affaires in the Netherlands, Liao Heshu, defected in February 1969, the *New York Times* ran the headline, "Defections by Chinese Red Officials Are a Rarity."[9] Still, those who disagreed with the government's stance were left with no choice. Unlike its American counterpart, China's foreign service has no "dissent channel." Defection or silence were the only options available for those who opposed the Party's policies.[10]

China quickly became a pariah state around the world. Group of Seven countries, made up of the world's largest economies, suspended high-level contacts with Beijing. The World Bank and the International Monetary Fund halted new loans. Congressional meetings with China's ambassador in Washington were abruptly canceled.[11] In London, protesters chanted "stop the killings" at the Chinese ambassador and spat at his car.[12]

Facing up to the international consequences of the massacre was humiliating. To diplomats on the front line, the West's response did not just feel like a simple moral protest—it seemed like a challenge to Communist Party rule. Chinese diplomats even found their reliable contacts unwilling to meet with them. Wu Jianmin, a political counselor at China's embassy in Brussels, found himself stood up for a previously arranged lunch appointment with a foreign diplomat. "They thought that the Chinese government was done for and so it didn't matter if you bullied or offended it," he remembered.[13]

***

The leadership's first instincts in the aftermath of the massacre oscillated between prickly denial and damage control. In the days immediately following June 4, diplomats in Beijing were given simple instructions: reassure the outside world that China has not gone off track and that the disruption will soon be resolved. They were shown the iconic image of the lone unarmed protester standing in front of a column of tanks on the empty six-lane Avenue of Eternal Peace that crossed Tiananmen Square and told to "expect a great deal of controversy when you return to your posts."[14]

The foreign ministry sent out videotapes to help bewildered diplomats overseas show local elites the "truth" about what had occurred.[15] Ambassadorial rotations were temporarily suspended as Beijing prepared to counter international criticism.[16]

It was a scary time to be a diplomat. Just like those who defended the Great Leap Forward in the aftermath of the "anti-rightist campaign" in the 1950s, the safest option was to stick to the official talking points. "It was clear that they were afraid. They didn't know what to do or say so they basically said nothing," remembered one former official on the State Department's China Desk. "It was tough on them."[17]

New arrivals at overseas embassies only added to the sense of fear and uncertainty. To make sure that its embassies maintained discipline, the ministry sent out Party loyalists to monitor the activities of others and enforce the new line. One such cadre was Liu Xiaoming, then thirty-three, who would later become China's ambassador to the UK. Liu was dispatched to Washington, where he kept tabs on colleagues and took up golf in his spare time (he was later hospitalized for breaking his jaw after being accidentally smacked in the face with a golf club).[18]

After the initial shock subsided, the government quickly became more assertive about its version of events. After telling American diplomats on June 7 that the situation in China was "complex," the foreign ministry grew more confident in the official narrative. James Lilley, the American ambassador to China, was summoned to the ministry later that month and dressed down over American media articles that claimed (accurately) that Chinese troops had opened fire on a diplomatic compound in Beijing.

"This is a fabrication," a vice minister told Lilley, insisting that the shots fired at the building had been taken to pursue a sniper. "You have insulted the Chinese government and military." Lilley replied that although he had only been a private in the infantry, "I know that you don't machine-gun a building from one end to the other and up nine stories to get one guy on the roof."[19] Propaganda efforts trace a similar path today: first, assess the facts; second, craft the Party's official line on how to describe what happened; third, push out that narrative repeatedly and at maximum volume.

Still, reciting suspect talking points and dressing down foreign diplomats would not be enough to dig China out of the hole. Top officials knew that a more robust fightback was needed to win China some breathing space and continue with economic reforms. At a conference for Chinese ambassadors in Beijing in July, Qian told the country's envoys that China would continue to focus on economic development. "An important task at the time was thinking of ways to get out, to break through the West's blockade and show that China's fundamental policies hadn't changed," Qian later wrote.[20]

***

China's leaders could not have picked a worse time to stress continuity. The earliest governments to recognize the People's Republic after 1949 were crumbling on live television. In August 1989, Polish Solidarity activist Tadeusz Mazowiecki became the first non-Communist head of government in the Soviet bloc. On November 9, protestors tore down the Berlin Wall.[21] The next day, Bulgaria's Communist Party ended the thirty-three-year dictatorship of Todor Zhivkov, paving the way for demonstrations and eventual democracy.[22] By the end of the month, the "velvet revolution" had ended one-party rule in Czechoslovakia.

Events in Romania were even more harrowing. On Christmas Day 1989, paratroopers hauled Romania's Communist dictator Nicolae Ceaușescu and his wife into a freezing courtyard next to a toilet block and mowed them down with Kalashnikovs.[23] A senior Chinese diplomat in Washington confided to Doug Paal, the then National Security Council's senior director for Asia, that the "old men" in Beijing had watched the video of the executions and were "terrified."[24]

It was in this context that Deng Xiaoping laid down a dictum that would guide Chinese foreign policy for the next two decades. Some in Beijing hoped that Deng would launch a series of polemical exchanges with Soviet leaders for allowing such chaos in the communist world—just as Mao had done with Khrushchev. Instead, Deng told cadres that his priority was "stability, stability, and more stability." Instead of seeking ideological confrontation, Deng believed that China should "observe the situation soberly, maintain our position, meet the challenge calmly, hide our capabilities, bide our time, remain free of ambitions, and never claim leadership."[25]

Deng's strategy would enable China to push back against its post-Tiananmen isolation. In the aftermath of the massacre, the country's diplomats made painstaking efforts to salvage China's international reputation. Channeling the same impulses they'd used to woo the world in the 1950s, the country launched a new charm offensive with its neighbors, embracing tools from economic diplomacy to sports diplomacy, media management and arms control to win friends.

During this period China played a weak hand skillfully. One key to this was its willingness to pursue a limited set of objectives with great focus. Understanding that they couldn't take on every challenge simultaneously, Chinese diplomats focused their energy on attracting investment, quieting criticisms of Beijing's human rights record, and stifling dissent over the Party's claims to sovereignty over Taiwan and Tibet. At the same time, they sought to enhance China's global reputation by rebranding it a "responsible power."

China succeeded on all of these fronts. Despite setbacks, the period after Tiananmen set in motion a series of events that would significantly bolster the Communist Party's international legitimacy. China's path to rehabilitation culminated in 2001 when Beijing was awarded the 2008 Summer Olympic Games. China emerged with a new sense of swagger and confidence in its global role, which often sat uneasily with the great insecurity that came with knowing how close things had come to unraveling during the summer of 1989.

***

That was all in the future. For now, turmoil in the Soviet bloc continued to preoccupy Chinese leaders. They were especially rattled by developments in Eastern Europe and, in August 1990, sought answers from their diplomats. The Chinese embassy in Yugoslavia sent a response. In a dispatch entitled "What is the meaning of the severe setback for socialism in Eastern Europe?" the authors argued that China's socialist brothers had been undone by a combination of nationalism and anti-communist sentiment. They also blamed Gorbachev for his weakness and Western policies of "peaceful evolution," which had worried Chinese leaders for decades.[26]

The unpleasant surprises kept coming. When Saddam Hussein invaded Kuwait in August 1990, Chinese leaders expected the United States to face a lengthy and difficult fight to drive him out. China's premier, Li Peng, confidently told Singapore's leader, Lee Kuan Yew, that Iraq would not be defeated easily.[27] In fact, American weaponry demolished Iraq's defenses rapidly with the use of F-117 stealth fighter-bombers, laser-guided bombs, and M1A1

Abrams tanks. It was a wakeup call for Chinese elites about just how much catching up they had to do.

The biggest shock came in the summer of 1991 with the disintegration of the Soviet Union. In public, leaders in Beijing were stoic. "If they shook any levels of government and power in Beijing, no one was owning up to it," remembered one Israeli diplomat who was posted in Beijing at the time. "The August 1991 coup d'etat against Gorbachev, Yeltsin's resistance and the collapse of the attempted putsch . . . were relegated to third and fourth items on the local television evening newscasts," he remembered. "Much more media prominence was given even to the visit of the Foreign Minister to the Comoros Islands."[28]

In private, though, Chinese officials were deeply shaken by the Soviet collapse and remain so to this day. "For us diplomats, the hardest thing for us to understand is also the most important thing for us to understand and that's the breakup of the Soviet Union," former foreign minister Li Zhaoxing wrote in 2014. "The unexpected disintegration of a superpower within just a few years leaves one with a deep impression."[29]

The world of the early 1990s appeared profoundly threatening to China's leaders. China was the only major communist government left standing while American commentators crowed about the "end of history" and the "unipolar moment." "Among our diplomatic corps, a degree of pessimism developed," one ambassador remembered.[30] What's more, the end of the Soviet Union had removed the primary reason for Sino-American cooperation. It had also left American officials with a grating sense of confidence in their way of doing things. "No matter what happened in the world, the United States had something to say about it," wrote one former Chinese diplomat.[31]

***

Chinese diplomats, led by Qian Qichen, met these challenges with skill, poise, and determination. The strategy, as journalist James Mann put it, saw Beijing work for a "slow, gradual desensitization of outrage. China incessantly pushed each foreign government to ease its sanctions or its shunning of Chinese leaders just a little bit, never too much; then, after each slight change, China began pressing once again until another small change was won."[32]

Beijing's neighbors were the easiest early targets. Chinese diplomats had for years been attempting to charm countries across Asia, but after Tiananmen, they stepped up their game. In the summer of 1990, China

established diplomatic relations with Singapore and Indonesia. It also continued to improve ties with South Korea, with which China would establish
formal relations in 1992. Japan watched from the sidelines until, in August
1991, Prime Minister Toshiki Kaifu became the first G-7 leader to visit
Beijing since the massacre.[33]

Britain was the next to succumb. The British government needed Chinese
approval for a new airport it hoped to build in its colony of Hong Kong, but
Beijing was clear that it expected the country's new prime minister John
Major to visit in order to secure its agreement. Major arrived in Beijing in
September 1991, becoming the first leader of a major Western country to do
so, and in the face of intense domestic criticism.[34]

The United States was a tougher sell, but the Gulf War provided a crucial
opening. Aware that Washington would require Beijing's support for United
Nations action against Saddam Hussein, Qian Qichen inserted China into
the political drama leading up to the war. He led the country's first attempt
at shuttle diplomacy, flying between Egypt, Saudi Arabia, Jordan, and Iraq
to engage local leaders and stress China's commitment to a peaceful resolution to the conflict. (At one point, Saddam Hussein irked Qian by comparing
Iraq's claim over Kuwait to China's claim to Hong Kong.)

It quickly became clear to the Americans that China's price for acqui-
escence to the war would be the high-level meetings denied to it since
Tiananmen. In early November, Qian met with Secretary of State James Baker
in Cairo. By the end of the month, Qian had landed a meeting with President
Bush himself, becoming the first high-level Chinese official to do so since the
massacre.[35] Foreign diplomats who visited the ministry in Beijing reported
that their Chinese counterparts were "delighted" with the outcome.[36]

As Party leaders tried to mend their image, they also turned to economic
diplomacy as reforms drove growth at home. In January and February 1992,
Deng Xiaoping began his famed "Southern Tour," an effort to kickstart
stalled economic reforms after the crackdown—to push market economics
while keeping a tight leash on political reform.

Chinese leaders quickly began to see the size of their country's markets
as an important source of diplomatic leverage. In early 1992, Premier Li
Peng attended the World Economic Forum in Davos and toured Western
Europe, making sure to visit business people on each stop, including Italy,
Switzerland, and Portugal. Li had been dubbed the "butcher of Beijing"
by the Western media after his leading role in the Tiananmen massacre,
but at Davos Li could play the darling of Western business. In his speech,

he talked up the opportunities presented by the Chinese market.[37] Chinese state-owned media eagerly played up Li's role as an international statesman, emphasizing his personal ties with Zhou Enlai in an attempt to soften his image at home.[38]

Investors and governments took notice, not least because Deng's economic reforms had started to show results: China's GDP jumped 12 percent in 1992.[39] In embassies from Vienna to Havana, diplomats reported that foreign politicians and investors had begun to ask them about the country's economic model.[40] They also noticed that living conditions in China had pulled ahead of those in many developing countries. Whereas Chinese diplomats visiting Africa for the first time in the 1960s had been amazed to see air conditioning and parking lots for the first time in their lives, by the 1990s they were shocked by the poverty in parts of the continent.[41]

At the same time, Chinese envoys began to take a more active interest in the resources China might gain access to by developing friendships with leaders in these countries, especially after it became a net importer of oil products in 1993. Suddenly, oil-rich states in the Middle East, Africa, and Latin America took on an increased importance for Beijing, together with access to the sea lanes that would enable its delivery.[42]

Still, the focus on economics was new to many Chinese envoys. In 1993, one Chinese diplomat in Canada was perplexed when local businessmen seemed to talk endlessly about public order and security. It was only later, after asking a member of his staff to investigate, that he realized they were referring to financial securities.[43]

***

Early gains aside, Beijing's fightback had a long way to go, as events in Washington would demonstrate. In September 1992, under pressure to secure reelection, President George H. W. Bush agreed to sell Taiwan F-16 fighter jets, military equipment the island's leaders had been trying to secure for at least a decade. The deal illustrated Washington's changed incentives in its relations with China: the lack of a common enemy in the Soviet Union gave it far fewer reasons to play nice. Initially furious, Beijing responded with caution, hoping in vain that Bush would win reelection. His opponent, Bill Clinton, was even less palatable.[44]

As governor of Arkansas, Clinton had visited Taiwan and his presidential campaign had been sharply critical of the Bush administration's post-Tiananmen policies. Clinton called for "an America that will never coddle tyrants, from Baghdad to Beijing" and advocated linking trade with human rights by putting conditions on the most-favored-nation trade privileges China enjoyed. "Of course if Bush wins, that's better," a senior Chinese scholar told the *New York Times*.[45]

In the end, Bush lost, leaving China's new president, Jiang Zemin, to deal with Clinton. An articulate if sometimes verbose man with a rectangular face and thick-rimmed square glasses, Jiang, now sixty-seven, had been hand-picked by Deng Xiaoping for his efficient handling of the 1989 student protests in Shanghai, but he was relatively inexperienced in foreign affairs.

Jiang's first big diplomatic test came in November 1993 when Clinton hosted leaders from twelve other Pacific Rim nations for the APEC summit on Blake Island, eight miles off the coast of Seattle. China had secured a one-on-one meeting between Clinton and Jiang, the first in-person dialogue between the Chinese and American heads of state since the Tiananmen Square massacre. Although the ninety-minute meeting consisted mostly of tightly scripted talking points, Jiang was so nervous about his own performance that he spent much of the time glancing across the room at Qian Qichen for reassurance.[46] The meeting achieved little of substance, but it was an important symbolic breakthrough. China, it seemed, was being welcomed back into the family of nations.

China's relations with the world had come a long way, but many inside the country chafed at the deference to foreign leaders its rehabilitation seemed to involve. China should not have to apologize for maintaining order within its own borders, they reasoned. The foreign ministry was singled out as a particular target. In July 1994, Hong Kong media reported that members of the Chinese military had written to Party leaders calling for Qian Qichen's resignation. Jiang defended his foreign policy chief in a subsequent meeting, citing Deng Xiaoping's praise of Qian as evidence of his political standing.[47]

Things were about to get even harder for Chinese diplomats who sought closer ties with America. In June 1995, Beijing reacted with fury when it heard that the United States planned to grant Taiwan's president Lee Teng-hui a visa, after explicit promises from Secretary of State Warren Christopher that it would not do so. China canceled two official visits to America while foreign ministry spokesman Shen Guofang warned that the United States would "pay the price" if the visit went ahead.[48]

During the visit, Lee delivered a speech that, to most observers, seemed innocuous. He talked at length about his time as a graduate student at Cornell as well as Taiwan's economic development. But to Chinese officials watching carefully for any sign of provocation, the speech was explosive.[49] Lee described the island as the "Republic of China on Taiwan" (as opposed to simply the Republic of China). He called for Taiwan to "demand the impossible" as it sought to break out of its diplomatic isolation. Lee also twisted the knife with comments hailing the "political miracle" of Taiwan's democratization, quoting Czech dissident-turned-president Václav Havel and declaring communism "dead or dying."[50]

Xinhua responded the next day, saying: "The issue of Taiwan is as explosive as a barrel of gunpowder. It is extremely dangerous to warm it up." Beijing followed its strong words with actions. In July and August 1995, it conducted missile tests, followed by surface and air military exercises in November and December, and more missile tests the following March as Lee campaigned for reelection. This time, the missiles landed near Taiwan's crucial ports of Keelung and Kaohsiung, signaling the possibility of a future blockade.

Clinton decided that China had gone too far. In March 1996, he deployed two aircraft carrier battle groups near Taiwan, humiliating China's military, which still lacked the capability to pose a threat to American ships so close to its coastline. In the short term, Beijing realized that there was no alternative to maintaining good relations with Washington, but with a steely eye on the long term, it doubled down on military modernization.

**

Lee's visit made clear to Beijing that it needed to step up its diplomacy in the United States, matching Taiwan by expanding its reach beyond political elites. The Chinese embassy began grassroots outreach to local governments and Chinese American groups across the country, which continue to this day.[51]

Jiang Zemin led by example during his 1997 tour, which involved visits to numerous regional cities including Honolulu, Los Angeles, Boston, New York, and Philadelphia, as well as a tour of technology companies and the Harvard campus. Jiang, now far more confident in public, broke into English in meetings and even cracked jokes as protesters gathered outside. He also promised a gathering of some 200 American business elites in New York that "China's market is open to you" as long as "some man-made obstacles" could be overcome.[52]

Beijing was also coming to the conclusion that it needed to do more to reassure its neighbors. In February 1995, China's occupation of the Mischief Reef had alarmed its Southeast Asian neighbors. The coral reef around 135 miles from the Philippines is part of the Spratly Islands, a chain of more than

100 tiny rock formations claimed in full or in part by China, the Philippines, Vietnam, Malaysia, Taiwan, and Brunei, and under which some say there are large oil reserves. "While we are hoping for the best, we must prepare for the worst," Fidel V. Ramos, the president of the Philippines, said. The 1995–1996 Taiwan Straits Crisis only exacerbated the perception that Beijing was willing to use military force to achieve its goals in the region.

Worse still, Beijing realized that its actions were drawing outside powers and rivals into affairs in its backyard. Countries such as Japan and Australia looked to strengthen their security ties with the United States, while Southeast Asian countries even began seeking ways to pull other powers into regional affairs. In December 1995, Indonesia and Australia penned a military cooperation agreement, while the Philippines signed a similar agreement with the UK in January 1996.[53] Beijing responded by recalibrating its regional policies and looking out for openings to improve ties with its neighbors.

Luckily for China, an opportunity came along quickly with the 1997 Asian Financial Crisis. As countries across the region faced economic headwinds and states such as Indonesia and Thailand grappled with financial meltdowns, the international community practically begged China not to devalue its currency for fear of triggering even further financial turmoil and destabilizing capital flight. Presenting itself as a responsible economic partner willing to make sacrifices for the greater good, Beijing acquiesced and kept its currency stable, winning praise and appreciation across the region and beyond. Even Bill Clinton chimed in: "China has shown great statesmanship and strength . . . by maintaining the value of its currency," he said.[54]

On the back of these plaudits, Chinese leaders began to sense an opportunity for greater regional leadership through greater participation in multilateral forums. Initially suspicious of these forums as tools for American influence, in the mid-1990s Beijing began sending observers to meetings of bodies such as the Association of Southeast Asian Nations (ASEAN) Regional Forum. As Cui Tiankai, one of the ministry's top Asia hands and future ambassador to Washington, later told China scholar David Shambaugh, "it was a gradual learning process for us, as we needed to become more familiar with how these organizations worked and to learn how to play the game."[55]

Gradually, Chinese diplomats gained confidence at these forums. China began holding annual meetings with top ASEAN officials in 1995. It also helped found ASEAN+3 in 1997, a grouping that brought China, Japan, and South Korea together with the ASEAN nations. China even began to experiment with leadership roles in these organizations. China went on to host the APEC summit in 2001 in Shanghai. It also offered itself as the headquarters for the "Shanghai Five" in 1996, an organization linking China with Russia and the Central Asian Republics and that would later evolve into the Shanghai Cooperation Organization.[56]

Chinese diplomats also updated their talking points. In 1996, the foreign ministry's Asia Department commissioned scholars to formulate a "new security concept," which presented "win-win" thinking as an alternative to the "zero-sum" mentality of the Cold War. It strongly echoed Zhou Enlai's Five Principles of Peaceful Coexistence, with its emphasis on "mutual trust, mutual benefit, equality, and cooperation." Pushing this new approach in particular were two officials in the foreign ministry's Asia Department: Fu Ying and the ministry's brightest rising star, Wang Yi.[57] Fu, a member of China's Mongolian ethnic minority who pursued postgraduate studies in England and later served as a translator for Deng Xiaoping, would go on to serve as China's second ever female vice foreign minister, ambassador to London, and a darling of the global elite. Wang would become foreign minister.[58]

Multilateral diplomacy also allowed Beijing to cast itself as a "responsible major power" on issues that mattered to the United States. Non-proliferation was particularly promising, as Chinese leaders realized that adhering to international rules could make the country safer *and* bring diplomatic accolades. After beginning to engage with the issue in the 1980s, China joined the Nuclear Non-Proliferation Treaty in 1992. It cut short its nuclear testing program in 1996 to join the Comprehensive Test Ban Treaty. In 1997, the foreign ministry upgraded its division for disarmament issues to department level, a move that increased staff numbers and strengthened its hand inside the Chinese bureaucracy. China's participation in the Conference on Disarmament in Geneva also became markedly less ideological over time and its diplomats gained genuine technical expertise by working with UN institutions.[59]

China also sought to strengthen ties with countries around the world through what it called "strategic partnerships." In doing so, it aimed to present an alternative vision for regional and global cooperation to America's alliance system, one that allowed it to seek closer ties with others without forcing them to abandon or take sides against the United States. In April 1996, Beijing upgraded its relationship with Russia from a "constructive partnership" to a "strategic cooperative partnership," while its relationship with America was labeled a "constructive strategic partnership" after a meeting between President Clinton and Jiang Zemin in 1997.[60] By 2016,

China analyst Peter Wood had identified twenty-two different levels of relationship Beijing was using to designate states around the world, ranging from the "all-weather strategic cooperative partnership" awarded to Pakistan to the cooler "mutually cooperative partners" reserved for Japan.[61]

Finally, China improved relations with its neighbors by settling long-standing border disputes. Between 1991 and 2003, it settled disputes with Kazakhstan, Kyrgyzstan, Laos, Russia, Tajikistan, and Vietnam. In most of these agreements, China ended up receiving 50 percent or less of the territory it had claimed.[62]

***

The next place to build its reputation was in the developing world. Most developing countries had not responded to the Tiananmen Square massacre as negatively as Europe or North America. These countries, most with the bitter aftertaste of colonialism still fresh, were much more receptive to the Chinese mantra of not interfering in other nations' "internal affairs." "At that time, Western diplomats would boycott our embassy events, but I always felt warmly welcomed in Africa and never felt in the slightest bit isolated," recalled one diplomat who was posted to Liberia at the time.[63] Diplomats in Rwanda, Colombia, Sri Lanka, and Indonesia recalled similar experiences.[64]

Egypt's president Hosni Mubarak told Chinese diplomats that the United States had put a lot of pressure on him to cool ties with China, but he accepted a visit from a top Chinese leader in 1989 anyway.[65] The president of Burkina Faso was the first foreign head of state to visit China after the massacre, and Foreign Minister Qian Qichen embarked on an eleven-country tour of Africa in the summer of 1989.[66] Qian later accompanied President Jiang Zemin on a 1996 tour of six African nations, during which Jiang signed trade deals and declared a new "milestone" in China's relations with the continent. Both China and Africa had "suffered enormously under colonialists and foreign aggression," Jiang said.[67]

International criticism of Beijing's human rights record actually became a way for China to forge bonds with some countries. In 1997, China's representatives at the United Nations said that the perpetrators of the Cambodian genocide were beyond the reach of any international tribunal. "The question of Pol Pot is Cambodia's internal affair" and "should be decided by Cambodians themselves without foreign interference."[68] That same year, during the deliberations of the United Nations Human Rights Commission, Chinese ambassador Wu Jianmin offered this warning: "We appeal to developing countries who genuinely care for human rights, because what happens to China today may well happen to them tomorrow."[69]

China's diplomacy in the developing world was also successful because it was willing to afford many countries a degree of respect that they wouldn't achieve anywhere else in the world. In Beijing, they would receive red carpet welcomes, banquets, and access to China's top leaders. One diplomat recalled that the department treated the prime minister of the Cook Islands as if he were the leader of a big country during a visit to China in 1998.[70] Where most other large nations concentrated on relations among big powers or regional neighbors, outwardly at least, Chinese diplomats pretended not to play favorites.

***

As China's international reach rapidly expanded, it was sometimes difficult for its diplomatic apparatus to keep up with the ministry's strict standards for discipline and secrecy. After diplomatic ties were established with Moldova in 1992, China's temporary embassy lacked a secure room for communications with Beijing. The ambassador was forced to drive 450 kilometers to the Chinese embassy in Romania just to send diplomatic cables. Forbidden from writing drafts beforehand, he would sketch out the contents in his head during the drive, committing them to memory in order to type them out quickly on arrival.[71]

Moves to professionalize Chinese diplomacy would continue in the 1990s, with further wage reforms and staff reductions. By 1994, most embassies had managed to cut 25 percent of their staff and were able to save even more money by hiring locals for the first time. One embassy in South America was reportedly able to save several hundred thousand dollars a year simply by hiring local drivers instead of shipping out Chinese ones. The ministry also provided clear job descriptions for diplomats, standardized promotion criteria, and increased training opportunities for mid-level diplomats.[72]

There was also a drive to infuse new talent by recruiting or borrowing officials from other agencies. The former vice presidents of the foreign ministry's think tank, the China Institute of International Studies, Su Ge and later Ruan Zongze, were assigned to the Chinese embassy in Washington. Cui Liru, head of the Americas program at the China Institute of Contemporary International Relations—a think tank that reports to China's lead intelligence agency—worked in China's mission to the United Nations in the 1990s.[73] Song Tao, a future foreign ministry vice minister and head of the

Party's International Department, was recruited to the diplomatic corps after serving in a series of provincial government and business roles in Fujian province.[74]

The foreign ministry itself got a swanky new headquarters in 1997 after its previous site grew too cramped for China's expanding diplomatic corps. The concrete and glass building on the southeast corner of where the imperial Chaoyang gate once stood in Beijing was designed in the shape of a fan to symbolize openness to the outside world, according to one former diplomat.[75] A stone relief in the ministry's 800-square-meter entrance hall depicted "Chinese Civilization," detailing the country's achievements from the Qin Dynasty through to the Long March 2 rocket launch system. The meeting and negotiation rooms were decorated with Chinese paintings and calligraphy, as well as Mao Zedong's poetry. Meeting room 216 displays Mao's poem "Ode to Plum Blossom," which Zhou Enlai had recited to Richard Nixon during his historic 1972 visit.[76] Unlike the State Department, all meeting rooms are on the first floor so no foreigners can actually visit the work space of their Chinese counterparts.[77]

Nothing symbolized China's enhanced global status better than the return of Hong Kong on July 1, 1997. The occasion was marked by a solemn ceremony watched by Britain's Prince Charles and Chinese president Jiang Zemin before the island reverted to Chinese rule after 156 years of colonial occupation. "The return of Hong Kong to the motherland after a century of vicissitudes indicates that from now on, our Hong Kong compatriots have become true masters of this Chinese land," Jiang told the assembled crowds.[78] As the ceremony progressed, the rain over the city's harbor front had turned from drizzle into a downpour. It was a poignant moment for Foreign Minister Qian Qichen, who had joined Jiang for the ceremony: the rain that day felt like it was "washing away China's century of national humiliation," he wrote later.[79] Deng Xiaoping, who had died that February after a long battle with Parkinson's disease, was unable to savor the historic moment he'd brought about through tough negotiations with Margaret Thatcher.

Chinese diplomats also began to feel a renewed sense of confidence in their political system. In a 1997 newspaper article, Liu Huaqiu, the director of the State Council's Foreign Affairs Office, boasted that the country had "withstood the impact from the drastic changes in Eastern Europe and the disintegration of the Soviet Union." China had also "smashed Western sanctions," he wrote.[80]

Still, deep insecurities continued to go hand in hand with this new confidence. Nearly four decades after being sent to have his first suit fitted during the Great Leap Forward, Li Jiazhong was now ambassador to Vietnam. He couldn't help feeling snubbed by the US ambassador, who never seemed to speak to him at diplomatic receptions. In return, Li didn't show up to American-hosted events and griped to other members of the diplomatic community. Even when his American counterpart later delivered an explicit message of friendship during a visit to the Chinese embassy, Li's guard stayed up. He decided to serve the ambassador tea, "but I didn't lay out dried fruit," he remembered. "I had no experience dealing with Americans and I felt it was better not to be too warm."[81]

Some Chinese diplomats who felt snubbed believed it was the result of flat-out racial prejudice. "When I was studying and working in Britain, I had a strong feeling that Europeans often unconsciously displayed the feelings of a superiority white people feel toward other ethnicities," remembered Ma Zhengang, China's ambassador to the UK from 1997 to 2002. "It doesn't matter whether it's British people, French, Germans or other Europeans, none of them will admit that this sense of superiority exists, but many Chinese people will have felt it."[82]

These feelings played out in the sheer pettiness of some embassy activities. When Deng Xiaoping died in 1997, the cultural attaché at the Chinese Embassy in New Zealand was sent out to note down which countries' embassies had failed to fly their flags at half-staff.[83] Other diplomats used their memoirs to highlight their struggles to remove Republic of China (Taiwan) flags from diplomatic receptions and trade fairs, or to prevent local television stations from showing documentaries about Tibet. "The Chinese delegation successfully carried out the important task the motherland had entrusted to us," wrote one diplomat who helped to remove Taiwan's flag from an event in Papua New Guinea. "We succeeded because our great motherland stood behind us."[84] It was hardly the stuff of great power leadership.

***

Insecure or not, the Chinese public increasingly expected their diplomats to act tough. In a bid to strengthen its position at home, the Communist Party had launched a "patriotic education campaign" in the aftermath of the Tiananmen Square massacre that stressed how foreign powers, especially Japan, had humiliated China. In 1995, the government commemorated the 100th anniversary of the Treaty of Shimonoseki, which ceded

Taiwan to Japan, by sponsoring a film recreating Japan's Second World War atrocities and opening public exhibitions that documented Japanese acts of aggression.[85]

These campaigns were useful for the Party in the sense that they helped unify the country against a common enemy, but they also created the problematic expectation that the Party should always stand up to perceived acts of foreign aggression. The problem was that this expectation had to be balanced against the need for strong economic relationships and to maintain the hard-won diplomatic gains of the 1990s.

These conflicting pressures meant the decision of a band of right-wing Japanese nationalists to build a lighthouse on a group of tiny windswept islands in the East China Sea in 1996 created an outsized problem for Beijing. The dispute over the uninhabited Senkaku Islands, known as the Diaoyu Islands in Chinese, had surfaced from time to time over previous decades but neither government had wanted to see it derail relations. As such, the Chinese foreign ministry responded to the lighthouse with strong verbal protests, but also stressed that it valued good relations with Japan. When protests broke out over the issue in Hong Kong, China's state media did not report on them, and censors deleted online postings that called for protests on the mainland.

The contrast between the government's caution and the nationalism of its own "patriotic education campaign" was palpable and left many Chinese—especially students—angry. Leading state media outlets received more than 37,000 letters, as well as petitions with over 150,000 signatures, demanding that the government defend China's claim to the islands. Hu Sheng, president of the Chinese Academy of Social Sciences, even warned that government attempts to suppress anti-Japanese sentiment risked unrest on a scale not seen since 1989.[86] Other parts of the government were angry too. Hong Kong media reported that the Chinese military was particularly frustrated by Qian Qichen's willingness to engage in dialogue with Japan.

The level of frustration with the government's caution was best encapsulated by the unlikely commercial success of the 1996 nationalist tract *China Can Say No*. The collection of essays on topics ranging from Hollywood to the CIA celebrated China's potential as a global leader, but also warned that to fulfill its potential China would need to learn to "say no" to outside powers determined to thwart its rise. The book's initial print run of 50,000 copies sold out within twenty days; it went on to sell more than 2 million copies in total.[87] The sequel, *China Can Still Say No*, was sharply critical of the government's Japan policy: "China has been too warm and accommodating towards Japan," the authors wrote.[88] It was banned just a month after its publication. As frustration built, nationalists online began referring to the foreign ministry as the ministry of traitors (*maiguobu*).[89]

As nationalist pressures intensified at home, the government also worried about slowing economic growth, rising unemployment, and sporadic unrest in rural China.[90] They also faced a series of international challenges. The United States reaffirmed its postwar security arrangements with Japan in a 1996 declaration that many officials in Beijing saw as a joint push to contain China.[91] India joined the ranks of the nuclear powers after a nuclear test in 1998, barely a week after Indian defense minister George Fernandes warned that China was India's "potential enemy number one."[92] Finally, Beijing watched Washington's increasing practice of humanitarian intervention with growing unease, including joint American-British air raids against Iraq in December 1998 that China opposed, together with France and Russia.[93]

The atmosphere in China grew even more fraught in 1999, as the People's Republic prepared to celebrate its fiftieth anniversary. In early April, China's reformist premier Zhu Rongji was pilloried as a weak "traitor" in online forums after he returned to China empty-handed when talks with the United States over China's accession to the World Trade Organization collapsed at the last minute.[94] Just a few weeks later, more than 10,000 members of Falun Gong, a spiritual group that practiced breathing exercises, gathered around the leadership compound of Zhongnanhai to protest official restrictions on the group.[95] Beijing's shock at the protests, the largest since those in Tiananmen Square ten years earlier, and its subsequent crackdown underlined just how vulnerable the leadership was feeling. The worst was yet to come.

***

In the early hours of May 8, 1999, Foreign Minister Tang Jiaxuan was woken by the constant ringing of his phone. He knew it was a bad sign.[96]

Tang's secretary broke the news to him: just ten minutes earlier, American bombs had crashed into the Chinese embassy in Belgrade, Yugoslavia. The foreign ministry was still struggling to gather all the facts but two things were already clear: there were Chinese casualties and a storm was coming in Sino-American relations.

The temperamentally quiet and soft-spoken Tang was overcome with anger. "I could not believe my ears," Tang remembered. "What a gross outrage: attacking an embassy of the People's Republic of China!"

Composing himself, Tang ordered his secretary to inform his superiors and contact the embassy by any means necessary. He ordered department heads to gather immediately in the foreign ministry, getting up out of bed and heading across Beijing to his office.

By the time he arrived at the ministry, the details were becoming clear. Three embassy staff accredited as journalists, who had been sleeping in the embassy compound, had been killed and twenty other diplomats, journalists, and family members had been wounded.[97] The embassy itself, a five-story building with a green, Chinese-style sloped roof, had been severely damaged. Eyewitnesses said it had been struck by three American missiles.[98]

Tang's next task was to report what had happened to China's top leadership. He traveled back across town to the Zhongnanhai compound to brief Jiang Zemin and other top leaders.

Tang knew the latest crisis would only exacerbate the leadership's existing outrage over NATO's actions. To China's leaders, the NATO campaign in Yugoslavia was just the latest expression of America's didactic post–Cold War triumphalism. They sympathized with what they saw as legitimate Serbian efforts to suppress the kind of separatism China faced in Xinjiang and Tibet. They had even provided behind-the-scenes cooperation to Serbian authorities who, in turn, had allowed Beijing access to study parts of an American F-117 stealth fighter shot down in March.[99]

Tang later described the scene inside Zhongnanhai as one of "tremendous grief and indignation." The leadership decided that it would "launch a solemn representation, resolutely protecting our state sovereignty and national dignity while also considering reform and opening and the long-term issues of our nation." In other words, they were going to impose the greatest diplomatic costs they could on the United States without totally derailing relations.

The Chinese leadership was highly dissatisfied with an almost casual public apology by President Clinton on May 8. The Chinese public, meanwhile, was taking its anger to the streets with the blessing and even facilitation of the government. The US embassy in Beijing was attacked with stones and eggs. Ambassador James Sasser was trapped inside as students outside the walls hurled rocks and screamed "kill Americans." Protesters surrounded the building. "This whole thing could spin out of control. We're just hoping that the police can continue to control them," Sasser told CBC news by telephone. "We are essentially hostages here."[100]

The protests were accompanied by a barrage of attacks in state media, which were quick to link the attacks to the wrongs committed against China in the past as part of the century of humiliation the post-Tiananmen patriotic education campaign had been drilling into the population. The *People's Daily* denounced the bombing as a "barbarian crime" and warned against American aspirations to become "Lord of the Earth."[101] Another editorial was headlined, "This is not 1899," in clear reference to the Boxer Rebellion during which foreign troops ransacked parts of Beijing.[102]

As the protests intensified, the embassy came close to being overrun. US Marines began the orderly destruction of classified documents, while Sasser and his team had retreated to the secure area inside of the embassy. As the turmoil reached a climax in Beijing, Secretary of State Madeleine Albright led a group of five American officials to the Chinese embassy in Washington to apologize for the bombing and explain the gravity of the situation unfolding in Beijing.

The visit served as a political gift to ambassador Li Zhaoxing. An avid amateur poet and later honorary head of the Chinese Shakespeare Society, Li launched into a truly theatrical performance. The transgression was "beyond imagination" and the American government must apologize, he said while gesticulating for dramatic effect for TV cameras ushered in to capture the moment. As the Americans left the embassy they were confronted by a mob of very angry Chinese "journalists" demanding an apology from Albright.[103]

Tensions were eventually reduced after several months of negotiations. Washington offered compensation for the lives lost and property damaged, fired the CIA operations officer involved in mistakenly targeting the embassy in Belgrade, and offered an official explanation for the bombings (which most educated Chinese still believe was deliberate).[104] China's leaders felt they'd made their point. "Our greatest accomplishment was the lesson we taught the United States: that today's China and its people cannot be bullied," the foreign minister, Tang Jiaxuan, later wrote.[105]

***

What followed was a period of profound uncertainty in Sino-American relations. The Belgrade bombings had shown just how fragile the recovery of ties in the 1990s had been.

To be sure, there were some positive signs. In November 1999, China and the United States agreed on terms for Beijing's accession to the World Trade Organization, removing a long-standing source of friction and uncertainty in their relationship. China's admission represented an opportunity for the country to continue, even accelerate, its remarkable economic rise as well as further recognition that it was accepted on equal terms by its global peers.

But there were also worrying trends. In November 2000, George W. Bush was elected president. Just a few months earlier, he had described China as a "strategic competitor" on the campaign trail. Beijing dispatched Yang Jiechi to Washington to deal with the new president, hoping his deep ties to the Bush family, which stretched back to his stint as a translator for George H. W. Bush in the 1970s, would be of use.[106]

Early hopes that things might stabilize proved fleeting as a new crisis emerged just months after Bush's inauguration. On April 1, 2001, a Chinese fighter jet clipped an American EP-3 spy plane in international airspace near the Chinese coast while attempting to intercept it. The Chinese pilot was killed in the collision while the damaged US plane was forced to make an emergency landing on China's Hainan Island.

On April 4, before setting off on a trip to Latin America, Jiang Zemin instructed the foreign ministry to secure an apology from the United States before releasing the crew.[107] He issued a simple instruction to the foreign ministry to pass along to the Americans: "You apologize, I release the men."[108]

It wasn't just the public that was angry, then foreign minister Tang Jiaxuan remembered. Chinese officials and the military were angry too. Multiple rounds of meetings in Beijing and Washington focused on the return of the American pilots but also how to phrase the apology in a way that would meet China's demands.

Inside the foreign ministry, English-language experts were brought in to study the gradations of meaning, using the *Oxford Advanced Learner's Dictionary* and *Webster's Encyclopedic Unabridged Dictionary of the English Language* to compare the meanings of "apologize," "sorry," and "regret." Finally, they settled on a formulation in which the United States said it was "very sorry." Tang put on a dark suit to accept the apology.[109]

The focus on the semantics of the apology might seem petty, but it also had deep historical roots. During the late Qing Dynasty, China's very first diplomats had been repeatedly dispatched across the world to apologize for infractions on Western interests, often under the threat of military action. In the early 1970s, a group of Chinese diplomats posted in New York stumbled upon the tombstone of a Qing diplomat sent to the United States on one such apology tour. "Weak countries get bullied. They have no real diplomacy to speak of," one of them later wrote. They, like Tang Jiaxuan and his successors, wanted nothing to do with this legacy.[110]

As if adding insult to injury, on April 24, the Bush administration announced a $12 billion package of arms sales to Taiwan.[111] In an interview with ABC News' *Good Morning America*, Bush went beyond the previous US position by stating that the country would do "whatever it takes" to defend the island.[112] Foreign ministry spokeswoman Zhang Qiyue responded that America had embarked on a "dangerous road," adding that "the Chinese government and people" were "strongly indignant."[113] China's domestic economic reforms and its conciliatory diplomacy had succeeded in pulling China back from the post-Tiananmen low point, but it was still unable to persuade large sections of the American political elite that its rise did not present a threat. The road ahead looked rocky.

***

The global response to the International Olympic Committee's July 2001 decision to award Beijing the 2008 Summer Olympic Games demonstrated the uneven progress of China's quest for global recognition. For Chinese envoys, the moment had been a long time coming. Decades earlier, Zhou Enlai had promised his diplomats: "one day, we will host a world-class sporting event."[114] After the success of "ping-pong diplomacy" in China's breakthrough with America, the country had expanded its use of sports to build ties with the outside world. In 1972 alone, it held 230 sports exchanges with 79 countries.[115]

China's drive for recognition in the world of sports had also been littered with disappointments. The country's previous 1993 bid to host the Summer Olympics in 2000 had been narrowly rejected after Western countries raised concerns over its human rights record. It was a sign that China was still considered a pariah by many around the world. One diplomat described the moment he found out that China had lost as "like being thrown into a pool of ice water."[116] For many Chinese citizens, it was simply a sign that much of the world looked down on China and its people.

When China pushed to host the 2008 games, it once again pulled out all the stops. This time, there was no room for failure. China committed nearly $22 billion to upgrade its infrastructure and improve environmental protection in the run up to the games, while embassies around the world were mobilized to lobby for it.[117] When the moment of victory arrived on July 13, 2001, the previous disappointments made it especially sweet. The atmosphere in the Chinese capital was feverish as the city erupted in flag waving, fireworks, and horn honking. "This victory did not come easily," remembered China's ambassador in Paris, one of the cities Beijing had beaten to host the games. "China's international status was enhanced!"[118]

The victory was a sign for many diplomats and for the Chinese public that the country was emerging from the weak and stigmatized status it had endured for more than a century. One Chinese diplomat who worked on the bid told a reporter that this was a victory for the Chinese people, who had once been described as the "sick man of Asia" and placed on the same level as dogs.[119]

Still, the moment was bittersweet. Chinese officials argued that the victory would help the country to improve human rights. Hosting the Olympics would help it make "advances in culture, health, education, sport and, not least of all, corresponding progress in human rights," Yuan Weimin, the country's minister of sport, argued.[120] But many foreign critics doubted the sincerity of these promises. "It is an absolute outrage that the IOC has decided to reward China's deteriorating human rights record by giving Beijing the honor of hosting the Olympics," an American congressman, Tom Lantos, said of the decision. François Loncle, head of France's foreign affairs committee, was more evocative: "How can one imagine, as is scheduled, that the triathlon and beach-volleyball can be organized on Tiananmen Square where the Chinese army bloodily wiped out the democratic movement of spring 1989?" he asked.[121]

Even after Beijing's decade-long charm offensive, many around the world still considered it a pariah. Reassuring these critics would become even more difficult given China's growing economic clout and the pace of its military modernization. Worse still, the Bush administration seemed set to continue treating China as a "competitor" and perhaps even a threat. Until, that is, one clear September morning changed everything.

10

Ambition Realized

Zhang Hongxi arrived late to work in Manhattan on September 11, 2001, after wishing his son a happy birthday. As soon as he got to the office, Zhang heard the piercing sound of sirens and watched from his window as what seemed like an endless line of emergency vehicles raced past.

To Zhang, China's consul general in New York, it looked as though the trucks were heading toward the World Trade Center, where he saw smoke billowing out of the North Tower. Figuring that whatever was happening would be big news, he told the political section of the consulate to film the unfolding events.

As his colleagues scrambled to follow his instructions, Zhang's eyes remained fixed on the towers just as an airplane appeared in the sky. Before he had time to process what was happening, the plane smashed into the South Tower, releasing a fireball on impact.

Zhang called an emergency meeting of the consulate's leadership and instructed staff to start monitoring the media. Diplomats headed outside to film as the first tower collapsed.[1]

Back in Beijing, President Jiang Zemin was glued to the television. He had watched virtually the whole incident unfold live on Hong Kong's Phoenix Television news channel as China's heavily censored domestic media wasn't reporting the news in detail yet.

After prying himself away from the screen, Jiang called a meeting of the Politburo Standing Committee to discuss China's response. They decided to condemn the attacks as terrorism. Within hours of the disaster and although it was by now past midnight in Beijing, Jiang called President George W. Bush, and followed up with another call the next day.[2]

China's leadership, along with its top diplomats, had spotted an opportunity amid the chaos. When Foreign Minister Tang Jiaxuan later met China's new ambassador in Washington, Yang Jiechi, both agreed the attacks represented an "important opportunity to improve and develop Sino-American relations."[3] It seemed likely that the United States would divert its attention from China to the Middle East, and even consider partnering with China to fight the war on terror, they reasoned.

China's leaders were right to think 9/11 would be a turning point. "The very first strong message of sympathy that came to President Bush was from China," former assistant secretary of state James Kelly later told an interviewer. "They were immediately on board with the war on terror and that just about shredded the agenda of anybody who wanted to get going with a new cold war."[4]

The fact that the attacks presented an opportunity didn't mean things would be easy. Like most residents in America, China's diplomatic corps was on edge in the weeks following 9/11. When the anthrax attacks began just a week after the towers fell, China's resident diplomats in the country took to opening letters inside glass boxes using gloves. The foreign ministry sent them additional medical supplies in case of emergency.[5]

There were also questions about what America's new focus on the Middle East would mean for China's influence in the wider region. In a bid to shore up its interests in Pakistan, China's closest diplomatic partner, Beijing dispatched a rising star to Islamabad: just over a week after the attacks, Wang Yi, China's youngest vice minister, arrived in Pakistan's capital to urge the country's leaders to cooperate with the United States and also seek reassurances that Beijing's own interests would not be harmed.[6]

Beijing seized the opportunity to reset ties with the world's sole superpower. It shared intelligence about terrorist activities and financing—even offering low-key military assistance in the form of minesweepers as America prepared to invade Afghanistan.[7] China would also allow the FBI to open an office in Beijing, with the explicit purpose of counter-terrorism cooperation.[8]

President Bush's meeting with Jiang Zemin during the APEC summit of Pacific Rim economies in Shanghai that October showed how much progress China had made. "You are president of a great nation," Bush told Jiang. "It is important for us to get to know each other." At the end of their talks, Jiang told Bush, "I've heard your determination and we agree with your views."[9] One month later, China acceded to the World Trade Organization, temporarily drawing a line under a decade of trade tensions. The Bush administration's 2002 National Security Strategy welcomed "the emergence of a strong, peaceful, and prosperous China."[10]

China's leaders were quick to spot the historical significance of the diplomatic turnaround. They began to talk about a "period of strategic opportunity" in which China would be free to grow its economy and benefit from its new access to global markets while America focused on the Middle East. It seemed that a great power conflict remained a remote possibility.[11] Jiang gave the idea his official stamp in late 2002 when he told Party leaders that the "first two decades of the 21st century are a period of important strategic opportunities."[12]

Everything seemed to go right for China in the period after 9/11. America was distracted by global terrorism and focused on the Middle East as the two powers found a way to cooperate over anti-terrorism. China's previous efforts to woo its neighbors after Tiananmen and especially after the 1995—1996 Taiwan Strait Crisis were also paying off. The period culminated with China hosting the 2008 Summer Olympics—the most significant moment of international validation for the regime since its founding. Former foreign minister Tang Jiaxuan later looked back on the progress China made in the 2000s, reflecting accurately that China's "comprehensive national power" and status had increased rapidly. The efforts of "the People's Liberation Army in civilian clothing," he wrote, had helped make that happen.[13]

There were limits to China's changing image. Washington retained its wariness of a potential peer competitor ruled by a communist dictatorship. Beijing feared Washington's pro-democracy agenda and encirclement by its network of allies. What's more, China was also never as zealous about counterterrorism as the Bush administration (outside of its perceived threat from its own Muslim minorities). Still, the two powers found a remarkable number of new areas to cooperate, starting with the danger of a nuclear North Korea.

***

In October 2002, the United States told North Korean officials that it had irrefutable evidence they were engaged in a secret program to develop the highly enriched uranium necessary to build a nuclear bomb.

Jiang Zemin had spent much of the 1990s brushing off American requests that Beijing rein in North Korea's nuclear ambitions. But Hu Jintao, who took over from Jiang Zemin as the head of the Communist Party in 2002, was starting to think differently about its irksome ally. Hu was a far more low-key, even dull, figure, a stark contrast to his ebullient predecessor. But he was younger and had new ideas. Hu was part of a new "fourth generation" of Chinese leaders, a group that was far less sentimental about China's ties with North Korea and had come to believe that the nuclear issue could be dealt with multilaterally.[14]

After taking over from Jiang, Hu initiated a review of China's policy on North Korea, soliciting opinions from across the Party-state. Eventually, he settled on a proposal advocated by the young vice foreign minister, Wang Yi, who had been dispatched to Pakistan soon after 9/11. Wang proposed shifting China's policy on North Korea to focus more on China's national interests than on ideological affinity with the North, and prioritized a strategy that prevented the North Koreans from developing nuclear weapons.[15]

In early 2003, just over a year after Bush had lumped North Korea in with Iran and Iraq in an "axis of evil," Hu decided something had to be done. Some 10,000 American troops were massing on Iraq's borders, preparing for re-gime change, and China needed to get more involved, if only to reduce the risk of American troops approaching Chinese borders as they had done in the early days of the Korean War. The task fell to Qian Qichen, the foreign ministry's fix-it man after Tiananmen.

Qian's plane jolted violently as it touched down at North Korea's Samjiyon Airport on March 8, 2003. The now seventy-five-year-old Qian and a small group of Chinese diplomats were on their way to Kim Jong-il's secret guest house at the foot of Mount Paektu, an active stratovolcano on the Chinese–North Korean border, which many consider the spiritual home of the Korean people and where the regime claimed Kim had been born.[16]

One member of Qian's small group looked up as he disembarked from the plane. "Why is North Korea so full of blue sky?" he asked himself. "China used to have blue skies like this when I was a kid." The observation highlighted the huge damage China's breakneck industrialization had done to its natural environment over the last twenty-five years, but it was also a function of the yawning gap in development that had now opened between the two Communist-ruled countries.

Qian's last trip to North Korea in July 1992 had been a tense affair. He'd been dispatched to secure the support of North Korea's founding father, Kim Il-sung, for China's desire to build ties with South Korea. Instead of the usual elaborate welcoming party, he'd been ushered to the most remote berth of Pyongyang's Sunan Airport before what Qian later described as Kim Il-sung's shortest ever meeting with a Chinese delegation.[17]

Qian's mission on this perfect spring day more than a decade later was no less significant. As the meeting commenced, he let Kim Jong-il get a few things off his chest. Qian listened patiently as the North Korean leader railed against American aggression and questioned China's involvement by insisting that the nuclear issue was a matter for North Korea and the United States alone.

Then, Qian came clean about his ask. He suggested that Kim considered three-way talks between the United States, North Korea, and China. "It doesn't really matter whether China is present or not," Qian reassured Kim, knowing that he craved the legitimacy that direct talks with America would bestow. "We will just listen to the discussion quietly."

Eventually, Kim relented. The outcome was a trilateral discussion among the powers, which later morphed into the Six-Party Talks with the addition of South Korea, Japan, and Russia. The mission was a success.

The first round of the Six-Party Talks began on August 27, 2003, in Beijing. The Chinese delegation was hosted by Wang Yi, who had accompanied Qian on his trip to see Kim Jong-il earlier that year. During the course of the talks, the North Koreans variously called Russia's representative a "dirty liar," boycotted a group discussion for negotiating a joint statement, and threatened the United States with a nuclear test.

Dealing with North Korea was exhausting even for China, a fellow communist regime. As Wang hosted the closing session of the talks two days later, North Korea's representative, deputy foreign minister Kim Yong-il, interjected: "This meeting is useless, and we have no interest in this. We will not participate in this kind of meeting any longer." Wang continued as if nothing had happened, concluding that "the participants in the Six-Party Talks agreed to continue the process of the Six-Party Talks and to decide as soon as possible through diplomatic routes the place and time of the next meeting."[18]

Hosting the talks provided the validation that Chinese leaders and diplomats had long sought. The foreign ministry specially created Six-Party Talks pencils, folders, and fans for the occasion.[19] State media broadcast constant coverage of the talks, summarizing coverage from the *New York Times* that emphasized China's new international importance while playing stock footage of Zhou Enlai to emphasize how Chinese diplomats today were following in his footsteps. A banner running across the screen read, "The eyes of the whole world are on the Beijing meeting."[20]

The talks themselves, which were held intermittently between 2003 and 2009, were a grueling process marked by dashed hopes, stalemates, and setbacks. But even if they ultimately failed to halt North Korea's quest for nuclear weapons, the talks achieved important breakthroughs. In 2005 North

Korea pledged to abandon its nuclear programs and in 2007 the parties agreed on steps to implement the 2005 agreement.

Perhaps even more important, the talks had helped maintain the positive momentum in post-9/11 Sino-American relations. "This whole Six-Party process has done more to bring the United States and China together than any other process I'm aware of," America's top negotiator, Christopher Hill, told ABC News at the time.[21]

Nevertheless, some in the Chinese capital were unsure about just how much global responsibility China should assume, just as some in Washington were torn about whether they really wanted to see China become an international leader. In 2006, then secretary of state Condoleezza Rice found herself "angry at Beijing" for its "policy of avoidance" over North Korea during meetings with China's foreign minister Li Zhaoxing. "I made a mental note to tell Li that China was a great power but never acted like one," Rice remembered. "Then a little voice inside my head whispered, *Maybe that's for the best*."[22]

***

As the Six-Party Talks unfolded in China, world attention was still focused on the US invasion of Iraq. Although the decision to invade a sovereign state horrified China's leaders, it also provided the Party with a major public relations opportunity.

Given the unpopularity of the Bush administration in many parts of the world, China's leaders could often score diplomatic points simply by showing up. This was evident in 2003 when Bush and Hu Jintao spoke on consecutive days at the Australian parliament. Hu was greeted far more enthusiastically than Bush, and Australia's *Financial Review* led with the headline, "Bush came, Hu conquered."[23] Anyone who's listened to a Hu Jintao speech will understand that the warm reception had more to do with American unpopularity than with the Chinese president's rhetorical flair.

The vacuum opened up just as Beijing was becoming more active in other aspects of its diplomacy—sending its leaders abroad far more frequently than in the past. China's top leaders (the president, the premier, the head of the National People's Congress, and the chairman of the Chinese People's Political Consultative Conference) made 424 overseas visits in the 1992–2006 period, up from 122 between 1981 and 1991.[24]

China's diplomats even began recommending that the country's leaders embrace forums they would previously have found uncomfortable, even distasteful. In 2003, Hu agreed to attend the Group of Eight Summit in Évian-les-Bains, France, at the urging of the foreign ministry and after a long debate among the country's top leadership. China had declined invitations to attend in 1996, 1999, and 2000 on the grounds that it shouldn't be associated with a club of rich countries. In 2003, it finally accepted.[25]

Still, Chinese leaders were extremely sensitive about how their new efforts would be perceived, and they worried about the potential backlash. The intense concern for China's reputation was encapsulated by the rise and fall of the slogan "peaceful rise," coined by the prominent Party intellectual Zheng Bijian in late 2003. Initially embraced by the Hu-Wen leadership in that year, in 2004 they opted instead to use the phrase "peaceful development," which they deemed less threatening.[26]

Enhancing the country's soft power seemed like a relatively low-risk strategy in the face of these concerns. In 2002, China had established a cultural center in Paris—its first cultural center in a major Western country—after a long period of debate among officials.[27] In 2004, the foreign ministry set up a Division of Public Diplomacy, citing the need to "catch up" with developed countries in this field.[28]

The soft-power push was most aggressive and most successful in China's Southeast Asian backyard. By the mid-2000s, China rivaled Japan as the largest donor in many of the region's countries, building schools in Cambodia and offering $500 million in assistance to a single high-profile railway project in the Philippines. Journalists and politicians from across the region were brought to China on paid junkets and polls across the region showed growing warmth toward Beijing.[29]

Perhaps the crowning achievement of China's initiatives came when it hosted the third China-Africa Summit in Beijing in November 2006. The outcome of increased engagement with Africa since the late 1990s, the summit was a deliberate push to improve China's image on the continent. In the run-up to the meeting, the foreign ministry's Policy Planning Department and the State Council Information Office convened meetings of Chinese government think tanks to discuss ways to boost China's soft power.[30]

No detail was too small. The government had a huge round table with a circumference of 62 meters made to symbolize the equality of all the participants. Hu Jintao made a point of meeting every head of state or government who attended the summit regardless of the size of their country.[31] As the event approached, Beijing was decorated with billboards showing elephants and giraffes roaming the savannah. Construction projects and traffic were curtailed to make way for temporary blue skies.[32]

The summit succeeded in attracting leaders from forty-eight African countries, including forty heads of state. Hu Jintao promised some $5 billion in cheap loans and buyers credits at the meeting, and pledged to build 100 new schools, train some 16,000 professionals, and promote Chinese culture across the continent.[33]

In its bid to charm the world, Beijing embraced countries the West had shunned. It courted Venezuela's Hugo Chávez, who described his relationship with China a "great wall" against American hegemony.[34] When Washington criticized Uzbekistan's leaders after a massacre of some 400 people in 2005, China expressed "resolute support" for the regime and gave its leader a twenty-one-gun salute during his visit to Beijing.[35] And as Western governments shunned the Sudanese regime in Khartoum, Beijing stepped up its support.[36]

China's reputation in the West suffered as a result of these friendships, especially as its preparations for the 2008 Summer Olympics opened the country up to more international scrutiny than at any time since the Tiananmen crackdown. As a result, Beijing began to moderate its approach. It strongly denounced North Korea's nuclear test in October 2006, voted to impose and tighten sanctions on Iran, supported the deployment of a United Nations–African Union force in Darfur, and condemned a crackdown in Myanmar.[37]

None of this was enough to stop human rights activists from labeling the gathering the "genocide Olympics" or Steven Spielberg withdrawing as an artistic adviser for the opening and closing ceremonies.[38] But it was undeniable that Beijing had made huge strides in bolstering its global reputation. Gradually, the soft power push became more central to the country's foreign policy. In a major speech in 2007, President Hu Jintao linked China's "rejuvenation" with its ability to project soft power, officially elevating its importance for Chinese diplomacy.[39]

***

China's rise and economic expansion also created new challenges for the country's diplomats. China's leaders began to articulate a "going out" strategy for Chinese companies in 1999 as a way to ensure access to the crucial raw materials the emerging superpower needed to sustain its rapid growth and to expose them to greater international competition. In 2002, the policy was given a top-level stamp of approval in Jiang Zemin's report to the 16th

Communist Party Congress.[40] By the end of 2005, China's cumulative foreign investment totaled $57.2 billion, up from just $7.6 billion in 2000.[41] As investments flowed overseas, so too did Chinese citizens.

It became apparent fairly quickly that problems accompanied this expansion. The year 2004 provided a wakeup call for the foreign ministry. In the space of just a few months, sixteen Chinese citizens were killed in attacks across Sudan, Afghanistan, and Pakistan where China's state-owned companies operated. The murders were widely covered in the Chinese media, intensifying public pressure for the ministry to step up its game.[42] The scale of the challenge continued to grow; in 2005, for example, Chinese tourists made some 30 million overseas trips, up from just 4.5 million in 1995.[43]

Providing support for its citizens abroad was a new challenge for the Communist Party. In the 1980s, most Chinese embassies devoted relatively little attention to the task—one former diplomat in Kenya estimated that there were only five Chinese non-diplomats in the country at that time.[44] But the diplomatic apparatus needed to change. The foreign ministry established a Department for External Security Affairs in 2004 charged with protecting citizens overseas. It established a Beijing-based hub for dealing with consular matters in 2005 and created a Center for Consular Protection in 2007.[45]

As the ministry evolved, the scale of the challenge and weight of expectations from the public grew exponentially. In early 2011, as governments fell across the Middle East during the Arab Spring, thousands of Chinese businesspeople found themselves stranded and afraid, especially those living and working in Libya, which began to slide into civil war. They looked to their government for help.

Anxious posts from trapped Chinese workers on the microblogging site Sina Weibo prompted other users to call the ministry in protest. "I just called the number 86-10-6596114 listed on the website of the Ministry of Foreign Affairs and a woman answered, sounding as if she'd just woken up," read one post. "As soon as the word 'Libya' left my mouth, she said, 'the leaders have all gone home, we'll deal with it tomorrow.'"[46]

The ministry wasn't entirely sure what it should be doing to meet this new challenge and turned to others for advice. But whereas they'd looked to socialist brother countries in the 1950s, in 2011 they asked the British embassy in Beijing for best practices on evacuating non-combatants.[47]

In the end, the evacuation of Chinese nationals from Libya was a major success. Over twelve days from late February to early March 2011, more than 35,000 Chinese citizens left the country by plane, ship, bus, and truck. It was the largest evacuation in China's history and the first to involve Chinese military airplanes.[48] Over the course of 2011, China evacuated more than 47,000 nationals living overseas, more than in all the decades since the 1949 founding of the People's Republic combined.[49]

Like the Six-Party Talks before it, China's increasingly active role in protecting its citizens overseas heralded a new stage in its march toward great power status. Just as activities of American Christian missionaries in Asia and the Middle East helped draw the United States slowly into a more global role before the First World War, Chinese students, tourists, and business-people overseas were now doing the same for China.[50]

As the Hu era drew to a close, the outgoing Chinese president highlighted the country's successes in protecting Chinese abroad in his report to the 18th Party Congress in 2012, signaling the increased importance the country's leadership now placed on protecting its citizens overseas.[51]

***

Paradoxically, China's growing global role weakened its foreign ministry. As Chinese businesspeople and tourists fanned out across the world, the ministry had to work together with—and sometimes compete with—other players such as the Ministry of Commerce, the Ministry of Public Security, and powerful state-owned companies. These organizations often had bigger budgets than the foreign ministry and at least equaled its political clout in Beijing.[52] The same was true across a wide range of complex global issues where China's influence was increasing from finance to healthcare, migra-tion, and the environment.[53] All of these new diplomatic players had their own ties to the central government and often posted their own representa-tives to embassies overseas.

It wasn't just the range of new actors that weakened the foreign ministry: it was also the kind of people attracted to diplomacy. The revolutionary elders were gone and so were the military recruits with strong ties across the lead-ership. They were replaced by professionals who were more knowledgeable about the intricacies of international diplomacy and fluent in foreign lan-guages, but who did not enjoy the prestige associated with military service and lacked close personal relationships with top Party leaders.[54]

Increasingly, officials in Beijing and across global capitals saw the for-eign ministry as a weak player. Susan Shirk, a former Clinton administra-tion official, recalled that "whenever I protested to Chinese diplomats about arrests of individuals for purely political offenses and reminded them about how damaging such arrests were to U.S.-China relations, they threw up their hands," explaining that "the Foreign Ministry can't do anything about it. The Ministries of State Security and Public Security are much more powerful. They won't even give us information about the cases."[55] Even state-owned companies could sometimes outflank the foreign ministry. "Sometimes we find companies doing things inconsistent with China's policies and interests," Le Yucheng, then head of the foreign ministry's Policy Planning Department, told China scholar David Shambaugh in 2010. "We tell them to stop, but they don't stop."[56]

Coordinating between so many disparate players was especially difficult in a political system like China's, which is designed to respond to orders from the top and where information is a closely guarded resource. In China, just like in the former Soviet Union, secrecy protocols limit the ability of ministries to share information with each other, forcing them instead to communicate through the top leadership.[57] The idea is to prevent any one part of the government from knowing too much. This feature of the system is often referred to as "stovepiping," a phrase that recalls a stovepipe's function as a kind of chimney for a fuel-burning stove: information flows vertically through top-down lines of control, instead of horizontally across organizations. Often only officials with vice minister rank are empowered to share information with other departments, making it tough to get things done if issues aren't worthy of being raised at that level.[58] "It's stovepiped because there is a fundamental lack of trust between these bureaucracies," said Robert Suettinger, a former CIA analyst.[59]

The foreign ministry's weakness and the Chinese government's culture of secrecy were on public display in January 2007 when the Chinese military destroyed one of China's weather satellites with a ballistic missile. When foreign governments asked Chinese diplomats for an explanation, they quickly concluded that the foreign ministry had not been informed about the test. Ten days after the incident, Li Zhaoxing, the foreign minister, said he had "not received any confirmed information" about the incident. It took the ministry two weeks to issue a statement even acknowledging that it had happened.[60] When foreign ministry spokespeople say they do not have information on a particular matter, they're usually telling the truth.

⁎⁎

If Chinese diplomats were increasingly hemmed in by the rest of the bureaucracy, they were also under increased pressure from the rapidly growing expectations of the Chinese public. Influenced by the patriotic education campaign of the 1990s, a new generation of young Chinese felt the leaders of their increasingly powerful country should be standing up for its interests more forcefully. The expectation hit up against China's cautious approach to reassuring its neighbors after Tiananmen.

In the mid-2000s, some nationalist citizens found a novel way to express their frustrations with the government: they began sending the foreign ministry calcium tablets in the post. The implication was that they should strengthen their weak backbones. As internet usage spread in China, Chinese citizens could vent their frustrations in real time, taking to online web forums and bulletin boards to complain about the ministry's conduct. Chinese diplomats paid attention. Officials charged with handling Japan in the ministry's Asia Department personally pored over online vitriol directed at them. Trainee diplomats at the China Foreign Affairs University also spent hours browsing nationalist forums.[61]

On one occasion, Li Zhaoxing, the foreign minister, vented his frustration to Secretary of State Condoleezza Rice. "You say you're under a lot of pressure, but it's not as much pressure as I face," Li said during a 2005 meeting in Beijing. "You Americans just have 300 million people, we have 1.3 billion. Now regular Chinese people are all voicing their opinions, saying China's foreign minister is too polite to America. I'm under more pressure."[62] Li's words were no doubt partly intended as a bargaining tactic, but the pressure was real.

It was China's relationship with Japan, however, that came in for the greatest criticism. Online anger erupted in 2003 after news emerged that a group of some 400 Japanese businessmen in the southern Chinese city of Zhuhai had hired more than 500 prostitutes for a three-day orgy from September 16–18, dates that coincided with the seventy-second anniversary of Japan's 1931 invasion of Manchuria.[63] Foreign ministry spokesperson Zhang Qiyue acknowledged that the incident had sparked "strong indignation and reactions" across China and urged Japan to "strengthen education for its citizens."[64]

Public frustration continued to build. In January 2004, Japanese prime minister Junichiro Koizumi once again provoked anger in China when he made his fourth visit to the Yasukuni Shrine, which honors Japan's war dead, including fourteen "Class A" war criminals. In spring 2005, a petition opposing Japan's bid for a permanent seat on the United Nations Security Council gathered more than 30 million signatures. In April that year, protests erupted over revisions to Japanese history textbooks that glossed over the country's wartime abuses. The government sought to manage the very real public anger by busing in student demonstrators to pre-arranged demonstration sites and allowing them to take turns throwing rocks.[65]

China's increasingly combustible domestic opinion made it difficult for the country's diplomats to even meet with their Japanese counterparts. In February 2006, Dai Bingguo, vice minister of foreign affairs, took a harsh stance during meetings, which the Japanese saw as an effort to "deflect domestic criticism of the MFA's handling of relations with Japan."[66] In an effort to keep a later trip to Japan quiet from the media, he wore sunglasses and asked his subordinates to call him "boss" instead of "minister" in an attempt to disguise his identity.[67] That same year, Foreign Minister Li Zhaoxing was reduced to meeting his Japanese counterpart in the men's room at the ASEAN Regional Forum in Malaysia because he believed it would be too difficult to meet with him in public.[68]

***

One way to appear strong in the face of a skeptical public was to present China as the equal of the powers that had once bullied it. Throughout the 2000s, the country developed a series of formal dialogues with other powers that aimed to reassure them about its intentions and signal to domestic audiences that China had arrived on the global stage. China insisted on calling these new forums, established with countries including the United States and Japan, "strategic dialogues," a term with which neither the Americans nor the Japanese were initially comfortable.[69] Foreign interlocutors would soon learn that China was often more interested in the pomp and optics of these dialogues than the substance.

By far the most important such dialogue was the one China established with the United States. In 2006, Hank Paulson, the US Treasury secretary, helped initiate the Strategic Economic Dialogue (SED) between the two countries.[70] The initial idea was to focus on "long-term strategic challenges," as Paulson felt that existing discussions were too mired in debating nitty-gritty problems.[71] The talks were renamed the Strategic and Economic Dialogue (S&ED) under the Obama administration, and expanded in scope to include a broader range of foreign policy issues. The negotiating process was often frustrating, not least because Chinese participants insisted on sticking closely to pre-approved talking points, but the meetings did make real progress on issues such as intellectual property theft, excess industrial capacity, and the expansion of the World Trade Organization's Information Technology Agreement.[72]

The success of the talks, however modest, owed a lot to Dai Bingguo. Dai, the young diplomat who had huddled with Chen Yi in the Zhongnanhai leadership compound at the start of the Cultural Revolution, had emerged as a close confidant of President Hu Jintao. After starting out in the foreign ministry as a young Soviet specialist, Dai had risen up the ranks before eventually heading the Party's International Department. Along the way, he had married the daughter of Huang Zhen, one of Zhou Enlai's original ambassador generals and the first head of China's liaison office in Washington in the 1970s.[73] In 2008, he was appointed state councilor, the rough equivalent of a cabinet member, charged with foreign affairs.[74]

Dai was an able interlocutor. Like Zhou Enlai and Qian Qichen, he stuck to the Party line but managed to find a way to make his delivery personal and accessible to American counterparts. "Sometimes I'd be subjected to long lectures about everything the United States was doing wrong in Asia, laced with sarcasm but always delivered with a smile," Secretary of State Hillary Clinton remembered. "Other times the two of us talked deeply and personally about the need to put the U.S.-China relationship on a sound footing for the sake of future generations." In one early meeting with Clinton, Dai pulled out a picture of his baby granddaughter, telling her, "this is what we're in it for." It struck a chord with Clinton. "It was concern for the welfare of children that got me into public service in the first place," Clinton later recalled.[75]

For Dai and other top Chinese diplomats, building this kind of rapport with American officials was useful in its own right, but perhaps more important, it demonstrated how profoundly China's international status had changed during their lifetimes. "Before the 21st century, which major country would agree to enter into a strategic dialogue with China like they do today?" Dai asked as he reflected on his career in 2016. "None of them!" he answered. "They looked down on you and thought you weren't qualified to enter into strategic dialogue with them."[76]

***

No one personified the mixture of pride and jumpiness better than Yang Jiechi, who took over as foreign minister in 2007—the youngest in the history of the People's Republic and the first born after the Communist Revolution. A slight man with slick-back hair, a round face, and spectacles, Yang was born in May 1950. He learned English after being admitted to the Shanghai

Foreign Languages School, one of only eleven such schools in China at the time.[77] Yang later recalled that he'd shivered inside unheated classrooms, his hands too cold to hold a pen.[78]

After leaving school during the Cultural Revolution, he worked for four years in the Pujiang Electricity Meter Factory before being chosen in 1972 as a trainee in the foreign ministry.[79] Zhou Enlai selected Yang to study in England together with a cohort from his school in Shanghai. He then served as an interpreter for the future president George H. W. Bush and his family on their tour of Tibet in the late 1970s, during which the Bushes nicknamed him "Tiger Yang." In 1998, Yang became the youngest vice foreign minister since the PRC was established. In late 2000, he was appointed ambassador to the United States.

Yang's career very nearly ended there. He suffered a massive heart attack in Washington in the winter of 2004. A chain smoker in an incredibly stressful job, Yang's prospects were not good when he was rushed to George Washington University Hospital. But Vice President Dick Cheney's heart doctor saved Yang's life and the ambassador left Washington shortly after. White House officials who met with him during this period said Yang appeared frail, and wondered whether they'd seen him for the last time.

But back home, Yang went on a disciplined health regimen in which he swam every single day—often at the foreign ministry-owned St. Regis Hotel in Beijing, which arguably had the best swimming pool in the capital. He not only survived but went on to greater heights as the leading voice on China's foreign policy—as foreign minister, state councilor, and eventually a member of the Politburo.[80]

In many ways, Yang personifies the foreign ministry's strengths and weaknesses. He has near perfect English and an exceptional grasp of American politics, culture, and history. He is always well briefed and makes sure his counterparts know it. People familiar with his daily routine say that he reads the New York Times each day from the news sections through to culture and the obituaries—and delights in dropping the details that he has gleaned into conversations with his counterparts, a technique younger diplomats consciously emulate. When making small talk before the start of official meetings, Yang comes across relaxed, often telling jokes or pithy anecdotes.[81]

But there's another side to Yang. When a foreign counterpart raises a sensitive topic, he wipes his smile from his face, turns red, and raises his voice. US embassy cables released by Wikileaks recount a meeting with American officials in 1997 on the topic of Britain's return of Hong Kong to Chinese rule. Yang became "visibly annoyed," as soon as the issue was raised, the cable said. "Noting that Britain did not have a bill of rights, Yang asked rhetorically why Hong Kong needed a bill of rights if Britain did not." Yang also lashed out at British condescension: the British "believed they could do whatever they liked," he said. China, he told the Americans, would "not swallow" Britain's attempt to put China "in its place."[82]

Yang's pushiness can be deeply off-putting for foreign counterparts. In contrast with the sense of connection Hillary Clinton felt with Dai Bingguo, she described Yang as "an unapologetic nationalist" with whom she had "our share of tense exchanges." Clinton recalled how during one late-night meeting in 2012, Yang began "waxing on about China's many superlative achievements, including its athletic dominance."[83]

Yang's Jekyll and Hyde approach to negotiation is deliberate and carefully controlled. "He's a guy who has this ability to, when necessary, turn on extreme charm and when necessary turn on extreme outrage. He does both well," said Dennis Wilder, one of Yang's long-term American interlocutors. "He's probably showing off to the rest of the delegation. They're all going to report on the meeting and it will go up the system," said Wilder. "He can flip that switch. It's an act of tremendous self-control and self-will. I have been in meetings that were just withering, where you wanted to run out of the room. But you never got the sense he was out of control."[84]

Yang's appointment drove continuity at the top of the foreign ministry, even extending to its hierarchical culture and regimented style. A protocol guide published in 2009 includes instructions on how to get along with your boss: don't disagree with him in front of others and give him credit when you achieve something, it suggests. When you go for a meeting with a superior, knock before entering and wait to be asked to sit or speak. Once seated, place your hands on your legs and maintain eye contact.[85]

The organization—staffed by some 4,000 diplomats by 2012[86]—also remained highly secretive. Even if the enforcement of the "buddy system" was laxer in the 2000s than it had been in previous decades, most diplomats were expected to follow the rule most of the time. Indeed, the first chapter of the same book on diplomatic protocol by former diplomat Zhang Guobin teaches readers that diplomats are not permitted any kind of personal contact with their hosts on overseas visits.[87]

The foreign ministry placed strict limits on cadres' personal lives. Unlike the vast majority of their counterparts around the world, Chinese diplomats are forbidden from marrying foreigners and even discouraged from marrying Chinese nationals whose political loyalty might be open to suspicion.[88] "Now that you are in the foreign ministry, the most important thing is that you put loyalty to the motherland and to the people first," former foreign minister Li Zhaoxing told a group of young diplomats. "In love and in marriage, you should also look for those who love their country."[89]

Chinese diplomacy continued to serve the Chinese Communist Party above all else. "If you want to understand China, you must understand the Communist Party, Dai Bingguo told American counterparts in the mid-2000s. "If you want to deal with China, you must deal with the Communist Party."[90]

**

The 2008 Summer Olympics put the Communist Party's newfound confidence on full display, together with its enduring insecurities. Beijing pulled out all the stops to host the games—the city improved its air quality every year for six years in the run-up to its hosting of the world's leading international sporting event, earmarked $1.6 billion to improve the water supply, seeded clouds to force rain, and evicted some 1.5 million residents from their homes to modernize the city. It also launched a public education campaign to curb public spitting, belching, and soup slurping, somewhat reminiscent of the training communist China's first diplomats had gone through in the 1950s.[91]

As China prepared for the games, opponents of the regime and its human rights violations used the occasion to step up their campaigns. Reporters Without Borders protested Beijing's hosting of the Olympics with a striking reimagining of the Olympic rings made out of handcuffs, while the Free Tibet Campaign employed a similar motif, using bullet holes instead.[92] Five months before the games were due to open in August, widespread and often violent protests broke out in Tibet in March. They were met with a fierce government crackdown and the effective imposition of martial law across the region.[93] As the Olympic torch relay made its way across the world through March and April, it too was met with widespread protests from Athens, through Paris, San Francisco, Delhi, and Bangkok.[94]

The government tasked Chinese diplomats with ensuring things went smoothly. Consular officers in San Francisco organized between 6,000 and 8,000 Chinese students in counter-demonstrations that aimed to drown out protesters, providing them with free transport, packed lunches, and T-shirts.

The government even flew in intelligence officials to help coordinate the activities. Similar operations took place in London, Canberra, Paris, and beyond. When anti-China activists were pelted with rocks in Seoul, a foreign ministry spokesperson refused to condemn the violence.[95]

Diplomats responded curtly to any criticism and attacked foreign media for its coverage of the protests. Fu Ying, then China's ambassador to London, wrote in the UK's *Daily Telegraph*, "Many complain about China not allowing enough access to the media. In China, the view is that the Western media needs to make an effort to earn respect."[96]

Nevertheless, the Olympic Games themselves were a huge success and a diplomatic, as well as a sporting, triumph for China. Beijing attracted eight heads of state and heads of government to the games, including President George W. Bush and his father former president George H. W. Bush. The pair attended a private lunch in the Communist Party leadership compound of Zhongnanhai with Hu Jintao. Yang Jiechi, who had served as a translator for Bush Senior three decades earlier, accompanied the two presidents to events including the US Olympic Men's Basketball Team's game against China.[97] The games were the most public validation of the regime since its founding in 1949. More than anything else, they symbolized the success of the country's decades-long quest for international respectability after the Tiananmen Square massacre of 1989.

***

Just three weeks after the closing ceremony of the Summer Olympics, Lehman Brothers, one of America's oldest and largest investment banks, filed for Chapter 11 bankruptcy. The venerable Wall Street institution, which traced its roots back to 1844, had become the largest victim of the subprime mortgage crisis that ravaged financial markets and led to the biggest economic downturn since the Great Depression. Negotiations to prevent the total meltdown of America's financial system were strained and acrimonious: at one point Treasury secretary Hank Paulson literally bent down on one knee to plead for the support of Nancy Pelosi, the House Speaker.[98] In October, the US unemployment rate surged to 10.2 percent, reaching double digits for the first time in twenty-six years.[99]

Less than two decades after the dynamism of American capitalism and ideals had propelled it to victory in the Cold War, the world's lone superpower suddenly seemed vulnerable. Global leaders in Beijing and beyond could feel the contours of global politics shifting beneath their feet. When

Dai Bingguo traveled to Paris that October, he was startled by French president Nicolas Sarkozy's frank assessment that the crisis had "shattered the American dream."[100] Whereas gaining the credibility needed to host the Olympics had taken two decades of painstaking work, the financial crisis changed China's international position faster than its leaders could ever have anticipated.

China's response was decisive. On November 9, Premier Wen Jiabao announced a 4 trillion yuan stimulus program, which would pump the equivalent of 15 percent of China's GDP into railways, airports, affordable housing, and industrial upgrading. Asian markets rallied on the news: stocks in Hong Kong, Shanghai, and Tokyo jumped more than 5 percent after having been depressed for much of the year.[101] Although these measures created significant distortions in its domestic economy, Chinese leaders nevertheless basked in the warm approval of the international media and governments around the world as they established their country as a bulwark against the worsening of the crisis.[102]

Just a few days after China announced its stimulus package, President Hu Jintao jetted off to Washington for a summit to discuss the world economy. During a formal dinner of leaders at the White House, Hu was seated directly to the left of Bush, President Luiz Inácio Lula da Silva of Brazil to his right. The meeting, the first of the grouping now known as the G-20, was a powerful symbol of how the global balance of power was shifting and of how quickly China found itself in a leadership role. Just five years earlier, its leaders had agonized over whether to even send Hu a Group of Eight summit as a guest. During the course of the G-20 summit, Hu even took Hank Paulson aside for a teachable moment: "I bet you're glad we didn't move the currency faster than we did. I hope you now understand why. Some of the things you wanted us to do would have been dangerous. Now we're stable and can stimulate the economy, and that's helping us and the whole world."[103] It was a humbling moment for American leadership and a signal to Chinese leaders that their economic model had come of age.

American actions inadvertently played into the sense that the global balance was tipping in China's favor. During a trip to Asia in early 2009, Secretary of State Hillary Clinton said that concerns over human rights couldn't "interfere" with efforts to combat the crisis and thanked Chinese policymakers for their "confidence in United States Treasuries."[104] Deputy Secretary of State James Steinberg talked about the importance of "strategic reassurance" with China.[105]

Chinese diplomats in Washington sensed a change in mood. "During my time in the United States, I felt a deep sense of 'American anxiety' filled every meeting and dialogue," wrote Ruan Zongze, a government scholar who was posted to the Chinese embassy in Washington between 2007 and 2011.[106] Against this backdrop, Chinese officials began to re-evaluate the status of their political system, which had for so long been criticized by the West. Some even began to speak openly about a "China model" that others might seek to emulate. Talking to a group of Chinese soldiers in 2009, Chen Jian, China's former ambassador to France, said "the fact that China was first to emerge from the financial crisis has significantly increased China's international status." He added that the crisis had "broken the myth that the Western model led by America is universal" and demonstrated the rise of a "China model."[107]

Soon, this new confidence began to creep into China's diplomatic playbook. At a conference for Chinese ambassadors in July 2009, Hu Jintao called for Chinese diplomats to adopt a more active international posture. He called for envoys to promote Chinese political and economic power, together with a strengthened image and moral persuasiveness; Foreign Minister Yang Jiechi and state media soon began referring to Hu's call as the "four strengths." Most notably of all, the conference added two Chinese characters to Deng Xiaoping's dictum for keeping a low international profile: it would now "maintain a low profile and bide its time while *actively* (*jiji*) getting something accomplished."[108]

When dealing with foreigners, a new sense of political high-handedness peppered China's usual jitters over foreign influence. China kept President Barack Obama on a tight leash during his first visit to the country in November 2009, permitting no questions during his "press conference" with the Chinese president—an appearance so stilted that it was parodied on *Saturday Night Live*.[109] Just one month later, in December, China effectively derailed the Copenhagen Climate Talks by pitting developing countries against the West and even sending a vice foreign minister to a plenary session in place of Wen Jiabao to discuss climate challenges with President Obama, Angela Merkel, Nicolas Sarkozy, Gordon Brown, and other global leaders.[110] In the aftermath of the summit, Britain's climate secretary, Ed Miliband, accused China of attempting to "hijack" the talks.[111]

As China's diplomats crowed, other agencies were also becoming more assertive. On March 8, 2009, five Chinese vessels shadowed and then maneuvered dangerously close to a US Navy vessel, the *Impeccable*, south of Hainan

Island in the South China Sea, ordering it to leave the area or "suffer the consequences."[112] In January 2010, China's military suspended exchanges with the United States over its proposed arms sales to Taiwan.[113] There was a more than threefold increase in mentions of China's "core interests" in the official *People's Daily* between 2008 and 2010.[114]

Tensions reached a climax at the ASEAN Regional Forum in July 2010. After Secretary of State Hillary Clinton rebuked China for its increasing assertiveness in the South China Sea, Foreign Minister Yang Jiechi launched into what witnesses describe as an angry diatribe. Staring directly at Clinton, Yang attacked the American position for some twenty-five minutes before turning to face Singapore's representative: "China is a big country, and other countries are small countries, and that is just a fact," he said. Then Assistant Secretary of State Kurt Campbell passed a note to a colleague that simply read, "Wow."[115] China was no longer willing to be lectured by the world and it was ready to let everyone know it.

The assertiveness continued. In September that year, Japan's detention of a Chinese fishing boat captain for operating in Japanese-claimed waters and steering the ship into a Japanese coast guard vessel prompted rage in Beijing. In December, Beijing reacted with fury to the decision by the Nobel Committee to award the Nobel Peace Prize to Chinese democracy activist Liu Xiaobo despite a vocal opposition campaign by Chinese diplomats. It launched a campaign to prevent other countries from attending the award ceremony and blocked salmon imports from Norway, a sign of its increasing willingness to back up its diplomatic priorities with coercive economic diplomacy.

Still, many in China's foreign policy establishment doubted the wisdom of the new assertiveness. In December 2010, State Councilor Dai Bingguo published an essay urging China to maintain its historic policy of keeping an international low profile, known as "hide and bide."[116] Privately, Dai told American officials that they should avoid over-interpreting China's actions and that the country's leaders still sought good relations.[117] As late as 2012, China's former ambassador to France, Chen Jian, published a book with a chapter entitled "Long Live the Spirit of Hide and Bide."[118]

There also seemed to be disagreement over the direction of foreign policy between different government departments. In November 2012, the powerful Ministry of Public Security angered Southeast Asian nations by issuing new passports to Chinese citizens containing maps that showed disputed islands in the South China Sea as part of China's territory. The passports, which prompted official protests from the Philippines and Vietnam, were without the consent of, or even advance warning to, the foreign ministry. Yang Jiechi was said to be "furious" on hearing the news.[119]

Another incident just a few weeks later raised similar questions about who was driving Chinese foreign policy and where it was headed. Hainan province, the tropical island where the American EP-3 spy plane had crash-landed just over a decade earlier, issued new regulations that authorized border public security officials to board and search foreign vessels. When foreign diplomats asked the foreign ministry about what exactly the regulations would mean in practice, Chinese diplomats were unaware of the changes and unprepared for the questions.[120]

Were these events signs of new assertiveness, bureaucratic incompetence, or a mixture of the two? In a 2012 paper on strategic mistrust between the two countries, Kenneth Lieberthal, a former senior director for Asia on the National Security Council, and Wang Jisi, a top adviser to Dai Bingguo, wrote that China's future was "undetermined."[121] It was a fair assessment of where much of the world stood on China at the time: wary but undecided. Within a few years that debate would effectively be over in the United States and much of the rest of the world. In China, meanwhile, public debate over the country's future would be muzzled as Xi Jinping took center stage.

11

Overreach

In December 2013, Australia's foreign minister, Julie Bishop, sat down for a meeting she knew would be difficult. She was scheduled to meet with Wang Yi, China's new foreign minister, on her first official visit to China.

Tensions were already running high. Bishop's ministry had previously called in China's ambassador in Canberra, Ma Zhaoxu, asking him to explain Beijing's provocative decision to declare an air defense identification zone in the disputed East China Sea.[1] Australia had sided with the United States and Japan by protesting the move, which required any aircraft traversing the zone to comply with identification procedures or face "defensive measures."[2]

Still, diplomatic norms should have prevented things from getting out of hand. By convention, top diplomats refrain from criticizing each other directly when they meet face-to-face. China had already had the chance to publicly protest Australia's actions, which foreign ministry spokesman Qin Gang had called "irresponsible" and "mistaken."[3] What's more, China was playing host. The chances of a public blowup seemed slim.

Bishop was shown into the meeting room in Beijing and seated at a long rectangular wooden table with fresh flowers arranged at the center. As host, Wang spoke first as television cameras captured the opening minutes of the meeting. He didn't hold back.

"I have to point out that what Australia has said and done with regard to China's establishment of the air defense identification zone in the East China Sea has jeopardized bilateral mutual trust and affected the sound growth of bilateral relations," Wang said, looking directly at Bishop from across the table.

For anyone accustomed to the opening of bilateral meetings anywhere—especially in China—Wang's actions were provocative. Such moments are usually reserved for pleasantries about the weather and bland statements about shared interests. The substance is usually reserved for after journalists are ushered out.

Not this time. Wang continued. "The whole of Chinese society and the general public are deeply dissatisfied with this," he said. "This is not what we want to see." Wang went on to tell Bishop the relationship between the two countries had entered a "critical period" and that he hoped Australia would view things from a "strategic and long-term perspective." To do so, Wang asserted, Australia should "move towards the same direction with China," and "properly handle sensitive issues."

Australia's ambassador to China, Frances Adamson, quietly slid Bishop a note that read simply, "This is going terribly badly."

Bishop responded to Wang coolly, saying that Australia respected "China's right to speak out on issues" and that she hoped China would extend the same rights to Australia. The pair then proceeded to dinner where they sat in near silence, staring past each other for an hour.[4]

During a hearing in Australia's senate, a senior Australian foreign affairs official would later say that he had "never in 30 years encountered such rudeness."[5] Others agreed. "It's the first time I've seen a senior Chinese, during the photo opportunity that precedes such bilateral meetings, vent a disagreement in this way with any country, even with the Japanese at difficult times in their relations," Stephen FitzGerald, Australia's first ambassador to the People's Republic, later told an interviewer.[6]

Bishop sought to play down tensions immediately after the meeting, saying that "friends don't always agree on every issue."[7] Recalling the incident years later, she was more frank, describing Wang's intervention as a "dressing down like you can't believe," which left her "furious." "That's why we have ambassadors," she said. "They then sort it out after you've left the country."[8]

Nervous insecurity was perhaps not the first explanation Bishop would have thought of for Wang's behavior. Beijing had emerged from the Global Financial Crisis as a leader in the G-20 and the Chinese economy had become a crucial driver of global growth. It had successfully hosted the Olympics. Virtually every government on earth recognized the People's Republic as China's legitimate government and few dared to directly question its claims to Tibet or Taiwan.

And yet all was not well inside China's foreign ministry. Wang had become minister that March, at the same time as Xi Jinping had been made China's head of state and less than six months after Xi had assumed leadership of the Communist Party. Wang needed to prove to his new boss that he and his ministry were capable of keeping up with Xi's confident and assertive style on the global stage. As the political atmosphere grew more intense at home, Chinese diplomats became ever more strident overseas.

Xi Jinping's foreign policy took the assertive turn which had begun under his predecessor and made it more confident, consistent, and ambitious. The change of approach would lead to a global pushback against China, which led many in the country to feel that Xi had overreached and was now raising the costs of China's continued rise. As Chinese diplomats played catch-up with Xi's ambitious agenda, they would find themselves hobbled by the same limitations and shortcomings that their predecessors had faced for generations.

***

Xi Jinping's hawkishness on foreign policy had long been rumored in Beijing, but it hadn't been put on public display until February 2009. The princeling son of a reform-minded vice premier, Xi Zhongxun, Xi was born in 1953. He spent his childhood in the rarefied world of Communist leadership compounds and schools reserved for children of the Party elite. Xi's father later found himself on the wrong side of Mao and was persecuted and imprisoned in Beijing. As a teenager, Xi was sent to live in the countryside in the village of Liangjiahe, just outside of Yan'an, where Mao had cemented his control of the Party at the end of the Long March.

Xi returned to Beijing in 1975 to attend Tsinghua University as a "worker-peasant-soldier" student. After graduating in 1979, Xi turned his attention to politics. His first job was serving as an aide to Geng Biao, one of the original ambassador generals who had peeked out at the Romanian ambassador presenting his credentials in 1950. Geng, a close friend of Xi's father, was now serving as defense minister, a position where he helped Deng Xiaoping gain full control over China's military. After a brief period working for Geng, Xi decided to leave Beijing for the provinces, realizing that he would need a power base independent of his father in order to realize his ambitions. He told a friend in Beijing that he "would be back one day."[9]

And so he was. After rising up the Party ranks in the coastal provinces of Fujian and Zhejiang, Xi returned to Beijing in 2007 as a member of the Politburo Standing Committee. In March the next year, he was appointed vice president—a sign that he was next in line to lead China. Following Party conventions, Xi maintained a low profile until his position was secure. When, as vice president, Xi met with George W. Bush and his father George H. W. Bush during the 2008 Olympics, he stuck closely to the administration's talking points, and came across as courteous and well-briefed, but unremarkable.[10]

Xi's first public foray into foreign policy came with a bang. During a February 2009 trip to Mexico, he addressed an audience of diplomats, businessmen, and students. "There are certain foreigners with full bellies who have nothing better to do than point the finger," Xi complained, referring to Western demands for human rights in China. "China does not export revolution, hunger, poverty, nor does China cause you any headaches," Xi said indignantly. "What else is there to say?"[11] The speech was not widely publicized inside China, but online nationalists who saw footage on Hong Kong television stations were impressed. "Boss Xi has set a good example for China's foreign policy!" wrote one commentator. "We are tired of the foreign ministry's diplomatic condemnations and protests. We want more plain talk like that! It's time for foreigners to get a taste of our temper!"[12]

The speech also caught the attention of some of the foreigners Xi presumably had in mind. The deputy chief of mission at the American embassy in Mexico cabled Washington to report Xi's "uncharacteristic outburst" that "sharply contrasted from the overall theme of his visit," which was supposed to focus on cooperation.[13]

Xi's remarks were no gaffe. In fact, his line on foreigners with "full bellies" was part of a set-piece speech he repeated at Chinese embassies around the world from Latin America to Europe as he prepared to grasp the levers of money and power in China.[14] To those who witnessed it, the message was clear: changes were coming for Chinese diplomacy.

Foreign leaders also began to realize that Xi Jinping would bring sweeping changes to Chinese domestic politics and foreign policy. Domestically, Xi seemed preoccupied with political stability. In the summer of 2011, when Xi hosted then vice president Joe Biden for a get-to-know-you discussion, Xi was intensely curious about the Arab Spring and the rising challenges to authoritarian ruling parties then under way in the Middle East. Their mistake, Xi told Biden, was to lose touch with the people, becoming self-satisfied and isolated. The Communist Party needed to avoid going down that road, he said.[15] Xi's approach to foreign policy, meanwhile, seemed to assume a far more central role for China in the world. During a 2012 trip to Washington aimed at building trust before he took power, Xi described the two countries' relationship as a "new type of relationship among major countries."[16] The phrase suggested a new parity between the two powers that made many in Washington uncomfortable.

Xi's reassessment of the global order was in many ways understandable. Events in the West in the lead-up to Xi's accession to power were hardly a picture of stability. In October 2011, Obama had announced a drawdown from Iraq, but the decade-long American conflict in Afghanistan continued. Eurozone unemployment was above 10 percent in March 2012. That same year, Vladimir Putin orchestrated a third term as Russia's president and Kim Jong-un successfully consolidated power in North Korea after the death of his father. In September, the ratings firm Moody's warned that America's triple-A credit rating was at risk if lawmakers failed to come up with a debt reduction plan.

When Xi finally took power in November 2012, he made his nationalist agenda even more explicit. One of his very first acts as leader was setting out his administration's framework slogan "the Chinese dream," which he defined as the "great rejuvenation of the Chinese people." Chinese leaders had been using the refrain for more than a century, but Xi put it front and center of his domestic and foreign policy ambitions. He never officially repudiated Deng Xiaoping's calls for China to "hide" its capabilities and "bide" its time, but his actions over the coming years would make it clear that he had done so in practice. It would present China's diplomats with their greatest challenge since the Tiananmen Square massacre.

***

The daunting task of keeping up with Xi's foreign policy ambitions fell to Wang Yi. Born in Beijing in 1953, the same year as Xi, Wang also spent a good chunk of his adolescence as a "sent down" youth during the Cultural Revolution, when he spent eight years laboring on a farm in the northeast. Always a harder worker than others, Wang taught himself literature and history, a former classmate told the *Christian Science Monitor*. He was "quite open minded. He did not just accept what he was told," the classmate remembered.[17]

After the Cultural Revolution, Wang was admitted to Beijing International Studies University, a foreign ministry feeder school. He then joined the Asian Affairs Department in the foreign ministry and started climbing the ranks as a Japan specialist.[18] He became fluent in both Japanese and English and even spent a year in Washington studying at Georgetown University from 1997 to 1998.

Wang's background was modest but, like Li Zhaoxing and Dai Bingguo before him, he married into China's foreign policy aristocracy. Wang's father-in-law, Qian Jiadong, had been one of Zhou Enlai's top aides and China's ambassador to the United Nations in Geneva.[19]

A smoother talker and far more naturally charming than his prede-cessor, Yang Jiechi, Wang proved to be popular inside the ministry. Chinese diplomats would later describe Wang as a true "politician," whereas Yang had been simply a "bureaucrat."[20] It didn't hurt that Wang was a looker. With bushy eyebrows and salt-and-pepper hair that cut a sharp contrast with the generic black dye used by his peers, even China's usually prudish state media dubbed him a "silver fox."[21]

Like any foreign ministry Japan hand, Wang had long been aware of the need to prove his nationalist credentials. He'd also fulfilled several high-stakes assignments from conveying China's wishes to Pakistan after 9/11 to helping shepherd the Six-Party Talks on North Korea. Ensuring that the for-eign ministry lived up to Xi's expectations was his greatest challenge yet.

Wang's solution was to double down on the founding values of the min-istry. After all, it had been set up to help a closed and paranoid political system cope with a more open outside world. Many of these founding princi-ples were perfectly suited to the emerging mood in Beijing.

Wang started with the rank and file. In August 2013, just under six months after being appointed foreign minister, he addressed a group of 251 fresh recruits in the ministry's Olive Room. He welcomed the "new comrades-in-arms" to the "diplomatic front," embracing the military metaphor that had helped Chinese diplomats understand their role since 1949.[22] "I hear that more than half of you were born in the 1990s. When I was your age, I was still laboring in the villages," he told them. "I didn't go to university until I was 24 years old, after the college entrance exam was reinstated, and so I envy you, but I'm also happy for you."

He framed their roles in terms of Xi's ambitions for China. "You've entered the diplomatic corps at a special and important time in our history," Wang told them. "Our country is closer to the goal of national rejuvenation than at any other time, and closer than ever before to becoming a global power," he said. "History has handed you the final baton."

Wang also acknowledged the view in some quarters that the ministry had been too weak in the past. "Ideals and convictions are our spiritual calcium. Without them we risk osteoporosis," he said, referring to the disease that softens the bones. "General Secretary Xi has told us that ideals guide our lives and convictions determine the success or failure of our cause." Wang's mes-sage was clear: under his leadership, the ministry would shake off the image for weakness that had prompted members of the public to post it calcium tablets in the 2000s.

Wang looked to foreign ministry traditions to fulfill Xi's ambitions. "Zhou Enlai will always be a model for diplomats," Wang told the group. "He famously said that diplomats are the People's Liberation Army in civilian clothing. A civilian army not only needs to maintain strict discipline and obedience to commands, but also needs to cultivate a strong character and work style . . . to serve the people like the PLA."

China's diplomats had to show more than just a newfound confidence. They had to demonstrate political obedience. Xi's rapid consolidation of power at home had been accompanied by a sweeping crackdown on free speech and civil society, as well as an anti-corruption campaign that would go on to ensnare more than 1.5 million officials.

In early 2013, a confidential directive called Document Number 9 began to circulate. It took aim at "Western constitutional democracy" and "universal values," while warning that "Western forces hostile to China" were "infiltrating the ideological sphere."[23] The document sent a chill through government ministries, educational institutions, and China's already embattled civil society. The following year, Qiao Mu, an outspoken liberal professor at Beijing Foreign Studies University, another foreign ministry feeder school, was removed from his teaching duties for unspecified "discipline violations."[24] China's diplomats would once again be operating in a high-stakes domestic environment, with serious consequences for perceived political mistakes.

***

The boldness continued. In June, Wang had accompanied Xi to Sunnylands, a 200-acre estate on Frank Sinatra and Bob Hope Drives outside Palm Springs, California. A somewhat unscripted "ties-off" meeting between Xi and Obama had been arranged to help the two leaders get to know each other and develop a working relationship. While Xi and Obama didn't build any personal chemistry, Wang began to develop a good relationship with Xi on this visit and subsequent international trips. Barriers broke down as they drank China's fiery Maotai liquor together, sometimes managing to outdrink other officials on the plane.[25]

Obama publicly dubbed the meeting "terrific" but in private there were signs that American patience with China over a range of issues was starting to wear thin.[26] At one point, Obama challenged Xi over Chinese hacking of American companies and government departments. Xi responded noncommittally with an allegory from Chinese opera about a warrior fighting an adversary in a dark room only to find out that he was battling against himself. The point was that the United States couldn't possibly know who was behind the attacks. Obama responded curtly, according to a person who witnessed the exchange: "The difference is that we know it's you."[27]

The significance of the foreign policy changes underway truly became clear a year later in Kazakhstan. In September 2013, Xi Jinping announced a vision for a "New Silk Road" in a speech to officials and students at Nazarbayev University in the capital, Astana. "I can almost hear the ring of the camel bells and wisps of smoke in the desert," he told his audience as he presented his vision for a prosperous and interconnected Asia, bankrolled by China.[28] The next month, speaking to the Indonesian parliament, he announced plans for a complementary "Maritime Silk Road." He also spoke of his intention to create an Asian Infrastructure Investment Bank that would help fund these initiatives.[29] These policies, later rebranded the "Belt and Road Initiative," marked the boldest departure yet from Deng Xiaoping's dictum that China should "hide" its capabilities and "bide" its time.

In October, Xi presided over a "work forum" on China's diplomacy toward its neighbors—the first such meeting since 2006. It was attended by the entire Politburo Standing Committee, top Party and government leaders, and a select group of Chinese ambassadors. Xi said China's foreign policy should be more "proactive" (*fen fa you wei*). Xi also used the phrase "top-level design" to describe his approach to diplomacy, an engineering term his predecessors had applied to economic policymaking. It was a hint that more centralized control was coming.[30]

Xi's actions on China's periphery seemed to further confirm the creeping assertiveness of the country's foreign policy. China had seized the Scarborough Shoal in the disputed South China Sea a few months before he took office. Xi followed up by declaring the Air Defense Identification Zone that Wang Yi would end up defending to Bishop in November 2013. Alarm in Washington escalated even more dramatically for those with the right kinds of security clearance. Unknown to the general public, American spy satellites began to pick up images of rapid Chinese island-building in the South China Sea in late 2013.[31] Over the next twenty months, China dredged and reclaimed seventeen times as much land as all the other claimants combined had dredged over the preceding four decades.[32] Beijing was now taking a far more provocative approach to its territorial claims in the South China Sea, through which $5 trillion in ship-borne trade passes each year. China's claims overlap with those of the Philippines, Malaysia, Vietnam, Taiwan, and Brunei.

In a March 2014 speech in Paris, Xi laid out the changes to Chinese foreign policy in the most explicit terms yet. "Napoleon Bonaparte once said that China 'is a sleeping lion,' and 'when China wakes up, it will shake the world,' " he said. "In fact, the lion of China has awoken, but what the world sees now is a peaceful, amiable, civilized lion."[33] In a speech in Shanghai in May that year he called on "the people of Asia to run the affairs of Asia."[34] The United States, Xi implied, was no longer welcome in China's neighborhood.

***

With such profound changes taking place in its foreign policy, Beijing needed its diplomats to reassure foreigners more than ever. This should have been China's civilian army's time to shine. Instead, it became harder and harder for them to have open and frank conversations with their foreign counterparts.

Foreign diplomats were quick to notice the shift. In 2013, a European Union official in Brussels scheduled a coffee with a longtime Chinese diplomat contact, hoping to draw on his decades of expertise on an important geopolitical hotspot. The European official was prepared for their usual frank and informative chat, but the Chinese diplomat showed up with an accomplice and was unwilling to discuss his area of expertise. The European official pressed on, wondering why their conversation had become so impersonal. Eventually, the Chinese diplomat made a gentle suggestion: "You may consult Google on these questions. You will find many useful resources there. I hope this helps."[35] An American official sensed the scale of the shift during a 2014 meeting. Anticipating the kind of constructive dialogue he'd become accustomed to from his counterpart during the course of their long relationship, he was astonished when his interlocutor flipped open a briefing book and began reading, verbatim, from a series of pre-approved talking points— and doing so in Chinese, despite his usual preference for English.[36]

The dramatic shift reflected the changed political atmosphere in Beijing under Xi Jinping. Many diplomats were still uneasy with Xi's hardline approach to foreign policy, and, more important, were fearful as a result of political changes at home. Rumors swirled around the foreign ministry about who might fall next in Xi's sweeping anti-corruption campaign.[37] Some believed that the Chinese president might not be willing to relinquish power after two terms in office. Already, some were speculating that Xi would become leader for life. The effect on the Chinese bureaucracy was stultifying.

Economic officials stopped approving projects for fear of making the wrong decision.[38] Diplomats kept their heads down and stuck closely to official talking points.

For the foreign ministry, this was history repeating itself. Just as Zhou Enlai had advised diplomats to stick closely to the wording of official Party documents during the Cultural Revolution, Chinese officials were now doing so out of instinct. American China hands recognized the pattern. "Whenever there is a more nationalist, orthodox administration that goes into power, the foreign ministry is the first suspected agency. That's where people go to root out traitors," said Susan Thornton, a former acting assistant secretary of state for East Asian and Pacific Affairs. "The foreign ministry went through that at the start of Xi Jinping. They felt like they didn't have much leeway and were all on edge."[39]

As a result, Chinese diplomacy became both more assertive and more stilted and inflexible. These changes played out in the high-level dialogues established in the 2000s. In 2014, Yang Jiechi, now a state councilor—the rough equivalent of an American cabinet official—made a visit to Washington. Yang was one of the Chinese diplomats most adept at shifting with the political currents in Beijing and had deployed performative anger throughout his career to showcase his nationalist credentials. On this occasion, Yang's approach hit up against the loquacious sincerity of John Kerry, the secretary of state.

Over the course of a lengthy discussion with Yang, Kerry broached the subject of Tibet—long one of the most acute points of tension in Washington's relationship with Beijing. If Yang just tried to get to know the Dalai Lama, Tibet's spiritual leader in exile, he'd discover that he wasn't such a bad guy, Kerry said. Boldly, some might say naïvely, Kerry hoped to change Yang's mind on the subject. Aware that Beijing would receive a readout of everything he discussed with Kerry, Yang launched into one of his signature diatribes. "He is a wolf in sheep's clothing," Yang exclaimed. "He is devious and he is tricking you," he added. Kerry, already late for his next meeting, continued making his point, but the conversation went nowhere.[40] If the secretary of state had known more about Chinese diplomats, he would have known the topic was a non-starter from the outset. After all, Yang's main audience was in Beijing.

Xi Jinping seemed to like the new mood and kept pushing it further. In November 2014, he gathered China's senior diplomats and military elite in Beijing for the Central Foreign Affairs Work Conference. Attended by top civilian and military officials and nearly every Chinese ambassador, the meeting was aimed at setting the tone for Chinese diplomacy in years to come. While he drew on many familiar themes, including Zhou Enlai's Five Principles of Peaceful Coexistence, a new focus was evident. It was time, Xi said, for China to embrace "major country diplomacy," while stressing the need to uphold China's "rights and interests."[41] In other words, it was time for China to assume a leading place in the world and take what rightfully belonged to it.

Xi also said that the Communist Party should "strengthen" its leadership of the country's foreign affairs process. The conduct of foreign policy should become more "coordinated," he said, and foreign affairs officials should "strengthen their ranks." Xi's remarks were a recognition that Chinese foreign policy making had become too fragmented in the 2000s. He planned to take back control.

Some in the foreign ministry relished the new call for toughness. One official scholar described it as a "diplomatic manifesto to secure the Chinese dream."[42] In late 2014, Chen Jin, a Communist Party scholar, said that the foreign ministry's leadership was now boasting that fewer and fewer people were sending them calcium in the mail.[43] Others were more apprehensive, but they kept their thoughts to themselves for now.

***

The push to act tough came as other ominous developments were making China's policies more difficult for its diplomats to sell, especially in Washington. In March 2015, the Chinese government announced plans to restrict the operations of foreign NGOs and their domestic partners in China by forcing them to register with the police.[44] In July, public security officials launched a sweeping crackdown on human rights lawyers across the country. Authorities detained about 250 lawyers and activists in the crackdown; some were paraded on television making humiliating confessions or portrayed as subversives or troublemakers.[45] Foreign diplomats looked on in horror. "A lot of our contacts, such as human rights lawyers, were being thrown into jail," remembered one former senior Obama administration official. "People were very upset."[46]

At the same time, American business groups were beginning to lose faith in China. Although the 2013 Third Plenum, a key Party meeting to map out economic policy, had promised a "decisive" role for market forces in the allocation of resources, the government's reform agenda had descended into a combination of piecemeal liberalization and foot-dragging. Xi pushed controversial industrial policies through an initiative called Made in China 2025. Launched in 2015, it included plans for China to become a leader in ten industries that would define the future of the world economy, including aerospace, new energy vehicles, artificial intelligence, robotics, and biotechnology. Some 77 percent of firms surveyed at the end of 2015 by the American Chamber of Commerce in China said they felt "less welcome" than before in China, up from 60 percent the previous year.[47] Foreign investors and executives, once China's most reliable friends in the West, began to quietly cheer America's hardening attitude.

Another area of tension was cybersecurity. State-backed hackers were targeting the US government and American companies. Tensions seemed set to come to a head as Xi prepared for his first state visit to America in September 2015. A threat by the Obama administration to impose sanctions over Chinese cyber espionage was averted only by an eleventh-hour visit to Washington by Meng Jianzhu, Xi's head of domestic security. "This is not just a matter of us being mildly upset," Obama said.[48]

Still, American officials emerged with signs of hope from the Obama-Xi summit. China had signaled that it would cut down on cyber spying, and Xi even stood on the South Lawn of the White House to publicly pledge that China would not militarize the disputed Spratly Islands in the South China Sea. For American officials who had spent months working to secure the promise, Xi's statement represented a major achievement, and a signal that the two sides might still be able to communicate in good faith. Before long, though, it became clear that China did indeed intend to militarize the islands, and that cyberattacks had resumed on their previous scale. The broken promises were an affront to American officials who'd taken them in good faith. One former top Pentagon official in the Obama administration described the moment as crucial to the deterioration of attitudes toward China in Washington.[49]

Although few of Xi's aggressive and imperious policies were the product of the foreign ministry, Chinese diplomats nevertheless took the rap from their foreign counterparts. They responded just as they had in the past when challenged abroad and under pressure at home: by lashing out. In June 2016, when a Canadian reporter asked the country's foreign minister, Stephane Dion, about human rights and the case of a Canadian citizen detained in China over alleged espionage, Wang Yi interjected. "Your question is full of arrogance and prejudice against China," he said. "This is totally unacceptable."[50]

Wang's performance went viral back home. His remarks resonated with online nationalists who had long hoped for greater assertiveness from the country's top envoys and prompted hundreds of messages of support on the Chinese social media platform Tianya. One netizen wrote, "Support Minister Wang's performance! I hope China can produce even more politicians of that caliber."[51] Wang's dressing-down of the reporter became a popular subject for GIFs. A fan club devoted to him on Weibo attracted more than 130,000 followers. The Communist Youth League gushed that Wang "has the look of a foreign minister" and is "handsome from whichever angle."[52]

For many Chinese citizens and an increasing number of diplomats, Western criticisms of China reeked of hypocrisy, and Wang's comments were a welcome refrain. After all, Western nations had their own share of problems. In April 2015, the death of twenty-five-year-old black man Freddie Gray in Baltimore sparked violent protests over police racism and brutality and helped reignite the Black Lives Matter movement. In November, terrorist attacks in Paris left 130 dead, leading French president François Hollande to declare "war" against the Islamic State. Over the course of the year, an influx of migrants from the Middle East and North Africa hit a Europe still struggling to recover from the 2008–2009 financial crisis, fueling a resurgence in far-right nationalist parties from Poland to Sweden and Denmark. The West, many Chinese officials felt, would be better off focusing on its own problems.

Chinese diplomats responded equally stridently to the July 2016 decision of an international tribunal in The Hague to rebuke China for its behavior in the South China Sea, arguing that its expansive claims to sovereignty over the region had no legal basis. The case, brought by the Philippines, was the first time the Chinese government had been summoned before the international justice system. China's ambassador to the Netherlands, Wu Ken, described the ruling as "wastepaper" and a "disgrace to international law." He also called on "certain countries who do not belong to this region" to cease "sabre rattling and fabricating disputes."[53]

Not everyone in China's foreign policy establishment was comfortable with the new tone. Chinese scholars visiting the United States in the months after the ruling confided in their American counterparts that many in the Chinese foreign policy community were embarrassed by the attacks on the judges.[54] Some former diplomats heard echoes of past mistakes. "As we head toward the center of the world stage, we have to be careful of our mindset," wrote Wu Jianmin, China's former ambassador to France. "There are some people who subconsciously want [China to] become a leader" and who believe that "hide and bide is outdated." Their mindsets, he said, were a relic of Cultural Revolution slogans about how China's revolution was at the center of the world.[55]

China's aggressive diplomacy continued anyway. Then Donald Trump came marching into the increasing uncertainty.

**

As in much of the world, Donald Trump's victory in November 2016 took Chinese diplomats by surprise. Cables sent back to Beijing from the Chinese embassy in Washington did not communicate the extent of the populist shift in American public opinion, in part because they failed to spot it and in part because of a pervasive fear of passing bad news up the chain in the Chinese bureaucracy. China spent the months before Trump's inauguration trying to make sense of the real estate mogul turned reality television star who had accused China of "raping" the United States during his election campaign, and promised to start a trade war.

Xi Jinping was clear from the outset that China would not submit to American pressure. During his final meeting with Barack Obama on the sidelines of the 2016 APEC summit in Peru just after Trump's election, Xi explained his approach to the incoming administration: "I will not throw the first punch, but I will not sit idly by and take one either," he said.[56] Still, it was clear that a head-on confrontation between the world's two largest economies would hurt both sides and was better avoided if possible. Officials in Beijing began citing an ancient Chinese saying from Sun Tzu's *The Art of War* as they brainstormed ways to avert an all-out breakdown in relations with America: you can kill 1,000 enemies, but you would also lose 800 soldiers.[57]

The first step in dealing with Trump was figuring out who he was and what he wanted. Just as Zhou Enlai had gathered information on Nixon and Kissinger's favorite books and movies, officials across government departments worked overtime in the weeks after his victory to gather insights. They trawled through Trump's Twitter account for clues on his policy positions, using VPN software to jump the Great Firewall to access the website, which was blocked in China.[58] Trump's book *The Art of the Deal* was scrutinized like an intelligence report as China's leaders sought to figure out how to handle him.

Next, officials needed to find ways to get through to Trump. At first, Beijing went through third parties. In January 2017, billionaire entrepreneur

Jack Ma, chairman of e-commerce giant Alibaba Group Holding Ltd., met with the president-elect in Trump Tower, after receiving an official nod from Xi Jinping to do so. Signaling the potential for China to support Trump's drive to create jobs in America, Ma promised to bring 1 million American small businesses onto his platform.[59] Then, Chinese diplomats approached the Trump family directly. Cui Tiankai, China's ambassador in Washington, established a backchannel to Trump through his son-in-law Jared Kushner in the weeks after Trump's inauguration. Cui even managed to get Ivanka Trump and the couple's daughter Arabella to attend the Chinese embassy's Lunar New Year Celebrations, where star-struck Chinese attendees whipped out their cellphones to record Ivanka and her daughter listening to traditional Chinese music, admiring crafts and playing with puppets.[60]

Still, Beijing remained confused about the president's end game. They reached out to anyone who could be helpful. Later that month, Yang Jiechi made his way to Washington, where he met with senior administration officials and sought information about Trump from longtime Republican contacts during a dinner at the Chinese embassy, including figures such as former national security adviser Brent Scowcroft and former secretary of commerce Barbara Franklin.[61] Well-connected as these individuals were, they were not Trump's people and were unable to offer Yang much help.

There were reasons for China to be cautiously optimistic. Ronald Reagan, Bill Clinton, and George W. Bush had all backed off from the confrontational policies they vowed to pursue as candidates once they reached office. Perhaps Trump would too. Soon, Trump began taking steps that created opportunities, not obstacles, for China. Within days of his January 2017 inauguration, he had withdrawn from the Trans-Pacific Partnership, a twelve-nation trade deal that aimed to help the United States compete with China's engagement in Asia. The decision reduced the pressure on Chinese officials to deliver liberalizing economic reforms because they no longer risked economic isolation in Asia.[62] Xi had moved to take advantage of the situation by positioning China as a champion of free trade and globalization, even delivering a speech at the 2017 World Economic Forum in Davos that compared protectionism to "locking yourself in a dark room."[63]

The quest to tame Trump continued, and Beijing now turned to money and flattery to alleviate tensions. This approach began with Xi's April 2017 meeting with Trump at the US president's Mar-a-Lago estate in Florida, but reached its climax in November of that year with Trump's state visit to Beijing. As rumors swirled among the CEOs who accompanied Trump that the White House was planning a tranche of anti-China moves, Beijing promised a quarter-trillion dollars' worth of deals and hosted the president in the private inner sanctums of the iconic Forbidden City.

This approach failed. A month after the president's Beijing visit, the Trump administration's National Security Strategy branded China a "strategic competitor" and "revisionist power." The following January, the administration launched tariffs on washing machines and solar cell imports, highlighting concerns about China's supply chain dominance and underpriced goods. The move kicked off a multiyear economic conflict that quickly spiraled into a broader geopolitical battle. By August 2018, tariffs on $34 billion of goods were already in effect and another $216 billion were in the pipeline. Trump had briefly kneecapped Chinese telecommunications giant ZTE Corp., alerting Chinese leaders to the vulnerability of their technology companies' access to American technology and markets.

The mood began to darken in Beijing as Chinese diplomats awoke to the seriousness of the situation. Strength in the face of foreign pressure became the only politically safe position. "No one dared to voice dovish opinions," said one Chinese trade negotiator. "Only very senior officials can advocate compromise with America; it's too risky for anyone else to speak up."[64] The mood was dark in Washington too. While some Democrats disagreed with Trump's tariffs or other specific policies, the need for a new approach became a rare point of bipartisan unity. In August 2017, the Senate's Democratic leader, Chuck Schumer, even encouraged Trump to move straight into retaliatory trade actions against Beijing over intellectual property without bothering with the customary investigation. On both sides of the Pacific, it was becoming increasingly clear that Sino-American ties were approaching a historic low.

Still, the United States was powerful enough that Chinese officials were forced to treat it with caution, even if they deplored its behavior. Chinese diplomats and state media generally refrained from criticizing Trump personally for fear of provoking the president, and even continued to tout Trump and Xi's personal "friendship." They did not afford the same deference to America's allies.

***

On April 22, 2017, the Chinese security chief, Meng Jianzhu, arrived in Sydney for an unlikely meeting with Bill Shorten, the head of Australia's opposition Labor Party. A slight and soft-spoken man with glasses and a habit of wearing suit jackets a couple of sizes too big for him, Meng headed China's formidable domestic security apparatus as the boss of its powerful Political and Legal Affairs Commission.

Meng took a seat in the Commonwealth Parliament Offices on Sydney's Bligh Street, a trendy new building filled with glass walls and ergonomic pods,[65] and prepared to deliver a stark message. Meng hoped that Shorten's party would support Australia's controversial extradition treaty with China in the face of criticism over Beijing's human rights record. It would be a shame, Meng said, if the Chinese government had to tell the overseas Chinese community in Australia that the Labor Party was not supportive of Australia-China ties.[66]

It was an extraordinary intervention. China had long touted its stance of non-interference in other countries' internal affairs, but now it was threatening to use its influence over a domestic constituency to alter the country's domestic politics. Meng's message came just weeks after China's ambassador to Australia, Chen Jingye, had delivered a similar warning to the party. These conversations were taking place as Australian politics was increasingly gripped by an acrimonious debate over Chinese interference.[67]

Australia was in the middle of a row over the extradition treaty and a burgeoning political scandal about the political influence of China in the country, including calls for legislation that would limit foreign interference. At issue was China's use of the same united front tactics that the country had once used to build coalitions of support in countries whose governments did not recognize the right of the Communists to rule China. Now, the aim was to shift opinion among elites and eventually official policy in a direction advantageous to Beijing. Where that wasn't possible, the policies would aim to silence dissent on sensitive issues like human rights, Taiwan, Tibet, and Xinjiang.

Concerns had been building for a while. In 2014, reports emerged that China had been developing networks of informants at leading universities, including Melbourne University and Sydney University, who were feeding information back to the Chinese consulate. Chen Yonglin, a Chinese diplomat who defected to Australia in 2005, said that "students are useful for welcoming leaders at airports and blocking protest groups from sight, and also collecting information." The Chinese consulate in Sydney described the claims as "totally groundless" and driven by "ulterior motives."[68]

As Meng met with Shorten in Sydney, the Labor Party was grappling with a rapidly evolving scandal involving Senator Sam Dastyari, who had allegedly taken money from pro-China donors in exchange for supporting the Chinese government's positions. Dastyari would eventually be forced to retire after the *Sydney Morning Herald* reported that he had recited Chinese government talking points on the South China Sea while standing next to a Chinese citizen who had been a donor. On another occasion, he asked the donor to place his phone aside to avoid surveillance.[69]

By December 2017, when *The Australian* first reported Meng's meeting with Shorten, Chinese interference had become a top issue in Australian politics. Later that month, Prime Minister Malcolm Turnbull described the threat of foreign interference in Australia as "unprecedented" and revealed that a government report into the issue had "galvanized" his government into action. "It's fair to say that our system as a whole had not grasped the nature and the magnitude of the threat," he said.[70]

As events unfolded in Australia, the world was watching. In February 2018, a senior Pentagon official, Randy Schriver, said Australia had "woken up" the world to China's influence operations.[71] The Pentagon's National Defense Strategy in 2018 grouped China's "influence operations" together with its "military modernization" and "predatory economics" as threats to the United States.[72] Similar assessments were taking place in London, Berlin, Ottawa, and beyond.[73]

The attention of these countries focused on Communist Party tools that dated back to the 1950s or even prior to the formation of the People's Republic. They included Party organs such as the United Front Work Department, International Liaison Department, and the Propaganda Department, as well as government bodies such as the foreign ministry, the education ministry, and the public security system overseen by Meng Jianzhu. The examinations also delved into how the Chinese government's efforts were complemented by a host of official and semi-official think tanks and "people-to-people" organizations.

Australia wasn't the only American ally to end up in Beijing's firing line, and increasingly China was willing to combine its diplomatic displeasure with crippling economic sanctions. In 2017, China ramped up a campaign of economic warfare against South Korea, which had installed an American missile defense system over Beijing's objections. China's foreign ministry blasted the South Korean government day after day for its decision, while a campaign of economic coercion knocked a third of a percentage point off South Korea's economic growth that year.[74] In 2018, Xi's government began a similar effort to pressure Canada, where the chief financial officer of Huawei

Technologies Co. Ltd. had been arrested in response to an American extradition request. Chinese spy agencies detained two Canadian citizens in apparent retaliation.

***

Back in Beijing, the political atmosphere grew increasingly tense as a cult of personality developed around Xi Jinping. Amidst Xi's push for political control, diplomats had to sit through Yan'an-style "self-criticism" sessions in the foreign ministry and "inspection tours," which tested their loyalty to the Party and willingness to follow orders.[75] At embassy events, they handed out copies of Xi's book, *The Governance of China*, in a strange echo of the way they once handed out Chairman Mao's "Little Red Book."[76] As the crucial 19th Party Congress approached in October 2017, rumors abounded that Xi might not name a successor, signaling his intention to stay in power indefinitely.[77] It was becoming increasingly clear that if you wanted to get ahead as a Chinese diplomat, you needed to be on board with Xi's agenda or face irrelevance, perhaps worse.

As usual, Yang Jiechi was out ahead of the political tides. In a *People's Daily* article in January 2017, Yang became one of the first Chinese officials to use the term "core" to refer to Xi's place in the Party, a designation his predecessors had dropped in favor of emphasizing collective leadership. He wrote that Xi's thoughts on diplomacy were "the most precious spiritual resources."[78] In July that year, Yang published an essay that hailed the "far-reaching" significance of "Xi Jinping thought on diplomacy," which he described as a "profound system of theories with rich connotations."[79] In private, Yang was also networking. American spies in China noted that he traveled to Shanghai to meet with one of his political patrons, the former president Jiang Zemin, in the run-up to the congress, just as he had done ahead of previous Party meetings where his professional success was at stake.[80]

Others were positioning themselves, too. In September 2017, just one month before the congress, Wang Yi praised Xi's "diplomatic thought" as a "compass" for foreign relations. "It innovates upon and transcends 300 years of traditional Western international relations theory," Wang gushed in an article for a Party publication. He hailed Xi as a "reformer and pioneer" who had "put forward many new ideas that his predecessors had not."[81]

Their efforts paid off. In the closing days of the 19th Party Congress, Yang was appointed to the twenty-five-member Politburo, becoming the first Chinese diplomat to serve on the body since Qian Qichen had retired in 2003. The move spoke to the increased importance of foreign affairs to a rising and increasingly powerful China. "It's a recognition of Yang personally and the entire foreign policy establishment," China's former ambassador to the United Kingdom, Ma Zhengang, told the *South China Morning Post*. "We are seeing an unprecedented transition of China's role, which will not be confined to domestic interests but demonstrate more interest in having a greater say on global issues."[82]

Domestic political changes emerging from the congress would also have profound implications for Chinese diplomacy. In a three-hour speech at the start of the congress, Xi repeated the leadership's line that China is in an "important period of strategic opportunity." He said China would become "a global leader in terms of comprehensive national strength and international influence" by the year 2050. China was "approaching the center of the world stage" and "standing tall and firm in the East," he said.[83] The congress also enshrined "Xi Jinping Thought" in the Communist Party's charter, echoing the doctrine of "Mao Zedong Thought" that Wang Jiaxiang had helped Mao develop in Yan'an.[84] Most important, Xi broke with convention and declined to anoint a successor, raising the prospect that he could continue to rule China for decades and effectively eliminating the possibility that he could become a lame duck during his second term.[85]

As Xi became more powerful, his words became gospel. He kept pushing the country toward greater assertiveness. In January 2018, after Xi called for Chinese ambassadors to play a more proactive role in the world at a conference in Beijing, China's envoy to the UK described his words as a "mobilization order" and a "bugle call."[86] It was as if the hopes of online nationalists in the 1990s and 2000s for a more assertive approach to diplomacy were now becoming official policy.

As Xi strengthened centralized control across the bureaucracy, he ordered a sweeping overhaul of the way Chinese embassies function. Aiming to overcome the unclear and overlapping responsibilities of different agencies that had sometimes hampered Chinese diplomacy in the 2000s, the Party initiated plans that would give ambassadors direct control over staff sent to embassies from other agencies as well as veto power over financial and personnel decisions.[87]

China's moves to strengthen its diplomatic corps came as the United States was weakening its own. While it is difficult to compare the size of Chinese and American diplomatic activities—given the sparse budget information from China and differing accounting practices—it was clear the two were headed in opposite directions. China's spending on diplomatic affairs rose to $7.8 billion in 2017, almost double the outlay in 2013. Trump's budget office, meanwhile, outlined a plan for a 37 percent spending cut by the State Department and the United States Agency for International Development, which had requested more than $50 billion.[88] The foreign ministry now employed some 6,000 diplomats; the new foreign ministry building, opened in 1997 to mark the country's newfound international prominence, was already overcrowded. "We did not anticipate how quickly China's position would change when the building was erected," said one diplomat.[89]

As the annual legislative gathering approached in spring 2018, Chinese diplomats began to fear that Wang Yi, China's "silver fox" foreign minister, might be becoming too high-profile. "There can only be one star," one diplomat said, referring to Xi Jinping.[90] Chinese diplomats worried that Wang's growing global prominence might incur Xi's wrath just as Zhou's success courting Nixon and Kissinger had aroused intense jealousy in Chairman Mao. When the National People's Congress came around, however, there was in fact good news in store for Wang. He stayed on as foreign minister and was simultaneously promoted to Yang Jiechi's previous job of state councilor.[91]

The gathering was also a historic turning point for Chinese politics: it made Xi's desire to stay on beyond his second term official by abolishing term limits on the presidency. The move would pave the way for Xi to become ruler for life by revoking the limits introduced in the 1982 constitution, which had aimed to prevent a return to one-man rule. Li Datong, a former senior editor at the official *China Youth Daily* newspaper, was one of the rare public voices raised against the change. "Removing term limitations on national leaders will subject us to the ridicule of the civilized nations of the world," he wrote in an open letter urging legislators to oppose the move. "It means moving backward into history and planting the seed once again of chaos in China."[92] In the end, China's rubber-stamp parliament approved the measure by 2,959 votes to 2. Chinese diplomats would adjust to political uncertainty at home the way they always had: through public displays of loyalty to the leadership and patriotic posturing.

***

In late 2018, a senior European diplomat arrived back in China after more than a decade away from the country. When she'd left in 2007, China was focused on hosting the Olympics. There was an infectious sense of optimism in Beijing that seemed to be shared by Chinese diplomats. They had communicated in a characteristically formal and scripted way, but their efforts to win over foreign opinion seemed sincere. Just over ten years later, the envoy noticed a much more aggressive and ideological tone from her Chinese counterparts. Their behavior, she said, displayed an intense sense of grievance, combined with increasing entitlement about China's international role.[93]

A similar pattern was repeating itself around the world. In September 2018, the leaders of eighteen Pacific island nations, plus delegations from non-member countries such as the United States and China, arrived in the tiny Micronesian state of Nauru, a country of around 12,000 inhabitants, for the Pacific Islands Forum. China's chief representative was Du Qiwen, its former ambassador to Greece. In keeping with the meeting's informal theme, Du arrived clad in a short-sleeved red shirt with flower petals on the sleeves. As regional leaders addressed the forum, Du raised his hand to speak. Nauru's president declined to allow Du's interjection as the prime minister of Tuvalu was due to speak next. But Du "insisted and was very insolent about it and created a big fuss and held up the meeting of leaders for a good number of minutes," said Nauru's president Baron Waqa. "Maybe because he was from a big country he wanted to bully us," Waqa told the media.

After around fifteen minutes of commotion, Nauru's president threatened to evict the Chinese delegation unless they allowed the meeting to continue. A leaked video of the meeting showed Waqa telling Du, "You are addressing ministers here. Show some respect." But Du too had reached his limit. "Finally, he was fuming, shouted at them very loudly and angrily, stood up and stormed out, but instead of heading for the nearest exit, he did a lap of the whole conference table to indicate his fury with each person," one participant told *The Guardian*. When reporters in Beijing asked the foreign ministry to account for Du's behavior, spokesperson Hua Chunying said, "What Nauru said is diametrically the opposite of the facts. It has totally confused right and wrong and they have made bogus accusations." She added: "It's actually the Nauru side who should reflect and apologize."[94]

The incidents kept coming. At the APEC Summit in Papua New Guinea in 2018, police were called after Chinese officials attempted to "barge" into the office of the country's foreign minister when their demands for changes to the summit's communiqué were not met.[95] In Canada, Chinese ambassador Lu Shaye publicly accused his hosts of "Western egotism and white supremacy" and repeatedly attacked the country's media for its "slanderous" reporting.[96]

In South Africa, China's chief emissary declared that Donald Trump's policies were making the United States the "enemy of the whole world."[97]

In Europe, Gui Congyou became the face of Chinese assertiveness. At fifty-seven with glasses and slick back hair, Gui had spent his whole career dealing with Russia and Central Asia before being appointed ambassador to Sweden in 2017. He inherited an already testy relationship: ties had been strained after Beijing's detention of Gui Minhai, a Chinese-born Swedish citizen who was snatched from a train bound for Beijing under the eyes of Swedish diplomats. Tensions escalated further in September 2018 after Swedish police forcibly ejected a Chinese man and his parents from a hotel in Stockholm after they refused to leave when hotel staff pointed out they had arrived a day early for their booking. Gui blasted the Swedish police as "inhumane and immoral," and the embassy issued a travel alert to its citizens warning of the country's "brutal treatment" of Chinese tourists.[98] Unabashed, he told Swedish public radio, "We treat our friends with fine wine, but for our enemies we have shotguns."

Gui took particular offense at the Swedish media. The Chinese embassy repeatedly contacted the country's print and television news outlets, instructing them to change their reporting. Gui later said the Swedish media's coverage of China was "like a 48-kilo lightweight boxer picking a fight with an 86-kilo heavyweight boxer." He explained that China had tolerated Sweden's behavior so far, but that its patience had limits: "The 86-kilo boxer out of courtesy and goodwill tells the 48-kilo boxer to mind his own business. But the lightweight boxer doesn't listen, he continues to provoke and forces himself into the heavyweight boxer's home. What choice does this 86-kilo boxer have?" Gui asked. The Swedish foreign minister said the ambassador's remarks were "an unacceptable threat," and three of the country's political parties called for him to be expelled.[99] In the space of just two years the ambassador was summoned by Sweden's foreign ministry more than forty times for his provocative comments.[100]

***

As these controversies unfolded, some in Beijing began to raise the alarm. In October 2018, Deng Pufang, the son of former paramount leader Deng Xiaoping, said in a speech that the Chinese government should "keep a sober mind and know our own place." In remarks reminiscent of his father's famous call for China to hide its strength and bide its time, Deng said China "should neither be overbearing nor belittle ourselves."[101] Weeks later, Long

Yongtu, the former trade negotiator who represented China in its World Trade Organization accession talks, criticized China's leaders for failing to "think deeply enough" in their approach to trade talks with Washington, especially the decision to slap tariffs on American soybeans.[102]

Foreign observers noted the shift in Chinese diplomacy too, and even came up with a new name for China's increasingly undiplomatic diplomats: "wolf warriors."[103] The name derived from a 2017 blockbuster movie, *Wolf Warrior 2*, which told the story of a group of Chinese soldiers sent to rescue a group of stranded civilian compatriots in a war-torn African nation. At one point, the film's hero, Leng Feng, uses a crossbow to fight American mercenaries. When he kills their boss, he tells them, "People like you will always be inferior to people like me." The film seemed to capture a sense among much of the Chinese public that the nation's moment had arrived: its tagline read, "Even though a thousand miles away, anyone who affronts China will pay."[104]

Some in the foreign ministry, especially younger officials, liked the new mood. "We can feel that people treat us differently when we walk into a room now. People seem to respect you more if you come from a powerful country," said one young Chinese diplomat. "It feels different from even a few years ago."[105] Others increasingly saw acting tough as a way to get ahead. "Everyone thinks he wants to see strength and won't accept criticism and so they act in line with that expectation," a former journalist for Chinese state media said of Xi Jinping. "It's like he looks left a little and this whole group of people under him goes charging off left, further than he ever intended."[106]

Others were motivated by insecurity. In January 2019, the former deputy head of the Party's powerful Organization Department, Qi Yu, was appointed as the foreign ministry's Party Secretary, a role usually reserved for foreign ministry veterans. He rose to the post despite a lack of diplomatic experience. The move handed Qi control over crucial and sensitive personnel decisions within the ministry.[107] Just after the appointment, one foreign ambassador said that Chinese diplomats were increasingly "scared."[108] Asked whether it was confidence or insecurity driving the country's recent behavior, one Chinese envoy said, "insecurity." "It's always insecurity," he explained. "It runs deeper than you know."[109] In this fraught atmosphere, one Chinese diplomat took to Twitter to push the boundaries of wolf warrior diplomacy.

***

In July 2019, Zhao Lijian, a forty-seven-year-old Chinese diplomat in Islamabad, decided he'd had enough of America's attacks on China. Beijing had come under intense criticism after human rights groups and the United Nations said it was detaining more than 1 million ethnic Uighur Muslims in "re-education camps" in its far western region of Xinjiang. American politicians had condemned the policy, which China, after initially denying the existence of the camps, was now defending.

A soft-spoken man who sometimes stumbles over his words, Zhao had served in Washington from 2009 to 2013, as America slowly recovered from the financial crisis. While there he'd joined Twitter, a platform banned in China. Zhao then served as a division director in the foreign ministry's Asia department, before landing a role in China's embassy in Islamabad where he briefly adopted the name "Muhammad" on his Twitter profile, before China's decision to curb the use of Islamic names in Xinjiang prompted him to take it down.[110]

Zhao grew increasingly angry as he watched Washington condemn China's policies toward its minorities, and in a flurry of tweets over a July weekend, he decided to make his frustrations public. American leaders who charged China with human rights were "hypocrites," he wrote, before referencing his understanding of the situation in the United States: "If you're in Washington DC, you know the white never go to the SW area, because it's an area for the black & Latin," he tweeted.

Zhao's tweets caught the eye of the former national security adviser under President Obama, Susan Rice. "You are a racist disgrace. And shockingly ignorant too," Rice wrote back to Zhao. She called on Ambassador Cui Tiankai to send the diplomat home, mistakenly believing that Zhao was still posted in Washington. Undeterred, Zhao shot back. "You are such a disgrace, too. And shockingly ignorant, too. I am based in Islamabad. Truth hurts."[111]

Engaging in such a shrill war of words with a senior member of the American foreign policy establishment while posted to a South Asian nation was unusual behavior, even for 2019. But Zhao believed he had a duty to speak out. "This is a time for Chinese diplomats to tell the true picture," he later said in an interview with *BuzzFeed News*. "Somebody is slandering you every day—like Pompeo, like Pence," he said: "They are badmouthing China. They are talking about Hong Kong. They are saying the protesters in Hong Kong are freedom fighters. This is totally wrong!"

Zhao conceded that his approach was unusual for a Chinese diplomat, even as the country's envoys were taking a tougher stance overseas. "People looked at me like I was a panda—like I was an alien from Mars," he told *BuzzFeed*.[112] Some in the ministry disliked his approach. Rice had enjoyed a strong working relationship with Yang Jiechi during her time in the Obama White House, and there was every reason to think she might serve in a future Democratic administration. In an attempt to limit the damage, Cui Tiankai, China's ambassador in Washington, quietly sent word to Rice, telling her that he did not approve of his tweet and that Zhao's Twitter account did not reflect China's official stance. The offending posts were soon deleted.[113]

Not everyone disapproved. In the past, Zhao's public freelancing might have earned him an official rebuke or even dismissal, but it came just as the foreign ministry was attempting to navigate Xi's calls for a more proactive and combative approach to diplomacy. Instead of being punished, Zhao was promoted. He was brought back to Beijing and made an official spokesman at the foreign ministry, a position that made him one of the most high-profile Chinese diplomats in the world.[114] On his return to the Chinese capital, Zhao was greeted by a group of young diplomats outside his office who had gathered to celebrate his elevation.[115] For them, Zhao represented a fresh and new voice for a country that had for too long tiptoed around global opinion. Like Zhao, they had grown up in the China of Deng Xiaoping's reforms, where living standards increased year on year and the country was becoming ever more influential in the world.

Other events seemed to confirm that Zhao's appointment was no fluke. Just a few weeks earlier, Hua Chunying, until Zhao by far the most outspoken foreign ministry spokesperson of the Trump era, was made head of the ministry's information department.[116] Lu Shaye, China's controversial ambassador to Canada, was also promoted to ambassador to France, a permanent member of the United Nations Security Council.[117] In late 2019, Xi Jinping issued the ministry a handwritten note calling on its diplomats to show more "fighting spirit" and adopt a tougher stance in the face of deteriorating relations with the United States.[118] Diplomats across the ministry noticed that the shift in tone was being rewarded—just as they too began opening their own Twitter accounts.

Although initially slow to embrace Twitter, by late 2019 nearly sixty Chinese diplomats had opened accounts—more than half of which were established that year.[119] Some were largely innocuous, posting official talking points or state media stories. Others quoted poetry or posted pictures of wildlife. China's ambassador to Nepal posted Instagram influencer-style selfies.[120] Others were far less banal. At times, some accounts adopted a distinctively Trumpian style, replete with sarcasm and capital letters. "#China has become powerful with U.S. money? LOL!" read one Tweet from Hua Chunying's account.[121]

The new presence of wolf warrior diplomats on Twitter established a whole new front for conflict as the spread of the Covid-19 pandemic sent ties skidding toward a new low.

***

On January 31, 2020, the Trump administration closed its borders to foreign nationals who had travelled to China within the last fourteen days. The novel coronavirus outbreak that had first been detected in the city of Wuhan in November had by then killed 213 people; nearly 10,000 cases had been identified worldwide. China responded angrily: "The US comments and actions are neither based on facts, nor helpful," foreign ministry spokesperson Hua Chunying said in a statement. "It is certainly not a gesture of goodwill."[122]

As the virus continued to spread across the world in February, it became increasingly clear that officials in Wuhan had failed to disclose it to central authorities, delaying the world's ability to prepare for the outbreak. On February 7, Li Wenliang, a thirty-four-year-old doctor in Wuhan, died of Covid-19 after being silenced in an early bid to warn of the dangers of the disease. Internet forums exploded with outrage, as censors took down hashtags such as "I Want Freedom of Speech" and links to "Do You Hear the People Sing?" from the musical *Les Misérables*.[123]

As international anger over Beijing's handling of the virus spread, the Communist Party began to position China as a global leader in disease control. Party officials announced plans to publish a book in six languages portraying Xi as a "major power leader" for his handling of the crisis. Xinhua ran stories featuring health experts from Russia, Cuba, and Belarus praising China's "openness" and "highly responsible attitude."[124] Zhao Lijian told reporters that "China has conducted itself as a responsible country. China's signature strength, efficiency, and speed in this fight has been widely acclaimed."[125] The rebranding was accompanied by the shipment of medical equipment to other countries, including Iran, Italy, Serbia, and South Korea. Wang Yi said the efforts amounted to a "silk road of healthcare," in a reference to Xi's Belt and Road Initiative.[126]

Anyone who questioned this narrative was hit fast and hard by Chinese diplomats on Twitter. "You speak in such a way that you look like part of the virus and you will be eradicated just like virus. Shame on you," Zha Liyou, China's consul-general in Kolkata, India, tweeted at one user.[127] In Brazil,

Ambassador Yang Wangming called the family of President Jair Bolsonaro "poison" after his son blamed the "Chinese dictatorship" for the pandemic.[128] The embassy in Venezuela went even further, instructing the country's officials to "put on a mask and shut up" after they referred to Covid-19 as the "Chinese coronavirus."[129]

On March 12, Zhao Lijian dropped a bomb. Without asking the permission of his superiors, Zhao tweeted a video of Robert Redfield, the director for the US Centers for Disease Control and Prevention, addressing a US congressional committee. Zhao wrote, "CDC was caught on the spot. When did patient zero begin in US? How many people are infected? What are the names of the hospitals? It might be US army who brought the epidemic to Wuhan. Be transparent! Make public your data! US owe us an explanation!"[130] Zhao followed up with another tweet urging his nearly 300,000 followers to share a story from a website promoting conspiracy theories, including articles lambasting the "Vaccine Deep State" and questioning whether Osama bin Laden really existed.[131]

The damage was immediate. Secretary of State Mike Pompeo urged Yang Jiechi to stop trying to "shift blame" for the virus. Trump himself was "enraged" by Zhao's tweet and intensified his criticisms of China for spreading the virus.[132] "As you know, China tried to say at one point—maybe they stopped now—that it was caused by American soldiers," he said on March 18. "That can't happen. It's not going to happen, not as long as I'm president. It comes from China."[133]

Zhao continued peddling the theory for more than a week before Cui Tiankai, already irritated by Zhao's previous spat with Susan Rice, stepped in. During an interview with "Axios on HBO," Cui said he stood by his previous statement that it was "crazy" to spread such theories. "Such speculation will help nobody. It's very harmful," said Cui, who holds a vice-ministerial rank in China's political hierarchy, two levels senior to Zhao. "Eventually, we must have an answer to where the virus originally came from. But this is the job for the scientists to do, not for diplomats." Asked why Zhao was making his claims, Cui responded, "Maybe you could go and ask him."[134]

Inside the ministry, officials were divided. One said that Zhao's approach had been vocally welcomed by many inside the foreign ministry. Another expressed relief that Cui had disowned Zhao's "dangerous" remarks, speculating that Zhao had made his comments under the assumption that Xi would approve.[135] Others in the Chinese foreign policy community were also alarmed. Scholars in research institutes in Beijing began cautioning the government that it should avoid making enemies internationally.[136] Two retired Chinese diplomats confided to a foreign counterpart that they were "disgusted" at how China was now behaving.[137]

Cui's comments seemed to quiet Zhao down, at least temporarily. The next day, Zhao posted an uncharacteristically innocuous tweet with photos of cherry blossoms and a plea to "unite to deal with the epidemic." Asked about his tweets at a press conference a few weeks later, Zhao stuck to the official line, but also defended his tweets as "a reaction to some American politicians stigmatizing China a while ago." The tweets, he said, reflected the anger of many Chinese people.[138]

***

Even if Zhao had beaten a tactical retreat, the combative behavior of Chinese envoys continued apace. On April 12, the Chinese embassy in Paris—led by Ambassador Lu Shaye, who had previously courted controversy in Canada—posted an article on its website entitled "Restoring distorted facts—Observations of a Chinese Diplomat Posted to Paris." In the post, an unnamed diplomat accused Western nursing homes of leaving residents to die and laying "siege" to the World Health Organization.[139] The article sparked public anger in France and a rebuke from the country's foreign ministry.[140]

Later that month, China's ambassador to Australia, Cheng Jingye, moved beyond strong language, threatening economic consequences after Australia called for an international inquiry into the origins of Covid-19. "Maybe also the ordinary people will say why should we drink Australian wine or to eat Australian beef?" he said in an interview with the *Australian Financial Review*. Simon Birmingham, Australia's trade minister, responded by saying his country would not bow to threats of "economic coercion."[141]

Other diplomats seemed more concerned about winning plaudits for Xi Jinping than salvaging China's reputation. Wu Ting, a diplomat in the Chinese consulate in Chicago, twice wrote to Wisconsin's Senate president, Roger Roth, asking him to pass a resolution praising the heroic steps China had taken to fight the virus. Roth replied with one word: "Nuts."[142] In Europe, Chinese diplomats approached German officials asking them to make positive statements about how Beijing was handling the crisis.[143]

It was quickly becoming clear that Beijing's international reputation had been severely damaged by the virus and its aftermath. In April, an internal report by a think tank under China's Ministry of State Security warned that anti-China sentiment was at its highest since the 1989 Tiananmen Square crackdown.[144] Chinese diplomats were a big part of the problem. As a former Australian prime minister, Kevin Rudd, wrote in May, "Whatever China's new generation of 'wolf-warrior' diplomats may report back to Beijing, the reality is that China's standing has taken a huge hit (the irony is that these wolf-warriors are adding to this damage, not ameliorating it)."[145]

Inside China, the debate over "wolf warrior" diplomacy continued to rage. Some applauded the more aggressive style. "What's behind China's perceived 'Wolf Warrior' style diplomacy is the changing strengths of China and the West," the *Global Times*, a nationalist tabloid run by the Communist Party, wrote in April. "As Chinese diplomacy increasingly reflects the interests of its people, they have become more astute in diplomatic affairs. They are no longer satisfied with a flaccid diplomatic tone."[146] Another story quoted online fans of Zhao Lijian. "I remember that many years ago, some citizens sent calcium tablets to the foreign ministry to express their dissatisfaction," said Vicky Chi, an eighteen-year-old who manages a 14,000-member fan site for Zhao. "Now I'm pleased to see our diplomats firmly say 'No' to the provocations and attacks."[147]

Wang Yi also defended his diplomats' tough new approach during a press conference in May. "We never pick a fight or bully others. But we have principles and guts. We will push back against any deliberate insult, resolutely defend our national honor and dignity, and we will refute all groundless slander with facts," he said.[148] Liu Xiaoming, China's ambassador in London and himself one of the country's most outspoken envoys, said the "wolf warrior" label represented a "misunderstanding" but defended the general approach: "Chinese diplomats need to fight wolf wars because there are wolves in this world," he said.[149]

Others were unimpressed. In September, Yuan Nansheng, China's former consul general in San Francisco, warned that "if we let populism and extreme nationalism flourish freely in China, the international community could misinterpret this as Beijing pursuing 'China First,'" referring to Trump's "America First" policy. Yuan called for a return to the low-key approach to diplomacy the country had followed in the 1990s and early 2000s. "Chinese diplomacy needs to be stronger, not just tougher," he said.[150] Still, as the months rolled on, it became clear that whether or not "wolf warrior" diplomacy was working internationally, the approach was here to stay for the time being, as events at a swanky hotel on the remote Pacific island of Fiji would demonstrate.

***

On October 8, 2020, around 100 distinguished guests, including Fijian ministers, foreign diplomats, scholars, and nonprofit employees, gathered at the Grand Pacific Hotel, an elegant early twentieth-century building on Victoria Parade, the main sea front of Fiji's capital, Suva. They were there to celebrate Taiwan's national day, an occasion marking the beginning of the 1911 uprising that overthrew the Qing Dynasty. Fiji has recognized Beijing since 1975, but like most countries around the world also maintains a friendly, unofficial relationship with Taiwan.

As the dignitaries mingled and made small talk, two uninvited diplomats from the Chinese embassy were seen photographing guests—a tactic Beijing often uses to intimidate those who oppose its interests. When confronted by Taiwanese officials and asked to leave, the Chinese diplomats initiated a fistfight, beating a Taiwanese official—a librarian at the trade office—so severely that he was hospitalized for concussion. Police were called, but the Chinese officials claimed diplomatic immunity.[151]

The incident came at a time of increased tensions between Beijing and Taipei. After the Solomon Islands and Kiribati switched ties to China in quick succession in 2019, the United States stepped in to shore up support for Taiwan in the region, urging Taipei's last four Pacific Island allies not to follow suit. Chinese diplomats in Fiji were on the lookout for any sign that the region's support for Beijing might be wavering. Still, the altercation seemed extreme: Beijing had been competing with Taipei for the past seventy years, and, by every possible metric, China was winning. It had steadily whittled away formal recognition of Taiwan, leaving Taipei with just fifteen official allies, mostly small Pacific and Latin American nations.

On one level, Beijing's envoys were acting tough, just as Xi Jinping had instructed. Wang Ting-yu, a Taiwanese legislator who specializes in foreign affairs, explained the dynamic well when he told the *New York Times* that the biggest problem in China now is that "under Xi Jinping's rule, their diplomats have turned to seeking private revenge. They have disregarded their country's diplomatic interests to follow the internal orders of the leaders."[152] In many ways, the behavior of Chinese diplomats in Fiji resembled the excesses of Beijing's envoys in the early 1950s and during the Cultural Revolution, when brazen outbursts were a way to signal loyalty to the leadership.

The Fiji incident also showed how Beijing's newfound "fighting spirit" was accompanied by the same insecurities about China's place in the world that were present at the creation of the foreign ministry in 1949. When asked about the fight in Fiji, Zhao Lijian denied Taiwan's allegations, stating that the island was "playing victim here" and a "thief crying 'stop thief.' " But then he added a revealing detail: the Chinese diplomats' actions were justified because Beijing had learned that a cake inside the venue was "marked with a false national flag."

China was now the second largest economy in the world and a permanent member of the United Nations Security Council; it possessed one of the world's most potent militaries. And yet, seventy years after its foundation, the country's diplomats could be goaded into a fistfight over what was—at worst—an inappropriately decorated cake. Like Zhou Enlai's fresh recruits in 1949, Chinese diplomats in 2020 were profoundly insecure about their country's place in the world. Also, like their predecessors, they were more concerned about looking weak in front of domestic audiences than truly improving China's reputation. In this sense, the People's Republic has had wolf warriors as long as it has had diplomats.

Conclusion

I met Wang Li in a Starbucks on the third floor of a Beijing mall in 2017. The meeting was technically against the rules. A newly minted Chinese diplomat, Wang was not supposed to be meeting with any foreigner by himself, let alone a journalist.[1]

Born in the mid-1990s, Wang was a child of local officials from a wealthy coastal province. His polished English was the result of parents who'd made sure he'd learned the language from an early age. He was perfectly at home in the international coffee chain as modal jazz played on the speaker system and the barista called out our drink orders using a mixture of Chinese, English, and Starbucks Italian: "grande *kabuqinuo* for Pete."

As a teenager, when Wang's teachers asked him about college applications, his parents had suggested he might consider a career as a diplomat. They'd even selected a challenging but strategically significant third language for his college major to help smooth the application process.

Like many children of a newly rich and powerful China, Wang's childhood had been comfortably sheltered in a way unimaginable to his parents' generation. His mother and father had lived through the Cultural Revolution, his grandparents the founding of the new China in 1949. Wang had worked hard to achieve all he had, but the path to success had been neatly laid out in front of him.

By the time we met, Wang had graduated college, passed the foreign ministry entrance exam, been through a month of mandatory military training, and completed two short rotations in different foreign ministry departments as part of his training. He'd just received his diplomatic passport and would be heading overseas in a matter of days.

For me, meeting Wang was an obvious choice. I wanted to understand what the future of Chinese diplomacy might look like. Wang's own motivations became clear during the course of our conversation. After a relaxed discussion about families, careers, relationships, and foreign policy, he asked an unexpected question: had the 1989 Tiananmen protests really been "a plot hatched and executed by the American Embassy?"

Wang had no shortage of information with which to answer his own question. He had read Chinese government accounts of events and had long used VPN software to access Chinese and Western explanations that were blocked in China. But that didn't make deciding whose account to believe any easier. Wang, like many of his contemporaries, knew better than to take everything his government told him at face value, but he also distrusted Western media and especially the US government.

I was a little startled at first. I'd heard these kinds of theories about Tiananmen plenty of times before, but they'd usually been presented to me with knowing confidence instead of open-minded inquisitiveness.

I did my best to share my perspective while stressing that I was no expert. While there's a lot that remains secret about that period—especially on the Chinese side—ambitious journalists, writers, and historians have been interested in the topic for three decades. Discovering a government plot on this scale would be the scoop of a lifetime, I said. Surely if compelling evidence existed, it would have come to light by now. What's more, while American diplomats and intelligence practitioners seem pretty smart to me, their ability to pull off something on this scale—*and keep it secret for three decades*—seemed pretty doubtful. Foreign governments were clearly sympathetic to the widespread calls for a more open and representative society, but hundreds of thousands of ordinary Chinese citizens and workers across industries demonstrated a spontaneous desire to rein in government excesses and address pocketbook issues including rampant inflation.

Wang thanked me for my perspective, but didn't seem particularly convinced by my point of view. We talked a bit more and then parted ways, but our conversation stuck with me for a long time after. Here was this smart, well-educated kid who was about to represent the second richest and most-powerful government in the world, but he was going to sit down in meetings with foreign counterparts facing the possibility that they knew more about certain aspects of his country's political history than he did. If I found myself in his position, I'd be on the hunt for explanations too.

In the coming decades, Wang and the next generation of Chinese diplomats will wrestle with the burgeoning ambitions of their country's leaders as well as growing expectations and scrutiny from the outside world. In many ways, Wang is a product of the profound changes that have taken place in Chinese diplomacy over the past seventy years, but is also emblematic of how, at the same time, so little has changed.

The group now on the front lines of China's foreign relations are in some ways unrecognizable from those who started out as the country's first diplomats in 1949. They are more professional, more cosmopolitan, and more expert than any previous generation, studying for advanced degrees at top global universities, mastering obscure languages, and developing specialized expertise on topics from global finance to nuclear weapons. To a great extent, they closely resemble the very best of their international counterparts.

And yet, in some fundamental ways very little has changed since Zhou Enlai set out his vision for creating a "civilian army" in 1949. "Under the close care and leadership of Premier Zhou Enlai, the foreign ministry from its establishment attached great importance to the way it does things, including the traditions of diligent study, careful work, and tight discipline," one former diplomat wrote in 2009. "The Party and the nation's guiding beliefs for strengthening and constructing the diplomatic corps have been handed down to [us] today . . . the basic spirit and requirements are the same."[2] Another wrote, "Zhou Enlai said the diplomatic corps is like the PLA in civilian clothing, it must have that kind of strict, iron discipline . . . for the last few decades, we haven't worn military uniforms, but we've always used this principle to guide our work."[3]

China's diplomats are unable to extricate themselves from the constraints of a secretive, paranoid political system. They will continue to be bound by institutions forged through underground revolutionary struggle and that matured at the height of the Cold War. It is a system for which small threats loom large and where enemies—internal and external—are always with you. It's a system where there's a constant tension between truth and political orthodoxy, which is at its most jarring when it rubs up against the outside world.

These constraints make Chinese diplomats good at formulating China's demands clearly and ruthlessly pursuing the country's objectives. These efforts have often been particularly effective—in the short term at least—when combined with Chinese campaigns of economic coercion against nations that step out of line. The system enables them to keep secrets, to get everyone on the same page, and to remain capable of keeping their interagency rivalries largely out of the media. No country in the world is in any doubt of China's policies on Taiwan or Tibet.

And yet, regardless of how well trained and cosmopolitan they might become, China's political system sets real limits on the ability of its diplomats to be persuasive. Chinese diplomats serve a political system that distrusts the outside world, which limits meaningful contact with foreigners and makes it difficult to win hearts and minds.

It's also a system that leaves its practitioners with little space to improvise and show flexibility, little room to take the initiative, and therefore not much chance of changing the viewpoints of people they interface with. It leaves them effective at garnering influence through inducements or threats but poorly equipped to make real friends. It's a system that's better at silencing critics than persuading others to share its point of view.

Today's Chinese diplomats and future generations will be weighed down by the sense—kept alive through propaganda—that the country was robbed of its rightful place in the world and it is their mission to retake it. Despite their country's growing power, they will likely remain sensitive to slights, insecure about the country's place in the world, and jumpy about domestic pressures. China's former ambassador to France, Chen Jian, wrote, "America has said that you need to be thick skinned to be a superpower—a characteristic which the Chinese people lack."[4]

In the early days, the core task was survival: warding off foreign threats and winning enough space internationally to make social revolution possible at home. Now China is on its way to becoming the largest economy in a multipolar world that's lost the superpower anchor that provided a modicum of stability and certainty. China possesses a formidable military with increasingly global ambitions, an innovative technology sector, and an ambitious space program. Yet despite the country's economic and technological progress, global public opinion polls show that China suffers from low trust and that the majority of citizens in many countries consider it a threat.

China's ability to win over other countries cannot rely on reserves of renminbi and its ability to wield a big stick alone. It will also depend on its ability to persuade. These challenges will require the kind of versatility and dexterity that Chinese diplomacy has only occasionally been able to demonstrate.

The path ahead is uncertain. The People's Republic of China has displayed an array of international personalities over time—some better suited to winning friends and influence than others.

One set of instincts led the Party to many successes over the years, from courting the US Army Observer Group in Yan'an to China's successes at Geneva and Bandung to the country's extraordinary fightback after Tiananmen, which culminated in its hosting of the 2008 Summer Olympics. These instincts have the power to take the country a long way even if they can't overcome every constraint laid down by domestic politics.

But as we've seen, each time China launches a charm offensive, its successes seem to eventually come undone by political campaigns at home. These pressures have driven an alternative set of instincts that have fueled core behaviors from Chinese diplomats from the early purges that took place in Yan'an through to Xi Jinping's push for political control today. These are the instincts that saw the lecturer tell his students that China only cared about "Mao Zedong law." They are also the instincts that compelled Wu Xiuquan to deliver his rasping diatribe at the United Nations in 1950. Above all, it's the impulse that drove China to wreck its international relationships during the Cultural Revolution.

Both instincts represent responses to the same political system. Both are subject to the same constraints and unfailing loyalty to China's one-Party state. They even employ many of the same techniques and features—from evasiveness to angry diatribes to the inherent insecurity surrounding China's place in the world.

But the charm instinct manifests itself in a desire for professionalism, an instinct to engage in real dialogue insofar as China's political system will allow it, and which seeks to persuade by meeting the world where it is. On the other hand, the instinct to bully creates an unapologetically bombastic approach to the outside world's misgivings about China. Here I stand, for I can be no other, it seems to say. Neither of these impulses makes it easy for Chinese diplomats to communicate with the outside world or gain acceptance. But the former has the power to take China far further toward its goal of global influence and prestige than the latter, which is far more likely to leave it isolated.

Today, as the Party approaches the 100th anniversary of its founding, China's political system is showing signs of reverting to the patterns that have held its diplomacy back in the past. Since 2008, foreign ministry officials have engaged in an assertive approach to diplomacy that echoes previous periods of outward aggression. Their behavior is the manifestation of a newfound confidence after the success of maneuvering through the Global Financial Crisis combined with fresh insecurities about regime legitimacy and long-term stability after the 2011 Arab Spring. The new approach was supercharged after 2012 by the ascendancy of Xi Jinping as he moved to neuter opponents and crack down on domestic opposition.

The mixture of self-declared confidence and jumpy insecurity manifested by the current leadership has pushed Chinese diplomats to display many of their least appealing but also most enduring qualities. Things could be different if the Party allowed its diplomats greater freedom to use their formidable skills to promote and protect their country. But free thought and independent action are far too threatening to China's political system to be tolerated for long. As a result, Chinese diplomats spend more of their time looking back over their shoulders than out into the world.

Notes

Introduction

1. Colin Packham and Philip Wen, "In APEC Host Papua New Guinea, China and the West Grapple over Strategic Port," *Reuters*, November 15, 2018, https://www.reuters.com/article/us-apec-summit-china/in-apec-host-papua-new-guinea-china-and-the-west-grapple-over-strategic-port-idUSKCN1NJ375.
2. Sophia Yan, "China Pledges More than $100 Billion in Belt and Road Projects," *CNBC*, May 14 2017, https://www.cnbc.com/2017/05/14/china-pledges-more-than-100-billion-in-belt-and-road-projects.html.
3. Xinhua, "Full Text of Xi's Signed Article on PNG Newspapers," *Xinhua*, November 14, 2018, http://www.xinhuanet.com/english/2018-11/14/c_137605468.htm.
4. Kate Lyons, "'The China Show': Xi Jinping Arrives in PNG for Start of Apec Summit," *The Guardian*, November 16, 2018, https://www.theguardian.com/world/2018/nov/16/the-china-show-xi-jinping-arrives-in-png-for-start-of-apec-summit; Charlotte Greenfield and Philip Wen, "PNG Lays On a Lavish Welcome for China's Xi as He Arrives for APEC," *Reuters*, November 15, 2018, https://www.reuters.com/article/apec-summit-china/png-lays-on-a-lavish-welcome-for-chinas-xi-as-he-arrives-for-apec-idUSL4N1XQ16E; AFP Videos, "APEC Summit: The Xi Show by the Sea Shore," *Agence France-Presse*, November 15, 2018, https://www.yahoo.com/news/apec-summit-xi-show-sea-025604035.html.
5. Toluse Olorunnipa and Dandan Li, "Pence-Xi Showdown at APEC Shows U.S.-China Divide Only Widening," *Bloomberg News*, December 17, 2018, https://www.bloomberg.com/news/articles/2018-11-17/pence-slams-china-says-u-s-offers-countries-better-option.
6. Natalie Whiting and Stephen Dziedzic, "APEC 2018: Chinese Officials Barge Into PNG Foreign Minister's Office after Being Denied Meeting," *ABC*, November 18, 2018, https://www.abc.net.au/news/2018-11-18/chinese-officials-create-diplomatic-storm-at-apec/10508812; AFP, "Police Called after Chinese Diplomats Attempt to 'Barge In' to APEC Host's Office," *Agence France-Presse*, November 18, 2018, https://www.yahoo.com/news/police-called-diplomats-apec-summit-tensions-boil-over-050420060.html; Josh Rogin, "Inside China's 'Tantrum Diplomacy' at APEC," *Washington Post*, November 20, 2018, https://www.washingtonpost.com/news/josh-rogin/wp/2018/11/20/inside-chinas-tantrum-diplomacy-at-apec/?utm_term=.5e61b31e4a0b.
7. Jason Scott, Dandan Li, and Toluse Olorunnipa, "APEC Ends in Disarray after U.S.-China Spat over Final Statement," *Bloomberg News*, November 18, 2018, https://www.bloomberg.com/news/articles/2018-11-18/apec-fails-to-agree-on-joint-statement-amid-u-s-china-tensions.

8. Scott, Li, and Olorunnipa, "APEC Ends in Disarray."

9. Charlotte Greenfield and Tom Westbrook, "Nauru Demands China Apologize for 'Disrespect' at Pacific Forum," *Reuters*, September 6, 2018, https://www.reuters.com/article/us-pacific-forum-china/nauru-demands-china-apologize-for-disrespect-at-pacific-forum-idUSKCN1LM0HM.

10. Peter Martin, "Diplomatic Outbursts Mar Xi's Plan to Raise China on the World Stage," *Bloomberg News*, March 7, 2019, https://www.bloomberg.com/news/articles/2019-03-06/diplomatic-outbursts-mar-xi-s-plan-to-raise-china-on-world-stage; The Economist, "Shotgun Diplomacy: How Sweden Copes with Chinese Bullying," *The Economist*, February 20, 2020, https://www.economist.com/europe/2020/02/20/how-sweden-copes-with-chinese-bullying.

11. Ashley Rodriguez, "China's Box Office Is Setting New Records–with a Bit of Hollywood Help," *Quartz*, November 22, 2017, https://qz.com/1134905/wolf-warrior-2-helped-chinas-box-office-to-new-records-in-2017/.

12. Ben Westcott and Steven Jiang, "China Is Embracing a New Brand of Foreign Policy. Here's What Wolf Warrior Diplomacy Means," *CNN*, May 29, 2020, https://edition.cnn.com/2020/05/28/asia/china-wolf-warrior-diplomacy-intl-hnk/index.html.

13. "Discovering Twitter: China Finds a Use Abroad for Twitter, a Medium It Fears at Home," *The Economist*, February 20, 2020, https://www.economist.com/china/2020/02/20/china-finds-a-use-abroad-for-twitter-a-medium-it-fears-at-home.

14. Alan Crawford and Peter Martin, "China's Coronavirus Diplomacy Has Finally Pushed Europe Too Far," *Bloomberg News*, April 22, 2020, https://www.bloomberg.com/news/articles/2020-04-21/china-s-coronavirus-diplomacy-has-finally-pushed-europe-too-far.

15. Bob Davis, Kate O'Keeffe, and Lingling Wei, "U.S.'s China Hawks Drive Hard-Line Policies after Trump Turns on Beijing," *Wall Street Journal*, October 16, 2020, https://www.wsj.com/articles/u-s-s-china-hawks-drive-hard-line-policies-after-trump-turns-on-beijing-11602867030.

16. Crawford and Martin, "China's Coronavirus Diplomacy Has Finally Pushed Europe Too Far."

17. Peter Martin, "China Seen Negatively at Record Rate in Nine Nations, Poll Says," *Bloomberg News*, October 6, 2020, https://www.bloomberg.com/news/articles/2020-10-06/china-seen-negatively-at-record-rate-in-nine-nations-poll-says.

18. Joint Chiefs of Staff, Joint Doctrine Note 1-18 (Washington, DC: Joint Chiefs of Staff, 2018), https://fas.org/irp/doddir/dod/jdn1_18.pdf.

19. Keith Zhai and Ting Shi, "China Uses Annual Congress to Tout Xi's Global Leadership Role," *Bloomberg News*, March 9, 2017, https://www.bloomberg.com/news/articles/2017-03-08/china-uses-annual-congress-to-tout-xi-s-global-leadership-role.

20. Lowy Institute, *2019 Lowy Institute Global Diplomacy Index*, https://globaldiplomacyindex.lowyinstitute.org/.

21. Mao, Zedong. *Selected Works of Mao Tse-Tung*, Vol. II (Beijing: Foreign Languages Press, 1965), 224.

22. Interview with Gao Zhikai, March 19, 2019.

23. Ji Chaozhu, *The Man on Mao's Right: From Harvard Yard to Tiananmen Square, My Life Inside China's Foreign Ministry* (New York: Random House, 2008), 151–152.

24. Interview in Beijing, January 2018.

25. Zhou Zhendong, "Zai Feizhou de Xinzang: Zhade," in *Dangdai Zhongguo shijie waijiao shengya*, ed. Waijiaobu Waijiaoshi Yanjiushi, Vol. V (Beijing: Shijie Zhishi Chubanshe, 1997), 308.

26. Fenghuang Wang, "Waijiaobu, Guofangbu liang wei 'yanzhi dandang' yin he shi hanjian tongkuang," *Fenghuang Wang*, November 4, 2019, http://news.ifeng.com/c/7rKXYgxThgI.

27. Interview in Beijing, 2017.

28. Chas W. Freeman Jr., "Diplomacy: A Rusting Tool of American Statecraft," Lecture to programs on Statecraft at American University, Harvard, and MIT, February 2018, https://chasfreeman.net/diplomacy-a-rusting-tool-of-american-statecraft/.

29. Peter Martin, "Diplomatic Outbursts Mar Xi's Plan to Raise China on the World Stage," *Bloomberg News*, March 7, 2019, https://www.bloomberg.com/news/articles/2019-03-06/diplomatic-outbursts-mar-xi-s-plan-to-raise-china-on-world-stage.

30. Xiao Gang, "Xi Jinping on Foreigners 'Pointing Fingers' at China (with Video)," *China Digital Times*, February 12, 2009, https://chinadigitaltimes.net/2009/02/xi-jinping-%E4%B9%A0%E8%BF%91%E5%B9%B3-on-foreigners-pointing-fingers-at-china-with-video/.

31. Keith Zhai and Yew Lun Tian, "In China, a Young Diplomat Rises as Aggressive Foreign Policy Takes Root," *Reuters*, March 31, 2020, https://www.reuters.com/article/us-china-diplomacy-insight/in-china-a-young-diplomat-rises-as-aggressive-foreign-policy-takes-root-idUSKBN21I0F8.

32. Adela Suliman, Ed Flanagan, and Justin Solomon, "China Jeers as George Floyd Protests Sweep U.S.," *NBC News*, June 1, 2020, https://www.nbcnews.com/news/world/china-jeers-george-floyd-protests-sweep-u-s-while-some-n1220186.

33. Interview in Beijing, spring 2020.

34. Cissy Zhou, "We're Not Wolf Warriors, We're Only Standing Up for China, Says Senior Official," *South China Morning Post*, December 5, 2020, https://www.scmp.com/news/china/diplomacy/article/3112733/were-not-wolf-warriors-were-only-standing-china-says-senior.

35. Kinling Lo, "Beijing Should Contain 'Extreme Conationalism', Ex-Diplomat Warns," *South China Morning Post*, September 30, 2020, https://www.scmp.com/news/china/diplomacy/article/3103550/us-china-relations-beijing-should-contain-extreme-nationalism.

36. This phase is drawn shamelessly from John Keegan, *The Face of Battle: A Study of Agincourt, Waterloo and the Somme* (London: Random House, 1976).

37. The major exception is Liu Xiaohong's excellent *Chinese Ambassadors: The Rise of Diplomatic Professionalism since 1949* (Seattle: University of Washington Press, 2001).

Chapter 1

1. Account drawn from: Ling Qing, *Cong Yanan dao Lianheguo: Ling Qing waijiao shengya* (Fuzhou: Fujian Renmin Chubanshe, 2008), 20–21, 68–70; Xu Jingli, *Jiemi Zhongguo waijiao dang'an* (Beijing: Zhongguo Dangan Chubanshe, 2005), 86–93; Xu Jingli, *Lingqi luzao: jueqi juren de waijiao fanglyue* (Beijing: Shijie

Zhishi Chubanshe, 1997), 191–198; Zhang Hanfu Bianxiezu, *Zhang Hanfu zhuan* (Beijing: Shijie zhishi chubanshe, 2003), 134–139; Tong Xiaopeng, *Fengyu sishinian*, Vol. 2 (Beijing: Zhongyang Wenxian Chubanshe, 1997), 321–322; and Qiao Songdu, *Qiao Guanhua yu Gong Peng: Wo de fumuqin* (Beijing: Zhonghuan Shuju, 2008), 102–106.

2. While all accounts of the meeting agree that Zhou compared armed struggle and diplomatic struggle, they differ on whether Zhou used the phrase "PLA in civilian clothing," which he had earlier used in a speech at Xibaipo. Ling Qing quotes him using the phrase, but the excerpt of the speech in Zhou's selected works on diplomacy does not.

3. Barry Naughton, *The Chinese Economy: Transformation and Growth* (Cambridge, MA: MIT Press, 2007), 50; S. S. Kantha, "Nutrition and Health in China, 1949 to 1989," *Progress in Food and Nutrition Science* 14, no. 2–3 (1990): 93–137.

4. Jiang Benliang, *Duonaohe zhi bo* (Chengdu: Sichuan Renmin Chubanshe, 2004), 76.

5. Interview in Beijing, 2018.

6. Gao Wenqian, *Zhou Enlai: The Last Perfect Revolutionary* (New York: Public Affairs, 2007), 21–27; Jin Chongji, *Zhou Enlai zhuan, 1898–1949* (Beijing: Zhongyang Wenxian Chubanshe, 1998), 3–7; Barbara Barnouin and Yu Changgen, *Zhou Enlai: A Political Life* (Hong Kong: Chinese University Press, 2006), 12–14; and Michael Dillon, *Zhou Enlai: The Enigma behind Chairman Mao* (London: I. B. Tauris, 2020), 1–12.

7. CIA, "Chou En-lai," CIA FOIA, November 4, 1974.

8. Nikita Khrushchev, *Khrushchev Remembers* (New York: Little Brown & Company, 1970), 405

9. Frank Dikotter, *Mao's Great Famine: A History of China's Most Devastating Catastrophe, 1958–62* (London: Bloomsbury, 2010), 18.

10. Gao, *Zhou Enlai*, 161.

11. Michael H. Hunt, *The Genesis of Chinese Communist Foreign Policy* (New York: Columbia University Press, 1996), 71–73.

12. Li Yan, "Zuji bian tianya: Chunfeng song wanjia," in *Zhou Enlai he ta de mishu men*, ed. Cheng Hua (Beijing: Zhongguo Guangbo Dianshi Chubanshe, 1992), 99; Lei Yingfu, "Yinrong wanzai en hui you meng," in *Zhou Enlai he ta de mishu men*, ed. Cheng, 119; Chen Hao, "Danxin yi pian, hongtu wanjuan," in *Zhou Enlai he ta de mishu men*, ed. Cheng, 186.

13. Li "Zuji bian tianya," in *Zhou Enlai he ta de mishu men*, ed. Cheng, 99; Lei, "Yinrong wanzai en hui you meng," in *Zhou Enlai he ta de mishu men*, ed. Cheng, 119; Chen, "Danxin yi pian, hongtu wanjuan," in *Zhou Enlai he ta de mishu men*, ed. Cheng, 186.

14. Zhang Ying, "Jiechu de nyu waijiaojia Gong Peng," in *Nyu Waijiaoguan*, ed. Cheng Xiangjun (Beijing: Renmin Tiyu Chubanshe, 1995), 457.

15. Xinhua, "Da shuju jiemi: buwei jiaban da pin," *CCTV.com*, July 19, 2015, http://news.cntv.cn/2015/07/19/ARTI1437264706858411.shtml.

16. Ma Lie, "Dang fanyi qiake de shihou," in *Zhou Enlai he ta de mishu men*, ed. Cheng, 231.

17. Yang Chun, "Taoli wuyan zi fenfang," in *Zhou Enlai he ta de mishu men*, ed. Cheng, 70; Li, "zuji bian tianya," in *Zhou Enlai he ta de mishu men*, ed. Cheng, 106.

18. Li, "Zuji bian tianya," in *Zhou Enlai he ta de mishu men*, ed. Cheng, 107; Guo Yinghui, "Zai Zhou Enlai yu Peng Dehuai zhi jian chuan xin," in *Zhou Enlai he ta de mishu men*, ed. Cheng, 134.

19. Ma, "Dang fanyi qiake de shihou," in *Zhou Enlai he ta de mishu men*, ed. Cheng, 230.

20. Tang Mingxin, *Feijia Taipingyang shangkong de hongqiao* (Chengdu: Sichuan Renmin Chubanshe, 2006), 13; Jiang, *Duonaohe zhi bo*, 90–92; Liu Yanshun, *Shan he hu hai hua Bolan* (Chengdu: Sichuan Renmin Chubanshe, 2006), 17–18; Zhang Xichang, *Sishi nian Faguo yuan* (Chengdu: Sichuan Renmin Chubanshe, 2006), 8–12; Ji, *The Man on Mao's Right:*, 151; Ke Hua, *Xin Zhongguo waijiao qisu Ke Hua 95 sui shuhuai* (Beijing: Wenhua Yishu Chubanshe, 2013), 97; Waijiaobu Waijiaoshi Bianjishi, *Xin Zhongguo waijiao fengyun*, Vol. 1 (Beijing: Shije Zhishi Chubanshe, 1990), 95–97; and Hua Liming, "wo mudu de Zhongdong fengyun," in *Ting dashi jiang gushi*, ed. Niu Li (Beijing: Xinhua Chubanshe, 2009), 4.

21. Jiang, *Duonaohe zhi bo*, 90; Zhang, *Sishi nian Faguo yuan*, 8–12; Cong Wenzi, "Zhou Enlai zongli dui waishi fanyi gongzuo de zhidao he guanhuai," in *Zhongguo waijiaoguan shouji*, ed. Li Tongcheng, Vol. 1 (Xiamen: Lujiang Chubanshe, 2001), 244–264; Ji, *The Man on Mao's Right*, 151; and Cheng Ruisheng, *Mulin waijiao sishi nian* (Chengdu: Sichuan Renmin Chubanshe, 2006), 39, 95, 97.

22. Lydia H. Liu, "Legislating the Universal: The Circulation of International Law in the Nineteenth Century," in *Tokens of Exchange: The Problem of Translation in Global Circulation*, ed. Lydia Liu (Durham, NC: Duke University Press, 1999), 145.

23. Masataka Banno, *China and the West 1858–1861: The Origins of the Tsungli Yamen* (Cambridge, MA: Harvard University Press, 1964).

24. William T. Rowe, *China's Last Empire: The Great Qing* (Cambridge, MA: Harvard University Press, 2009), 223.

25. S. C. M. Paine, *The Sino-Japanese War of 1894–1895: Perceptions, Power, and Primacy* (New York: Cambridge University Press, 2003), 32–33.

26. Odd Arne Westad, *Restless Empire: China and the World since 1750* (New York: Basic Books, 2012), 99–104.

27. Antonia Finnane, *Changing Clothes in China: Fashion, History, Nation* (New York: Columbia University Press, 2008), 69.

28. Li Zhaoxing, *Shuo bu jin de waijiao: Wo de kuaile huiyi* (Beijing: Zhongxin Chubanshe, 2014), 34–35.

29. Orville Schell and John Delury, *Wealth and Power: China's Long March to the Twenty-First Century* (New York: Random House, 2013), 320.

30. Brendan Scott, "Memories of China's 1895 Shame Loom over Envoy's High-Stakes Talks," *Bloomberg News*, May 9, 2019, https://www.bloomberg.com/news/articles/2019-05-09/china-trade-envoy-s-unflattering-comparison-shows-high-stakes.

31. Jennifer Rudolph, *Negotiated Power in Late Imperial China: The Zongli Yamen and the Politics of Reform* (Ithaca, NY: Cornell University Press, 2008), 405.

32. Gao, *Zhou Enlai*, 27.

33. Wang Dong, *China's Unequal Treaties: Narrating National History* (Plymouth, MA: Lexington, 2008), 10.

34. Wang, Zheng, *Never Forget National Humiliation: Historical Memory in Chinese Politics and Foreign Relations* (New York: Columbia University Press, 2012), 151.

35. Gao, *Zhou Enlai*, 28.

36. Gao, *Zhou Enlai*, 28–29; Barnouin and Yu, *Zhou Enlai*, 14–16.

37. Wu Jianmin, *Tan waijiao* (Beijing: Zhongxin Chubanshe, 2015), 6–7, 148; and Wu Jianmin and Shi Yanhua, *Zai Faguo de waijiao shengya* (Beijing: Zhongguo Renmin Daxue Chubanshe 2010), 12–13.

38. Wu, *Tan waijiao*, 6–7, 148; Wu and Shi, *Zai Faguo de waijiao shengya*, 12–13.

39. Gao, *Zhou Enlai*, 3; Lu Peixin, "Jiemi waijiao liyi beihou de jiaofeng," in *Bie yang feng yu*, ed. Zhang Bing (Beijing: Xinhua Chubanshe, 2007), 221–222.

40. Tang Jiaxuan, *Jin yu xu feng* (Beijing: Shijie Zhishi Chubanshe, 2009), 81.

41. Xu Guoqi, *Strangers on the Western Front: Chinese Workers in the Great War* (Cambridge, MA: Harvard University Press, 2011).

42. Xu Guoqi, *China and the Great War: China's Pursuit of a New National Identity and Internationalization* (Cambridge, UK: Cambridge University Press, 2005), 187.

43. Xu, *China and the Great War*, 245.

44. Margaret MacMillan, *Peacemakers: Six Months That Changed the World* (London: John Murray, 2001), 332–333, 340–341.

45. Rana Mitter, *A Bitter Revolution: China's Struggle with the Modern World* (Oxford: Oxford University Press, 2004), 3–4, 7–10.

46. Gao, *Zhou Enlai*, 29–42; Barnouin and Yu, *Zhou Enlai*, 18–21.

47. Paul Bailey, "The Chinese Work-Study Movement in France," *The China Quarterly* 115 (September 1988): 441–461.

48. Gao, *Zhou Enlai*, 39–45; Barnouin and Yu, *Zhou Enlai*, 25–27.

49. Hunt, *The Genesis of Chinese Communist Foreign Policy*, 71–73.

50. Jay Taylor, *The Generalissimo: Chiang Kai-shek and the Struggle for Modern China* (Cambridge, MA: Harvard University Press, 2009), 157.

51. See Lenin's 1920 call for the Bolsheviks to act with "military ruthlessness, with military discipline and self-sacrifice" in Christopher Read, *Lenin: A Revolutionary Life* (London: Routledge, 2005), 254.

52. Barnouin and Yu, *Zhou Enlai*, 32.

53. Taylor, *The Generalissimo*, 55.

54. Gao, *Zhou Enlai*, 48.

55. Gao, *Zhou Enlai*, 55–57.

56. Jin, *Zhou Enlai zhuan, 1898–1949*, 291–295; Matthew James Brazil, "The Darkest Red Corner: Chinese Communist Intelligence and Its Place in the Party, 1926–1945," PhD diss., University of Sydney, 2012; Barnouin and Yu, *Zhou Enlai*, 44–45.

57. Jin, *Zhou Enlai zhuan, 1898–1949*, 326–328.

58. Gao, *Zhou Enlai*, 68–69.

59. Benjamin Yang, "The Zunyi Conference as One Step in Mao's Rise to Power: A Survey of Historical Studies of the Chinese Communist Party," *The China Quarterly* 106 (1986): 235.

60. Yang, "Taoli wuyan zi fenfang," in *Zhou Enlai he ta de mishu men*, ed. Cheng, 61; Li, "Zuji bian tianya: Chunfeng song wanjia," in *Zhou Enlai he ta de mishu men*, ed. Cheng, 108.

61. Gao, *Zhou Enlai*, 235.
62. Interview with Sidney Rittenberg, March 2017.
63. Li Zhisui, *The Private Life of Chairman Mao: The Memoirs of Mao's Personal Physician* (New York: Random House, 1994), 509–510.
64. Tang, *Feijia Taipingyang shangkong de hongqiao*, 16.
65. Shi Zhe, *Zai lishi juren shenbian* (Beijing: Zhongyang Wenxian Chubanshe, 1991), 539–544.
66. Waijiaobu Waijiaoshi Bianjishi, *Xin Zhongguo waijiao fengyun*, Vol. 1, 80.
67. Chen, "Danxin Yi Pian," in *Zhou Enlai he ta de mishu men*, ed. Cheng, 195.
68. Gao, *Zhou Enlai*, 4.
69. Frederic E. Wakeman, *Spymaster: Dai Li and the Chinese Secret Service* (Berkeley: University of California Press, 2003), 178.
70. Steve Tsang, "Target Zhou Enlai: The 'Kashmir Princess' Incident of 1955," *The China Quarterly* 139 (September 1994): 774.
71. Gao, *Zhou Enlai*.
72. Li Weihan, *Huiyi yu yanjiu* (Beijing: Zhonggong Dangshi Ziliao Chubanshe, 1984), 363.
73. Michael Ellman, "Soviet Repression Statistics: Some Comments," *Europe-Asia Studies*, Vol. 54, No. 7 (2002), p. 1162

Chapter 2

1. Huang Hua, *Qinli yu jianwen: Huang Hua huiyilu* (Beijing: Shijie Zhishi Chubanshe, 2007), 2–38.
2. Jeremy Tai, " Opening Up the Northwest: Reimagining Xi'an and the Modern Chinese Frontier," unpublished doctoral dissertation, UC Santa Cruz (2015).
3. For a detailed look at Li's role in Chinese intelligence see Peter L. Mattis, "Li Kenong and the Practice of Chinese Intelligence," *International Journal of Intelligence and CounterIntelligence* 28, no. 3 (2015): 540–556.
4. Pauline Keating, "The Ecological Origins of the Yan'an Way," *The Australian Journal of Chinese Affairs* 32 (July 1994): 123–153.
5. Kai Cheng, *Li Kenong: Yi ge yinbi zhanxian de zhuoyue lingdaoren* (Beijing: Zhongguo Youyi Chuban Gongsi, 1996), 101.
6. S. Bernard Thomas, *Season of High Adventure: Edgar Snow in China* (Berkeley: University of California Press, 1996), 13–27; John Maxwell Hamilton, *Edgar Snow: A Biography* (Bloomington: Indiana University Press, 1988), 5–15.
7. Anne-Marie Brady, *Making the Foreign Serve China: Managing Foreigners in the People's Republic* (Lanham, MD: Rowman & Littlefield, 2003), 43–45.
8. Julia Lovell, "The Uses of Foreigners in Mao-Era China: 'Techniques of Hospitality' and International Image-Building in the People's Republic, 1949–1976," *Transactions of the RHS* 25 (2015): 135–158.
9. Brady, *Making the Foreign Serve China*, 43–45.
10. Brady, *Making the Foreign Serve China*, 43–45.

11. James Griffiths, "Trump to Become First Foreign Leader to Dine in Forbidden City since Founding of Modern China," *CNN*, November 8, 2017, https://www.cnn.com/2017/11/07/politics/trump-forbidden-city-beijing-china/index.html; "Xi Hosts Trump with Iconic Chinese Culture," *Xinhua*, November 8, 2017, http://www.xinhuanet.com//english/2017-11/08/c_136737845.htm.

12. "Remarks by President Trump and President Xi of the People's Republic of China before Bilateral Meeting," Osaka, Japan, June 29, 2019, https://www.whitehouse.gov/briefings-statements/remarks-president-trump-president-xi-peoples-republic-china-bilateral-meeting-osaka-japan/.

13. Brady, *Making the Foreign Serve China*, 45.

14. Brady, *Making the Foreign Serve China*, 45–47.

15. Kai, *Li Kenong*, 101–112.

16. Edgar Snow, *Red Star over China* (New York: Grove Press, 1968), 90, 124.

17. Andrew G. Walder, *China under Mao: A Revolution Derailed* (Cambridge, MA: Harvard University Press, 2017), 7, 25–26.

18. Jin Cheng, *Yan'an Jiaojichu huiyilu* (Beijing: Zhongguo Qingnian Chubanshe, 1985), 40–49, 136–137, 157, 198–218.

19. Fang Kecheng, "Shei shi 'Zhongguo renmin de lao pengyou'?," *Nanfang Zhoumo*, March 3, 2011, http://www.infzm.com/content/55879; Lee Kuan Yew, *From Third World to First: Singapore and the Asian Economic Boom* (New York: HarperCollins, 2000), 608.

20. Foreign Ministry Spokesperson Lu Kang's Regular Press Conference on December 7, 2016, http://www.fmprc.gov.cn/mfa_eng/xwfw_665399/s2510_665401/t1422213.shtml.

21. Interview with Robert Suettinger, July 22, 2019.

22. Yi Fei, *Fengyun jidang, yi ge laowuguan de waijiao shengya* (Shenyang: Liaoning renmin chubanshe, 2003), 60–61; see also Peter Mattis, "Contrasting China and Russia's Influence Operations," *War on the Rocks*, January 16, 2018, https://warontherocks.com/2018/01/contrasting-chinas-russias-influence-operations/.

23. Richard H. Solomon, *Chinese Negotiating Behavior: Pursuing Interests Through "Old Friends,"* new ed. (Washington, DC: United States Institute of Peace Press, 1999), 100–102.

24. Huang, *Qinli yu jianwen*, 39–47.

25. Kishan S. Rana, *Asian Diplomacy: The Foreign Ministries of China, India, Japan, Singapore, and Thailand* (Washington, DC: Woodrow Wilson Center Press, 2007), 27; Interviews in Beijing.

26. Shi, *Zai lishi juren shenbian*, 200–201; Shi Changwang, *Wang Jiaxiang zhuan* (Hefei: Anhui Renmin Chubanshe, 1999), 89–90; Xu Zehao, *Wang Jiaxiang zhuan* (Beijing: Dangdai Zhongguo Chubanshe, 1996), 120–127; Hunt, *The Genesis of Chinese Communist Foreign Policy*, 227.

27. Li, *Huiyi yu Yanjiu*, 376; Cheng Zhongyuan, *Zhang Wentian zhuan* (Beijing: Dangdai Zhongguo Chubanshe, 2000), 186–189; Kai, *Li Kenong*, 101.

28. Tong Xiaopeng, *Fengyu sishinian*, Vol. 1 (Beijing: Zhongyang Wenxian Chubanshe, 1994), 155, 315–316; Jin, *Zhou Enlai zhuan, 1898–1949*, 513–514, 590, 603–604, 651, 663, 790.

29. Hunt, *The Genesis of Chinese Communist Foreign Policy*, 227.

30. Ling, *Cong Yanan dao Lianheguo*; Qiao, *Qiao Guanhua yu Gong Peng*, 40.

31. Qiao, *Qiao Guanhua yu Gong Peng*, 40.

32. John Pomfret, *The Beautiful Country and the Middle Kingdom: America and China, 1776 to the Present* (New York: Henry Holt, 2016), 328.

33. Hunt, *The Genesis of Chinese Communist Foreign Policy*, 143.

34. Gao Hua, *How Did the Red Sun Rise?: The Origin and Development of the Yan'an Rectification Movement, 1930–1945* (Hong Kong: Chinese University Press, 2018), 319–334.

35. Huang, *Qinli yu Jianwen*, 46–47; Jin, *Zhou Enlai zhuan, 1898–1949*, 682–683; Shi, *Zai lishi juren shenbian*, 242.

36. Ke, *Xin Zhongguo waijiao qisu Ke Hua 95 sui shuhuai*, 64–65.

37. Timothy Cheek, "The Fading of Wild Lilies: Wang Shiwei and Mao Zedong's Yan'an Talks in the First CPC Rectification Movement," *The Australian Journal of Chinese Affairs* 11 (1984): 25–58.

38. Huang, *Qinli yu jianwen*, 46–47.

39. Huang, *Qinli yu jianwen*, 46–47; Jin, *Zhou Enlai zhuan, 1898–1949*, 682–683; Wu Xiuquan, *Wo de licheng* (Beijing: Jiefangjun Chubanshe, 1984), 162–164.

40. Petr Parfenovich Vladimirov, *The Vladimirov Diaries: Yenan, China, 1942–1945* (New York: Doubleday, 1975), 240.

41. Tong, *Fengyu sishinian*, vol. 2, 253–266; Jin, *Zhou Enlai zhuan, 1898–1949*, 679–693.

42. Barnouin and Yu, *Zhou Enlai*, 92.

43. Jin, *Yan'an Jiaojichu huiyilu*, 89.

44. Interview with Robert Suettinger, July 22, 2019.

45. This section draws on Ling, *Cong Yanan dao Lianheguo*, 21–22, 28–30; Huang, *Qinli yu jianwen*, 48–71; Pomfret, *The Beautiful Country and the Middle Kingdom*, 320–331.

46. Huang, *Qinli yu Jianwen*, 55.

47. Hunt, *The Genesis of Chinese Communist Foreign Policy*, 152.

48. Huang, *Qinli yu jianwen*, 55; Ling, *Cong Yanan dao Lianheguo*, 28–30.

49. Ling, *Cong Yanan dao Lianheguo*, 28–30; Jin, *Yan'an Jiaojichu huiyilu*, 190–197.

50. John S. Service, *Lost Chance in China: The World War II Dispatches of John S. Service* (New York: Random House, 1974), 181.

51. Niu Jun, *From Yan'an to the World: The Origin and Development of Chinese Communist Foreign Policy* (Norwalk, CT: Eastbridge, 2005), 165–167.

52. Daniel Kurtz-Phelan, *The China Mission: George Marshall's Unfinished War, 1945–1947* (New York: W. W. Norton, 2018), eBook; Huang, *Qinli yu jianwen*, 65–69.

53. "Special Message to the Congress on Greece and Turkey: The Truman Doctrine," March 12, 1947, https://www.trumanlibrary.gov/library/public-papers/56/special-message-congress-greece-and-turkey-truman-doctrine.

54. Odd Arne Westad, *The Cold War: A World History* (London: Penguin Random House, 2017), 142.

55. Ho Feng-Shan, *My Forty Years as a Diplomat* (Pittsburgh: Dorrance, 2010), 125; Jonathan Clements, *Makers of the Modern World—Wellington Koo, China* (London: Haus Publishing, 2008), 21–22; Xu, *Jiemi Zhongguo waijiao dang'an*, 106–112.

56. Ling, *Cong Yanan dao Lianheguo*, 58–61; Waijiaobu Waijiaoshi Bianjishi, *Xin Zhongguo waijiao fengyun*, Vol. 2 (Beijing: Shije Zhishi Chubanshe, 1994), 163–164; Xu, *Lingqi luzao*, 36.

57. Ling, *Cong Yanan dao Lianheguo*, 58–61.

58. Ling, *Cong Yanan dao Lianheguo*, 64–65.

59. Huang, *Qinli yu jianwen*, 72–88; Xu, *Jiemi Zhongguo waijiao dang'an*, 22–23.

60. Interview with Sidney Rittenberg, March 2017.

61. Kenneth T. Young, *Negotiating with the Chinese Communists: The United States Experience, 1953–1967* (New York: McGraw-Hill, 1968), 30.

62. China Daily, "Former Mao Translator, Diplomat Huang Dies," *People's Daily online*, November 25, 2010, http://en.people.cn/90001/90782/90873/7210273.html.

63. Huang, *Qinli yu Jianwen*, 72–88; Xu, *Jiemi Zhongguo waijiao dang'an*, 22–23.

64. Xu, *Jiemi Zhongguo waijiao dang'an*, 78; Ling Qing, *Cong Yanan dao Lianheguo*, 66; Zhang Rong "Zhou Enlai de 'erduo he zuiba'—Wang Bingnan," in *Kaiqi guomen: Waijiaoguan de fengcai*, eds. Fu Hao and Li Tongcheng (Beijing: Zhongguo Huaqiao Chubanshe, 1995), 120–122, 127; Luo Yisu, "Wang Bingnan tieshi: Yi waijiaojia Wang Bingnan," in *Dangdai Zhongguo shijie waijiao shengya*, ed. Waijiaobu Waijiaoshi Yanjiushi (Beijing: Shije Zhishi Chubanshe, 1994), Vol. VI, 30–31.

65. Xu, *Jiemi Zhongguo waijiao dangan*, 76–81; Ruan Hong, *Han Xu zhuan* (Beijing: Shijie Zhishi Chubanshe, 2004), 40.

66. Yi, *Fengyun jidang*, 5; Hao Rui, *Huang tudi shang zoulai de waijiaojia: Fu Hao* (Beijing: Jiefangjun Chubanshe, 2001), 38–39.

Chapter 3

1. Pieced together from Zong Daoyi, *Zhou Nan koushu: Yaoxiang dangnian yu shan lun jin* (Jinan: Qilu Shushe, 2007), 103; Zhou Yihuang, "Jiangjun Dashimen," in *Zhongguo waijiaoguan shouji*, ed. Li Tongcheng, Vol. 2 (Xiamen: Lujiang Chubanshe, 2001), 704; Pei Monong, "Ciya dalu shang de teming quanquan dashi: Xin Zhongguo di yi dai waijiaojia Yuan Zhongxian," in *Kaiqi guomen*, eds. Fu and Li, 302–308; Yin Jiamin, "Pingfeng hou biye de jiangjun dashi," in *Shenmi zhi men: Gongheguo waijiao shilu*, ed. Cao Ying (Beijing: Tuanjie Chubanshe, 1993), 296–298.

2. Yi, *Fengyun jidang*; Hao, *Huang tudi shang zoulai de waijiaojia*, 38–39.

3. Jin Chongji, *Zhou Enlai zhuan, 1949–1976* (Beijing: Zhongyang Wenxian Chubanshe, 1998), 5; Bo Yibo, *Ruogan zhongda juece yu shijian de huigu* (Beijing: Zhonggong Zhongyang Dangxiao Chubanshe, 1992), 11; the exception was a small group of Nationalist diplomats awarded a purely advisory role.

4. Xu, *Lingqi luzao*, 190–191.

5. Yi, *Fengyun jidang*, 6.

6. Zhang Hanzhi, *Wo yu Qiao Guanhua* (Beijing: Zhongguo Qingnian Chubanshe, 1994), 251.

7. Kai, *Li Kenong*, 364.

8. Ling Qing, *Cong Yan'an dao Lianheguo*, 68.

9. Chen Xiuxia, *Xianshen duiwai jiaoliu: Jiating, liuxue shengya ji duiwai gongzuo jiaoliu huodong jishi* (Beijing: Shijie Zhishi Chubanshe, 2001), 21–35.

10. Liu, *Chinese Ambassadors*, 14–18.

11. Yi, *Fengyun Jidang*, 5.

12. Zhou, "Jiangjun Dashimen," in *Zhongguo waijiaoguan shouji*, ed. Li, Vol. 2, 701; Zhang Rong, "Huang tudi zou lai de waijiaoguan—Fu Hao," in *Kaiqi guomen*, eds. Fu and Li, 94.

13. Han Nianlong, "Waijiao shengya huigu yu diandi tihui," in *Dangdai Zhongguo shijie waijiao shengya*, ed. Waijiaobu Waijiaoshi Yanjiushi (Beijing: Shijie Zhishi Chubanshe, 1994), 176; Zhou, "Jiangjun dashimen," in *Zhongguo waijiaoguan shouji*, ed. Li, Vol. 2, 701–703.

14. Yi, *Fengyun jidang*, 11–15.

15. Yin, "Pingfeng hou biye de jiangjun dashi," in *Shenmi zhimen*, ed. Cao, 192.

16. Jiang, *Duonaohe zhi bo*, 11.

17. Yi, *Fengyun jidang*, 8.

18. Zong, *Zhou Nan koushu*, 390.

19. Ji, *The Man on Mao's Right*, 122.

20. Esther Cheo Ying, *Black Country to Red China: One Girl's Journey from War-torn England to Revolutionary China* (London: Penguin Random House, 2009), eBook.

21. Shi, *Zai lishi juren shenbian*, 379.

22. Cheo, *Black Country to Red China*, eBook; Luo Yisu, "Wang Bingnan tieshi: Yi waijiaojia Wang Bingnan," *Dangdai Zhongguo shijie waijiao shengya*, ed. Waijiaobu Waijiaoshi Yanjiushi, Vol. VI, 32.

23. Max Weber, "The Meaning of Discipline," *From Max Weber: Essays in Sociology*, eds. Hans Gerth and C. Wright Mills (New York: Oxford University Press, 1958), 253.

24. Michel Foucault, *Discipline and Punish: The Birth of the Prison* (New York: Vintage Books, 1995), 166.

25. Ling, *Cong Yanan dao Lianheguo*, 65; interviews in Beijing.

26. Wang Guoquan, *Wang Guoquan huiyilu* (Beijing: Zhongguo Shehui Chubanshe, 1996), 70; Zhou, "Jiangjun dashimen," in *Zhongguo waijiaoguan shouji*, ed. Li, Vol. 2, 703.

27. Ji Pengfei, "Chushi minzhu Deguo jishi," in *Dangdai Zhongguo shijie waijiao shengya*, ed. Waijiaobu Waijiaoshi Yanjiushi, Vol. I, 168.

28. Christopher R. Hughes, *Chinese Nationalism in the Global Era* (London: Routledge, 2006), 40.

29. Li, *Shuo bu jin de waijiao*, 343–344.

30. Susan Thornton interviewed by James Green, US-China Dialogue Podcast, March 31, 2019, https://uschinadialogue.georgetown.edu/podcasts/stapleton-roy.

31. Interview with Susan Thornton, July 9, 2019.

32. Li, *Shuo bu jin de waijiao*, 161–162.

33. Interview with David Mulroney, July 11, 2019.

34. Interview with David Mulroney, July 11, 2019

35. Xu, *Jiemi Zhongguo waijiao dang'an*, 98–101; Zhou, "Jiangjun dashimen," in *Zhongguo waijiaoguan shouji*, ed. Li, Vol. 2, 703.

36. Zong, *Zhou Nan koushu*, 113.

37. Xu, *Jiemi Zhongguo waijiao dang'an*, 98–101; Zhou, "Jiangjun dashimen," in *Zhongguo waijiaoguan shouji*, ed. Li, Vol. 2, 703.

38. Elizabeth McGuire, "Sino-Soviet Romance: An Emotional History of Revolutionary Geopolitics," *Journal of Contemporary History* 52, no. 4 (2017): 867–868.

39. Elizabeth McGuire, *Red at Heart: How Chinese Communists Fell in Love with the Russian Revolution* (New York: Oxford University Press, 2018), 285; Cheng, *Zhang Wentian zhuan*, 80.

40. Wang, *Wang Guoquan huiyilu*, 193.

41. Jiang, *Duonaohe zhi bo*, 17.

42. Li, *Shuo bu jin de waijiao*, 317.

43. Yi, *Fengyun jidang*, 18; Xu, *Jiemi Zhongguo waijiao dang'an*, 98–101; Xu, *Lingqi luzao*, 268–269.

44. Yin, "Pingfeng hou biye de jiangjun dashi," in *Shenmi zhi men*, ed. Cao, 299–300.

45. Interviews in Beijing.

46. Zhang Guobin, *Waijiaoguan shuo liyi* (Beijing: Huawen Chubanshe, 2009), 37–38, 114, 159, 261–262.

47. Kang Maozhao, *Waijiaoguan huiyilu* (Beijing: Zhongyang wenxian chubanshe, 2001), 21.

48. Shi Shi, "Peng Mingzhi chushi Bolan shiji," in *Dangdai Zhongguo shijie waijiao shengya*, ed. Wiajiaobu Waijiaoshi Yanjiushi, Vol. I, 41.

49. Liu, *Chinese Ambassadors*, 46.

50. Liu Ying, "Bu xunchang de dashi: Yi Zhang Wentian chushi Mosike," in *Dangdai Zhongguo shijie waijiao shengya*, ed. Wiajiaobu Waijiaoshi Yanjiushi, Vol. II (Beijing: Shijie Zhishi Chubanshe, 1994), 6.

51. Cheng, *Mulin Waijiao Sihi Nian*, 15–16.

52. Shi Shi, "Peng Mingzhi chushi Bolan shiji," in *Dangdai Zhongguo shijie waijiao shengya*, ed. Wiajiaobu Waijiaoshi Yanjiushi, 42.

53. Jiang, *Duonaohe zhi bo*, 21–22.

54. Yi, *Fengyun jidang*, 27.

55. Xie Heng, "Zai guowai de rizili," in *Nyu waijiaoguan*, ed. Cheng, 578.

56. Ke, *Xin Zhongguo waijiao qisu Ke Hua 95 sui shuhuai*, 88–89.

57. Xu, *Wang Jiaxiang zhuan*, 477; Zhu Zhongli, "Wang Jiaxiang waijiao shengya zongyi," in *Dangdai Zhongguo shijie waijiao shengya*, ed. Wiajiaobu Waijiaoshi Yanjiushi (Beijing: Shijie Zhishi Chubanshe, 1994), 25; Shi Shi, "Peng Mingzhi chushi Bolan jishi," in *Dangdai Zhongguo shijie waijiao shengya*, ed. Wiajiaobu Waijiaoshi Yanjiushi, 41; Zhu Xiangzhong, *Lamei qinliji* (Chengdu: Sichuan Renmin Chubanshe, 2004), 11–12.

58. Geng Biao, "waijiao shengya diandi," in *Dangdai Zhongguo shijie waijiao shengya*, ed. Wiajiaobu Waijiaoshi Yanjiushi, Vol. I, 110; Pei Monong, "yingjie Zhong Yi youhao gaochao de shouren dashi Yuan Zhongxian," in *Dangdai Zhongguo shijie waijiao shengya*, ed. Wiajiaobu Waijiaoshi Yanjiushi, Vol. I, 110; Xie, "Zai guowai de rizili," in *Nyu waijiaoguan*, ed. Cheng, 578; Liu, *Chinese Ambassadors*, 24–25.

59. Zong, *Zhou Nan koushu*, 102–103.

60. Quoted in Liu, *Chinese Ambassadors*, 102.

61. Shen Jian, "Churen zhu yindu dashi de qianqian houhou," in *Dangdai Zhongguo shijie waijiao shengya*, ed. Wiajiaobu Waijiaoshi Yanjiushi, Vol. III (Beijing: Shijie Zhishi Chubanshe, 1994), 18.

62. Ma Xinghan, "Fengyun tuqi: Liangci jinji zhaojian," in *Waijiao fengyun: Waijiaoguan haiwai miwen*, eds. Fu Hao and Li Tongcheng (Beijing: Zhongguo huaqiao chubanshe), 179.

63. Cheng Yuanxing, *Zhongguo shewai shijian miwen* (Beijing: Zuojia Chubanshe, 2006), 188–191.

64. Li Jiazhong, *Cong Weiminghu dao Huanjiahu: Wo yu Yuenan* (Chengdu: Sichuan Renmin Chubanshe, 2004), 9.

65. Dylan M. H. Loh, "Diplomatic Control, Foreign Policy, and Change under Xi Jinping: A Field Theoretic Account," *Journal of Current Chinese Affairs* 47, no. 3 (2018): 126; see also Lyu Congmin, *Waijiao Rensheng: Wo de huiyi he ganwu* (Beijing: Zhongxin Chubanshe, 2009), 205.

66. Liu, *Chinese Ambassadors*, 28.

67. Ji, *The Man on Mao's Right*, 151–152.

68. Gu Ji, "Waijiao shengya er san shi," Mi Guojun, "1976 nian 1 yue 9 ri zai Dongjing," in *Dangdai Zhongguo shijie waijiao shengya*, ed. Wiajiaobu Waijiaoshi Yanjiushi, Vol. IV (Beijing: Shijie Zhishi Chubanshe, 1996), 115.

69. Shi, *Wang Jiaxiang zhuan*, 283; Xu, *Wang Jiaxiang zhuan*, 478.

70. Margaret Atwood, *The Handmaid's Tale* (London: Vintage Books, 1996), 71.

71. Li, *Cong Weiminghu dao Huanjiahu*, 11–12.

72. Zhang, *Waijiaoguan shuo liyi*, 26.

73. Interviews in Beijing; see also Loh, "Diplomatic Control, Foreign Policy, and Change under Xi Jinping," 127.

74. Interview in Washington DC, July 2019.

75. Interview in Beijing.

76. Interview with Gao Zhikai, March 19, 2019.

77. Wu, *Tan Waijiao*, 16.

78. Gregg A. Brazinsky, *Winning the Third World: Sino-American Rivalry During the Cold War* (Chapel Hill: University of North Carolina Press, 2017), 50.

79. Byron S. Weng, "Communist China's Changing Attitudes toward the United Nations," *International Organization* 20, no. 4 (Autumn 1966): 684.

80. "Telegram from Zhou Enlai to Wu Xiuquan and Qiao Guanhua," December 3, 1950, History and Public Policy Program Digital Archive, Zhonggong zhongyang wenxian yanjiushi (CPC Central Historical Documents Research Office) and Zhongyang dang'anguan (Central Archives), eds., Jianguo yilai Zhou Enlai wengao (Zhou Enlai's Manuscripts since the Founding of the PRC), vol. 3 (Beijing: Zhongyang wenxian chubanshe, 2008), 575–576. Translated by Jingxia Yang and Douglas Stiffler, https://digitalarchive.wilsoncenter.org/document/114235.

81. Wu Xiuquan, *Zai Waijiaobu ba nian de jingli* (Beijing: Shijie Zhishi Chubanshe, 1983), 52, 41.

82. Wu, *Zai Waijiaobu ba nian de jingli*, 43, 46.

83. Hampton Sides, *On Desperate Ground: The Marines at the Reservoir, the Korean War's Greatest Battle* (New York: Doubleday, 2018), 212.

84. Wu, *Zai Waijiaobu ba nian de jingli*, 52–57; "Chinese Intervention in Korea Has Become Aggression," *Daily Mercury*, November 30, 1950, https://trove.nla.gov.au/newspaper/article/171310405; "The Road to Paris," *Time*, December 11, 1950, http://content.time.com/time/subscriber/article/0,33009,814060,00.html.

85. Ji, *The Man on Mao's Right*, 92.

86. Yang Guanqun, *Chaotouxishui sanshi nian* (Chengdu: Sichuan Renmin Chubanshe, 2006), 46–47.

87. Zong, *Zhou Nan koushu*, 105.

88. John W. Garver, *China's Quest: The History of the Foreign Relations of the People's Republic of China* (Oxford: Oxford University Press, 2016), 92–93.

89. Kathryn Weathersby, "Stalin, Mao, and the End of the Korean War," in *Brothers in Arms: The Rise and Fall of the Sino-Soviet Alliance*, ed. Odd Arne Westad (Stanford, CA: Stanford University Press, 1998), 108–109.

90. Westad, *The Cold War*, 233.

91. Hua-yu Li, *Mao and the Economic Stalinization of China, 1948–1953* (Lanham, MD: Rowman & Littlefield, 2006), 155–161.

92. Shi, *Zai lishi juren shenbian*, 516–517; Lin, "Bu xunchang de dashi," in *Dangdai Zhongguo shijie waijiao shengya*, ed. Wiajiaobu Waijiaoshi Yanjiushi, Vol. II, 15; Jin, *Zhou Enlai zhuan, 1949–1976*, 116–117; Bo, *Ruogan Zhongda Juece yu shijian de huigu*, 284–287.

93. Deborah Kaple, "Agents of Change: Soviet Advisers and High Stalinist Management in China, 1949–1960," *Journal of Cold War Studies* 18, no. 1 (2016): 5–30.

94. Geoffrey Roberts, "A Chance for Peace? The Soviet Campaign to End the Cold War, 1953–1955," Cold War International History Project, Woodrow Wilson International Center for Scholars, working paper no. 57 (October 2008).

95. Quoted in Liu, *Chinese Ambassadors*, 6.

Chapter 4

1. Chen Jian, "China and the First Indo-China War, 1950–54," *The China Quarterly* 133 (March 1993): 85–110.

2. Chen, "China and the First Indo-China War," 107.

3. Kevin Ruane, "Anthony Eden, British Diplomacy and the Origins of the Geneva Conference of 1954," *The Historical Journal* 37, no. 1 (March 1994): 156–172

4. Quoted in Zhai Qiang, "China and the Geneva Conference of 1954," *The China Quarterly* 129 (March 1992): 119.

5. " 'Preliminary Opinions on the Assessment of and Preparation for the Geneva Conference,' Prepared by the PRC Ministry of Foreign Affairs," March 2, 1954, History and Public Policy Program Digital Archive, PRC FMA 206-Y0054. Translated by Chen Zhihong https://digitalarchive.wilsoncenter.org/document/111963.

6. Wang Bingnan, *Zhongmei huitan jiu nian huigu* (Beijing: Shijie Zhishi Chubanshe, 1985), 6; Li Yueran, *Waijiao wutai shang de xin Zhongguo lingxiu* (Beijing: Waiyu jiaoxue yu yanjiu chubanshe, 1994), 46.

7. "Transcript, Zhou Enlai's presentation at the meeting of members of the Chinese delegation attending the Geneva Conference (excerpt), 5:00 a.m.," April 20, 1954, History and Public Policy Program Digital Archive, *Zhou Enlai nianpu, 1949–1976*, Vol. l, 361; Xiong, 19–20. Translated for CWIHP by Chen Jian, https://digitalarchive.wilsoncenter.org/document/121144.

8. Ji, *The Man on Mao's Right*, 123.

9. Kai, *Li Kenong*, 408.

10. Xu, Jiemi *Zhongguo waijiao dang'an*, 254.

11. Wang, *Zhongmei huitan jiu nian huigu*, 6–7.

12. Xu, *Jiemi Zhongguo waijiao dang'an*, 253; Qiao, *Qiao Guanhua yu Gong Peng*, 139; Kai, *Li Kenong*, 409.

13. Xu, Jiemi, *Zhongguo waijiao dang'an*, 256.

14. Yang, *Chaotouxishui sanshi nian*, 67–69.

15. Ruan, *Han Xu zhuan*, 65; Xinhua, "Feature: Villa of Montfleury witnesses New China's emergence on int'l arena," *Xinhua* January 14, 2017, http://www.xinhuanet.com/english/2017-01/14/c_135982721.htm.

16. Chen, "China and the First Indo-China War," 108–110.

17. Shi Zhe, "Zhou Enlai chuxi Rineiwa Huiyi de shangceng Neimu," in *Shenmi zhi men*, ed. Cao, 121–123.

18. Qiao, *Qiao Guanhua yu Gong Peng*, 139; Li, *Waijiao wutai shang de xin Zhongguo lingxiu*, 47.

19. Tang, *Feijia Taipingyang shangkong de hongqiao*, 187–188; Ruan, *Han Xu zhuan*, 67; Xinhua, "Feature: Villa of Montfleury Witnesses New China's Emergence on int'l arena"; John Sbardellati and Tony Shaw, "Booting a Tramp: Charlie Chaplin, the FBI, and the Construction of the Subversive Image in Red Scare America," *The Pacific Historical Review* 72, no. 4 (November 2003): 495–530.

20. Tom Buchanan, *East Wind: China and the British Left, 1925–1976* (Oxford: Oxford University Press, 2012), 144.

21. Quoted in Zhai, "China and the Geneva Conference of 1954," 121.

22. Xiong Xianghui, *Wo de qingbao yu waijiao shengya* (Beijing: Zhonggong dangshi chubanshe, 1999), 89.

23. Qiao, *Qiao Guanhua yu Gong Peng*, 106–110.

24. Rosemary Foot, "Chinese Power and the Idea of a Responsible State," in *Power and Responsibility in Chinese Foreign Policy*, eds. Yongjin Zhang and Greg Austin (Acton: ANU Press, 2013), 21–47.

25. Michael M. Sheng, "Mao and China's Relations with the Superpowers in the 1950s: A New Look at the Taiwan Strait Crises and the Sino-Soviet Split," *Modern China* 34, no. 4 (October 2008): 480–487; Thomas J. Christensen, *Useful Adversaries: Grand Strategy, Domestic Mobilization, and Sino-American Conflict, 1947–1958* (Princeton: Princeton University Press: 1996), 194–195.

26. Kuo-kang Shao, "Zhou Enlai's Diplomacy and the Neutralization of Indo-China, 1954–55," *The China Quarterly* 107 (September 1986): 489.

27. Report by British Embassy in Tokyo cited by Amitav Acharya, "Who Are the Norm Makers? The Asian-African Conference in Bandung and the Evolution of Norms," *Global Governance* 20, no. 3 (July–September 2014): 407.

28. "Talk with the American Correspondent Anna Louise Strong," August 6, 1946, History and Public Policy Program Digital Archive, *Mao Zedong xuanji* (Selected Works of Mao Zedong), vol. 4 (Beijing: Renmin chubanshe, 1996), 1191–1192. Translation from the Ministry of Foreign Affairs of the People's Republic of China and the Party Literature Research Center under the Central Committee of the Communist Party of China, eds., Mao Zedong on Diplomacy (Beijing: Foreign Languages Press, 1998), 45–48, https://digitalarchive.wilsoncenter.org/document/121327.

29. "Report from the Chinese Foreign Ministry, 'Draft of the Tentative Working Plan for Participating in the Asian-African Conference,'" January 16, 1955, History and Public Policy Program Digital Archive, PRC FMA 207-00004-03, 22–25, http://digitalarchive.wilsoncenter.org/document/113189; Wang Junyan, "Zhong Ri lingdaoren Wanglong Huiyi fijian jinxing zhanhou shouci jiechu," in *Wanlong jingshen puzhao dadi: Jinian Yazhou Huiyi 50 zhounian*, ed. Zhang Yan (Beijing: Shijie Zhishi Chubanshe, 2005), 148.

30. Quoted in Acharya, "Who Are the Norm Makers?," 408.

31. Tsang, "Target Zhou Enlai," 766–782.

32. "Supplementary Speech of Premier Zhou Enlai at the Plenary Session of the Asian African-Conference," April 19, 1955, History and Public Policy Program Digital Archive, PRC FMA 207-00006-02, 1–13. Translation from China and the Asian-African Conference (Documents) (Peking: Foreign Languages Press, 1955), 21–27, http://digitalarchive.wilsoncenter.org/document/114673.

33. Yang Gongsu, *Cang sang jiushi nian: Yi ge waijiao teshi de huiyi* (Haikou: Hainan Chubanshe, 1999), 214–215.

34. Ji, *The Man on Mao's Right*, 140.

35. Yinghong Cheng, "Beyond Moscow-Centric Interpretation: An Examination of the China Connection in Eastern Europe and North Vietnam during the Era of De-Stalinization," *Journal of World History* 15, no. 4 (December 2004): 493–494.

36. Lucy Hornby, "Xi Harks Back to China's 1950s Foreign Policy," *Financial Times The World Blog*, June 29, 2014, https://www.ft.com/content/5c572122-fcba-3546-bc50-22aead4148ec; Xi Jinping, "Carry Forward the Five Principles of Peaceful Coexistence to Build a Better World through Win-Win Cooperation," July 7, 2014, http://www.china.org.cn/world/2014-07/07/content_32876905.htm.

37. Jin, *Zhou Enlai zhuan, 1949–1976*, 213; Huang, *Qinli yu jianwen*, 112; John Kotelawala, *An Asian Prime Minister's Story* (London: George G. Harrap, 1956), 185–187; Nicholas Tarling, "'Ah-Ah': Britain and the Bandung Conference of 1955," *Journal of Southeast Asian Studies* 23, no. 1 (March 1992): 99.

38. Carlos Peña Romulo, *The Meaning of Bandung* (Chapel Hill: University of North Carolina Press, 1956), 11; Lisandro E. Claudio, "The Anti-Communist Third

World: Carlos Romulo and the Other Bandung," *Southeast Asian Studies.* 4, no. 1 (April 2015): 141.

39. Tarling, "'Ah-Ah,'" 103.

40. Sally Percival Wood, "'CHOU GAGS CRITICS IN BANDOENG' or How the Media Framed Premier Zhou Enlai at the Bandung Conference, 1955," *Modern Asian Studies* 44, no. 5 (September 2010): 1022.

41. "Upset at Bandung," *Time*, May 2, 1955, http://wilpattuhouse.com/MiscStuff/time_before66/19550502_UpsetatBandung.html.

42. Cited in Naoko Shimazu, "Diplomacy as Theatre: Staging the Bandung Conference of 1955," *Modern Asian Studies* 48, no. 1 (2013): 225–252.

43. Garver, *China's Quest*, 108–109.

44. Ho, *My Forty Years as a Diplomat*, 154–208.

45. Amanda Lee, "China Refuses to Give Up 'Developing Country' Status at WTO despite US demands," *South China Morning Post*, April 6, 2019, https://www.scmp.com/economy/china-economy/article/3004873/china-refuses-give-developing-country-status-wto-despite-us.

46. Liu, *Chinese Ambassadors*, 63.

47. Zhang Hanfu Bianxiezu, *Zhang Hanfu zhuan*, 310.

48. Ke, *Xin Zhongguo waijiao qisu Ke Hua 95 sui shuhuai*, 88–90.

49. Alice Miller, "The CCP Central Committee's Leading Small Groups," *China Leadership Monitor* 26 (Fall 2008), https://media.hoover.org/sites/default/files/documents/CLM26AM.pdf.

50. Beiwai had existed in an earlier incarnation as the foreign affairs school (*waishi xuexiao*) in Shijiazhuang, Hebei, before being put under MFA leadership in 1949 when existing students were sent to recruit others with good political credentials from around the country around the country. See Zong, *Zhou Nan koushu*, 87–93.

51. Cheng, *Zhang Wentian zhuan*, 389–390; David L. Shambaugh, "China's National Security Research Bureaucracy," *The China Quarterly* 110 (June 1987): 291–296.

52. Liu, *Chinese Ambassadors*, 67.

53. Ke, *Xin Zhongguo waijiao qisu Ke Hua 95 sui shuhuai*, 94; Yang, *Cang sang jiushi nian*, 289.

54. Zhu, *Wo de Lamei waijiao shengya*, 23.

55. Hu Shiyan, *Chen Yi zhuan* (Beijing: Dangdai Zhongguo Chubanshe, 1991), 536.

56. Interview with Sidney Rittenberg, August 30, 2017.

57. Han, "Tuoxia wuzhuang huan wenzhuang," in *Kaiqi guomen*, eds. Fu and Li, 180.

58. Gao Yan and Qi lu, "Bu zhi 'quanquan' de 'zhongguo teming quanquan dashi'—Jiao Ruoyu," in *Kaiqi Guomen*, eds. Fu and Li, 258–259.

59. Mao, "Always Keep to the Style of Plain Living and Hard Struggle" (October 26, 1949), *Selected Works of Mao Tse-tung*, 5:23.

60. Wu, *Nantai buliaoqing*, 2; see also Zhu, *Wo de lamei waijiao shengya*, 23.

61. Zhou Zhendong and Ke Yi, *Yi dui waijiaoguan fufu de rensheng huimou* (Beijing: Shijie Zhishi Chubanshe, 2010), 246–247.

62. Xie Junzhen, *Cong banmendian dao Zhijiage* (Chengdu: Sichuan Renmin Chubanshe, 2006), 87.

63. Wu, *Nantai buliaoqing*, 2–3.

64. Chen, *Xianshen duiwai jiaoliu*, 134–135.

65. Wu, *Zai waijiaobu ba nian de jingli*, 92–94.

66. Tang, *Feijia Taipingyang shangkong de hongqiao*, 12; Li Zhongxiao, *Lianheguo de Zhongguo nyu waijiaoguan* (Beijing: Zhongguo Wenlian Chubanshe, 1997), 79–104.

67. For example, Michael David-Fox, *Showcasing the Great Experiment: Cultural Diplomacy and Western Visitors to the Soviet Union, 1921–1941* (Oxford: Oxford University Press, 2011).

68. Gerry Groot, *Managing Transitions: The Chinese Communist Party, United Front Work, Corporatism and Hegemony* (New York: Routledge, 2004).

69. Wang Jialong, *Huoyue zai renmin waijiao wutai shang: Zhongguo Gonghui guoji huodong de huigu* (Beijing: Zhongyang Wenxian Chubanshe, 1995), 337–346.

70. Henry Pu Yi, *The Last Manchu: The Autobiography of Henry Pu Yi, Last Emperor of China* (New York: Skyhorse Publishing, 2010), eBook.

71. Cheng, *Zhongguo shewai shijian miwen*, 14–98; Sergei I. Kuznetsov and Sergei V. Karasov, "The Last Emperor of China: Internment in the Soviet Union," *Journal of Slavic Military Studies* 18, no. 2 (2005): 207–226.

72. Tang, *Feijia Taipingyang shangkong de hongqiao*, 100–106.

73. Tang, *Feijia Taipingyang shangkong de hongqiao*, 110–111.

74. Li Hongshan, "Building a Black Bridge: China's Interaction with African-American Activists during the Cold War," *Journal of Cold War Studies*. 20, no. 3 (2018): 114–152.

75. Buchanan, *East Wind*, 114–178.

76. Lorenz M. Lüthi, "Rearranging International Relations? How Mao's China and de Gaulle's France Recognized Each Other in 1963–1964," *Journal of Cold War Studies* 16, no. 1 (Winter 2014): 119; Donald W. Klein, "Peking's Evolving Ministry of Foreign Affairs," *The China Quarterly* 4 (October–December 1960): 28–39.

77. Wang Guanhua, "'Friendship First': China's Sports Diplomacy during the Cold War," *Journal of American-East Asian Relations* 12, no. 3/4 (Fall–Winter 2003): 133–143.

78. Wang, *Huoyue zai renmin waijiao wutai shang*, 184.

79. Wang Shu, "Ji du feizhou xing: kaipi sahala yinan feizhou de gongzuo," in *Dangdai Zhongguo shijie waijiao shengya*, ed. Waijiaobu Waijiaoshi Yanjiushi, Vol. V, 84; Waijiaobu Waijiaoshi Bianjishi, *Xin Zhongguo waijiao fengyun*, Vol. 2, 64.

80. János Rádvanyi, "The Hungarian Revolution and the Hundred Flowers Campaign," *The China Quarterly* 43 (July–September 1970): 121.

81. Peter Wesley-Smith, "Chinese Consular Representation in British Hong Kong," *Pacific Affairs* 71, no. 3 (Autumn 1998): 371–375; interviews in Beijing.

82. Chen, "China and the First Indo-China War, 1950–54," 105.

83. Garrett Martin, "Playing the China Card? Revisiting France's Recognition of Communist China, 1963–1964," *Journal of Cold War Studies* 10, no. 1 (Winter 2008): 52–55.

84. Garver, *China's Quest*, 225.

85. Peter Van Ness, *Revolution and Chinese Foreign Policy: Peking's Support for Wars of National Liberation* (Berkeley: University of California Press, 1971), 94, 112–113, 169, 193, 207, 193.

86. Anne-Marie Brady, "Magic Weapons: China's Political Influence Activities under Xi Jinping," paper presented at the conference on "The Corrosion of Democracy under China's Global Influence," Arlington, Virginia, USA, September 16–17, 2017, https://www.wilsoncenter.org/sites/default/files/for_website_magicweaponsanne-mariesbradyseptember2017.pdf.

87. For example, John Garnaut, "How China Interferes in Australia and How Democracies Can Push Back," *Foreign Affairs*, March 9, 2018, https://www.foreignaffairs.com/articles/china/2018-03-09/how-china-interferes-australia.

88. Report of the Working Group on Chinese Influence Activities in the United States, "Chinese Influence & American Interests: Promoting Constructive Vigilance," November 29, 2018, https://asiasociety.org/center-us-china-relations/chinese-influence-american-interests-promoting-constructive-vigilance.

89. Cheng, *Zhang Wentian zhuan*, 377; Lin, "Bu Xunchang de Dashi," in *Dangdai Zhongguo shijie waijiao shengya*, ed. Waijiaobu Waijiaoshi Yanjiushi, Vol. II, 24.

90. Wu Xiuquan, *Zai Waijiaobu Ba Nian de Jingli*, 94.

91. Wu Lengxi, *Shi nian lunzhan: Zhong Su guanxi huiyilu* (Beijing: Zhongyang Wenxian Chubanshe, 1999), 1–6.

92. Lorenz M. Lüthi, *The Sino-Soviet Split: Cold War in the Communist World* (Princeton: Princeton University Press, 2010), 76–77; Wu, *Shi Nian Lunzhan*, 138.

93. CIA, "Khrushchev—A Personality Sketch," CIA FOIA, June 5, 1961.

94. Wu, *Shi nian lunzhan*, 6–9.

95. Bo, *Ruogan zhongda juece yu shijian de huigu*, 574–577.

96. Bo, *Ruogan zhongda juece yu shijian de huigu*, 327, 485, 528.

97. Lawrence R. Sullivan, "Leadership and Authority in the Chinese Communist Party: Perspectives from the 1950s," *Pacific Affairs* 59, no. 4 (Winter 1986–1987): 623–627.

98. Ji, *The Man on Mao's Right*, 155–157.

99. Bo, *Ruogan zhongda juece yu shijian de huigu*, 573.

100. Yen-lin Chung, "The Witch-Hunting Vanguard: The Central Secretariat's Roles and Activities in the Anti-Rightist Campaign," *The China Quarterly* 206 (June 2011): 391–411; Zong, *Zhou Nan koushu*, 170–171.

101. Zong, *Zhou Nan koushu*, 170–171.

102. Bo, *Ruogan zhongda juece yu shijian de huigu*, 1041.

103. Ke, *Xin Zhongguo waijiao qisu Ke Hua 95 sui shuhuai*, 114.

104. Ji, *The Man on Mao's Right*, 174–177; Wu, *Zai Waijiaobu ba nian de jingli*, 41; Liu, *Chinese Ambassadors*, 108–109.

105. Ke, *Xin Zhongguo waijiao qisu Ke Hua 95 sui shuhuai*, 114–115.

106. Zong, *Zhou Nan Koushu*, 170.

107. Ji, *The Man on Mao's Right*, 175.

108. Li, *The Private Life of Chairman Mao*, 221.

109. Michael Schoenhals, "Mao Zedong: Speeches at the 1957 'Moscow Conference,'" *Journal of Communist Studies* 2, no. 2 (1986): 109–126.

Chapter 5

1. Li, *Cong Weiminghu dao huanjianhu*, 3–9.
2. Dikotter, *Mao's Great Famine*, xii–xiii.
3. Dikotter, *Mao's Great Famine*, 27.
4. Zhou and Ke, *Yidui waijiaoguan fufu de rensheng huimou*, 19.
5. Michael M. Sheng, "Mao and China's Relations with the Superpowers in the 1950s: A New Look at the Taiwan Strait Crises and the Sino-Soviet Split," *Modern China* 34, no. 4 (October 2008): 498–499; Christensen, *Useful Adversaries*, 217–225.
6. Zhonggong Zhongyang Wenxian Yanjiushi, *Zhou Enlai waijiao wenxuan* (Beijing: Zhongyang Wenxian Chubanshe, 1990), 265.
7. Christensen, *Useful Adversaries*, 217.
8. Dai Bingguo, *Zhanlyue duihua: Dai Bingguo huiyilu* (Beijing: Zhongxin Chubanshe, 2016), 19.
9. Dikotter, *Mao's Great Famine*, 70.
10. Dikotter, *Mao's Great Famine*, 80.
11. Zhu, *Wo de Lamei waijiao shengya*, 27–29.
12. Zong, *Zhou Nan koushu*, 171.
13. Zhu, *Wo de Lamei waijiao shengya*, 28.
14. Wu, *Tan waijiao*, 41.
15. Qiao, *Qiao Guanhua yu Gong Peng*, 197–198.
16. Zong, *Zhou Nan koushu*, 171; Geng Biao, *Geng Biao huiyilu* (Nanjing: Jiangsu Renmin Chubanshe, 1998), 162–167.
17. Zhu, *Wo de Lamei waijiao shengya*, 28.
18. Kang Maozhao, *Waijiaoguan huiyilu*, 89.
19. Thomas P. Bernstein, "Mao Zedong and the Famine of 1959–1960: A Study in Wilfulness," *The China Quarterly* 186 (June 2006): 425–427; Dikotter, *Mao's Great Famine*, 87–89.
20. Wang, *Wang Guoquan huiyilu*, 79; Wang Guoquan, "Wo de Dashi Shengya," in *Dangdai Zhongguo shijie waijiao shengya*, ed. Waijiaobu Waijiaoshi Yanjiushi, Vol. II (Beijing: Shijie Zhishi Chubanshe, 1994), 145–147.
21. Dikotter, *Mao's Great Famine*, eBook.
22. Jin, *Zhou Enlai Zhuan, 1949–1976*, 508.
23. Cheng, *Zhang Wentian zhuan*, 401.
24. Liu, *Shan he hu hai hua Bolan*, 30–32.
25. Dikotter, *Mao's Great Famine*, eBook.
26. Shi, *Zai lishi juren shenbian*, 270.
27. Dikotter, *Mao's Great Famine*, eBook; Cheng, *Zhang Wentian zhuan*, 413–419; Bo, *Ruogan zhongda juece yu shijian de huigu*, 859.
28. Cheng, *Zhang Wentian zhuan*, 139–140.

29. Cheng, *Zhang Wentian zhuan*, 401–413.

30. Liu, *Chinese Ambassadors*, 41.

31. Cheng, *Zhang Wentian zhuan*, 299–300.

32. Shen Zhihua and Xia Yafeng, "The Great Leap Forward, the People's Commune and the Sino-Soviet Split," *Journal of Contemporary China* 20, no. 72 (2011): 876–877.

33. Niu Jun, "1962: The Eve of the Left Turn in China's Foreign Policy," Cold War International History Project, Woodrow Wilson International Center for Scholars, working paper no. 48 (October 2005), 7–8; Wu, *Shi nian lunzhan*, 203–204.

34. Bo, *Ruogan zhongda juece yu shijian de huigu*, 861.

35. Tong, ed., *Fengyu sishinian*, Vol. 2, 378; Zong, *Zhou Nan koushu*, 172.

36. Bo, *Ruogan Zhongda juece yu shijian de huigu*, 863.

37. Wu Xiuquan, *Huiyi yu huainian* (Beijing: Zhonggong Zhongyang Dangxiao Chubanshe, 1991), 328–332.

38. Dikotter, *Mao's Great Famine*, eBook.

39. Gao, *Zhou Enlai*, 187–188.

40. Liu, *Chinese Ambassadors*, 109.

41. Zong, *Zhou Nan Koushu*, 171.

42. "Journal of Soviet Ambassador to the DPRK A.M. Puzanov for 29 September 1960," September 29, 1960, History and Public Policy Program Digital Archive, AVPRF fond 0102, opis 16, delo 7, 102–129. Translated by Gary Goldberg, https://digitalarchive. wilsoncenter.org/document/119468.

43. Bo, *Ruogan zhongda juece yu shijian de huigu*, 1143.

44. Ruan, *Han Xu zhuan*, 57.

45. Alexander V. Pantsov with Steven I. Levine, *Deng Xiaoping: A Revolutionary Life* (Oxford: Oxford University Press, 2015), 207.

46. Pantsov with Levine, *Deng Xiaoping*, 207.

47. Yang Jisheng, *Tombstone: The Great Chinese Famine, 1958–1962* (New York: Farrar, Straus & Giroux, 2013), chapter 1.

48. Chen Tao, "East German Pragmatism, China's Policy of Differentiation, and Soviet Miscalculation: Hermann Matern's 1961 Trip to China Revisited," *Cold War History* (2018): 7; Jin, *Zhou Enlai Zhuan, 1949–1976*, 459.

49. Jasper Becker, *Hungry Ghosts: Mao's Secret Famine* (New York: Henry Holt, 1998), 291.

50. Brady, *Making the Foreign Serve China*, 121–122.

51. Lovell, "The Uses of Foreigners in Mao-Era China," 151.

52. Xia Kunbao, *Huanjing waijiaoguan shouji* (Beijing: Zhongguo Huanjingkexue Chubanshe, 2009), 12–13.

53. Jiang, *Duonaohe zhi bo*, 11, 31–35.

54. Edward Wong, "A Trip to Tibet, with My Handlers Nearby," *New York Times*, July 31, 2010, https://www.nytimes.com/2010/08/01/weekinreview/01wong.html.

55. Peter Martin, "How China Is Defending Its Detention of Muslims to the World," *Bloomberg News*, April 19, 2019, https://www.bloomberg.com/news/articles/2019-04-19/how-china-is-defending-its-detention-of-muslims-to-the-world.

56. Interviews in Beijing.

57. Xu, *Wang Jiaxiang zhuan*, 515; A. Doak Barnett, *The Making of Foreign Policy in China: Structure and Process* (Boulder, CO: Westview Press, 1985), 46.

58. David Shambaugh, "China's 'Quiet Diplomacy': The International Department of the Chinese Communist Party," *China: An International Journal* 5, no. 1 (March 2007): 26–54; Peter Martin and Alan Crawford, "China's Influence Digs Deep into Europe's Political Landscape," *Bloomberg News*, April 4, 2019.

59. Xu, *Wang Jiaxiang Zhuan*, 554–557; Wu, *Huiyi yu huainian*, 374–375; Zhu Zhongli, *Mao Zedong, Wang Jiaxiang zai wo de shenghuo zhong* (Beijing: Zhonggong Zhongyang Dangxiao Chubanshe, 1995), 209, 216–222.

60. Shi, *Wang Jiaxiang Zhuan*, 246; Xu, *Wang Jiaxiang zhuan*, 375; Zhu, *Mao Zedong, Wang Jiaxiang zai wo de shenghuo zhong*, 60, 120–123.

61. Xu, *Wang Jiaxiang zhuan*, 554–557; Xia Yafeng. "Wang Jiaxiang: New China's First Ambassador and the First Director of the International Liaison Department of the CCP," *American Journal of Chinese Studies* 16, no. 2 (2009): 137–155.

62. Zhu, *Mao Zedong, Wang Jiaxiang zai wo de shenghuo zhong*, 223; Xu, *Wang Jiaxiang zhuan*, 321–323.

63. Wu, *Shi Nian Lunzhan*, 208.

64. Enrico Maria Fardella, "Mao Zedong and the 1962 Cuban Missile Crisis," *Cold War History* 15, no. 1 (2014): 73–88.

65. Fardella, "Mao Zedong and the 1962 Cuban Missile Crisis."

66. Fardella, "Mao Zedong and the 1962 Cuban Missile Crisis."

67. Wu, *Shi nian lunzhan*, 515.

68. Pantsov with Levine, *Deng Xiaoping*, 230.

69. Ylber Marku, "Communist Relations in Crisis: The End of Soviet-Albanian Relations, and the Sino-Soviet Split, 1960–1961," *International History Review*, 42, no. 4 (2020): 813–832.

70. Sun Yixian, *Zai damo nabian: Qinli Lin Biao zhuiji shijian he Zhong Meng guanxi bo zhe* (Beijing: Zhongguo Qingnian Chubanshe, 2001), 38.

71. Cheng Yinghong, "Sino-Cuban Relations during the Early Years of the Castro Regime, 1959–1966," *Journal of Cold War Studies* 9, no. 3 (2007): 78–114.

72. Zhu Xiangzhong, *Lamei qinliji* (Chengdu: Sichuan Renmin Chubanshe, 2004), 39–40; see also Sun, *Zai damo nabian*, 87–88.

73. He Ying, "Dui Yuanjian Tanzan Tielu juece de huigu," in *Xin Zhongguo waijiao fengyun*, ed. Waijiaobu Waijiaoshi Bianjishi, Vol. 3 (Beijing: Shije Zhishi Chubanshe, 1994), 31–42; Wei Song, "Seeking New Allies in Africa: China's Policy towards Africa during the Cold War as Reflected in the Construction of the Tanzania-Zambia Railway," *Journal of Modern Chinese History* 9, no. 1 (2015): 46–65.

74. Martin, "Playing the China Card?," 52–80; Lüthi, "Rearranging International Relations?," 111–145.

75. "The Situation Surrounding the Establishment of Diplomatic Relations between China and France and Related Issues," 1964, History and Public Policy Program Digital Archive, PRC FMA 110-01998-01, 27–44. Translated by Fan Chao, https://digitalarchive.wilsoncenter.org/document/119197.

76. Wang Guoquan, "Wo de dashi shengya," in *Dangdai Zhongguo shijie waijiao shengya*, ed. Waijiaobu Waijiaoshi Yanjiushi, Vol. II, 152; Ruan, *Han Xu zhuan*, 95.

77. Westad, *The Cold War*, 248–249.

78. "Cable from the Chinese Embassy in Czechoslovakia to the Ministry of Foreign Affairs, 'Our Contacts with Middle- and Lower-Level Personnel,'" December 3, 1964, History and Public Policy Program Digital Archive, PRC FMA 109-02736-03, 27-29. Translated by Xi Zhao, https://digitalarchive.wilsoncenter.org/document/119202.

79. Jiang Benliang, Duonaohe zhi bo, 49–50; Liu Fang, "Bu chang de renqi, nanwang de niandai: Chushi Luomaniya de yixie huiyi," in *Dangdai Zhongguo shijie waijiao shengya*, ed. Waijiaobu Waijiaoshi Yanjiushi, Vol. III (Beijing: Shijie Zhishi Chubanshe, 1994), 7–11; see also Cezar Stanciu, "Fragile Equilibrium: Romania and the Vietnam War in the Context of the Sino-Soviet Split, 1966," *Journal of Cold War Studies* 18, no. 1 (2016): 161–187.

80. Ma Jisen, *The Cultural Revolution in the Foreign Ministry of China* (Hong Kong: Chinese University Press: 2004), 3; Zhu, *Wo de Lamei waijiao shengya*, 29.

81. Dai, *Zhanlyue duihua*, 22–23.

82. Liu Xinsheng and Pan Zhengxiu, *Feixiang shiwai taoyuan* (Chengdu: Sichuan Renmin Chubanshe, 2004), 403–405.

83. Lin Song, "Wode waijiao shengya pianduan," in *Dangdai Zhongguo shijie waijiao shengya*, ed. Waijiaobu Waijiaoshi Yanjiushi, Vol. III (Beijing: Shijie Zhishi Chubanshe, 1994), 169–173.

84. Zeng Tao, *Waijiao shengya shiqi nian* (Nanjing: Jiangsu Renmin Chubanshe, 1997), 109–118.

Chapter 6

1. Dai, *Zhanlue duihua*, 24.

2. Ke, *Xin Zhongguo waijiao qisu Ke Hua 95 sui shuhuai*, 126.

3. Ke, *Xin Zhongguo waijiao qisu Ke Hua 95 sui shuhuai*, 126.

4. Ji, *The Man on Mao's Right*, 225.

5. Yang, *Cang sang jiushi nian*, 291.

6. Cheng, *Zhongguo shewai shijian miwen*, 242–243.

7. Qiao, *Qiao Guanhua yu Gong Peng*, 215.

8. Ma, *The Cultural Revolution in the Foreign Ministry of China*, 7–19.

9. Kang, *Waijiaoguan huiyilu*, 171.

10. Wang, *Wang Guoquan huiyilu*, 226–227.

11. Wang, *Wang Guoquan huiyilu*, 228; Wu, *Tan waijiao*, 63; Cheng, *Zhongguo shewai shijian miwen*, 246–247; Ma, *The Cultural Revolution in the Foreign Ministry of China*, 73–75.

12. Wang, *Wang Guoquan huiyilu*, 228; Zeng, *Waijiao shengya shiqi nian*, 110; Sun, *Zai damo nabian*, 95; Cheng, *Zhongguo shewai shijian miwen*, 248.

13. Ke, *Xin Zhongguo waijiao qisu Ke Hua 95 sui shuhuai*, 182.

14. Li Tongcheng, *Zai yiguo xingkongxia* (Chengdu: Sichuan Renmin Chubanshe, 2004), 19, 37.

15. CIA, "Mao's Red Guard Diplomacy: 1967," CIA FOIA, June 21 1968.

16. Li, *Cong Weiminghu dao huanjianhu*, 274.

17. Sun, *Zai Damo nabian*, 95–96.

18. Yuan Jie, "Nan Wang de Waijiao zhi Lyu," in *Nyu waijiaoguan*, ed. Cheng, 376.

19. Yang, *Cang sang jiushi nian*, 291.

20. Yang, *Cang sang jiushi nian*, 291.

21. Zhu, *Lamei qinliji*, 92.

22. Walder, *China Under Mao*, 279.

23. Ji, *The Man on Mao's Right*, 231.

24. "Telegram number 3725-59 from M. Lucien Paye," November 16, 1966, History and Public Policy Program Digital Archive, Documents Diplomatiques Français, 1966 tome 2 (1 Jun–31 Dec) (Bruxelles: Peter Lang, 2006), 874–878. Translated by Garret Martin, https://digitalarchive.wilsoncenter.org/document/116518.

25. "The Polish-Soviet Talks in Moscow: October 10–15, 1966," October 1966, History and Public Policy Program Digital Archive, Andrzej Paczkowski, ed. Tajne Dokumenty Biura Politycznego PRL-ZSRR, 1956-1970. London: Aneks Publishers, 1996. Translated by Malgorzata K. Gnoinska, http://digitalarchive.wilsoncenter.org/document/113556.

26. "The DPRK Attitude Toward the So-called 'Cultural Revolution' in China," March 7, 1967, History and Public Policy Program Digital Archive, AVPRF f. 0102, op. 23, p. 112, d. 24, 13–23. Obtained by Sergey Radchenko and translated by Gary Goldberg, http://digitalarchive.wilsoncenter.org/document/114570.

27. Ji, *The Man on Mao's Right*, 227.

28. Ke, *Xin Zhongguo waijiao qisu Ke Hua 95 sui shuhuai*, 182.

29. Zong, *Zhou Nan koushu*, 140.

30. Chen Yi Zhuan Bianxiezu, *Chen Yi zhuan*, 606.

31. Kang, *Waijiaoguan huiyilu*, 172–173.

32. For example, Wang, *Wang Guoquan huiyilu*, 109–113, 235–236; Hao, *Huang tudi shang zoulai de waijiaojia*, 84–85; Ma, *The Cultural Revolution in the Foreign Ministry of China*, 77–81.

33. Qiao, *Qiao Guanhua yu Gong Peng*, 231.

34. Huang, *Qinli yu jianwen*, 134–139.

35. Yi, *Fengyun jidang*, 235–242. Confusingly, after the author details the unprompted phone call from Beijing, he goes on to blame the listening devices on the CIA.

36. Chen Yi Zhuan Bianxiezu, *Chen Yi Zhuan*, 612; Wang, *Wang Guoquan huiyilu*, 111; Ma, *The Cultural Revolution in the Foreign Ministry of China*, 207–212; Interview with Sidney Rittenberg, August 30, 2017.

37. Chen Yi Zhuan Bianxiezu, *Chen Yi zhuan*, 612; Ke, *Xin Zhongguo waijiao qisu Ke Hua 95 sui shuhuai*, 189–191; Ma, *The Cultural Revolution in the Foreign Ministry of China*, 203–204.

38. Qiao, *Qiao Guanhua yu Gong Peng*, 225.

39. Chen Yi Zhuan Bianxiezu, *Chen Yi zhuan*, 612; Wang, *Wang Guoquan huiyilu*, 111.

40. CIA, "China's Foreign Policy—Who Is in Charge?," CIA FOIA, July 20, 1967.

41. Zhang Hanfu Bianxiezu, *Zhang Hanfu zhuan*, 316–321.

42. Hao, *Huang tudi shang zoulai de waijiaojia*, 88.

43. Qian Jiadong, "Haishi Rang Women Tan Zongli Ba," in *Zhou Enlai he ta de mishu men*, ed. Cheng, 250.

44. Zhao Maofeng, "Pingfan Zhong Jian Jingshen," in *Zhou Enlai he ta de mishu men*, ed. Cheng, 319.

45. Ling, *Cong Yanan dao Lianheguo*, 118.

46. Zeng, *Waijiao shengya shiqi nian*, 112.

47. Xu, *Wang Jiaxiang zhuan*, 572–581; Shi, *Wang Jiaxiang zhuan*, 324–325; Zhu, *Mao Zedong, Wang Jiaxiang zai wo de shenghuo zhong*, 231–235.

48. Wu, *Huiyi yu huainian*, 403–439.

49. Zhang "Zhou Enlai de 'erduo he zuiba,'" in *Kaiqi guomen*, eds. Fu and Li, 132–33; Cheng, *Zhongguo shewai shijian miwen*, 200–223.

50. James McGregor, *One Billion Customers: Lessons from the Front Lines of Doing Business in China* (New York: Simon & Schuster, 2005), 213–216.

51. Zhang Hanzhi, *Kuaguo houhou de dahongmen* (Shanghai: Wenhui Chubanshe, 2004), 19–20.

52. CIA, "Mao's Red Guard Diplomacy: 1967," CIA FOIA, June 21, 1968; Liu, *Chinese Ambassadors*, 116.

53. "Red Diplomats Armed with Mao Tse-tung's Thought Are Dauntless," *Peking Review* 37, September 8, 1967, https://www.marxists.org/history/erol/china/pr-1967-37.pdf.

54. Westad, *Restless Empire*, 354–355.

55. Wang, *Wang Guoquan Huiyilu*, 100.

56. "Note from the Ministry of Foreign Affairs of the Czechoslovak Socialist Republic to the Embassy of the People's Republic of China in Prague," February 9, 1967, History and Public Policy Program Digital Archive, National Archives of the Czech Republic (NA), 021/136/67-3. Obtained by East China Normal University, Shanghai, and translated by Mike Kubic, https://digitalarchive.wilsoncenter.org/document/176522.

57. Westad, *Restless Empire*, 334–335.

58. Han Kehua, "Nan wang si guo xing," in *Dangdai Zhongguo shijie waijiao shengya*, ed. Waijiaobu Waijiaoshi Yanjiushi, Vol. VI, 90.

59. Jiang, *Duonaohe zhi bo*, 76–85; "Telegrams from Romanian Embassy, Beijing, to Romanian Ministry of Foreign Affairs, 22–24 August 1968," August 24, 1968, History and Public Policy Program Digital Archive, Romanian Foreign Ministry Archives (AMAE), fond Telegrams, Pekin 1968, Vol II, pp. 272–274. Republished in Romulus Ioan Budura, coordinator, Relațiile Româno-Chineze 1880–1974: Documente [Romanian-Chinese Relations 1880–1974: Documents], București, Ministerul Afacerilor Externe [Foreign Affairs Ministry], Arhivele Naționale [National Archives], 2005, 901–902. Translated for CWIHP by Mircea Munteanu, http://digitalarchive.wilsoncenter.org/document/113289.

60. Henry Kissinger, *The White House Years* (New York: Little, Brown, 1979), 183.

61. Song Ke and Zhu Jianfei, "Architecture at a Political Turning Point: Diplomatic Buildings in 1970s Beijing," *ABE Journal* [En ligne], 12 | 2017, mis en ligne le 26

janvier 2018, consulté le 26 décembre 2019, http://journals.openedition.org/abe/3759.

62. Chen Jian, *Mao's China and the Cold War* (Chapel Hill: University of North Carolina Press, 2001), 245.

63. First Inaugural Address of Richard Milhous Nixon, January 20, 1969, https://avalon.law.yale.edu/20th_century/nixon1.asp.

64. Chen, *Mao's China and the Cold War*, 238.

65. See a detailed account from the group's notetaker: Xiong, *Wo de qingbao yu waijiao shengya*, 165–193.

66. Chen Yi Zhuan Bianxiezu, *Chen Yi Zhuan*, 614.

67. Zhu, *Lamei Qinliji*, 3–5.

68. Yang, *Cang Sang Jiushi Nian*, 297.

69. Zhang Huixin, Yang Chengxu, and Xing Geng, "Yi Waijiao Shijie Wang Yutian," in *Dangdai Zhongguo shijie waijiao shengya*, ed. Waijiaobu Waijiaoshi Yanjiushi, Vol. II, 188.

70. Walder, *China under Mao*, 201.

71. Zong, *Zhou Nan Koushu*, 176.

72. Zhang Bing, *Nyu waijiaoguan shouji* (Chengdu: Sichuan Renmin Chubanshe, 2004), 1–3, 327–364.

73. Zhou and Ke, *Yidui waijiaoguan fufu de rensheng huimou*, 223–224.

74. Xia, *Huanjing Waijiaoguan shouji*, 20.

75. Zong, *Zhou Nan koushu*, 177; Barnouin and Yu, *Zhou Enlai*, 245.

76. Xia, *Huanjing waijiaoguan shouji*, 24; Zhang, *Nyu waijiaoguan shouji*, 327–364.

77. Xiong, *Wo de qingbao yu waijiao shengya*, 207.

78. Zhang, *Kuaguo houhou de dahongmen*, 232; Gao, *Zhou Enlai*, 15.

79. Interview with J. Stapleton Roy, July 8, 2019.

80. Jing Zhicheng interviewed on Nixon's China Game, pbs.org, September 1999, http://wwz.html.

81. Henry Kissinger, *On China* (London: Penguin, 2012), 220–221.

82. Kissinger, *On China*, 225–226.

83. Thomas, *Season of High Adventure*, 320–332.

84. Kissinger, *On China*, 225–226.

85. Kissinger, *On China*, 229–231.

86. Gao, *Zhou Enlai*, 15.

87. Kissinger, *On China*, 238.

88. Ruan, *Han Xu Zhuan*, 130.

89. Kissinger, *The White House Years*, 742–745.

90. Peter Martin and Jennifer Jacobs, "What Does Trump Want? China Scours Twitter, Cocktail Parties for Clues," *Bloomberg News*, February 21, 2017, https://www.bloomberg.com/news/articles/2017-02-21/over-twinkies-and-tweets-china-ponders-what-does-trump-want.

91. Interviews with businesspeople and diplomats in Beijing, July 2018.

92. Chen, *Mao's China and the Cold War*, 269.

93. Jin, *Zhou Enlai Zhuan, 1949–1976*, 1083–1085.

94. Xing Jisheng, *Cong Taihangshan dao Jialebihai: Wang Jin dashi de waijiao shengya* (Beijing: Zhongguo Wenlian Chubanshe, 2006), 82.

95. Pieced together from Weng Ming, "'256' hao sanchaji yuejing zhihou," in *Zhongguo waijiaoguan shouji*, ed. Li, Vol. 2, 527–544; Jin, *Zhou Enlai zhuan, 1949–1976*, 1040–1041; Wu Wenyi, "Lishi fuyu wo de yi xiang teshu shiming," in *Xin Zhongguo waijiao fengyun*, ed. Waijiaobu Waijiaoshi Bianjishi, Vol. 1, 153–176; Fu Hao, "Jiu yisan shijian bubai," in *Xin Zhongguo waijiao fengyun*, ed. Waijiaobu Waijiaoshi Bianjishi, Vol. 1, 177–187; Sun Yixian, Chen Qingyi, and Wang Zhongyuan, "Shicha Lin Biao pantao feiji zhuihui xianchang jishi," in *Xin Zhongguo waijiao fengyun*, ed. Waijiaobu Waijiaoshi Bianjishi, Vol. 1, 188–196; Sun, *Zai damo nabian*, 163–285.

96. Guo Jiading, "Chu jin Lianheguo," in *Xin Zhongguo waijiao fengyun*, ed. Waijiaobu Waijiaoshi Bianjishi, Vol. 3 (Beijing: Shije Zhishi Chubanshe, 1994), 98.

97. Chen Jian, *Waijiao, rang shijie geng hexie* (Beijing: Zhongguo Renmin Daxue Chubanshe, 2012), 5–6.

98. Xiong, *Wo de qingbao yu waijiao shengya*, 336.

99. Weng Ming, "Lin xing dian jiang: 'Qiao Lao Ye' shou ci shuai tuan fu Lianda," in *Jing tian wei di: Waijiaoguan zai Lianheguo*, eds. Fu Hao and Li Tongcheng (Beijing: Zhongguo Huaqiao Chubanshe, 1995), 8.

100. Zhang, *Kuaguo houhou de dahongmen*, 277–278; Wu Miaofa, *Qiao Guanhua zai Lianheguo de rizi* (Taiyuan: Beiqiu Wenyi Chubanshe, 1998), 29.

101. Xiong, *Wo de qingbao yu waijiao shengya*, 346–350.

102. Xiong, *Wo de qingbao yu waijiao shengya*, 350–353; Wu, *Qiao Guanhua zai Lianheguo de rizi*, p. 30; Guo Jiading, "Chu jin Lianheguo," in *Xin Zhongguo waijiao fengyun*, ed. Waijiaobu Waijiaoshi Bianjishi, Vol. 3, 116–117.

103. Wu, *Qiao Guanhua zai Lianheguo de rizi*, 30–31.

104. Pieced together from Hao, *Huangtudi shang zoulai de waijiaojia*, 104–105; Fu Hao, "Bu mian zhi ye: Mao Zedong mianshou jiyi Zhongnanhai," in *Jing Tian Wei Di*, eds. Fu and Li, 1–6; Xiong, *Wo de qingbao yu waijiao shengya*, 353–356; Guo, "Chu jin Lianheguo," in *Xin Zhongguo waijiao fengyun*, ed. Waijiaobu Waijiaoshi Bianjishi, Vol. 3, 99; Tian Jin and Yu Mengjia, *Zhongguo zai Lianheguo: Gongheguo dizao geng meihao de shijie* (Beijing: Shijie Zhishi Chubanshe, 1998), 35.

105. Wu, *Qiao Guanhua zai Lianheguo de rizi*, 38.

Chapter 7

1. Zhang, *Kuaguo houhou de dahongmen*, 283–284; Wu, *Qiao Guanhua zai Lianheguo de rizi*, 120–121; He Liliang, "Zai Lianheguo de rizi li," in *Nyu Waijiaoguan*, ed. Cheng, 274–277.

2. Wu Miaofa, "Waijiao dubai: Lianheguo jishi," in *Jing tian wei di: Waijiaoguan zai Lianheguo*, eds. Fu Hao and Li Tongcheng (Beijing: Zhongguo Huaqiao Chubanshe, 1995), 206.

3. Samuel S. Kim, "International Organization Behavior," in *Chinese Foreign Policy*, eds. Robinson and Shambaugh, 405–407.

4. *China's National Defense in 2008*, http://www.china.org.cn/government/whitepaper/node_7060059.htm.

5. United Nations Secretariat, "Assessment of Member States' Contributions to the United Nations Regular Budget for the year 2019," December 24, 2018, https://undocs.org/en/ST/ADM/SER.B/992.

6. "Is China Contributing to the United Nations' Mission?," CSIS ChinaPower, https://chinapower.csis.org/china-un-mission/; David Wainer, "China Is Eyeing a Widening Void at the UN Thanks to Trump," *Bloomberg News*, February 1, 2019, https://www.bloomberg.com/news/articles/2019-02-01/china-sees-trump-s-america-first-policies-widening-void-at-un.

7. CGTN, "UN Echoes China's Concept of Building 'Community of Shared Future for Mankind," http://english.scio.gov.cn/2017-11/09/content_41867418.htm.

8. Guo, "Chu jin lianheguo," in *Xin Zhongguo waijiao fengyun*, ed. Waijiaobu Waijiaoshi Bianjishi, Vol. 3, 120–123; Li Songling, "Yi zhang yi chi: 'Zhongguo xuanfeng' Xijuan Lianheguo," in *Jing tian wei di*, eds. Fu and Li, 16.

9. Wu, *Qiao Guanhua zai Lianheguo de rizi*, 140.

10. Wu, *Tan waijiao*, 79.

11. Zong, *Zhou Nan koushu*, 223.

12. Wu, *Tan waijiao*, 77.

13. Waijiaobu Waijiaoshi Bianjishi, *Xin Zhongguo waijiao fengyun*, Vol. 3, 125.

14. Andrew Scobell and Alireza Nader, *China in the Middle East: The Wary Dragon* (Santa Monica, CA: RAND Corporation, 2016), 4 https://www.rand.org/pubs/research_reports/RR1229.html.

15. FMPRC, "The Third Wave of Establishing Diplomatic Relations with Other Countries," https://www.fmprc.gov.cn/mfa_eng/ziliao_665539/3602_665543/3604_665547/t18014.shtml.

16. Yi, *Fengyun jidang*, 290.

17. Richards J. Heuer Jr., *Psychology of Intelligence Analysis* (Washington, DC: Center for the Study of Intelligence, 1999), 70–71; Frank Watanabe, *15 Axioms for Intelligence Analysts: How to Succeed in the DI* (Washington, DC: Center for the Study of Intelligence, 1997).

18. Interview, July 10, 2019.

19. Dai, *Zhanlue duihua*, 346–347.

20. Ling Qing, *Cong Yanan dao Lianheguo*, 111; Li, *Shuo bu jin de waijiao*, 152–153.

21. Li, *Shuo bu jin de waijiao*, 151–58; Michael Chege, "Economic Relations Between China and Kenya, 1963–2007," in *U.S. and Chinese Engagement in Africa: Prospects for Improving U.S.-China-Africa Cooperation*, ed. Jennifer G. Cooke (Washington, DC: CSIS Press, 2008), 21–22.

22. Ke, *Xin Zhongguo waijiao qisu Ke Hua 95 sui shuhuai*, 207.

23. Chen Yi Zhuan Bianxiezu, *Chen Yi zhuan*, 620–625; Shishi, "Mao Zedong Poli Chuxi Chenyi Zhuidaohui," in *Xin Zhongguo waijiao fengyun*, ed. Waijiaobu Waijiaoshi Bianjishi. Vol. 3, 10–12; Jin, *Zhou Enlai zhuan, 1949–1976*, 1053; Kang, *Waijiaoguan huiyilu*, 215.

24. Margaret MacMillan, *Seize the Hour: When Nixon Met Mao* (London: John Murray, 2006), 25.

25. MacMillan, *Seize the Hour*, 33.

26. Transcript, Nixon-Mao conversation, Beijing, February 21, 1972, in *The Kissinger Transcripts: The Top Secret Talks with Beijing and Moscow*, ed. William Burr (New York: New Press, 1998), 59–65.

27. Jiang Chengzong, "Yu xiwei chujian gaoda," in *Zhongguo waijiaoguan shouji*, ed. Li, Vol. 2, 753.

28. Zhang, *Kuaguo houhou de dahongmen*, 256.

29. Peter Martin, "Beijing Puts Its Best Foot Forward for Xi's Summit," *Bloomberg News*, May 14, 2017, https://www.bloomberg.com/news/articles/2017-05-14/beijing-suddenly-has-blue-skies-clean-air-as-xi-hosts-summit; Interviews with Beijing bar owners, May 2017.

30. Kissinger, *The White House Years*, 1056.

31. Gao, *Zhou Enlai*, 17.

32. Gao, *Zhou Enlai*, 17, 237–238.

33. Zhang, *Kuaguo houhou de dahongmen*, 296.

34. R. W. Apple Jr., "U.S. and China Will Soon Set Up Offices in Capitals for Liaison; Peking to Free Two Americans," *New York Times*, February 23, 1973, https://www.nytimes.com/1973/02/23/archives/us-and-china-will-soon-set-up-offices-in-capitals-for-liaison.html; David Kirkpatrick and Este Bruce, "The U.S. Liaison Chief for Peking," *New York Times*, March 16, 1973, https://www.nytimes.com/1973/03/16/archives/the-us-liaison-chief-for-peking-david-kirkpatrick-este-bruce.html.

35. James Lilley, *China Hands: Nine Decades of Adventure, Espionage, and Diplomacy in Asia* (New York: Public Affairs, 2004), 162; Ivian C. Smith and Nigel West, *Historical Dictionary of Chinese Intelligence* (Lanham, MD: Scarecrow Press, 2012), 291–292; interviews with five former US intelligence officials.

36. Yi Jiamin, "Jintian shifou tianqing: Leng nuan Huashengdun," in *Lu si shei shou: Waijiaoguan zai Meiguo*, eds. Fu Hao and Li Tongcheng (Beijing: Zhongguo Huaqiao Chubanshe, 1995), 13–14; Ruan, *Han Xu zhuan*, 172, 203.

37. Zong, *Zhou Nan koushu*, 220–221; Zhang, *Kuaguo houhou de dahongmen*, 299.

38. Guo Jingan and Wu Jun, *Chushi feizhou de suiyue* (Chengdu: Sichuan Renmin Chubanshe, 2006), 201–202.

39. Li, *Zai Yiguo xingkong xia*, 194–199.

40. Shi Shi, "'Woniu' Shijian Shimo," in *Xin Zhongguo waijiao fengyun*, ed. Waijiaobu Waijiaoshi Bianjishi, Vol. 2, pp. 176–180; Zhou and Ke, *Yidui waijiaoguan fufu de rensheng huimou*, 120.

41. Li, *The Private Life of Chairman Mao*, 573; Gao, *Zhou Enlai*, 236.

42. Li, *Cong Weiminghu dao huanjianhu*, 182–186; Jin, *Zhou Enlai zhuan, 1949–1976*, 1133.

43. SCMP Reporter, "LSE's Role in Guiding China's Budding Diplomats," *South China Morning Post*, December 14, 2010, https://www.scmp.com/article/733308/lses-role-guiding-chinas-budding-diplomats; Zhou Wenzhong, *Dou er bu po: Zhongmei boyi yu shijie zai pingheng* (Beijing: Zhongxin Chuban Jituan, 2017), 106.

44. Li, *Cong Weiminghu dao Huanjianhu*, 182–186.

45. Tong Xiaopeng, *Fengyu sishinian*, Vol. 2 (Beijing: Zhongyang Wenxian Chubanshe, 1997), 521.

46. Li, *The Private Life of Chairman Mao*, 577; Tong, *Fengyu sishinian*, Vol. 2, 520.

47. Gao, *Zhou Enlai*, 257; Xia Yafeng, "Gao, Zhou Enlai: The Last Perfect Revolutionary, A Biography, 2007," H-Diplo Review Essay, July 30, 2009, https://issforum.org/essays/PDF/Xia-Wenqian.pdf.

48. Wu Miaofa, "Huiyi Deng Xiaoping canjia di liu jie tebie Lianda," in *Zhongguo waijiaoguan shouji*, ed. Li, Vol. 1, 61.

49. Wu, *Qiao Guanhua zai Lianheguo de rizi*, 178; Ezra Vogel, *Deng Xiaoping and the Transformation of China* (Cambridge, MA: Harvard University Press, 2011), eBook.

50. Kang, *Waijiaoguan huiyilu*, 226.

51. Yi Jiamin, "Jintian shifou tianqing: Leng nuan huashengdun," in *Lu si shei shou*, eds. Fu and Li, 46.

52. Memorandum of Conversation: Beijing, December 2, 1975, 4:10–6:00 p.m., FRUS 18, 859.

53. Cheng, *Mulin waijiao sihi nian*, 151.

54. Dai Yan, *Yi ge putong waijiaoguan de chengzhang licheng* (Beijing: Huiyi Jiujiu Chupin, 2015), 75; Ke, *Xin Zhongguo waijiao qisu Ke Hua 95 sui shuhuai*, 221; Mi Guojun, "1976 nian 1 yue 9 ri zai Dongjing," in *Dangdai Zhongguo shijie waijiao shengya*, ed. Waijiaobu Waijiaoshi Yanjiushi, Vol. IV (Beijing: Shijie Zhishi Chubanshe, 1996), 91–92; Interview with Charles Liu, February 26, 2019.

55. Zhang, *Wo yu Qiao Guanhua*, 88–89; Yi, "Jintian shifou tianqing," in *Lu si shei shou*, eds. Fu and Li, 40; Zong, *Zhou Nan koushu*, 221.

56. Ji, *The Man on Mao's Right*, 285; Ke, *Xin Zhongguo waijiao qisu Ke Hua 95 sui shuhuai*, 222.

57. Wen-Hsuan Tsai, "Framing the Funeral: Death Rituals of Chinese Communist Party Leaders," *The China Journal* 77 (September, 2016): 58, 68.

58. Wang Chuanbin, *Kuayue shiji de huiyi* (Beijing: Shijie Zhishi Chubanshe, 2010), 265; Mi, "1976 nian 1 yue 9 ri zai Dongjing," in *Dangdai Zhongguo shijie waijiao shengya*, ed. Waijiaobu Waijiaoshi Yanjiushi, Vol. IV, 97; Xie, *Cong Banmendian dao Zhijiage*, 153.

59. James Palmer, *Heaven Cracks, Earth Shakes: The Tangshan Earthquake and the Death of Mao's China* (New York: Basic Books, 2012), eBook.

60. Zhang, *Nyu waijiaoguan shouji*, 276.

61. Zhang Bing, *Yuanli zuguo de lingtu* (Beijing: Xinhua Chubanshe, 2008), 65.

62. Zhang, *Nyu waijiaoguan shouji*, 275–280; Zhang, *Yuanli zuguo de lingtu*, 67; Wu Deguang, *Cong libinguan dao zonglingshi* (Beijing: Xinhua Chubanshe, 2008), 52.

63. Palmer, *Heaven Cracks, Earth Shakes*, eBook.

64. Zhang, *Nyu waijiaoguan shouji*, 275–280.

65. Li, *The Private Life of Chairman Mao*, 18.

66. Li Tongcheng, *Zai yiguo xingkongxia*, 171.

67. Xing, *Cong Taihangshan dao Jialebihai*, 119–200.

68. Li, *The Private Life of Chairman Mao*, 18.

69. Li, *The Private Life of Chairman Mao*, 20.

70. Lee, *From Third World to First*, 579–586.

71. Han Kehua, "Nan wang si guo xing," in *Dangdai Zhongguo shijie waijiao shengya*, ed. Waijiaobu Waijiaoshi Yanjiushi, Vol. VI, 103; see also Xing, *Cong Taihangshan dao Jialebihai*, 122.

72. Zhou and Ke, *Yidui waijiaoguan fufu de rensheng huimou*, 121; Yi, "Jintian shifou tianqing," in *Lu Si Shei Shou*, eds. Fu and Li, 50; Xing, *Cong Taihangshan dao Jialebihai*, 122.

73. Zhu Xiaodi, *Thirty Years in a Red House: A Memoir of Childhood and Youth in Communist China* (Boston: University of Massachusetts Press, 1999), 170.

74. Ling, *Cong Yanan dao Lianheguo*, 125.

75. Zhang, *Wo yu Qiao Guanhua*, 94–103, 280; Zhang, "Jiechu de nyu waijiaojia Gong Peng," in *Nyu Waijiaoguan*, ed. Cheng, 472

76. Kang, *Waijiaoguan Huiyilu*, 242; Yi, "Jintian Shifou Tianqing" in *Lu Si Shei Shou*, eds. Fu and Li, 50

77. "Notes on Meetings Held in the Great Hall of the People in Peking, on 3 and 4 August 1977 at 3 PM," September 23, 1977, History and Public Policy Program Digital Archive, S-0987-0007-06, United Nations Archives and Records Management Section. Obtained for CWIHP by Charles Kraus, https://digitalarchive.wilsoncenter.org/document/118489.

78. Zhu Xiaodong, "Understanding China's Growth: Past, Present, and Future," *Journal of Economic Perspectives* 26, no. 4 (Fall 2012): 103.

79. Justin Yifu and Zhongkai Shen, "Reform and Development Strategy," in *China's 40 Years of Reform and Development: 1978–2018*, eds. Ross Garnaut, Ligang Song, and Cai Fang (Acton: ANU Press, 2018), 121.

80. Michael Schoenhals, "The 1978 Truth Criterion Controversy," *The China Quarterly* 126 (1991): 243–268.

81. Huang Jing, *Factionalism in Chinese Communist Politics* (Cambridge, UK: Cambridge University Press, 2000), 363.

82. Pantsov with Levine, *Deng Xiaoping*, 145.

83. Liu Shuqing, "San ren dashi, san zhong ganshou: Dashi shengya pianduan huiyi," in *Dangdai Zhongguo shijie waijiao shengya*, ed. Waijiaobu Waijiaoshi Yanjiushi, Vol. II, 232.

84. Interview with Stapleton Roy, July 8, 2019.

85. Wang, *Kuayue shiji de huiyi*, 278.

86. N.R. Kleinfeld, "Coca-Cola to Go on Sale in China As U.S. and Peking Expand Ties," *New York Times*, Dec. 20, 1978 https://www.nytimes.com/1978/12/20/archives/cocacola-to-go-on-sale-in-china-as-us-and-peking-expand-ties-moves.html?sq=j%2520paul%2520austin&scp=14&st=cse

Chapter 8

1. Huang, *Qinli yu jianwen*, 251–256; Chai Zemin, *Zhongmei jianjiao fengyu lu* (Shanghai: Shanghai Cishu Chubanshe, 2010), 115–130; The White House Historical

Association, "History of China State Visits to the White House," https://www. whitehousehistory.org/history-of-chinese-state-visits-to-the-white-house.

2. Chen Jian, "From Mao to Deng: China's Changing Relations with the United States," Cold War International History Project, Woodrow Wilson International Center for Scholars, working paper no. 92 (November 2019).

3. Richard Cockett, *Thinking the Unthinkable: Think-tanks and the Economic Counter-revolution, 1931–83* (London: Fontana Press, 1995).

4. US State Department Cable, "Portrait of Vice President Xi Jinping: 'Ambitious Survivor' of the Cultural Revolution," November 16, 2009, https://wikileaks.org/plusd/cables/09BEIJING3128_a.html.

5. Interview with former British official, April 2019.

6. Ke, *Xin Zhongguo waijiao qisu Ke Hua 95 sui shuhuai*, 257–264.

7. Zhong Zhendi, "Dayang Bian: Yi Zhijiage," in *Lu si shei shou*, eds. Fu and Li, 74.

8. Li, *Lianheguo de Zhongguo nyu waijiaoguan*, 40–41.

9. Liu, "San ren dashi, san zhong ganshou," in *Dangdai Zhongguo shijie waijiao shengya*, ed. Waijiaobu Waijiaoshi Yanjiushi, Vol. II, 233.

10. Ruan Hong, "Gongheguo di yi wei nyu dashi," in *Nyu waijiaoguan*, ed. Cheng, 11–13.

11. Ruan Hong, "Waishi shengya liushi nian: Fang Gong Pusheng," in *Nyu waijiaoguan*, ed. Cheng, 449; Wang Mingle, "How Ireland's Free Trade Zone Model Inspired the Shenzhen SEZ," *China Daily*, October 15, 2018, http://www.chinadaily.com.cn/a/201810/15/WS5bc4b2b8a310eff3032827b6.html.

12. James Mann, *About Face: A History of America's Curious Relationship with China from Nixon to Clinton* (New York: Alfred Knopf, 1998), 116.

13. Huang, *Qinli yu jianwen*, 260.

14. Mann, *About Face*, 125; Huang, *Qinli yu jianwen*, 262–264; Chai, *Zhongmei jianjiao fengyu lu*, 167–174.

15. Jeffrey A. Bader, *Obama and China's Rise: An Insider's Account of America's Asia Strategy* (Washington, DC: Brookings Institution Press, 2012), 76.

16. Young, *Negotiating with the Chinese Communists*, 30.

17. Nicholas D. Kristof, "Better Relations Depend on U.S., Deng Tells Nixon," *New York Times*, November 1, 1989, https://www.nytimes.com/1989/11/01/world/better-relations-depend-on-us-deng-tells-nixon.html.

18. Huang, *Qinli yu jianwen*, 278, 281, 325.

19. "The State of Foreign Policy," June 8, 1982, History and Public Policy Program Digital Archive, Mongolian Foreign Ministry Archive, Ulaanbaatar, fond 2, dans 1, kh/n 467. Obtained and translated for CWIHP by Sergey Radchenko, https://digitalarchive.wilsoncenter.org/document/113334.

20. "Sino-Soviet Relations: President Brezhnev's Speech, Tashkent, March 24, 1982 (excerpts)," *Survival: Global Politics and Strategy* 24, no. 4 (1982).

21. Huang, *Qinli yu jianwen*, 357–358.

22. Qian Qichen, *Waijiao shiji* (Beijing: Shijie Zhishi Chubanshe, 2003), 205–213.

23. Qian, *Waijiao Shiji*, 3–6; Li, *Shuo bu jin de waijiao*, 61.

24. Zou Jianhua, *Waijiaobu fayanren jiemi* (Beijing: Shizhi Zhishi Chubanshe, 2005), 64.

25. Jin Guihua, "Qiong Ren Jia Zhouchu de Fayanren," in *Ting dashi jiang gushi*, ed. Niu, 132.

26. FMPRC, "Foreign Ministry Spokesperson Hua Chunying's Regular Press Conference," July 29, 2019, http://pk.chineseembassy.org/eng/fyrth/t1684227.htm.

27. Zou, *Waijiaobu fayanren jiemi*, 122–123, 146–151.

28. Wu, *Tan waijiao*, 215.

29. Qian, *Waijiao shiji*, 7–11; Ministry of Foreign Affairs of the People's Republic of China, "Xi Jinping Pays State Visit to Finland and Travels to Florida, US for China-US Presidents' Meeting," https://www.fmprc.gov.cn/mfa_eng/topics_665678/xjpdfljxgsfwbfmgflldjxzmyshw/.

30. Hu Yaobang's Speech at First Plenum of 12th Party Central Committee (September 13, 1982), *Beijing Review* 25, no. 44 (November 1, 1982).

31. Liu, *Chinese Ambassadors*, 156–157.

32. Liu, *Chinese Ambassadors*, 158–159; Straits Times, "9 Chinese embassy staff shot dead," *The Straits Times*, August 1, 1982, https://eresources.nlb.gov.sg/newspapers/Digitised/Page/straitstimes19820801-1.1.1; AP, "Attache Kills Nine in Shooting at Embassy," *Eugene Register-Guard*, July 31, 1982, https://news.google.com/newspapers?id=GvNVAAAAIBAJ&sjid=R-IDAAAAIBAJ&hl=de&pg=6651%2C7213285.

33. Liu, *Chinese Ambassadors*, 158–159.

34. Sergey Radchenko, *Unwanted Visionaries: The Soviet Failure in Asia at the End of the Cold War* (Oxford: Oxford University Press, 2014), 36–37.

35. Liu, *Chinese Ambassadors*, 159; CIA, "China's Second Revolution," CIA FOIA, May 15, 1986.

36. Martin Childs, "Huang Hua: Politician and Diplomat Who Played a Leading Role in Bringing China Out of International Isolation," *The Independent*, December 7, 2010, https://www.independent.co.uk/news/obituaries/huang-hua-politician-and-diplomat-who-played-a-leading-role-in-bringing-china-out-of-international-2152957.html; David Barbosa, "Huang Hua, 97, a Diplomat Who Served China, Dies," *New York Times*, November 24, 2010, https://www.nytimes.com/2010/11/25/world/asia/25huang.html; Xinhua, "Funeral Held in Beijing for Former Chinese Vice Premier Huang Hua," *People's Daily online*, December 2, 2010, http://en.people.cn/90001/90776/90785/7217960.html.

37. Miller, "The CCP Central Committee's Leading Small Groups."

38. Liu, *Chinese Ambassadors*, 156–159.

39. Liu, *Chinese Ambassadors*, 161–162.

40. Liu, *Chinese Ambassadors*, 160–161.

41. Ma, *The Cultural Revolution in the Foreign Ministry of China*, 84–85.

42. CIA, "China's Diplomats in the United States: The Maturing of an Embassy," CIA FOIA, 5 September 1986.

43. Wang Zhiyun, "Caijun fengyun xiaoji," in *Nyu waijiaoguan*, ed. Cheng, 36–56; Barnett, *The Making of Foreign Policy in China*, 79–81; Alastair Iain Johnston, "Learning versus Adaptation: Explaining Change in Chinese Arms Control Policy in the 1980s and 1990s," *The China Journal* 35 (January 1996): 38–41.

44. Interview with Gao Zhikai, March 19, 2019.

45. CIA, "China's Role in International Organizations," CIA FOIA, May 4, 1984.

46. Interview with Hank Levine, July 24, 2019.

47. Xia, *Huanjing waijiaoguan shouji*, 73; Wang Zhijia, *Zhongguo huanjing waijiao* (Beijing: Zhongguo Huanjing Kexue Chubanshe, 1999), 125–156.

48. Dai, *Yi ge putong waijiaoguan de chengzhang licheng*, 108.

49. Interview with Charles Liu, February 26, 2019.

50. Xie, *Cong Banmendian dao Zhijiage*, 167–170.

51. Margaret Thatcher, "Speech at Dinner for Chinese General Secretary (Hu Yaobang)," June 9, 1986, https://www.margaretthatcher.org/document/106417.

52. Xie, *Cong Banmendian dao Zhijiage,*. 160; Zong, *Zhou Nan Koushu*, 231–233.

53. Zhang Tingyan, "Chaoxian Bandao de banshengyuan," in *Ting dashi jiang gushi*, ed. Niu Li (Beijing: Xinhua Chubanshe, 2009), 155–156.

54. Qian, *Waijiao shiji*, 139–160.

55. Interview, July 19, 2019.

56. Interview with Gao Zhikai, March 19, 2019.

57. Interview with Doug Paal, July 18, 2019.

58. Qian, *Waijiao shiji*, 28–29.

59. Ma, "Bashi niandai Dongou wenti huimou," in *Dangdai Zhongguo shijie waijiao shengya*, ed. Waijiaobu Waijiaoshi Yanjiushi, Vol. V, 167–182.

60. Christopher S. Wren, "China Cracking Down on Progeny of Powerful," *New York Times*, February 17, 1984, https://www.nytimes.com/1984/02/17/world/china-cracking-down-on-progeny-of-powerful.html.

61. Archie Brown, *The Rise and Fall of Communism* (New York: HarperCollins, 2009), 528–533.

62. James Green interview with Stapleton Roy, US-China Dialogue Podcast, April 19, 2019, https://uschinadialogue.georgetown.edu/podcasts/stapleton-roy.

63. Interview with a former US official, July 10, 2019.

64. Liu, *Chinese Ambassadors*, 163–164.

65. Interview with former US official, July 22, 2019.

66. Qian, *Waijiao shiji*, 36; Liu Xinsheng and Zhao Guomin, *Waijiaoguan lishi qinli ji* (Beijing: Jiuzhou Chubanshe, 2013), 23.

67. Bill Keller, "Gorbachev Visits Beijing for Start of Summit Talks," *New York Times*, May 15, 1989, https://www.nytimes.com/1989/05/15/world/gorbachev-visits-beijing-for-start-of-summit-talks.html.

Chapter 9

1. Qian, *Waijiao Shiji*, 165–170.

2. Wang Yusheng, "Yi ge dashi de huanle yu kunao," in *Dangdai Zhongguo shijie waijiao shengya*, ed. Waijiaobu Waijiaoshi Yanjiushi, Vol. II, 303.

3. Ruan Hong, *Han Xu zhuan* (Beijing: Shijie Zhishi Chubanshe, 2004), 370.

4. Orville Schell, *Mandate of Heaven: The Legacy of Tiananmen Square and the Next Generation of China's Leaders* (New York: Simon & Schuster, 1995), 175.

5. Human Rights Watch, "The Persecution of Human Rights Monitors, December 1988 to December 1989: A Worldwide Survey," *Human Rights Watch* (December 1989), 220.

6. Liu, *Chinese Ambassadors*, 163–164; Zong, *Zhou Nan koushu*, 337–339; Wang Yusheng, "Yi ge dashi de huanle yu kunao," in *Dangdai Zhongguo shijie waijiao shengya*, ed. Waijiaobu Waijiaoshi Yanjiushi, Vol. II, 305.

7. Liu, *Chinese Ambassadors*, 163–164.

8. Lyu, *Waijiao Rensheng*, 206.

9. Tillman Durdin, "Defections by Chinese Red Officials Are a Rarity," *New York Times*, February 8, 1969, https://www.nytimes.com/1969/02/08/archives/defections-by-chinese-red-officials-are-a-rarity-pekings.html.

10. Liu, *Chinese Ambassadors*, 163–164. The one exception was a young diplomat in Paris whose resignation was accepted by the ambassador.

11. Wu Jianmin, *Waijiao anli* (Beijing: Renmin Daxue Chubanshe, 2007), 59–60.

12. Ji, *The Man on Mao's Right*, 328.

13. Wu, *Tan Waijiao*, 54.

14. Ji, *The Man on Mao's Right*, 328.

15. Sun Dagang, "Yi ci nan wang de guoqing zhao dai hui," in *Dangdai zhongguo shijie waijiao shengya*, ed. Waijiaobu Waijiaoshi Yanjiushi, Vol. III, 304; Zhang Zai, "Benboqin guoming kangkai le nan tian: chushi aodaliya jishi," in *Dangdai Zhongguo shijie waijiao shengya*, ed. Waijiaobu Waijiaoshi Yanjiushi, Vol. III, 323.

16. Liu, *Chinese Ambassadors*, 164.

17. Interview with Dick Williams, July 19, 2019.

18. Interviews with multiple former senior US officials, summer 2019.

19. Lilley, *China Hands*, 329.

20. Qian, *Waijiao shiji*, 255–256.

21. Brown, *The Rise and Fall of Communism*, 533–544.

22. Kemal Kirişc, "Beyond the Berlin Wall: The Forgotten Collapse of Bulgaria's 'Wall,'" *Brookings Institution*, November 5, 2019, https://www.brookings.edu/blog/order-from-chaos/2019/11/05/beyond-the-berlin-wall-the-forgotten-collapse-of-bulgarias-wall/.

23. Emma Graham-Harrison, "'I'm Still Nervous,' Says Soldier Who Shot Nicolae Ceausescu," *The Guardian*, December 6, 2014, https://www.theguardian.com/world/2014/dec/07/nicolae-ceausescu-execution-anniversary-romania.

24. Interview with Doug Paal, July 18, 2019.

25. Michael Yahuda, "Deng Xiaoping: The Statesman," *The China Quarterly* 135 (September 1993): 564.

26. Ma "Bashi Niandai Dongou Wenti Huimou," in *Dangdai Zhongguo shijie waijiao shengya*, ed. Waijiaobu Waijiaoshi Yanjiushi, Vol. V, 179–182.

27. Lee, *From Third World to First*, 635.

28. E. Zev Sufott, *A China Diary: Towards the Establishment of China-Israel Diplomatic Relations* (London: Frank Cass, 1997), 85–86.

29. Li, *Shuo bu jin de waijiao*, 71–72.

30. Wang, "Yi ge dashi de huanle yu kunao," in *Dangdai Zhongguo shijie waijiao shengya*, ed. Waijiaobu Waijiaoshi Yanjiushi, Vol. II, 304.

31. Zhang, *Nyu waijiaoguan shouji*, 146–147.

32. Mann, *About Face*, 246.

33. Kathy Chenault, "Kaifu Tells Chinese That Reform Key to Improving Relations," *AP*, August 12, 1991, https://apnews.com/article/255988a4477db1c560cfee0a3cd2 6c4b.

34. Sheryl Wudunn, "British Visit Breaks Ice with China," *New York Times*, September 3, 1991, https://www.nytimes.com/1991/09/03/world/british-visit-breaks-the-ice-with-china.html.

35. Qian, *Waijiao Shiji*, 75–107; Wu, *Waijiao anli*, 106–143; Tai Huasun, *Chushi lianheguo* (Beijing: Xinhua Chubanshe, 2010), 17.

36. Thomas L. Friedman, "Chinese Official Is Invited to Washington in Response to Gulf Stance," *New York Times*, November 28, 1990, https://www.nytimes.com/1990/11/28/world/mideast-tensions-chinese-official-invited-washington-response-gulf-stance.html.

37. Wu, *Waijiao anli*, 154–177.

38. Robert Benjamin, "China's Prime Minister Regains Face," *Baltimore Sun*, January 30, 1991.

39. David Holley, "Economy Grew 12% in 1992, China Says," *Los Angeles Times*, December 31, 1992, https://www.latimes.com/archives/la-xpm-1992-12-31-mn-4309-story.html.

40. Hu Benyao, "Zhong Ao guanxi shi shang de xin pianzhang," in *Dangdai zhongguo shijie waijiao shengya*, ed. Waijiaobu Waijiaoshi Yanjiushi, Vol. V, 338; Xu Yicong, "Zai Hawana Meihao de Huiyi," in *Dangdai Zhongguo shijie waijiao shengya*, ed. Waijiaobu Waijiaoshi Yanjiushi, Vol. V, 368.

41. Guo Jingan and Wu Jun, *Chushi feizhou de suiyue* (Chengdu: Sichuan Renmin Chubanshe, 2006), 124.

42. Sergei Troush, "China's Changing Oil Strategy and Its Foreign Policy Implications," *Brookings Institution*, September 1, 1999, https://www.brookings.edu/articles/chinas-changing-oil-strategy-and-its-foreign-policy-implications/.

43. Zhang, *Nyu waijiaoguan shouji*, 148–149.

44. Mann, *About Face*, 269.

45. Nicholas D. Kristof, "China Worried by Clinton's Linking of Trade to Human Rights," *New York Times*, October 9, 1992, https://www.nytimes.com/1992/10/09/world/china-worried-by-clinton-s-linking-of-trade-to-human-rights.html.

46. Mann, *About Face*, 292; Winston Lord interview by Charles Stuart Kennedy and Nancy Bernkopf Tucker, Association for Diplomatic Studies and Training Foreign Affairs Oral History Project, Initial Interview, April 28, 1998, 576.

47. Robert L. Suettinger, *Beyond Tiananmen: The Politics of U.S.-China Relations, 1989–2000* (Washington, DC: Brookings Institution Press, 2003), 208; Garver, *China's Quest*, 610.

48. Rone Tempest, "China Threatens U.S. over Taiwan Leader's Visit: Diplomacy: Beijing Recalls Two Delegations, Vows Further Action over Perceived Nod to Taipei," *Los*

Angeles Times, May 26, 1995, https://www.latimes.com/archives/la-xpm-1995-05-26-mn-6275-story.html.

49. Thomas J. Christensen, *The China Challenge*, eBook.

50. Lee Teng-hui, "Always in My Heart," speech delivered at Cornell University, June 9, 1995, https://taiwantoday.tw/news.php?post=3961&unit=4,29,31,45.

51. Calder, *Asia in Washington*, 149.

52. FMPRC, "President Jiang Zemin Visited the United States," *FMPRC* https://www.fmprc.gov.cn/mfa_eng/ziliao_665539/3602_665543/3604_665547/t18030.shtml; Seth Faison, "Analysis: U.S. Trip Is Everything Jiang Expected," *New York Times*, November 3, 1997, https://archive.nytimes.com/www.nytimes.com/library/world/110397us-china-assess.html.

53. Allen S. Whiting, "ASEAN Eyes China: The Security Dimension," *Asian Survey* 37, no. 4 (April 1997): 299–322; Ian James Storey, "Creeping Assertiveness: China, the Philippines and the South China Sea Dispute," *Contemporary Southeast Asia* 21, no. 1 (April 1999): 95–118.

54. Michael Laris, "Chinese Openly Debate Whether to Devalue Yuan," *Washington Post*, July 16, 1998, https://www.washingtonpost.com/archive/politics/1998/07/16/chinese-openly-debate-whether-to-devalue-yuan/ff892f47-ee5e-4d26-ae90-35cac3977221/.

55. David Shambaugh, "China Engages Asia: Reshaping the Regional Order," *International Security* 29, no. 3 (Winter 2004/05): 68; Wang Yusheng, *Qinli APEC: Yi ge Zhongguo gaoguan de ticha* (Beijing: Shijie Zhishi Chubanshe, 2000), 135–157.

56. Evan S. Medeiros and M. Taylor Fravel, "China's New Diplomacy," *Foreign Affairs* 82, no. 6 (November/December 2003): 25; Shambaugh, "China Engages Asia," 68–70.

57. Susan Shirk, *Fragile Superpower: How China's Internal Politics Could Derail Its Peaceful Rise* (Oxford: Oxford University Press, 2007), 128–129; David Shambaugh, *China Goes Global: The Partial Power* (Oxford: Oxford University Press, 2013), 97.

58. Lionel Barber, "Lunch with the FT: Madam Fu Ying," *The Financial Times*, January 30, 2010, https://www.ft.com/content/867f123c-0c78-11df-a941-00144feabdc0.

59. Alastair Iain Johnston, *Social States: China in International Institutions, 1980–2000* (Princeton: Princeton University Press, 2008), 52–55, 67–69.

60. Avery Goldstein, "An Emerging China's Emerging Grand Strategy: A Neo-Bismarckian Turn?" in *International Relations Theory and the Asia-Pacific*, eds. G. John Ikenberry and Michael Mastanduno (New York: Columbia University Press, 2003), 74–83; Rex Li, *A Rising China and Security in East Asia: Identity Construction and Security Discourse* (Abingdon: Routledge, 2009), 180–181.

61. Peter Wood, "China's Foreign Relations," *Ashtray Analytics*, September 18, 2016, https://www.ashtreeanalytics.com/posts/2016/09/18/chinas-foreign-relations.

62. Medeiros and Fravel, "China's New Diplomacy," 26.

63. Guo and Wu, *Chushi Feizhou de suiyue*, 301.

64. Tain Yimin, "Qian qiu zhi guo: Luwangda," in *Dangdai Zhongguo shijie waijiao shengya*, ed. Waijiaobu Waijiaoshi Yanjiushi, Vol. II, 294–295; Wang, "Yi ge dashi de huanle yu kunao," in *Dangdai Zhongguo shijie waijiao shengya*, ed. Waijiaobu Waijiaoshi Yanjiushi, Vol. II, 304; Zhang Ruijie, "Zai sililanka renzhi de rizi li," in

Dangdai Zhongguo shijie waijiao shengya, ed. Waijiaobu Waijiaoshi Yanjiushi, Vol. III, 283–284; Qian, *Waijiao shiji*, 127, 255–56; Lyu, *Waijiao rensheng*, 38–39.

65. Liu Baolai, *Chushi Zhongdong* (Beijing: Xinhua Chubanshe, 2009), 141.

66. Jiang Xiang, "Nan wang de feizhou suiyue," in *Dangdai Zhongguo Shijie waijiao shengya*, ed. Waijiaobu Waijiaoshi Yanjiushi, Vol. VI, 309–310; Zhang Qingmin, "China's Relations with Developing Countries: Patterns, Principles, Characteristics, and Future Challenges," in *Handbook on China and Developing Countries*, ed. Carla P. Freedman, 59.

67. Julia C. Strauss, "The Past in the Present: Historical and Rhetorical Lineages in China's Relations with Africa," *The China Quarterly* 199 (September 2009): 789–791.

68. James D. Seymour, "Human Rights in Chinese Foreign Relations," in *China and the World: Chinese Foreign Policy Faces the New Millennium*, ed. Samuel S. Kim (Boulder, CO: Westview Press, 1998), 229.

69. Peter Van Ness, "China and the Third World: Patterns of Engagement and Indifference," in *China and the World*, ed. Kim, 154.

70. Zhang, *Nyu waijiaoguan shouji*, 190.

71. Jiang, *Duonaohe zhi bo*, 299–309.

72. Liu, *Chinese Ambassadors*, 164–167; Barnett, *The Making of Foreign Policy in China*, 75–92.

73. Bonnie S. Glaser, "Chinese Foreign Policy Research Institutes and the Practice of Influence," in *China's Foreign Policy: Who Makes It, and How Is It Made?*, ed. Gilbert Rozman (New York: Palgrave Macmillan, 2012), 113.

74. Lin Yunshi, "Song Tao jieti Wang Jiarui ren Zhonglianbu buzhang," *Caixin*, November 26, 2015, http://china.caixin.com/2015-11-26/100878667.html.

75. Zhu, *Wo de Lamei waijiao shengya*, 30.

76. FMPRC, "Tour the Ministry," https://www.fmprc.gov.cn/mfa_eng/wjb_663304/cgwjb_665383/; Mao Zedong, Willis Barnstone, *The Poems of Mao Zedong* (Berkeley: University of California Press, 2010), 115–116.

77. Interview, June 2020.

78. Edward A. Gargan, "China Resumes Control of Hong Kong, Concluding 156 Years of British Rule," *New York Times*, July 1, 1997, https://www.nytimes.com/1997/07/01/world/china-resumes-control-of-hong-kong-concluding-156-years-of-british-rule.html.

79. Qian, *Waijiao Shiji*, 349.

80. Cited in Avery Goldstein, "The Diplomatic Face of China's Grand Strategy: A Rising Power's Emerging Choice," *The China Quarterly* 168 (December 2001): 838.

81. Li, *Cong Weiminghu dao Huanjianhu*, 258–263.

82. Ma Zhengang, "Ouzhouren kan Zhongguoren," in *Bie yang feng yu*, ed. Zhang, 18.

83. Qiu Bingjun, *Hunqian mengrao Xinxilan* (Changchun: Jilin Renmin Chubanshe, 2000), 262.

84. Zhang, *Nyu waijiaoguan shouji*, 225–227; Liu and Pan, *Feixiang shiwai taoyuan*, 189–191; Dai Ping, "You yi xixin: Waijiao shengya diandi," in *Dangdai Zhongguo shijie waijiao shengya*, ed. Waijiaobu Waijiaoshi Yanjiushi, Vol. III, 190–191; Dai, *Yi ge putong waijiaoguan de chengzhang licheng*, 144–45; Wang, *Qinli APEC*, 193.

85. Maggie Farley, "China Enlists WWII Fervor to Foster National Strength," *Los Angeles Times*, August 12, 1995, https://www.latimes.com/archives/la-xpm-1995-08-12-mn-34201-story.html.

86. Erica Strecker Downs and Phillip C. Saunders, "Legitimacy and the Limits of Nationalism: China and the Diaoyu Islands," *International Security* 23, no. 3 (Winter 1998–1999): 137–138.

87. Jude D. Blanchette, *China's New Red Guards: The Return of Radicalism and the Rebirth of Mao Zedong* (New York: Oxford University Press, 2019), eBook.

88. Peter Hays Gries, *China's New Nationalism: Pride, Politics, and Diplomacy* (Berkeley: University of California Press, 2004), 123–124.

89. Thomas J. Christensen, "More Actors, Less Coordination? New Challenges for the Leaders of a Rising China," in *China's Foreign Policy: Who Makes It, and How Is It Made?*, ed. Gilbert Rozman (New York: Palgrave Macmillan, 2012), 29.

90. Albert Keidel, "China's Social Unrest: The Story behind the Stories," *Carnegie Endowment for International Peace Policy Brief* 28 (September 2006), https://carnegieendowment.org/files/pb48_keidel_final.pdf.

91. Banning Garrett and Bonnie Glaser, "Chinese Apprehensions about Revitalization of the U.S.-Japan Alliance," *Asian Survey* 37, no. 4 (April 1997): 383–401.

92. John F. Burns, "India Sets 3 Nuclear Blasts, Defying a Worldwide Ban," *New York Times*, May 12, 1998, https://www.nytimes.com/1998/05/12/world/india-sets-3-nuclear-blasts-defying-a-worldwide-ban-tests-bring-a-sharp-outcry.html.

93. "International Reactions to US Strikes on Iraq," *James Martin Center for Nonproliferation Studies*, December 17, 1998, https://www.nonproliferation.org/international-reactions-to-us-strikes-on-iraq/.

94. Joseph Fewsmith, "China and the WTO: The Politics behind the Agreement," *NBR Analysis* 10, no. 5, December 1, 1999, https://www.nbr.org/publication/china-and-the-wto-the-politics-behind-the-agreement/.

95. Seth Faison, "10,000 Protesters in Beijing Urge Cult's Recognition," *New York Times*, April 26, 1999, http://movies2.nytimes.com/library/world/asia/042699china-protest.html.

96. Tang, *Jin yu xu feng*, 166–193.

97. The common understanding in Washington is that these three members of staff were intelligence officials from the Ministry of State Security.

98. Later investigations would show that a B-2 stealth bomber had dropped five precision-guided missiles on the building.

99. BBC, "China Stealth Fighter 'Copied Parts from Downed US Jet,'" *BBC News*, January 24, 2011, https://www.bbc.com/news/world-asia-pacific-12266973.

100. Cited in Rebecca MacKinnon et al., "Chinese in Belgrade, Beijing Protest NATO Embassy Bombing," *CNN*, May 9, 1999, http://edition.cnn.com/WORLD/asiapcf/9905/09/china.protest.03/.

101. Quoted in Bates Gill, *Rising Star: China's New Security Diplomacy* (Washington, DC: Brookings Institution, 2010), 113.

102. Quoted in Westad, *Restless Empire*, 397.

103. Madeleine Albright, *Madam Secretary: A Memoir*, eBook; Interviews in Washington, DC, July 2019; Interviews in Shanghai.

104. David M. Lampton, *Same Bed, Different Dreams: Managing U.S.-China Relations, 1989–2000* (Berkeley: University of California Press, 2002), 61.

105. Tang Jiaxuan, *Jin yu xu feng*, 192.

106. Jim Mann, "China's Tiger Is a Pussycat to Bushes," *Los Angeles Times*, December 20, 2000, https://www.latimes.com/archives/la-xpm-2000-dec-20-mn-2466-story.html.

107. Wu, *Waijiao anli*, 327.

108. Zhou, *Dou er bu po*, 15–16.

109. Tang, *Jin yu xu feng*, 266–287; Zhou, *Dou er bu po*, 17–18.

110. Wu, *Qiao Guanhua zai Lianheguo de rizi*, 143–144.

111. CNN, "White House Announces Arms Sale to Taiwan," *CNN*, April 24, 2001, https://edition.cnn.com/2001/ALLPOLITICS/04/24/us.taiwan.arms/index.html.

112. Kelly Wallace, "Bush Pledges Whatever It Takes to Defend Taiwan," *CNN*, April 25, 2001, https://edition.cnn.com/2001/ALLPOLITICS/04/24/bush.taiwan.abc/index.html.

113. "Bush's Taiwan Comments a Move on 'Dangerous Road'—FM Spokeswoman," http://www.china.org.cn/english/11913.htm.

114. Tang, *Feijia taipingyang shangkong de hongqiao*, 48.

115. Wang, "'Friendship First,'" 147.

116. Yuan Tao, "Aoyun qinghuai," in *jianzheng Aolinpike*, eds. Tang Mingxin, Feng Guijia, and Zhang Bing (Beijing: Xinhua Chubanshe, 2007), 102.

117. Zhou Xiaopei, "Shensheng de yi piao," in *Jianzheng Aolinpike*, eds. Tang, Feng, and Zhang, 280.

118. Wu and Shi, *Zai Faguo de waijiao shengya*, 248.

119. Tang, *Feijia Taipingyang shangkong de hongqiao*, 45–46.

120. Jere Longman, "Beijing Wins Bid for 2008 Olympic Games," *New York Times*, July 14, 2001, https://www.nytimes.com/2001/07/14/sports/olympics-beijing-wins-bid-for-2008-olympic-games.html.

121. Nic Hopkins, "Beijing Celebrates Olympic Vote," *CNN*, July 13, 2001, https://edition.cnn.com/2001/fyi/news/07/13/beijing.olympics/index.html; Guardian Unlimited Sport, "Reaction to Beijing's Olympic success," *The Guardian*, July 13, 2001, https://www.theguardian.com/sport/2001/jul/13/1.

Chapter 10

1. Zhang Hongxi, "Muni '9.11,'" in *Bie yang feng yu*, ed. Zhang, 205–207.

2. Wu, *Waijiao Anli*, 342–343; Yoichi Funabashi, *The Peninsula Question: A Chronicle of the Second Korean Nuclear Crisis* (Washington, DC: Brookings Institution Press, 2007), 266–267.

3. Tang, *Jin yu xu feng*, 297.

4. Cited in Funabashi, *The Peninsula Question*, 267.

5. Zhang, "Muni '9.11,'" in *Bie yang feng yu*, ed. Zhang, 209.

6. Andrew Small, *The China-Pakistan Axis: Asia's New Geopolitics* (London: Hurst & Co, 2015), 131–132; Willy Wo-Lap Lam, "Smoke Clears over China's U.S. Strategy," *CNN*, September 26, 2001, https://edition.cnn.com/2001/WORLD/asiapcf/east/09/25/willy.column/.

7. Small, *The China-Pakistan Axis*, 130; Michael D. Swaine, *America's Challenge: Engaging a Rising China in the Twenty-First Century* (Washington, DC: Carnegie Endowment for International Peace, 2011), 231–232.

8. "US opens FBI office in Its Beijing embassy," October 25, 2002, http://www.china-embassy.org/eng/sgxx/sggg/fyrth/t34936.htm.

9. Alex Frew McMillan and Major Garrett, "U.S. Wins Support from China," *CNN*, October 19, 2001, https://www.cnn.com/2001/WORLD/asiapcf/east/10/19/bush.jiang.apec/index.html.

10. National Security Council, *The National Security Strategy of the United States* (Washington, DC: The White House, 2002), https://georgewbush-whitehouse.archives.gov/nsc/nss/2002/.

11. Xu Jian, "Rethinking China's Period of Strategic Opportunity," *China International Studies*, March/April 2014, 51–70; Cui Liru, "China's 'Period of Historic Opportunities,'" *China-U.S. Focus*, February 1, 2018, https://www.chinausfocus.com/foreign-policy/chinas-period-of-historic-opportunities.

12. "Full Text of Jiang Zemin's Report at 16th Party Congress," December 10, 2002, http://en.people.cn/200211/18/eng20021118_106983.shtml.

13. Tang, *Jin yu xu feng*, 461.

14. Funabashi, *The Peninsula Question*, 277.

15. Funabashi, *The Peninsula Question*, 275–276.

16. This account draws extensively from Funabashi's meticulously researched *The Peninsula Question*, 262–266.

17. Qian, *Waijiao shiji*, 157–159.

18. Funabashi, *The Peninsula Question*, 337–345.

19. Victor Cha, *The Impossible State: North Korea, Past and Future*, eBook.

20. Shirk, *Fragile Superpower*, 125.

21. Cited in Bonnie S. Glaser and Liang Wang, "The North Korea Nuclear Crisis and U.S.-China Cooperation," in *China and the United States: Cooperation and Competition in Northeast Asia*, ed. Suisheng Zhao (New York: Palgrave Macmillan, 2008), 143.

22. Condoleezza Rice, *No Higher Honor: A Memoir of My Years in Washington* (New York: Random House, 2011), 474.

23. Cited in Joseph Fewsmith, *China Since Tiananmen: From Deng Xiaoping to Hu Jintao*, 2nd ed. (Cambridge, UK: Cambridge University Press, 2008), 2.

24. Evan S. Medeiros, *China's International Behavior: Activism, Opportunism, and Diversification* (Santa Monica: RAND Corporation, 2009), 72–77.

25. Tang, *Jin yu xu feng*, 357–358; Wu and Shi, *Zai faguo de waijiao shengya*, 306; Wu Jianmin, *Waijiao anli* (Beijing: Renmin Daxue Chubanshe, 2007), 206–218; Willy Wo-Lap Lam, "China's Hu Set for Global Debut," *CNN*, May 27, 2003, https://edition.cnn.com/2003/WORLD/asiapcf/east/05/25/china.hu/index.html.

26. Robert L. Suettinger, "The Rise and Descent of 'Peaceful Rise,'" *China Leadership Monitor,* no. 12 (Fall 2004), https://media.hoover.org/sites/default/files/documents/clm12_rs.pdf.

27. Wu and Shi, *Zai Faguo de waijiao shengya,* 209–210.

28. Anne-Marie Brady, *Marketing Dictatorship: Propaganda and Thought Work in Contemporary China* (Lanham, MD: Rowman and Littlefield, 2008), 87.

29. Joshua Kurlantzich, *Charm Offensive: How China's Soft Power Is Transforming the World* (New Haven, CT: Yale University Press, 2007), 68–69, 83, 103.

30. Glaser, "Chinese Foreign Policy Research Institutes and the Practice of Influence," in *China's Foreign Policy,* ed. Rozman, 101.

31. Tang, *Jin yu xu feng,* 443–445.

32. Joseph Kahn, "China Opens Summit for African Leaders," *New York Times,* November 2, 2006.

33. Michal Meidan, "China's Africa Policy: Business Now: Politics Later," *Asian Perspective* 30, no. 4 (2006): 69–70.

34. Jonathan Watts, "Chavez Says China Deal 'Great Wall' against US," *Guardian,* August 26, 2006, https://www.theguardian.com/world/2006/aug/26/china.venezuela.

35. Stephen Blank, "Islam Karimov and the Heirs of Tiananmen," *Eurasia Daily Monitor* 2, no. 115, June 14, 2005.

36. Daniel Large, "China's Sudan Engagement: Changing Northern and Southern Political Trajectories in Peace and War," *The China Quarterly* 199 (September 2009): 610–626.

37. Stephanie Kleine-Ahlbrandt and Andrew Small, "China's New Dictatorship Diplomacy: Is Beijing Parting with Pariahs?," *Foreign Affairs* (January/February 2008).

38. Peter Sanders and Geoffrey A. Fowler, "Spielberg Severs Olympics Tie," *Wall Street Journal,* February 13, 2008, https://www.wsj.com/articles/SB120285499475363491.

39. "Hu Calls for Enhancing 'Soft Power' of Chinese Culture," *Xinhua,* October 15, 2007, http://www.china.org.cn/english/congress/228142.htm.

40. Jiang Zemin, "Build a Well-off Society in an All-Round Way and Create a New Situation in Building Socialism with Chinese Characteristics," November 8, 2002, http://www.china.org.cn/english/2002/Nov/49107.htm.

41. David M. Lampton, "The Faces of Chinese Power," *Foreign Affairs* 86, no. 1 (January/February 2007): 122.

42. Jonas Parello-Plesner and Mathieu Duchatel, *China's Strong Arm: Protecting Citizens and Assets Abroad* (London: IISS/Routledge, 2015), 37–40.

43. Kurlantzich, *Charm Offensive,* 23.

44. Parello-Plesner and Duchatel, *China's Strong Arm,* 33.

45. Parello-Plesner and Duchatel, *China's Strong Arm,* 41–42.

46. Josh Chin, "China's Other Problem with Protests Abroad," *Wall Street Journal, China Real Time Report,* February 23, 2011, https://blogs.wsj.com/chinarealtime/2011/02/23/chinas-other-problem-with-protests-abroad/.

47. Parello-Plesner and Duchatel, *China's Strong Arm,* 38.

48. Parello-Plesner and Duchatel, *China's Strong Arm,* 12–13.

49. Parello-Plesner and Duchatel, *China's Strong Arm,* 11.

50. Ian Tyrrell, *Reforming the World: The Creation of America's Moral Empire* (Princeton: Princeton University Press, 2010).

51. Hu Jintao, "Firmly March on the Path of Socialism with Chinese Characteristics and Strive to Complete the Building of a Moderate Prosperous Society in all Respects," November 8, 2012, http://www.china.org.cn/china/18th_cpc_congress/2012-11/16/content_27137540.htm.

52. Parello-Plesner and Duchatel, *China's Strong Arm*, 41–60; Lucy Corkin, "Redefining Foreign Policy Impulses toward Africa: The Roles of the MFA, the MOFCOM and China Exim Bank," *Journal of Current Chinese Affairs* 40, no. 4 (2011): 61–90.

53. Linda Jakobson and Dean Knox, "China's New Foreign Policy Actors," Stockholm Peace Research Institute, Stockholm SIPRI policy paper no. 26 (2010).

54. Liu, *Chinese Ambassadors*, 206–207.

55. Shirk, *Fragile Superpower*, 224.

56. Shambaugh, *China Goes Global*, 69.

57. Ken Jowitt, *New World Disorder: The Leninist Extinction* (Berkeley: University of California Press, 1992), 134–136.

58. Rana, *Asian Diplomacy*, 38–39.

59. Interview with Robert Suettinger, July 22, 2019.

60. Bates Gill and Martin Kleiber, "China's Space Odyssey: What the Antisatellite Test Reveals about Decision-Making in Beijing," *Foreign Affairs* 86, no. 3 (May–June 2007), 2–6.

61. Interviews in Beijing; Shirk, *Fragile Superpower*, 101–102; Zou, *Waijiaobu fayanren jiemi*, 38.

62. Li, *Shuo bu jin de waijiao*, 24.

63. Joseph Kahn, "China Angered by Reported Orgy Involving Japanese Tourists," *New York Times*, September 30, 2003, https://www.nytimes.com/2003/09/30/world/china-angered-by-reported-orgy-involving-japanese-tourists.html.

64. China Daily, "Japan Urged to Be Aware of China's Laws," *China Daily*, October 10, 2003, http://www.chinadaily.com.cn/en/doc/2003-10/10/content_270604.htm.

65. Joseph Kahn, "China Is Pushing and Scripting Anti-Japanese Protests," *New York Times*, April 15, 2005, https://www.nytimes.com/2005/04/15/world/asia/china-is-pushing-and-scripting-antijapanese-protests.html.

66. US State Department Cable, "Japanese Readout: Dai Bingguo Uncompromising on Yasukuni Seeks 'Positive' Signals from Japan," February 13, 2006, https://wikileaks.org/plusd/cables/06TOKYO775_a.html.

67. Dai, *Zhanlue duihua*, 320.

68. Li, *Shuo bu jin de waijiao*, 139; John Aglionby, "The Art of Toilet Diplomacy," *The Guardian*, July 27, 2006, https://www.theguardian.com/world/2006/jul/27/worlddispatch.johnaglionby.

69. Dai, *Zhanlyue duihua*, 118, 301.

70. Kerry Dumbaugh, "China-U.S. Relations: Current Issues and Implications for U.S. Policy," *CRS Report for Congress*, June 14, 2007, https://china.usc.edu/sites/default/files/legacy/AppImages/crs-us-china-relations-07.pdf.

71. US Department of the Treasury, "Fact Sheet: Creation of the U.S.-China Strategic Economic Dialogue," September 20, 2006, https://www.treasury.gov/press-center/press-releases/Pages/hp107.aspx.

72. Claire Reade, "The U.S.-China S&ED: Time to Tinker, Not to Toss," *CSIS*, June 27, 2016, https://www.csis.org/analysis/us-china-sed-time-tinker-not-to-toss.

73. Bo Zhiyue, *China's Elite Politics: Political Transition and Power Balancing* (Singapore: World Scientific, 2007), 163–164; Cheng Li, *China's Leaders: The New Generation* (Lanham, MD: Rowman & Littlefield, 2001), 138.

74. CCTV, "China's New Cabinet Members Approved," *CCTV*, March 18, 2008, http://www.china.org.cn/government/NPC_CPPCC_sessions2008/2008-03/18/content_12899026.htm.

75. Hillary Rodham Clinton, *Hard Choices* (London: Simon & Schuster, 2014), 61–62.

76. Dai, *Zhanlyue duihua*, 367–368.

77. Yi Wang, "Yang Jiechi: Xi Jinping's Top Diplomat Back in His Element," *China Brief* 17, no. 16, December 8, 2017, https://jamestown.org/program/yang-jiechi-xis-top-diplomat-back-element/; Li Xing and Lyndon Cao, "Yang a Popular Choice as FM," *China Daily*, April 28, 2007, http://www.chinadaily.com.cn/china/2007-04/28/content_862385.htm.

78. Clinton, *Hard Choices*, 62.

79. Wang, "Yang Jiechi"; Li and Cao, "Yang a Popular Choice as FM."

80. Interview with former US official, July 2019.

81. Interviews in Beijing, March 2018; Interview with former US official, July 2019.

82. U.S. State Department Cable, "Codel Ackerman Meeting with Assistant Minister of Foreign Affairs Yang Jiechi, January 28," January 31, 1997, https://wikileaks.org/plusd/cables/97BEIJING3816_a.html.

83. Clinton, *Hard Choices*, 62–63.

84. Interview with former US official, July 2019.

85. Zhang, *Waijiaoguan shuo liyi*, 2–8.

86. Shambaugh, *China Goes Global*, 66.

87. Zhang, *Waijiaoguan shuo liyi*, 26.

88. Interviews.

89. Li, *Shuo bu jin de waijiao*, 342.

90. Dai, *Zhanlyue duihua*, 114.

91. Preeti Bhattacharji and Carin Zissis, "Olympic Pressure on China," *CFR*, June 17, 2008, https://www.cfr.org/backgrounder/olympic-pressure-china; Lindsay Beck, "Beijing to Evict 1.5 Million for Olympics," *Reuters*, June 5, 2007, https://uk.reuters.com/article/uk-olympics-beijing-housing/beijing-to-evict-1-5-million-for-olympics-idUKSP31431820070605; Wang Nan and Nick Mulvenney, "Olympics—Beijing Stops Cars for Games Clean Air Test," *Reuters*, August 17, 2007, https://www.reuters.com/article/idUSPEK207929; Jim Yardley, "No Spitting on the Road to Olympic Glory, Beijing Says," *New York Times*, April 17, 2007, https://www.nytimes.com/2007/04/17/world/asia/17manners.html.

92. Nicholas J. Cull, "The Public Diplomacy of the Modern Olympic Games and China's Soft Power Strategy," in *Owning the Olympics: Narratives of the New China*, eds.

Monroe E. Price and Dayan Daniel (Ann Arbor: University of Michigan Press, 2008), 136.

93. Jim Yardley, "Violence in Tibet as Monks Clash with the Police," *New York Times*, March 15, 2008, https://www.nytimes.com/2008/03/15/world/asia/15tibet.html.

94. Candida Ng, "Timeline: Olympic Torch Protests around the World," *Reuters*, April 28, 2008, https://www.reuters.com/article/us-olympics-torch-disruptions-idUSSP17070920080428.

95. Bethany Allen-Ebrahimian and Zach Dorfman, "China Has Been Running Global Influence Campaigns for Years," *The Atlantic*, May 14, 2019, https://www.theatlantic.com/international/archive/2019/05/beijing-olympics-china-influence-campaigns/589186/; NBC, "Pro-Beijing Crowds Drown Torch Protesters," *NBC*, April 24, 2008, http://www.nbcnews.com/id/24268336/ns/beijing_olympics-beijing_olympics_news/t/pro-beijing-crowds-drown-out-torch-protesters/#.XoLuP5MzbsF; Jon Herskovitz, Jack Kim, and Ben Blanchard, "S. Korea Probes Chinese Violence at Torch Relay," *Reuters*, April 29, 2008, https://www.reuters.com/article/us-olympics-torch-korea/s-korea-probes-chinese-violence-at-torch-relay-idUSSEO12376920080429; James Jiann Hua To, *Qiaowu: Extra-Territorial Policies for the Overseas Chinese* (Leiden: Brill Academic, 2014), 31–34.

96. Fu Ying, "Western Media Has Demonized China," *The Daily Telegraph*, April 13, 2008, https://www.telegraph.co.uk/comment/personal-view/3557186/Chinese-ambassador-Fu-Ying-Western-media-has-demonised-China.html.

97. White House photo by Eric Draper, President George W. Bush attends the US Olympic Men's Basketball Team's game against China with his father, former President George H. W. Bush and China's Foreign Minster Yang Jiechi Sunday, Aug. 10, 2008, https://georgewbush-whitehouse.archives.gov/news/releases/2008/08/images/20080810_d-1287-515h.html.

98. David M. Herszenhorn, Carl Hulse, and Sheryl Gay Stolberg, "Talks Implode during a Day of Chaos; Fate of Bailout Remains Unresolved," *New York Times*, September 25, 2008, https://www.nytimes.com/2008/09/26/business/26bailout.html.

99. Peter S. Goodman, "U.S. Unemployment Rate Hits 10.2%, Highest in 26 Years," *New York Times*, November 6, 2009, https://www.nytimes.com/2009/11/07/business/economy/07jobs.html.

100. Dai, *Zhanlue duihua*, 350.

101. David Barboza, "China Unveils Sweeping Plan for Economy," *New York Times*, November 9, 2008, https://www.nytimes.com/2008/11/10/world/asia/10china.html.

102. Albert Keidel, "China's Stimulus Lesson for America," Carnegie Endowment for International Peace, November 2008, http://carnegieendowment.org/files/chinas_stimulus_lesson_for_america.pdf.

103. Henry M. Paulson Jr., *Dealing with China: An Insider Unmasks the New Economic Superpower* (New York: Machete, 2015), 259.

104. Reuters Staff, "Clinton Says Appreciates China Confidence in US Debt," *Reuters*, February 21, 2009, https://uk.reuters.com/article/china-clinton-treasuries/clinton-says-appreciates-china-confidence-in-us-debt-idUSNPEK32176320090221.

105. Josh Rogin, "The End of the Concept of 'Strategic Reassurance'?," *Foreign Policy*, November 6, 2009, https://foreignpolicy.com/2009/11/06/the-end-of-the-concept-of-strategic-reassurance/.

106. Ruan Zongze, *Yi ge Waijiaoguan de Meiguo Mitan* (Nanjing: Jiangsu Renmin Chubanshe, 2012), 14.

107. Chen, *Waijiao, rang shijie geng hexie*, 83–84.

108. Bonnie S. Glaser and Benjamin Dooley, "China's 11th Ambassadorial Conference Signals Continuity and Change in Foreign Policy," *Jamestown China Brief* 9, no. 22 (November 4, 2009).

109. Bader, *Obama and China's Rise*, 54–61; Clinton, *Hard Choices*, 65–66.

110. Bader, *Obama and China's Rise*, 61–68; Clinton, *Hard Choices*, 415–425.

111. John Vidal, "Ed Miliband: China Tried to Hijack Copenhagen Climate Deal," *The Guardian*, December 20, 2009, https://www.theguardian.com/environment/2009/dec/20/ed-miliband-china-copenhagen-summit.

112. Michael Green, Kathleen Hicks, Zack Cooper, John Schaus, and Jake Douglas, "Counter-coercion Series: Harassment of the USNS Impeccable," *CSIS*, May 9, 2017, https://amti.csis.org/counter-co-harassment-usns-impeccable/.

113. Andrew Browne and Jay Solomon, "China Threatens U.S. Sanctions over Arms Sale to Taiwan," *Wall Street Journal*, January 31, 2010, https://www.wsj.com/articles/SB10001424052748703389004575034240303883892.

114. Michael D. Swaine, "China's Assertive Behavior Part One: On 'Core Interests'," *China Leadership Monitor*, no. 34, 4, https://carnegieendowment.org/files/CLM34MS_FINAL.pdf.

115. Interviews, summer 2019; Bader, *Obama and China's Rise*, 104–106; Clinton, *Hard Choices*, 70–71.

116. Bader, *Obama and China's Rise*, 123.

117. Interview with former US official, July 11, 2019.

118. Chen, *Waijiao, Rang shijie geng hexie*, 50.

119. Linda Jackobson, "Domestic Actors and the Fragmentation of China's Foreign Policy," in *China in the Era of Xi Jinping*, eds. Robert S. Ross and Jo Inge Bekkevold, eBook; Manuel Mogato, "China Angers Neighbors with Sea Claims on New Passports," *Reuters*, November 22, 2012, https://www.reuters.com/article/us-china-southchinasea/china-angers-neighbors-with-sea-claims-on-new-passports-idUSBRE8AL09Q20121122.

120. Jackobson, "Domestic Actors and the Fragmentation of China's Foreign Policy," in *China in the Era of Xi Jinping*, eds. Ross and Bekkevold, eBook; John Ruwitch, "As China's Clout Grows, Sea Policy Proves Unfathomable," *Reuters*, December 9, 2012, https://uk.reuters.com/article/china-sea-policy/analysis-as-chinas-clout-grows-sea-policy-proves-unfathomable-idUKL4N09H0OZ20121209.

121. Kenneth Lieberthal and Wang Jisi, "Addressing U.S.-China Strategic Distrust," Brookings Institution, John L. Thornton China Center Monograph Series, No. 4, March 2012, https://www.brookings.edu/wp-content/uploads/2016/06/0330_china_lieberthal.pdf.

Chapter 11

1. Karen Barlow, "Australia Expresses Concern over China Air Defence Zone," *ABC*, November 26, 2013, https://www.abc.net.au/news/2013-11-26/an-aust-calls-in-china-ambassador-over-air-defence-zone-announc/5117974.

2. John Kerry, "Statement on the East China Sea Air Defense Identification Zone," U.S. Department of State, November 23, 2013, https://2009-2017.state.gov/secretary/remarks/2013/11/218013.htm; Catherine McGrath, "China, Australia Spat over Air Defence Identification Zone Highlights 'Troubled Relations' in Region," *ABC*, November 28, 2013, https://www.abc.net.au/news/2013-11-28/australia-taking-sides-in-china-defence-zone-stoush/5122756.

3. Stephen McDonnell and Jane Cowan, "China Warns Julie Bishop's 'Irresponsible' Criticism of New Air Zone Could Hurt Relations," *ABC*, November 28, 2013, https://www.abc.net.au/news/2013-11-27/china-rejects-australian-criticism-of-new-air-zone/5120920.

4. Stephen McDonell, "East China Sea Row Escalates, as Wang Yi Tells Julia Bishop That Australia Has 'Jeopardised Trust'," *ABC*, December 7, 2013, https://www.abc.net.au/news/2013-12-07/east-sea-dispute-between-china-and-australia-escalates/5142080; Michael Martina, "Australia Foreign Minister Downplays China Air Defense Zone Tension in Visit," *Reuters*, December 7, 2013, https://in.reuters.com/article/us-australia-china-idUSBRE9B603620131207; FMPRC, "Wang Yi: China and Australia Should Nurture Rather Than Damage Mutual Trust," FMPRC, December 6, 2013, https://www.fmprc.gov.cn/ce/cgjb/eng/zxxx/t1107386.htm; Jade Macmillan, "Julie Bishop Recalls Meeting with Her Chinese Counterparts after Diplomatic Dispute," *ABC*, August 14, 2019, https://www.abc.net.au/news/2019-08-14/julie-bishop-recalls-meeting-with-her-chinese-counterpart/11411462.

5. David Wroe, "China's Rebuke of Julie Bishop 'Rudest' Conduct Seen in 30 Years, Says Senior Foreign Affairs Official," *SMH*, February 27, 2014, https://www.smh.com.au/politics/federal/chinas-rebuke-of-julie-bishop-rudest-conduct-seen-in-30-years-says-senior-foreign-affairs-official-20140227-33jid.html.

6. Stephen FitzGerald, "Australia's Baffling Dealings with China," *The China Story Journal*, January 30, 2014, https://www.thechinastory.org/2014/01/australias-baffling-dealings-with-china/.

7. "Transcript—Media Doorstop in Beijing," https://www.foreignminister.gov.au/minister/julie-bishop/transcript-eoe/transcript-media-doorstop-beijing; ABC News, "Julie Bishop Downplays Diplomatic Spat with China over New Air Defence Zone," *ABC*, December 7, 2013, https://www.abc.net.au/news/2013-12-07/bishop-downplays-diplomatic-spat-with-china-over-air-defence/5142548.

8. Macmillan, "Julie Bishop Recalls Meeting with Her Chinese Counterparts after Diplomatic Dispute."

9. U.S. State Department Cable, "Portrait of Vice President Xi Jinping: 'Ambitious Survivor' of the Cultural Revolution," November 16, 2009, https://wikileaks.org/plusd/cables/09BEIJING3128_a.html.

10. Interview with former US official, July 2019.

11. Xiao Gang, "Xi Jinping on Foreigners 'Pointing Fingers' at China (with Video)," *China Digital Times*, February 12, 2009, https://chinadigitaltimes.net/2009/02/xi-jinping-%E4%B9%A0%E8%BF%91%E5%B9%B3-on-foreigners-pointing-fingers-at-china-with-video/.

12. Austin Ramzy, "A Chinese Leader Talks Tough to Foreigners," *Time*, February 13, 2009, https://world.time.com/2009/02/13/a-chinese-leader-talks-tough-to-foreigners/; Willy Lam, "Xi Jinping: China's Conservative Strongman-in-Waiting," *Jamestown China Brief* 11, no. 16, September 2, 2011, https://jamestown.org/wp-content/uploads/2011/09/cb_11_39.pdf?x73213.

13. U.S. State Department Cable, "Chinese VP Trip to Mexico—Journey Begins with a Five-Step Proposal," March 10, 2009, https://wikileaks.org/plusd/cables/09MEXICO701_a.html.

14. Interviews in Beijing.

15. Peter Martin and Daniel Ten Kate, "Biden Championed Close China Ties and Then Xi Came Along," *Bloomberg Businessweek*, April 23, 2020, https://www.bloomberg.com/news/articles/2020-04-23/a-biden-presidency-wouldn-t-mean-better-u-s-china-relations.

16. Xi Jinping, "Work Together for a Bright Future of China-US Cooperative Partnership," FMPRC, February 15, 2012, https://www.fmprc.gov.cn/mfa_eng/wjdt_665385/zyjh_665391/t910351.shtml.

17. Peter Ford, "The New Face of Chinese diplomacy: Who Is Wang Yi?" *Christian Science Monitor*, March 18, 2013, https://www.csmonitor.com/World/Asia-Pacific/2013/0318/The-new-face-of-Chinese-diplomacy-Who-is-Wang-Yi.

18. "Wang Yi," *China Vitae*, http://www.chinavitae.com/biography/Wang_Yi%7C416/bio.

19. Cheng Li, *Chinese Politics in the Xi Jinping Era: Reassessing Collective Leadership* (Washington, DC: Brookings Institution Press, 2016), 270; Fengmian Xinwen, "Waijiaobu 12 wei lingdao quanbu gongbu yinyu zhuangkuang," *Fengmian Xinwen*, November 12, 2016, http://politics.gmw.cn/2016-11/12/content_22949065.htm.

20. Interviews in Beijing.

21. Ben Blanchard and Christian Shepherd, "China's Confident 'Silver Fox Steps into Diplomatic Limelight," *Reuters*, August 25, 2017, https://www.reuters.com/article/us-china-congress-wang-idUSKCN1B50GU.

22. FMPRC, "Wei shixian waijiao bao guomeng er nuli fendou," FMPRC, August, 23, 2013, https://www.fmprc.gov.cn/ce/cohk/chn/xwdt/wsyw/t1069032.htm.

23. Chris Buckley, "China Takes Aim at Western Ideas," *New York Times*, August 19, 2013, https://www.nytimes.com/2013/08/20/world/asia/chinas-new-leadership-takes-hard-line-in-secret-memo.html?_r=0.

24. Tom Phillips, "'It's Getting Worse': China's Liberal Academics Fear Growing Censorship," *The Guardian*, August 6, 2015, https://www.theguardian.com/world/2015/aug/06/china-xi-jinping-crackdown-liberal-academics-minor-cultural-revolution.

25. Interviews in Beijing.

26. Elizabeth Economy, "The Xi-Obama Summit: As Good as Expected—and Maybe Even Better," *The Atlantic*, June 11, 2013, https://www.theatlantic.com/china/archive/

2013/06/the-xi-obama-summit-as-good-as-expected-and-maybe-even-better/
276733/.

27. Interview with former US official, August 2019.

28. Xi Jinping, "Promote Friendship between Our People Work Together to Build a
Bright Future," *FMPRC*, September 7, 2013, https://www.fmprc.gov.cn/ce/cebel/eng/
zxxx/t1078088.htm.

29. Wu Jiao, "President Xi Gives Speech to Indonesia's Parliament," *China Daily*, October
2, 2013, https://www.chinadaily.com.cn/china/2013xiapec/2013-10/02/content_
17007915_2.htm.

30. Xi Jinping, "Let the Sense of Common Destiny Take Deep Root in Neighboring
Countries," *FMPRC*, October 25, 2013, https://www.fmprc.gov.cn/mfa_eng/
wjb_663304/wjbz_663308/activities_663312/t1093870.shtml; Timothy Heath,
"Diplomacy Work Forum: Xi Steps Up Efforts to Shape a China-Centered Regional
Order, *Jamestown China Brief* 13, no. 22, November 7, 2013, https://jamestown.org/
program/diplomacy-work-forum-xi-steps-up-efforts-to-shape-a-china-centered-
regional-order/; Michael D. Swaine, "Chinese Views and Commentary on Periphery
Diplomacy," *China Leadership Monitor*, no. 44 (Summer 2014), https://www.hoover.
org/sites/default/files/research/docs/clm44ms.pdf.

31. Interviews with former US officials, July and August, 2019.

32. Ritchie B. Tongo, "China's Land Reclamation in South China Sea Grows: Pentagon
Report," *Reuters*, August 21, 2015, http://www.reuters.com/article/us-southchinasea-
china-pentagon-idUSKCN0QQ0S920150821.

33. "Xi Jinping Looks Ahead to New Era of China-France Ties," CCTV.com, March 28,
2014, http://english.cntv.cn/2014/03/28/VIDE1395981962032239.shtml.

34. Xi Jinping, "New Asian Security Concept for New Progress in Security Cooperation,"
FMPRC, May 21, 2014, https://www.fmprc.gov.cn/mfa_eng/zxxx_662805/t1159951.
shtml.

35. Interview, February 2020.

36. Interview with former US official, August 2019.

37. Interview with former US official, August 2019.

38. Peter Martin, "The Humbling of the NDRC: China's National Development and
Reform Commission Searches for a New Role Amid Restructuring," *Jamestown China
Brief* 14, no. 5, March 6, 2014, https://jamestown.org/program/the-humbling-of-the-
ndrc-chinas-national-development-and-reform-commission-searches-for-a-new-
role-amid-restructuring/.

39. Interview with Susan Thornton, July 2019.

40. Interview with two former US officials, July 2019.

41. "Xi Jinping Chuxi Zhongyang Waishi Gongzuo Huiyi Bing Fabiao Zhongyao
Jianghua," *Xinhua*, November 29, 2014, http://www.xinhuanet.com//politics/2014-
11/29/c_1113457723.htm; Michael D. Swaine, "Xi Jinping's Address to the Central
Conference on Work Relating to Foreign Affairs: Assessing and Advancing Major
Power Diplomacy with Chinese Characteristics," *China Leadership Monitor*, no. 46
(Winter 2015), https://carnegieendowment.org/files/Michael_Swaine_CLM_46.pdf.

42. Chen Xianggang, "A Diplomatic Manifesto to Secure the Chinese Dream," China-US Focus, December 31, 2014, https://www.chinausfocus.com/foreign-policy/a-diplomatic-manifesto-to-secure-the-chinese-dream/.

43. Guanchazhewang, "Waijiaobu lingdao: gei waijiaobu ji gaipian de ren yue lai yue shao," *Guangchawang*, December 9, 2014, https://www.guancha.cn/strategy/2014_12_09_302831.shtml?luicode=10000011&lfid=1076031956994364&u=http%3A%2F%2Fwww.guancha.cn%2Fstrategy%2F2014_12_09_302831.shtml.

44. Maya Wang, "China's New Foreign NGO Law Will Help Silence Critics," *Human Rights Watch*, April 13, 2015, https://www.hrw.org/news/2015/04/13/chinas-new-foreign-ngo-law-will-help-silence-critics.

45. Andrew Jacobs and Chris Buckley, "China Targeting Rights Lawyers in a Crackdown," *New York Times*, July 22, 2015, https://www.nytimes.com/2015/07/23/world/asia/china-crackdown-human-rights-lawyers.html; Amnesty International, "China's Crackdown on Human Rights Lawyers: A Year On," July 9, 2016, https://www.amnesty.org/en/latest/campaigns/2016/07/one-year-since-chinas-crackdown-on-human-rights-lawyers/.

46. Interview with former US official, July 2019.

47. Xu Yangjingjing and Simon Denyer, "Six Charts That Explain Why U.S. Companies Feel Unwelcome in China," *Washington Post WorldViews*, January 20, 2016, https://www.washingtonpost.com/news/worldviews/wp/2016/01/20/six-charts-that-explain-why-u-s-companies-feel-unwelcome-in-china/.

48. Philip Ewing, "How Tough Will Obama Be with Xi?" *Politico*, September 23, 2015, https://www.politico.com/story/2015/09/president-obama-xi-jinping-state-visit-213997.

49. Interview with former US official, August 2019.

50. Ashifa Kassam and Tom Philips, "Chinese Minister Vents Anger When Canadian Reporter Asks about Human Rights," *The Guardian*, June 2, 2016, https://www.theguardian.com/law/2016/jun/02/chinese-foreign-minister-canada-angry-human-rights-question.

51. Blanchard and Shepherd, "China's Confident 'Silver Fox' Steps into Diplomatic Limelight."

52. Beimeng Fu, "People Are Super Thirsty over This Diplomat And It's Kinda Weird," *BuzzFeed News*, July 20, 2016, https://www.buzzfeednews.com/article/beimengfu/these-diplomats-are-now-basically-pop-stars-and-its-super-we.

53. "International Law Dishonored by Illegal Award on South China Sea Arbitration: Interview with Ambassador Wu Ken," http://nl.china-embassy.org/eng/xwdt/t1380919.htm.

54. Elizabeth C. Economy, *The Third Revolution: Xi Jinping and the New Chinese State* (New York: Oxford University Press, 2018), 90.

55. Wu, *Tan Waijiao*, 147.

56. Interview, November 2017.

57. Keith Zhai, Ken Wills, Jeff Kearns, and Kevin Hamlin, "China Cites 'The Art of War' as Trump Signals Trade Battle," *Bloomberg News*, November 28, 2016, https://www.bloomberg.com/news/articles/2016-11-28/china-turns-to-the-art-of-war-as-trump-signals-battle-on-trade.

58. Peter Martin, Jennifer Jacobs, and Steven Yang, "What Does Trump Want? China Scours Twitter, Cocktail Parties for Clues," *Bloomberg News*, February 21, 2017, https://www.bloomberg.com/news/articles/2017-02-21/over-twinkies-and-tweets-china-ponders-what-does-trump-want.

59. Selina Wang, "Alibaba's Ma Meets with Trump to Talk about Creating Jobs," *Bloomberg News*, January 10, 2017, https://www.bloomberg.com/news/articles/2017-01-09/alibaba-s-jack-ma-meets-with-trump-in-pledge-to-create-new-jobs; Interviews in Beijing.

60. Jennifer Jacobs and Peter Martin, "China Woos Ivanka, Jared Kushner to Smooth Ties with Trump," *Bloomberg News*, February 7, 2017, https://www.bloomberg.com/news/articles/2017-02-07/china-courts-ivanka-jared-kushner-to-smooth-ties-with-trump.

61. Teddy Ng, "China's Top Diplomat on Two-Day Mission to US," *SCMP*, February 26, 2017, https://www.scmp.com/news/china/diplomacy-defence/article/2074209/chinas-top-diplomat-two-day-mission-us; Interviews in Washington, July 2019.

62. Interviews in Beijing and Washington.

63. Noah Barkin and Elizabeth Piper, "In Davos, Xi Makes Case for Chinese Leadership Role," *Reuters*, January 17, 2017, https://www.reuters.com/article/us-davos-meeting-china-idUSKBN15118V.

64. Interview in Beijing.

65. Schiavello Construction, "Commonwealth Parliament Offices," https://www.schiavello.com/construction/projects/commercial/commonwealth-parliament-office.

66. Primrose Riordan, "China's Veiled Threat to Bill Shorten on Extradition Treaty," *The Australian*, December 4, 2017, https://www.theaustralian.com.au/nation/foreign-affairs/chinas-veiled-threat-to-bill-shorten-on-extradition-treaty/news-story/ad793a4366ad2f94694e89c92d52a978.

67. Primrose Riordan, "China's Veiled Threat to Bill Shorten on Extradition Treaty," *The Australian*, December 4, 2017, https://www.theaustralian.com.au/nation/foreign-affairs/chinas-veiled-threat-to-bill-shorten-on-extradition-treaty/news-story/ad793a4366ad2f94694e89c92d52a978.

68. John Garnaut, "Chinese Spies Keep Eye on Leading Universities," *Sydney Morning Herald*, April 21, 2014, https://www.smh.com.au/national/chinese-spies-keep-eye-on-leading-universities-20140420-36yww.html; John Garnaut, "China Spreads Its Watching Web of Surveillance across Australia," *Sydney Morning Herald*, April 26, 2014, https://www.smh.com.au/national/china-spreads-its-watching-web-of-surveillance-across-australia-20140425-379om.html.

69. Nick McKenzie, James Massola, and Richard Baker, "Labor Senator Sam Dastyari Warned Wealthy Chinese Donor Huang Xiangmo His Phone Was Bugged," *Sydney Morning Herald*, November 29, 2017, https://www.smh.com.au/politics/federal/labor-senator-sam-dastyari-warned-wealthy-chinese-donor-huang-xiangmo-his-phone-was-bugged-20171128-gzu14c.html; Nick McKenzie, James Massola, and Richard Baker, "All at Sea: 'Shanghai Sam' Dastyari, the 'Whale' and the 'Lost' Tape Recording," *Sydney Morning Herald*, November 30, 2017, https://www.smh.com.au/national/all-at-sea-

shanghai-sam-dastyari-the-whale-and-the-lost-tape-recording-20171127-gztmwc.html.

70. Malcolm Turnbull, "Speech Introducing the National Security Legislation Amendment (Espionage and Foreign Interference) Bill 2017," December 7, 2017, https://www.malcolmturnbull.com.au/media/speech-introducing-the-national-security-legislation-amendment-espionage-an.

71. Peter Hartcher, "Australia Has 'Woken Up' the World on China's Influence: US Official," *SMH*, February 27, 2018, https://www.smh.com.au/politics/federal/australia-has-woken-up-the-world-on-china-s-influence-us-official-20180226-p4z1un.html.

72. Jim Mattis, *Summary of the 2018 Defense Strategy of the United States of America: Sharpening the American Military's Competitive Edge* (Washington, DC: Department of Defense, 2018), 2, https://dod.defense.gov/Portals/1/Documents/pubs/2018-National-Defense-Strategy-Summary.pdf.

73. Charles Parton, "China-UK Relations: Where to Draw the Border Between Influence and Interference?" *RUSI Occasional Papers*, 20 February 2019, https://rusi.org/publication/occasional-papers/china-uk-relations-where-draw-border-between-influence-and; Thorsten Benner, Jan Weidenfeld, Mareike Ohlberg, Lucrezia Poggetti, and Kristin Shi-Kupfer, "Authoritarian Advance: Responding to China's Growing Political Influence in Europe," Report by MERICS and GPP, February 2, 2018, https://merics.org/en/report/authoritarian-advance-responding-chinas-growing-political-influence-europe.

74. James Mayger and Jiyeun Lee, "China's Missile Sanctions Are Taking a Heavy Toll on Both Koreas," *Bloomberg News*, August 29, 2017, https://www.bloomberg.com/news/articles/2017-08-29/china-s-missile-sanctions-are-taking-a-heavy-toll-on-both-koreas.

75. Peter Martin, "Diplomatic Outbursts Mar Xi's Plan to Raise China on the World Stage," *Bloomberg News*, March 7, 2019, https://www.bloomberg.com/news/articles/2019-03-06/diplomatic-outbursts-mar-xi-s-plan-to-raise-china-on-world-stage.

76. I attended one such event in New Delhi in 2015. See also FMPRC, "Xi Jinping, The Governance of China Was Launched in London," Chinese Embassy in London, April, 16, 2015, http://www.chinese-embassy.org.uk/eng/ambassador/dshd/2015year/t1257353.htm.

77. Chris Buckley, "Xi Jinping May Delay Picking China's Next Leader, Stoking Speculation," *New York Times*, October 4, 2016, https://www.nytimes.com/2016/10/05/world/asia/china-president-xi-jinping-successor.html.

78. Shi Jiangtao, "The Man behind the Xi-Trump Summit," *SCMP*, April 1, 2017, https://www.scmp.com/news/china/diplomacy-defence/article/2083810/man-behind-xi-trump-summit.

79. Yang Jiechi, "Study and Implement General Secretary Xi Jinping's Thought on Diplomacy in a Deep-going Way and Keep Writing New Chapters of Major-Country Diplomacy with Distinctive Chinese Features," *Xinhua*, July 17, 2017, http://www.xinhuanet.com/english/2017-07/19/c_136456009.htm.

80. Interview in Washington, DC, July 2019.

81. Michael Martina, "China Says Xi Transcends West as a Diplomatic 'Pioneer,'" *Reuters*, September 1, 2017, https://www.reuters.com/article/us-china-congress-diplomacy/china-says-xi-transcends-west-as-a-diplomatic-pioneer-idUSKCN1BC4KQ.

82. Shi Jiangtao, "Diplomat's Rise a Sign of Xi's Global Ambitions," *SCMP*, October 25, 2017, https://www.scmp.com/news/china/policies-politics/article/2116978/ its-good-day-chinas-diplomats-foreign-policy-chief.

83. Ting Shi, "Xi Plans to Turn China into a Leading Global Power by 2050," *Bloomberg News*, October 18, 2017, https://www.bloomberg.com/news/articles/2017-10-17/ xi-to-put-his-stamp-on-chinese-history-at-congress-party-opening.

84. Ting Shi, Keith Zhai, and Peter Martin, "Xi's Key Milestone Positions Him to Rule China for Decades," *Bloomberg News*, October 24, 2017, https://www. bloomberg.com/news/articles/2017-10-24/xi-s-new-milestone-positions-him-to- rule-china-for-decades-more.

85. Peter Martin, Ting Shi, and Keith Zhai, "Xi's Iron Grip on Power Adds Pressure to Deliver on Reforms," *Bloomberg News*, October 26, 2017, https://www. bloomberg.com/news/articles/2017-10-25/xi-s-iron-grip-on-power-adds- pressure-to-deliver-china-reforms.

86. Xinhuawang, "Wei xinshidai zhongguo waijiao puxie xin de huacai yuezhang: wo zhuwaishijie shenru xuexi xi Jinping zai zhuwaishijie gongzuo huiyi shang de zhongyao jianghua," Xinhua, January 4, 2018, http://www.xinhuanet.com/2018-01/ 04/c_1122212110.htm.

87. Peter Martin, Keith Zhai, and Ting Shi, "As U.S. Culls Diplomats, China Is Empowering Its Ambassadors," *Bloomberg News*, February 7, 2018, https://www. bloomberg.com/news/articles/2018-02-07/as-u-s-culls-diplomats-china-is- empowering-its-ambassadors.

88. Zhai and Shi, "China Uses Annual Congress to Tout Xi's Global Leadership Role."

89. Interviews in Beijing.

90. Interview in Beijing, spring 2018.

91. Christian Shepherd, "China Makes 'Silver Fox' Top Diplomat, Promoted to State Councilor," *Reuters*, March 19, 2018, https://www.reuters.com/article/us-china- parliament-diplomacy/china-makes-silver-fox-top-diplomat-promoted-to-state- councilor-idUSKBN1GV044.

92. Li Datong, "Li Datong's Open Letter," translated by David Bandurski, February 28, 2018, https://chinamediaproject.org/2018/02/28/li-datongs-open-letter/.

93. Interview in Beijing, February 2019.

94. Charlotte Greenfield and Tom Westbrook, "Nauru Demands China Apologize for 'Disrespect' at Pacific Forum," *Reuters*, September 6, 2018, https://www.reuters.com/ article/us-pacific-forum-china/nauru-demands-china-apologize-for-disrespect- at-pacific-forum-idUSKCN1LM0HM; Ben Doherty and Helen Davidson, "Chinese Envoy Walks Out of Meeting after Row with Nauru President amid 'Bullying' Claims," *The Guardian*, September 5, 2018, https://www.theguardian.com/world/ 2018/sep/05/chinese-envoy-walks-out-of-meeting-after-row-with-nauru- president-amid-bullying-claims.

95. Natalie Whiting and Stephen Dziedzic, "APEC 2018: Chinese Officials Barge Into PNG Foreign Minister's Office after Being Denied Meeting," *ABC*, November 18 2018, https:// www.abc.net.au/news/2018-11-18/chinese-officials-create-diplomatic- storm-at-apec/10508812; AFP, "Police Called after Chinese Diplomats Attempt to

'Barge In' to APEC Host's Office," *Agence France-Presse*, November 18, 2018, https://www.yahoo.com/news/police-called-diplomats-apec-summit-tensions-boil-over-050420060.html; Josh Rogin, "Inside China's 'Tantrum Diplomacy' at APEC," *Washington Post*, November 20, 2018, https://www.washingtonpost.com/news/josh-rogin/wp/2018/11/20/inside-chinas-tantrum-diplomacy-at-apec/?utm_term=.5e61b31e4a0b.

96. RSF,"ChineseDiplomatLuShaye,theBaneofCanadianMedia,AppointedAmbassador to France," *Reporters Without Borders*, June 17, 2019, https://rsf.org/en/news/chinese-diplomat-lu-shaye-bane-canadian-media-appointed-ambassador-france.

97. FMPRC, "Elements of Remarks by H.E. Ambassador Lin Songtian at South African National Editors Forum (SANEF)," *Chinese Embassy in South Africa*, August 22, 2018, http://za.china-embassy.org/eng/sgxw/t1587417.htm.

98. Björn Jerdén and Viking Bohman, "China's Propaganda Campaign in Sweden, 2018–2019," Swedish Institute for International Affairs, April 2019, https://www.ui.se/globalassets/ui.se-eng/publications/ui-publications/2019/ui-brief-no.-4-2019.pdf.

99. AFP, "Sweden Summons Chinese Ambassador over Criticism of Country and Media," *AFP*, January 22, 2020, https://hongkongfp.com/2020/01/22/sweden-summons-chinese-ambassador-criticism-country-media/.

100. The Economist, "Shotgun Diplomacy: How Sweden Copes with Chinese Bullying," *The Economist*, February 20, 2020, https://www.economist.com/europe/2020/02/20/how-sweden-copes-with-chinese-bullying.

101. Jun Mai, "Deng Xiaoping's Son Urges China to 'Know Its Place' and Not Be 'Overbearing'," *South China Morning Post*, October 30, 2018, https://www.scmp.com/news/china/politics/article/2170762/deng-xiaopings-son-uses-unpublicised-speech-urge-china-know-its.

102. Frank Tang, "China's Former Chief Trade Negotiator Criticizes Beijing's 'Unwise' Tactics in US Tariff War," *South China Morning Post*, November 18, 2018, https://www.scmp.com/economy/china-economy/article/2173779/chinas-former-chief-trade-negotiator-criticises-beijings.

103. David Bandurski says the term first appeared in a BBC Chinese-language commentary: David Bandurski, "Xi Jinping: Leader of the Wolf Pack," *Global Asia* 15, no. 3 (September 2020), https://www.globalasia.org/v15no3/focus/xi-jinping-leader-of-the-wolf-pack_david-bandurski.

104. Ben Westcott and Steven Jiang, "China Is Embracing a New Brand of Foreign Policy. Here's What Wolf Warrior Diplomacy Means," *CNN*, May 29, 2020, https://edition.cnn.com/2020/05/28/asia/china-wolf-warrior-diplomacy-intl-hnk/index.html.

105. Interview in Beijing.

106. Interview in Beijing, December 2018.

107. ShiJiangtao,"DiplomaticNovicePickedforTopCommunistPartyJobatChina'sForeign Ministry amid Deteriorating Relations with US," *SCMP*, January 30, 2019, https://www.scmp.com/news/china/diplomacy/article/2184367/diplomatic-novice-picked-top-communist-party-job-chinas-foreign.

108. Interview in Beijing, February 2019.

109. Interview in Beijing, spring 2019.

110. Ananth Krishnan, "China Diplomat in Pakistan Changes Twitter Name after 'Muhammad Ban'," *India Today*, April 28, 2017, https://www.indiatoday.in/world/story/chinese-diplomat-zhao-lijian-islamic-names-banned-muhammad-974035-2017-04-28.

111. Laura Zhou, "Susan Rice Calls Chinese Diplomat Zhao Lijian 'a Racist Disgrace' after Twitter Tirade," *SCMP*, July 15, 2019, https://www.scmp.com/news/china/diplomacy/article/3018676/susan-rice-calls-chinese-diplomat-zhao-lijian-racist-disgrace.

112. Ben Smith, "Meet the Chinese Diplomat Who Got Promoted for Trolling the US on Twitter," *BuzzFeed News*, December 2, 2019, https://www.buzzfeednews.com/article/bensmith/zhao-lijian-china-twitter.

113. "Discovering Twitter: China Finds a Use Abroad for Twitter, a Medium It Fears at Home," *The Economist*, February 20, 2020, https://www.economist.com/china/2020/02/20/china-finds-a-use-abroad-for-twitter-a-medium-it-fears-at-home.

114. Owen Churchill, "Chinese Diplomat Zhao Lijian, Known for His Twitter Outbursts, Is Given Senior Foreign Ministry Post," *SCMP*, August 24, 2019, https://www.scmp.com/news/china/diplomacy/article/3024180/chinese-diplomat-zhao-lijian-known-his-twitter-outbursts-given.

115. Zhai and Yew, "In China, a Young Diplomat Rises as Aggressive Foreign Policy Takes Root."

116. CGTN, "China's Foreign Ministry Spokeswoman Hua Chunying Promoted to Department Head," *CGTN*, July 22, 2019, https://news.cgtn.com/news/2019-07-22/China-s-FM-spokeswoman-Hua-Chunying-promoted-to-department-head-IxiFNBXmhO/index.html.

117. Keegan Elmer, "China's 'Outspoken' Lu Shaye Leaves Canada to Become Ambassador to France," *SCMP*, August 9, 2019, https://www.scmp.com/news/china/diplomacy/article/3022175/chinas-outspoken-lu-shaye-leaves-canada-become-ambassador.

118. Zhai and Yew, "In China, a Young Diplomat Rises as Aggressive Foreign Policy Takes Root."

119. Zhaoyin Feng, "China and Twitter: The Year China Got Louder on Social Media," *BBC*, December 29, 2019, https://www.bbc.com/news/world-asia-china-50832915.

120. Jing Xuan Teng, "'LOL!': China's Informal, Confrontational Twitter Diplomacy," *AFP*, January 14, 2020, https://news.yahoo.com/lol-chinas-informal-confrontational-twitter-diplomacy-020225229.html.

121. https://twitter.com/MFA_China/status/1202221440646336513?s=20.

122. Yuliya Talmazan, "China Criticizes U.S. Border Closure as Coronavirus Death Toll Rises," *NBC*, February 1, 2020, https://www.nbcnews.com/news/world/china-criticizes-u-s-border-closure-coronavirus-death-toll-rises-n1128161.

123. Daniel Ten Kate and Peter Martin, "The Death of a Doctor Poses the Greatest Threat to China's Xi Yet," *Bloomberg Businessweek*, February 13, 2020, https://www.bloomberg.com/news/articles/2020-02-13/the-death-of-a-doctor-poses-the-greatest-threat-to-china-s-xi-yet.

124. Javier C. Hernández, "China Spins Coronavirus Crisis, Hailing Itself as a Global Leader," *New York Times*, February 28, 2020, https://www.nytimes.com/2020/02/28/world/asia/china-coronavirus-response-propaganda.html.

125. FMPRC, "Foreign Ministry Spokesperson Zhao Lijian's Regular Press Conference on March 5, 2020," *FMPRC*, March 5, 2020, https://www.fmprc.gov.cn/mfa_eng/xwfw_665399/s2510_665401/t1752564.shtml.

126. Keith Zhai and Huizhong Wu, "As Outbreak Goes Global, China Seeks to Reframe Narrative," *Reuters*, March 6, 2020, https://www.reuters.com/article/us-health-coronavirus-china-diplomacy-an-idUSKBN20T14C.

127. "Discovering Twitter."

128. Tom Phillips, "Bolsonaro's Son Enrages Beijing by Blaming China for Coronavirus Crisis," *The Guardian*, March 19, 2020, https://www.theguardian.com/world/2020/mar/19/coronavirus-bolsonaro-son-china-row.

129. Shashank Bengali and Alice Su, "'Put On a Mask and Shut Up': China's New 'Wolf Warriors' Spread Hoaxes and Attack a World of Critics," *Los Angeles Times*, May 4, 2020, https://www.latimes.com/world-nation/story/2020-05-04/wolf-warrior-diplomats-defend-china-handling-coronavirus.

130. Ben Westcott and Steven Jiang, "Chinese Diplomat Promotes Conspiracy Theory That US Military Brought Coronavirus to Wuhan," *CNN*, March 14, 2020, https://edition.cnn.com/2020/03/13/asia/china-coronavirus-us-lijian-zhao-intl-hnk/index.html; interviews in Beijing.

131. Jason Scott and Iain Marlow, "Chinese Official Pushes Conspiracy Theory U.S. Spread Virus," *Bloomberg News*, March 13, 2020, https://www.bloomberg.com/news/articles/2020-03-13/chinese-official-pushes-conspiracy-theory-u-s-army-behind-virus.

132. Bob Davis, Kate O'Keeffe, and Lingling Wei, "U.S.'s China Hawks Drive Hard-Line Policies after Trump Turns on Beijing," *Wall Street Journal*, October 16, 2020, https://www.wsj.com/articles/u-s-s-china-hawks-drive-hard-line-policies-after-trump-turns-on-beijing-11602867030.

133. Quint Forgey, "Trump on 'Chinese Virus' Label: 'It's Not Racist at All,'" *Politico*, March 18, 2020, https://www.politico.com/news/2020/03/18/trump-pandemic-drumbeat-coronavirus-135392.

134. Jonathan Swan and Bethany Allen-Ebrahimian, "Top Chinese Official Disowns U.S. Military Lab Coronavirus Conspiracy," *Axios*, March 22, 2020, https://www.axios.com/china-coronavirus-ambassador-cui-tiankai-1b0404e8-026d-4b7d-8290-98076f95df14.html.

135. Interviews in Beijing, March 2020; see also Wendy Wu, "Is It Time for China to Leash Its Wolf Warrior Diplomats?," *South China Morning Post*, August 12, 2020, https://www.scmp.com/news/china/diplomacy/article/3097134/it-time-china-leash-its-wolf-warrior-diplomats?mc_cid=ebbb2a3033&mc_eid=911ee2620b.

136. Zhai and Yew, "In China, a Young Diplomat Rises as Aggressive Foreign Policy Takes Root."

137. Interview in Beijing, March 2020.

138. Sharon Chen, Jing Li, and Dandan Li, "China Spokesman Defends Virus Tweets Criticized by Trump," *Bloomberg News*, April 7, 2020, https://www.bloomberg.com/news/articles/2020-04-07/china-spokesman-defends-virus-tweets-criticized-by-trump.

139. John Irish, "Outraged French Lawmakers Demand Answers on 'Fake' Chinese Embassy Accusations," *Reuters*, April 16, 2020, https://www.reuters.com/article/us-health-coronavirus-france-china/outraged-french-lawmakers-demand-answers-on-fake-chinese-embassy-accusations-idUSKCN21X30C.

140. Alan Crawford and Peter Martin, "China's Coronavirus Diplomacy Has Finally Pushed Europe Too Far," *Bloomberg News*, April 22, 2020, https://www.bloomberg.com/news/articles/2020-04-21/china-s-coronavirus-diplomacy-has-finally-pushed-europe-too-far.

141. Georgia Hitch and Jordan Hayne, "Federal Government Calls Chinese Ambassador on Trade Boycott over Coronavirus Inquiry," *ABC News*, April 28, 2020, https://www.abc.net.au/news/2020-04-28/government-calls-chinese-ambassador-boycott-coronavirus-inquiry/12191984.

142. Edward Wong and Paul Mozur, "China's 'Donation Diplomacy' Raises Tensions with U.S.," *New York Times*, April 14, 2020, https://www.nytimes.com/2020/04/14/us/politics/coronavirus-china-trump-donation.html.

143. Andreas Rinke, "Germany Says China Sought to Encourage Positive COVID-19 Comments," *Reuters*, April 26, 2020, https://www.reuters.com/article/us-health-coronavirus-germany-china/germany-says-china-sought-to-encourage-positive-covid-19-comments-idUSKCN2280JW.

144. Reuters Staff, "Internal Chinese Report Warns Beijing Faces Tiananmen-like Global Backlash over Virus," *Reuters*, May 4, 2020, https://www.reuters.com/article/us-health-coronavirus-china-sentiment-ex-idUSKBN22G19C.

145. Kevin Rudd, "The Coming Post-COVID Anarchy," *Foreign Affairs*, May 6, 2020, https://www.foreignaffairs.com/articles/united-states/2020-05-06/coming-post-covid-anarchy.

146. Global Times, "West Feels Challenges by China's New 'Wolf Warrior' Diplomacy," *Global Times*, April 16, 2020, https://www.globaltimes.cn/content/1185776.shtml.

147. Huang Lanlan, "Young Chinese Idolize FM Spokespersons, Welcome 'Wolf Warrior' Diplomats," *Global Times*, May 21, 2020, https://www.globaltimes.cn/content/1189118.shtml.

148. Westcott and Jiang, "China Is Embracing a New Brand of Foreign Policy."

149. Beijing Ribao, "Zhuying dashi: yinwei shijie shang you lang, zhongguo waijiaoguan cai yao zuo lang zhan," *Beijing Ribao*, May 24, 2020, http://www.bjd.com.cn/a/202005/24/WS5eca85fde4b00aba04d1e437.html.

150. Kinling Lo, "Beijing Should Contain 'Extreme Conationalism,' Ex-Diplomat Warns," *South China Morning Post*, September 30, 2020, https://www.scmp.com/news/china/diplomacy/article/3103550/us-china-relations-beijing-should-contain-extreme-nationalism.

151. Samson Ellis and Cindy Wang, "Taiwan Diplomat Hurt in Scuffle With China Officials in Fiji," *Bloomberg News*, October 19, 2020, https://www.bloomberg.com/news/articles/2020-10-19/taiwanese-diplomat-hurt-in-scuffle-with-china-officials-in-fiji; Ben Boherty, Sheldon Chanel, Helen Davidson, and Lily Kuo, "Taiwan Official in Hospital after Alleged 'Violent Attack' by Chinese Diplomats in Fiji," *The Guardian*, October 19, 2020, https://www.theguardian.com/world/2020/oct/19/taiwan-official-in-hospital-after-alleged-violent-attack-by-chinese-diplomats-in-fiji; Amber Wang, "Cake Fight: Taiwan, China Officials Scuffle at Fiji Soiree,"

AFP, October 19, 2020, https://news.yahoo.com/taiwan-says-chinese-diplomats-assaulted-051404468.html; Will Glasgow, "China Blames Flag Cake as Diplomats Brawl with Taiwan Embassy Staff," *The Australian*, October 20, 2020, https://www.theaustralian.com.au/world/china-blames-flag-cake-as-diplomats-brawl-with-taiwan-embassy-staff/news-story/32b08c91203ffc2b389b6382e0b6458b.

152. Javier C. Hernández, "Latest Clash between China and Taiwan: A Fistfight in Fiji," October 19, 2020, https://www.nytimes.com/2020/10/19/world/asia/china-taiwan-fiji-fight.html.

Conclusion

1. Interview in Beijing, 2017. "Wang Li" is a pseudonym.
2. Lyu, *Waijiao Rensheng*, 200, 205.
3. Li Jiazhong, "Qinli Yuezhan de Zhongguo Waijiaoguan," in *Ting Dashi Jiang Gushi*, ed. Niu, 38–39.
4. Chen, *Waijiao, rang shijie geng hexie*, 119.

Index

For the benefit of digital users, indexed terms that span two pages (e.g., 52–53) may, on occasion, appear on only one of those pages.